The iOS 16 iPhone Guidebook

In this book, we get to the heart of the iPhone and iOS 16. For beginners, there's a guide to setting up your iPhone and using its key features. We break down the iPhone's key apps, with tutorials on both their basic functions and more advanced features, and our guides to the iPhone's more advanced capabilities is great for when you want to take things further. It's all in The iOS 16 iPhone Guidebook.

Contents

12: First Steps with Your iPhone

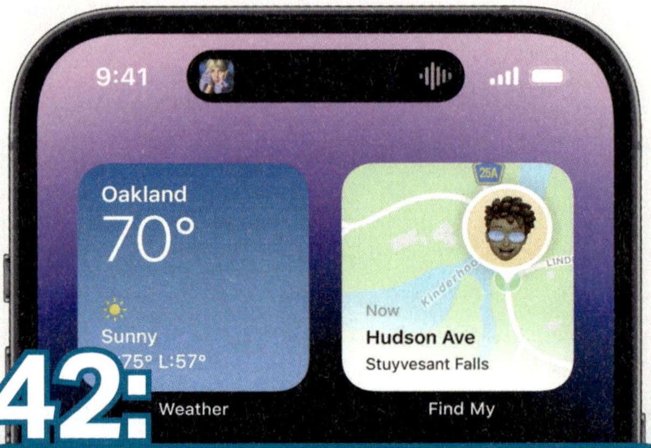

42: Your iPhone's Built-in Apps

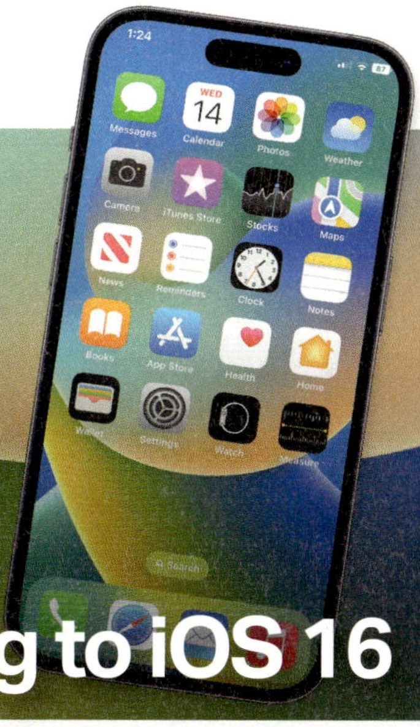

126: Updating to iOS 16

118: Your iPhone's Advanced Functions

40: New Lock Screen

The Lock Screen has had a major overhaul. We show you how to use its great new features.

Free Digital Magazine

See page 146 for download details

Can You Run iOS 16?

Older iPhones cannot be updated to the new operating system, so if you want to upgrade your iPhone to iOS 16, it must be one of the following models. If you're unsure which iPhone you own, go to https://apple.co/35BofOC.

iPhone 8/8 Plus
iPhone SE (2nd gen or later)

iPhone XS/XS Max
iPhone XR
iPhone X

iPhone 14 models
iPhone 13 models
iPhone 12 models
iPhone 11 models

The Ten Most Asked Questions We Get About iOS 16

What's iOS 16 all about? We answer ten of your most-asked questions about the iPhone's latest operating system.

What is iOS 16, and why should we be excited about it?

iOS 16 is the latest version of the operating system that runs on Apple's iPhone. It's packed with great new features and improvements to functions you already have, and like all versions of iOS, it's free too! A new Apple operating system is always an event, and with iOS 16 there's plenty to celebrate. There's a great new lock screen with increased functionality, new Focus features, the ability to recall emails and messages you sent before they were ready, multi-stop routing in Maps, Live Text in videos, iCloud Shared Photo Library and more.

Apple identified a security flaw in iOS 15. Is iOS 16 going to be safe to use?

The security flaw is patched in the new operating system. iOS 16 has been extensively tested, both internally and as a developers' and public beta release. Apple is dedicated to making its software secure and safe, and also to safeguard your privacy. A new feature, Safety Check, lets victims of abusive relationships review and reset the access they've granted others to make sure they're not sharing information with someone they'd rather not. In fact, iOS is the most secure, private operating system on any mobile device.

How do I install iOS 16?

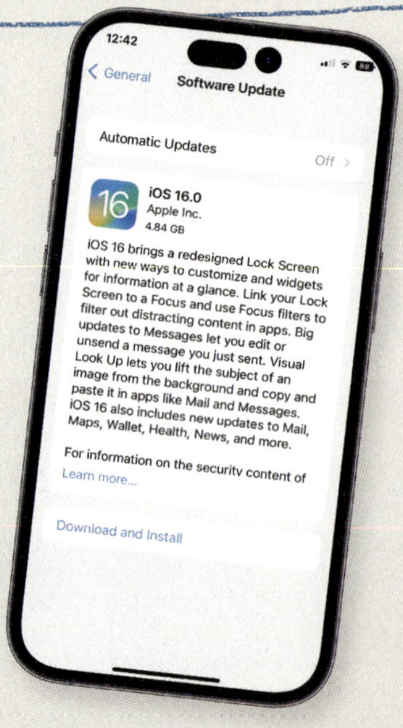

iOS 16 is easy – and free – to install. Open the Settings app, tap the General option and then tap Software Update. Your iPhone checks whether a new version of iOS is available, and if there is, invites you to download it. Follow the on-screen instructions.

Tell me about the new lock screen?

The lock screen has been completely overhauled. You can add widgets to the lock screen, and change the font and colour of the numbers used to show the time too. The new lock screen is multi-layered, so if you use a photograph, you can have the time shown between the main photo object and its background. It looks amazing. Best of all, you can make multiple lock screens and switch between them at will. You can even set a Focus for each lock screen, so when you switch to it, your chosen Focus is turned on too.

What's the new Photo Sharing feature I've heard about?

This one's great for families. You can now set up a photo album that's shared with the people in your family group. When you post a picture, it's instantly available to everyone else in the group – just the thing to keep them in the loop on holidays or events. Everyone in the group has equal rights to post and edit pictures, and you can even set your phone to automatically send a photo to the album as you take it. It's an amazing feature, and great fun to use.

Can you really recall an email in the Mail app?

You certainly can! If you send an email and notice you've made a mistake or forgot to add an attachment, you have ten seconds in which you can recall it. You just tap the Undo Send button at the foot of the screen. You're then taken back to the composition screen, where you can correct your mistakes before sending it again. It's an amazing feature which will save a lot of frustration.

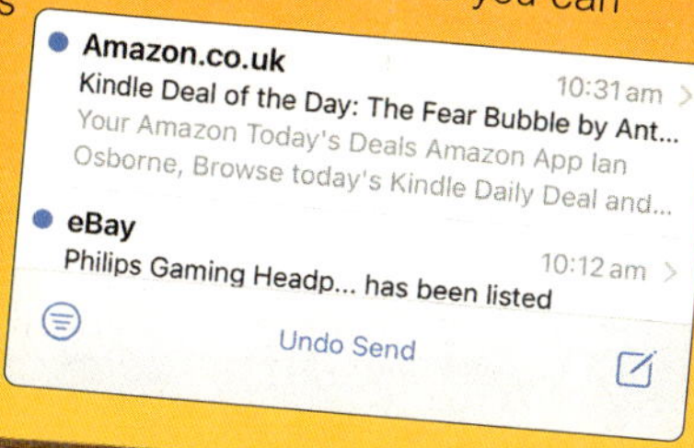

I use Maps as an in-car GPS. Has it changed?

The redesign of the Maps app continues apace, with more detail, cycling information, Look Around and better 3D being rolled out in more and more territories. One of the best new features in iOS 16 Maps is Multistop Routing. When setting a route, you can now add up to 15 stops along that route. Just the thing for long journeys where you might want to factor in stops for fuel, refreshments and more.

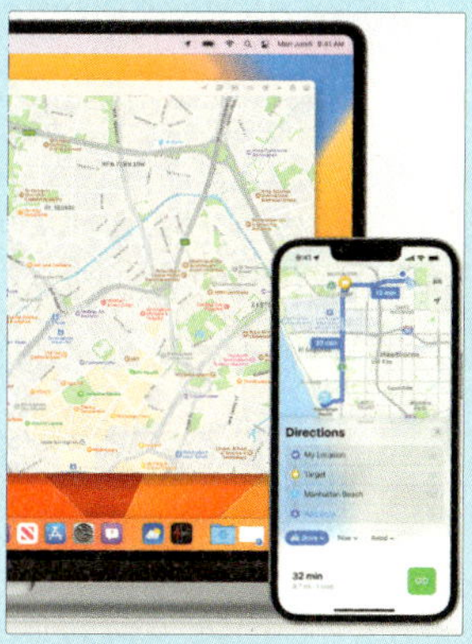

I use Messages more than Mail these days. Can I unsend a message too?

Yes, but there are a few limitations. You can recall a message for up to two minutes after sending it, but unless the recipient also has an iPhone on iOS 16, an iPad on iPadOS 16 or a Mac on macOS Ventura, it still gets through even though it disappears from your screen. You can edit and resend a message for up to 15 minutes, but again, unless your recipient has an up-to-date Apple device, they get the old message as well as the new one. It's still a great feature for when the auto-correct causes problems just as you send your message, though.

What else is new? Anything interesting?

Plenty! The Live Text feature that lets you copy words and numbers from photographs can now be achieved with videos too. Just pause the video, and tap the words on the screen. Wallet IDs and Wallet Keys are rolling out in more areas, and the Dictation feature has been improved, with the keyboard now appearing on the screen while you speak, so you can seamlessly switch between the two. And that's not all. Check our tutorials for lots more tips and features in iOS 16.

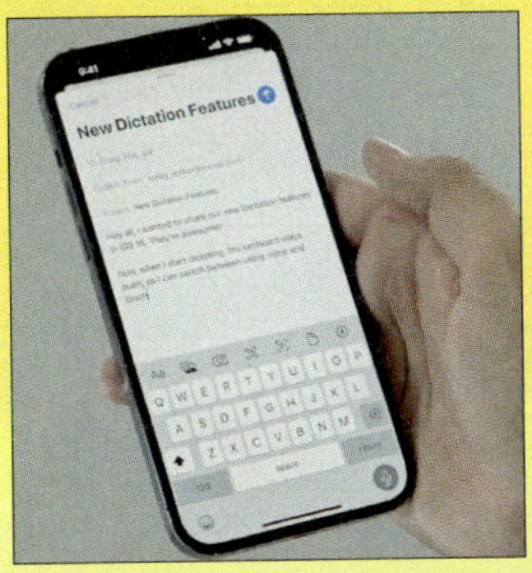

What do I need to run iOS 16?

To install iOS 16, your iPhone must be an iPhone SE (2nd generation or later), or an iPhone 8 or later. If you're unsure which model your iPhone is, go to: https://support.apple.com/en-gb/HT201296.

New iPhones

Apple's brand new iPhone 14 series is here, and they're looking great.

The iPhone 14 Pro and Pro Max

Apple's flagship phones

To no one's surprise, the iPhone 14 range includes an iPhone 14 Pro and iPhone 14 Pro Max. These are Apple's high-end models, top-of-the-range models for top-of-the-range needs. As expected, there was a price increase over the launch prices of the iPhone 13 Pro and Pro Max, but this wasn't as hefty as we thought it might be. So let's take a look at the iPhone 14 Pro, and its larger stable mate, the iPhone 14 Pro Max.

New Colours

iPhone 14 Pro and iPhone 14 Pro Max are made from surgical grade stainless steel, and are available in four new colours, namely space black, silver, gold, and a gorgeous deep purple design that looks far better than the more lilac model in the non-Pro iPhone 14 range.

Better Screens

Once again, the Pro iPhones come in two sizes; the regular model, with a 6.1-inch screen (measured corner to corner), and the larger Pro Max with a 6.7-inch display. The screen makes significant advances over the previous model. It has smaller borders and is brighter than before, in fact, it has the highest outdoor peak brightness in a smartphone, of up to 2000 nits, which is twice as bright as iPhone 13 Pro.

But most significantly, it's always on. Instead of turning off when the iPhone is idle, it merely dims, so you can still see the time and information like the new Lock Screen widgets without picking up the phone or tapping the display. This is made possible by some great new power-efficient features. The screen refresh rate can go as low as one hertz with a new low power mode, and uses far less power when it does refresh. It works intelligently too, with wallpaper photos dimming without losing the correct skin tones.

The always-on display dims when the iPhone is idle.

New Class of Camera

The new iPhone 14 Pro and Pro Max's camera is designed to deliver the best results for any photographer, from the casual snapper to the most demanding professional. They introduce a brand new class of camera to the iPhone – a 48MB offering with a quad-pixel sensor. It's the largest sensor yet, and is 65% larger than the one on the iPhone 13 Pro/Max. It also offers up to two times' improvement in low light conditions. The Telephoto lens has an extra telephoto option. You can now choose between 0.5x, 1x, 2x and 3x magnification.

The Ultra Wide camera has a larger sensor and more focus pixels, and is up to three times better in low light conditions than its predecessor. It's perfect for macro photography, that is, focussing on subjects very close to the camera.

The flash has been redesigned with a new adaptive behaviour based on the focal length of the photo. Its nine LEDs control the power and intensity of the light, for perfectly lit pictures. It's up to twice as bright as before too.

Fundamental to the pro camera system, A16 Bionic powers incredible computational photography features. The CPU, GPU, Neural Engine, and image signal processor seamlessly work together to support the new camera hardware and perform up to four trillion operations per photo. It also makes possible the new Action Mode, which when switched on, stabilises your video photography without needing an extra device such as a gimbal.

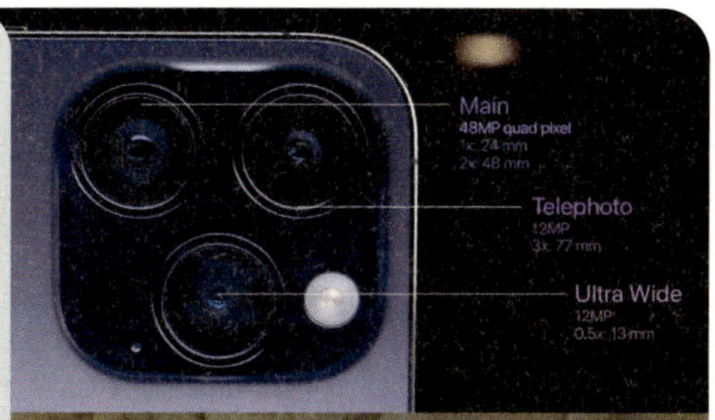

The New A16 Bionic Chip

The new iPhone Pro range is again powered by an Apple Silicon system-on-a-chip, this time the new A16 Bionic. With almost 16 billion transistors, two high-performance cores and four high-efficiency cores, the new six-core CPU is up to 40% faster than the competition. It features an accelerated five-core GPU with 50% more memory bandwidth for graphics-intensive games and apps, and its new 16-core Neural Engine is capable of nearly 17 trillion operations per second.

The A16 Bionic chip was built with power efficiency, the new screen features and photography in mind.

Prices and Release Date

The iPhone 14 Pro and Pro Max are available to preorder and go on sale on 16th September at the following prices:

iPhone 14 Pro

128GB	£1,099/$999/1.299 €
256GB	£1,209/$1099/1.429 €
512GB	£1,429/$1299/1.689 €
1TB	£1,649/$1499/1.949 €

iPhone 14 Pro Max

128GB	£1,199/$1099/1.449,00 €
256GB	£1,309/$1199/1.579,00 €
512GB	£1,529/$1399/1.839,00 €
1TB	£1,749/$1599/2.099,00 €

Dynamic Island

Those who listened to the rumour mill ahead of the iPhone 14 Pro/Pro Max's launch expected the notch atop the screen to go in favour of a pill-shaped window a little down from the top edge, but no one predicted what we got. The new iPhone's Dynamic Island feature is arguably the most innovative and exciting change to the user interface we've seen in years.

This window, of course, houses the TrueDepth camera, which has been re-engineered to fit into a 30% smaller space. For the first time, the proximity sensor which powers Face ID is positioned behind the display. This allows the Dynamic Island window to do far more than house the camera. Instead, it adapts dynamically to show alerts, background activities, notifications and current information too.

For example, when you get a phone call, the Dynamic Island expands to house the notification about who's calling, and also the accept and reject call buttons. When you use Face ID, it becomes square-shaped as it shows you the progress of your scan. It also shows when your iPhone is muted, charging or playing music, and shows upcoming directions when using the Maps. It's great for ongoing background activities too, like a countdown timer. It can also house iOS 16's Live Activities information too, such as the current score in a sporting event or keeping an eye on when your taxi will arrive.

The animations associated with Dynamic Island are fluid and intuitive, and they're available to third-party developers to use with their own apps too.

The iPhone 14 and iPhone 14 Plus

A new phone in five exciting colours

As expected, the Autumn refresh also brought us a regular iPhone 14 model with a 6.1-inch screen (measured corner to corner), but we also got an iPhone 14 Plus, a larger model with a 6.7-inch screen. This is a first for the regular iPhone – previously, only the iPhone's Pro models came in regular and larger sizes. One thing we didn't get is an iPhone 14 mini. This is surprising considering the iPhone 12 and 13 series enjoyed a smaller version, but perhaps they weren't selling.

Whichever size of iPhone 14 you buy, it retains the 'notch' housing the TrueDepth camera. No Dynamic Island here.

Unusually for a non-Pro model, the iPhone 14 comes in regular 6.1-inch and a 'Plus' 6.7-inch models.

Five Exciting Colours

The iPhone 14 and iPhone 14 Plus come in five different colours; midnight, blue, starlight, purple, and the fundraising (PRODUCT)RED, where some of the profits go to AIDS charities.

Improved Performance

The regular-sized iPhone 14 offers all-day battery life, and the iPhone 14 Plus goes even further, offering the best battery life ever in an iPhone.

At the heart of the iPhone 14/14 Plus is the Apple Silicon A15 Bionic system-on-a-chip, which debuted last year with the iPhone 13 Pro models. It has a five-core GPU that's 18% faster than the iPhone 13's. Its six-core CPU offers two high-performance and four high-efficiency cores, and it also boasts a 16-core neural engine for machine learning.

Also worth noting is the A15 Bionic's custom Image Signal Processor which powers some great features in the iPhone 14/14 Plus camera system.

The Build

Both sizes of the iPhone 14 are made from aerospace-grade aluminium. They have an updated internal design for better thermal performance. This prevents overheating during peak-needs use such as gaming, so you can play for longer. The screens boast Super Retina XDR displays with OLED technology that supports 1200 nits of peak HDR brightness, a 2,000,000:1 contrast ratio, and Dolby Vision. And if you're prone to dropping your phone, you'll be glad to learn the Ceramic Shield front cover — exclusive to iPhone and tougher than any other smartphone glass — returns.

Action Mode

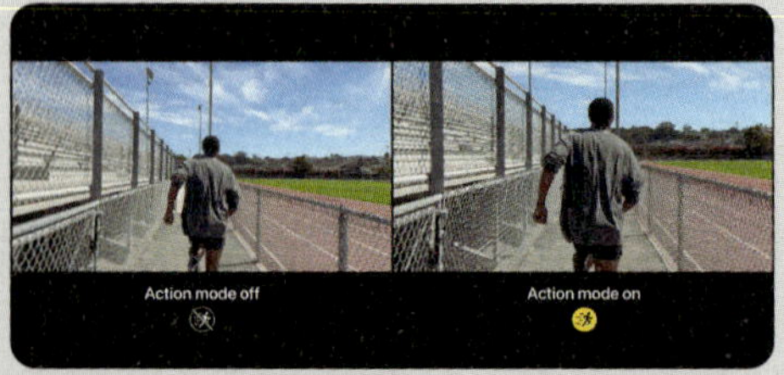

When recording video, Cinematic Mode is now available in 4K at 30 fps and 4K at 24 fps. Dolby Vision HDR is available too, exclusive to iPhone. But the best enhancement to video recording is the new Action Mode. Toggled on and off with a tap, Action Mode is a stabilisation tool that adjusts to significant shakes, motion, and vibrations while you record your video. Where you might expect footage to be shaky, it's now silky smooth.

The iPhone 14/14 Plus Camera System

As expected, the regular iPhone 14 models have a two-camera system that gives great photos across the entire range of light. In bright light, colours come alive. In low light, moody shadows dominate.

The new 12MP main lens has a larger image sensor than before, and larger pixels at 1.9 microns. The aperture is faster for better motion freezing when you take a still picture of an object in motion, and it boasts a 49% improvement in low-light photos compared to the iPhone 13's camera.

The Ultra Wide camera offers a unique perspective for wider shots, and the improved True Tone flash is 10% brighter and has better uniformity for more consistent lighting.

Around the front, the iPhone 14/14 Plus has a new 12MP TrueDepth camera with a faster aperture giving a 38% improvement in low light imaging. For the first time, the front-facing camera has auto focus, allowing it to focus clearly at multiple distances. It can focus faster too, for all-round better selfies.

In a first for a non-Pro iPhone, the TrueDepth camera offers auto focus, so it can focus on multiple objects at varying distances.

Prices and Release Date

The iPhone 14 goes on sale on 16th September and the iPhone 14 Plus on 7th October, at the following prices:

iPhone 14	
128GB	£849/$799/999 €
256GB	£959/$899/1.129 €
512GB	£1,179/$1,099/1.389 €
iPhone 14 Plus	
128GB	£949/$899/1.149,00 €
256GB	£1,059/$999/1.279,00 €
512GB	£1,279/$1199/1.539,00 €

Emergency!

Health and safety is a keen interest at Apple, and both the regular and Pro models of the iPhone 14 boast some great new features that might just save your life.

With Crash Detection, your new iPhone can tell if you've been in a car crash and alert the emergency services automatically. It achieves this using a combination of old and new components and some nifty software.

Emergency SOS can get help to you even in remote locations with no Wi-Fi or cellular coverage. Your iPhone 14 contacts the emergency services using an overhead communication satellite. Because bandwidth is so limited, a voice connection is impossible. If the service you need accepts text messages, you're put in touch directly. If not, Apple has set up a series of relay centres that can take your messages and read them to the emergency service. This satellite connectivity can also be used to share your location using the Find My app.

Emergency SOS via Satellite is included with all iPhone 14 models free for two years. The service launches in November 2022, in the USA and Canada only, but it will spread to other territories over time.

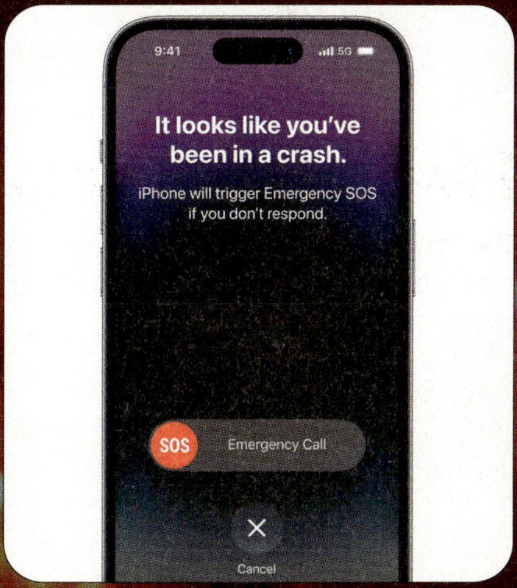

The iPhone 14 can tell if you've been in a car crash, and automatically contact the emergency services.

How Emergency SOS Works

Make sure you're outdoors, and launch Emergency SOS. Tap Report Emergency.

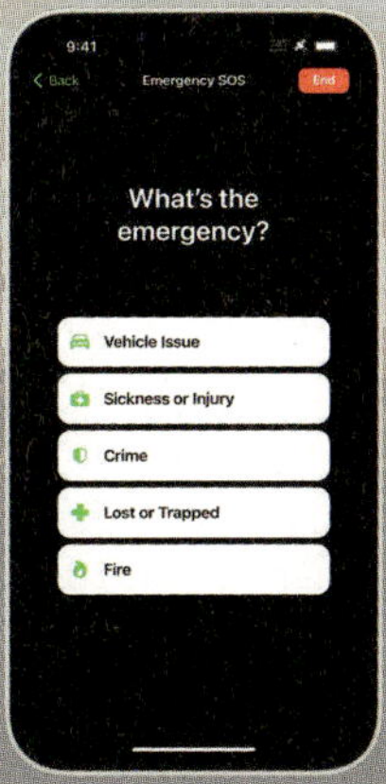

You're questioned about the emergency. Do so, using one of the on-screen buttons.

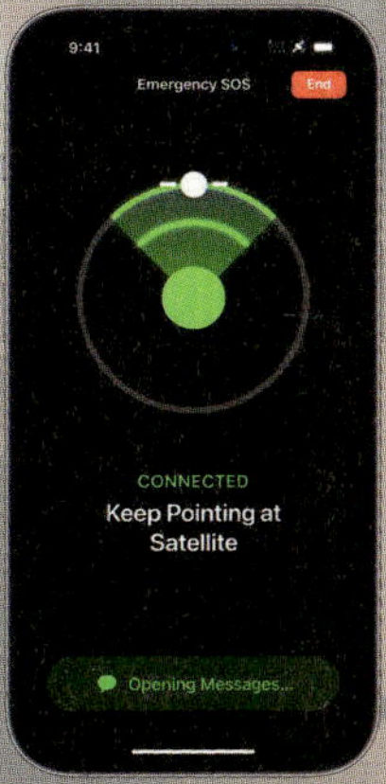

Keep the phone pointed at the satellite, and the Messages app opens.

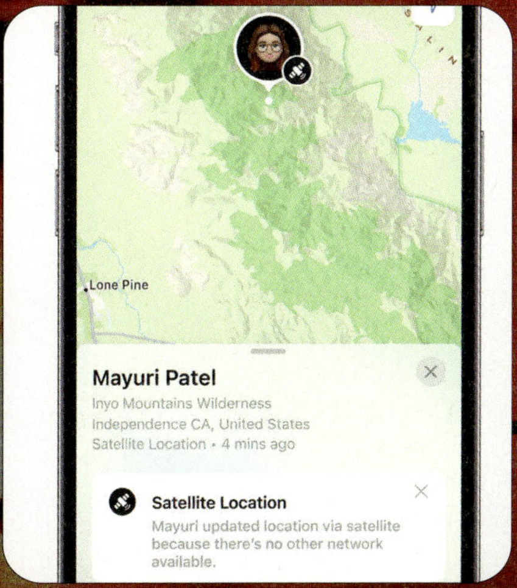

You can use satellite connectivity to share your location with the Find My app.

First Steps with Your iPhone

Here we show you the iPhone's basics, such as the various buttons and ports on your iPhone, setting up the iPhone out of the box, setting up your Internet connection and email accounts, using the virtual keyboard, touchscreen gestures, Control Centre, the lock screen and more.

Mon 6 72°
9:41
JUN
24.8
MI

Buttons & Ports

The latest iPhones have a very similar control layout. They all have Face ID, whether it's in a notch or the iPhone 14 Pro's new Dynamic Island, they all have a side button, volume controls and a Lightning port. And, of course, they all have an excellent Retina display. Sizes may vary, but whatever phone you have, the screen is amazing. Let's take a look at your iPhone's controls.

What's at the front

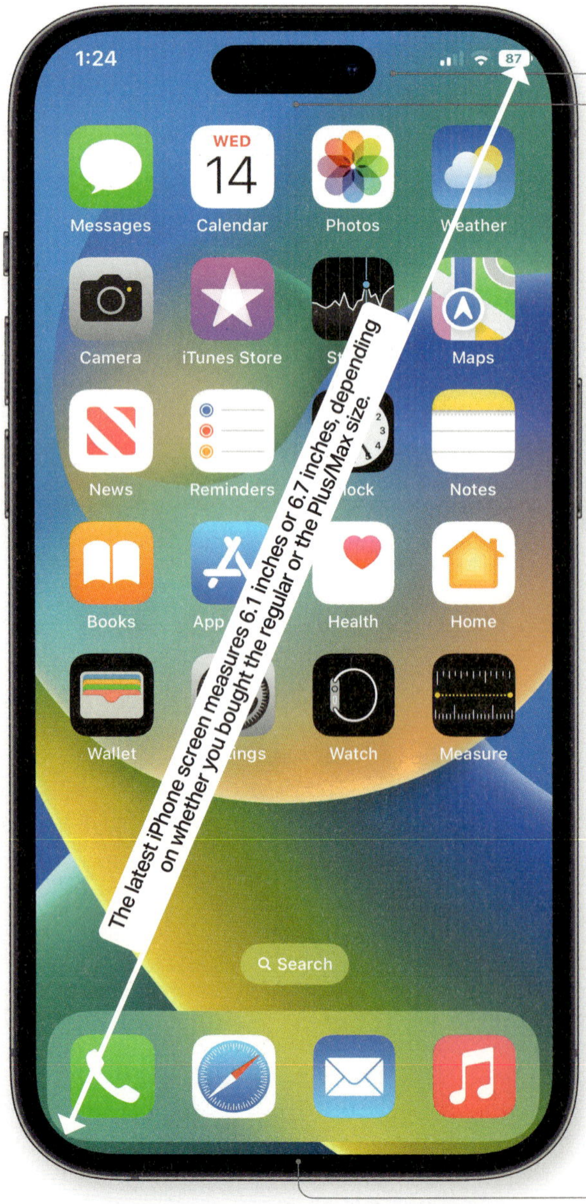

The very latest Pro-level iPhones, the 12MP TrueDepth camera, infrared projector and proximity sensor are housed in a pill-shaped space called Dynamic Island. This island can also carry information gleaned from apps, show incoming messages and more. Previous generations of iPhone have a notch instead of the Dynamic Island.

To unlock your iPhone, enter a password or confirm a purchase, just hold it up so it can see your face. Face ID does its work, with no further input needed.

The iPhone's Side Button is here. On some iPhones, this button is located on the top instead of on the side. It's a multi-function button that can summon Siri, launch Face ID, access Apple Pay and more.

On the base of your iPhone is the Lightning Connector/audio EarPods connection port, and also the built-in microphone and stereo speakers. Older iPhones might have a 3.5mm earphones port here.

Home Button iPhones Models

The older iPhone models still share many of the same side-button locations and functions

The rear-facing camera, flash and mic. The specs of the camera, including the number of lenses, depends on the model.

The front-facing camera for selfies and FaceTime video conversations. Obviously, this camera doesn't support Face ID.

The Home button. Press it to get back to the Home screen, and place your finger on it to use the Touch ID fingerprint reader.

Rear and side features

The latest Pro-level iPhones have a three-lens camera system; a regular camera, a wide angle lens and a telephoto lens. The non-Pro iPhone 14 has a two-lens camera system, and some earlier iPhones have a single camera lens.

The iPhone's camera system has a built-in flash, which also doubles as a torch; just open the Control Centre and tap the Torch icon to light it up.

Also found in the rear camera of recent iPhones is the LiDAR scanner, which measures how long it takes light to reflect back from objects.

This is the Ring silent switch. Click it to turn Silent Mode on and off.

These are the volume buttons. The upper one increases the volume and the lower button lowers it. In Apple's Camera and many third-party photography apps, you can also use the volume buttons to take a photo instead of the on-screen shutter button.

Use an ejector tool to eject the SIM tray, which is found here. This is where you insert your nano SIM, supplied by your mobile service supplier. Some very recent iPhones dispense with a physical SIM in favour of an eSIM, though this is limited to the USA at the moment.

iPhone 14 Pro: 3.05 inches (77.6 mm),
iPhone 14: 2.81 inches (71.5 mm)

iPhone 14 and iPhone 14 Pro: 0.31 inch (7.85 mm)

Getting Set Up

If you're setting up your new iPhone straight out of the box, follow this guide as we take you through the extremely important first time setup. Learn how to set up all the core functions of your iPhone, from switching it on for the first time to making your first phone call. Whichever model of iPhone you own, with our help you'll soon be up and running.

Inserting your Nano-SIM card

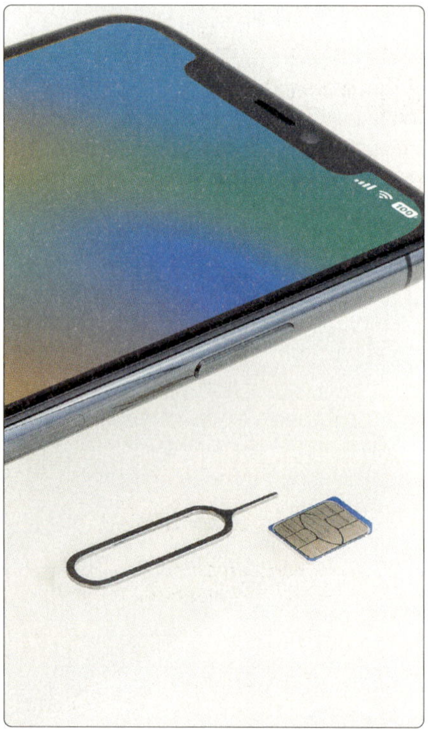

1 To activate your iPhone, you must first insert the Nano-SIM card provided by your mobile phone network provider. An eSim card is non-removal as detailed below.

2 Use a SIM eject tool like the one pictured here, or maybe a straightened paper clip, and insert it into the small hole next to the SIM slot. The tray then pops out as shown.

3 Place the SIM card in the tray (there's only one way it can go in) and slide the tray back in the slot. Push it in firmly so it snaps into place. Your iPhone should recognise it.

eSIM explained

The dual sim functionality introduced with the 2018 iPhone models, enables users to access two sim cards in one iPhone. Unlike the standard sim card, the eSIM card is built into the phone itself and is accessed via software, with your coverage purchased via mobile networks. By using dual sims you can now access two mobile networks and numbers in one device.

The initial set up of your iPhone

1 The opening screen shows 'Hello' in different languages. Press the Home button or flick the screen up. Select your language, followed by the country, or region, in which you're to use the phone.

2 If you already have an iPhone or an iPad running iOS 11 or later handy, you can set up your new iPhone by bringing them together as shown to sign in automatically. If not, tap Set Up Manually.

3 Choose your network from the list, then enter the password supplied with (or printed on) your router. Tap Next, then on the next screen, tap Continue after reading about Data & Privacy.

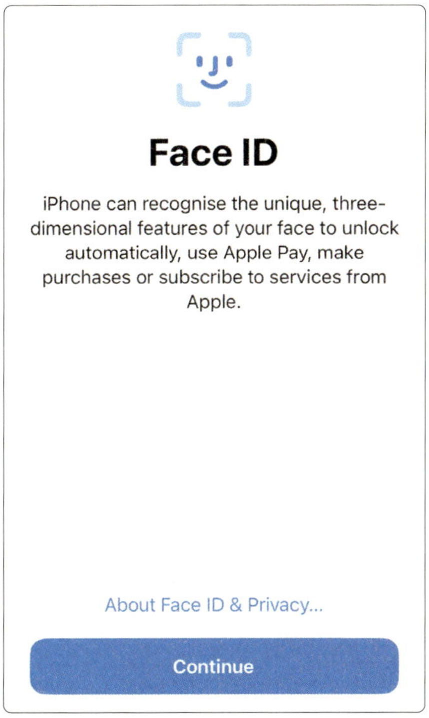

4 The next step is setting up your Face ID (or on older iPhones, Touch ID). If you wish to do this now, see the tutorials later in this book for the relevant step-by-step guides.

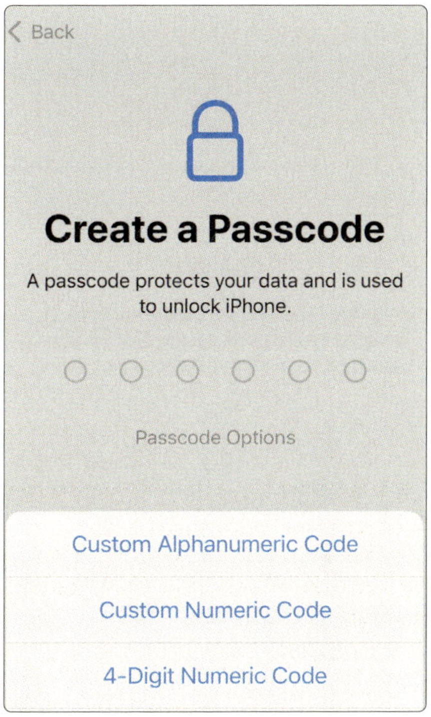

5 Choose a six-figure passcode used to unlock your iPhone. Alternatively, tap Passcode Options to add a different type of code; or skip it altogether (not recommended).

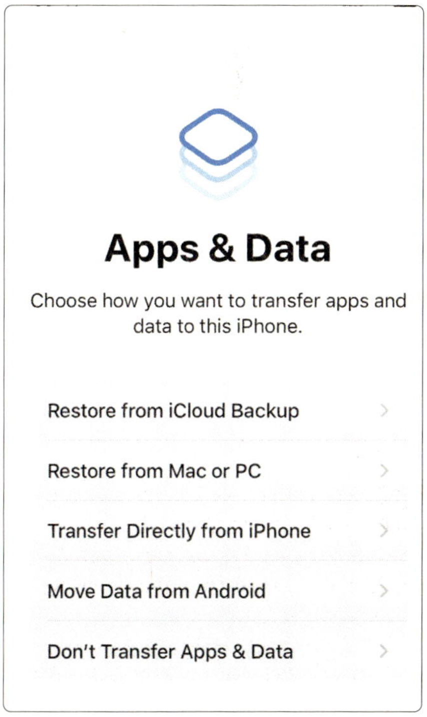

6 After setting your passcode, you can transfer data from your other phone (iPhone or Android) or a backup if you wish. If this is your first iPhone, choose the last option.

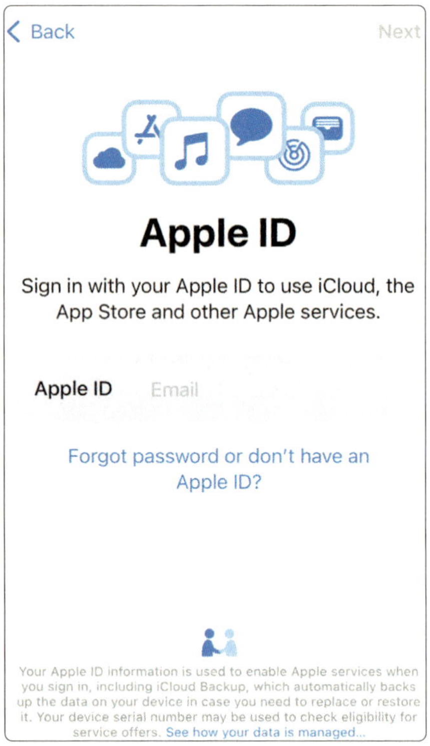

7 Enter your Apple ID. This is your email address and password. If you don't have one, tap the link below the Password field and follow the tutorial on Your Apple ID – How to Set it Up.

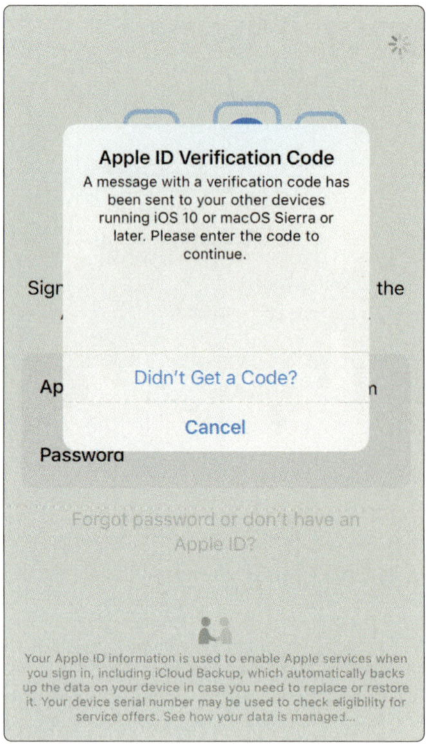

8 If you have other recent Apple devices signed into the same Apple ID you just used, you're sent a verification code. Read it off your other Apple device and type it here. Agree to the T&Cs.

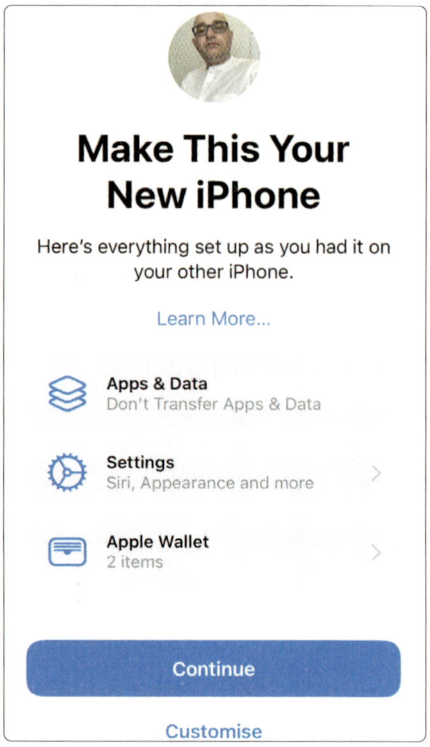

9 If you've previously had an iPhone, you set it up in the same way as before. Tap Continue to do so, or Customise Settings to decline. Next is info about staying up to date; tap Continue.

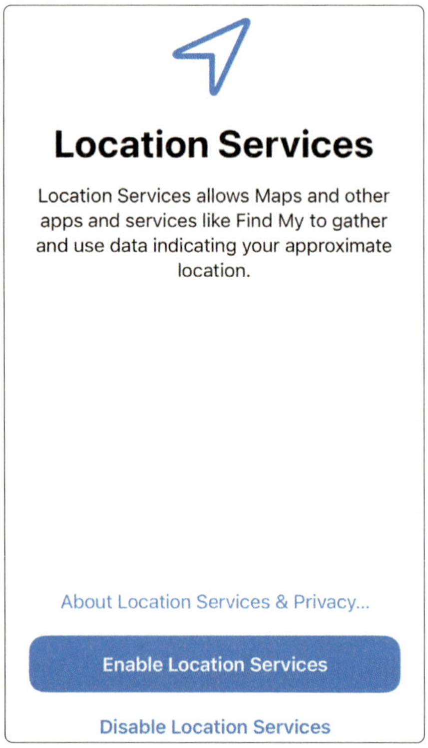

10 Do you wish to enable Location Services; we suggest you should because, whilst this enables your iPhone to gather data about where you are, it is essential for apps like Find My and Maps.

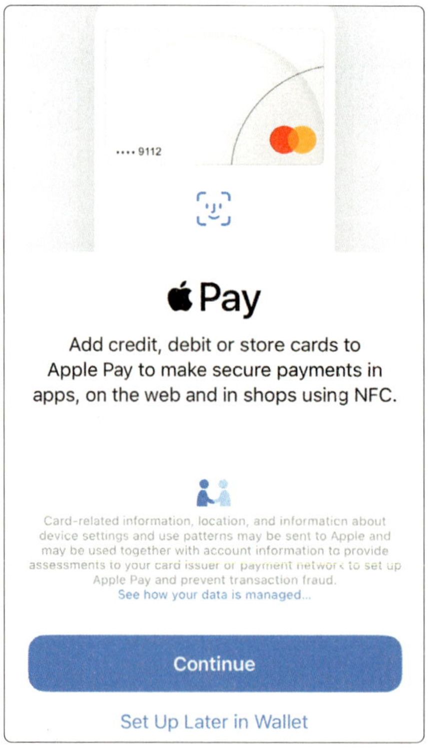

11 Do you set up Apple Pay now, or later in the Wallet app? If you decide to do it now, follow the on-screen instructions. Naturally, if you don't want to use it at all, you can ignore this feature.

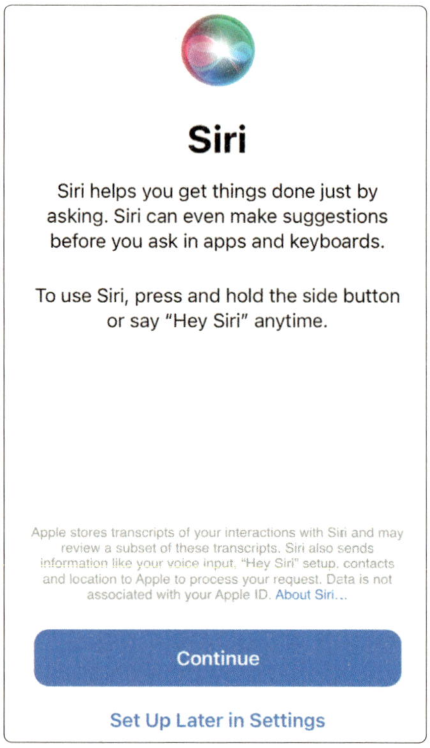

12 You can now train Siri to recognise your voice. Again, if you want to do it now, follow the on-screen instructions. If not, tap Set Up Later in Settings; you can do it any time you like.

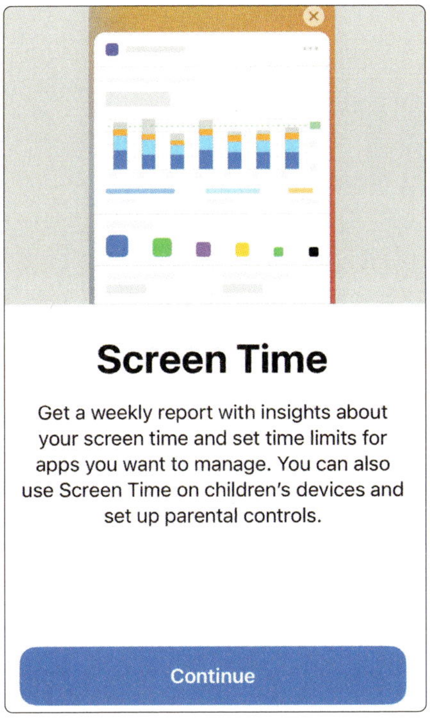

13 You can now set up Screen Time, a feature that gives you a weekly report on how you use your iPhone. There's a full tutorial on it later in this book. Set it up now, or later as you wish.

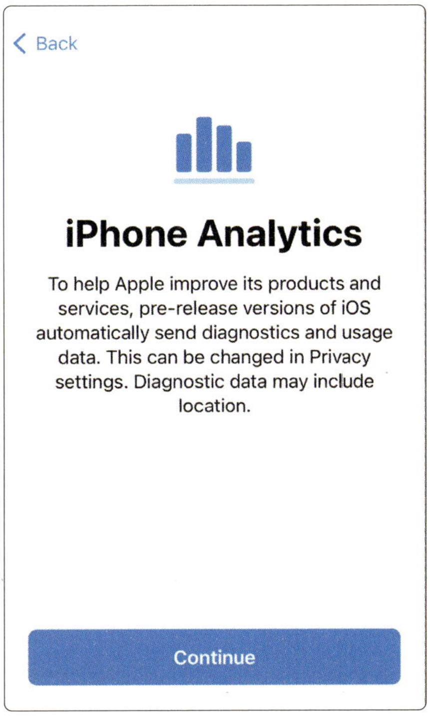

14 The next two screens ask if you want to share iPhone Analytics and iCloud Analytics with Apple and its developers. It's up to you, and you can change your mind in Settings later.

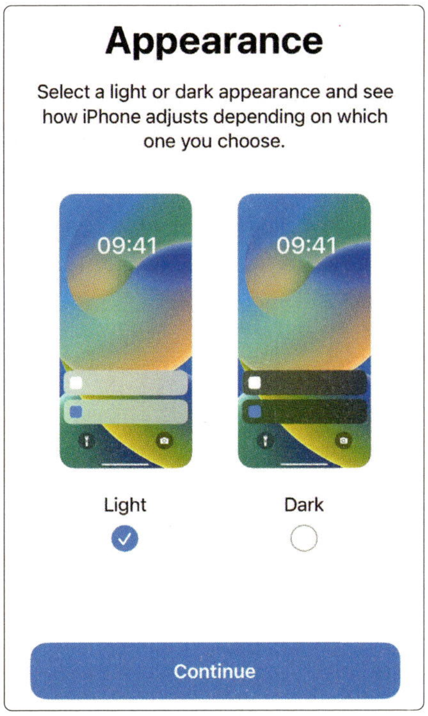

15 Decide whether to use Light Mode or Dark Mode (this is another option you can change later, in Settings). You're then welcomed to the iPhone and are ready to get started.

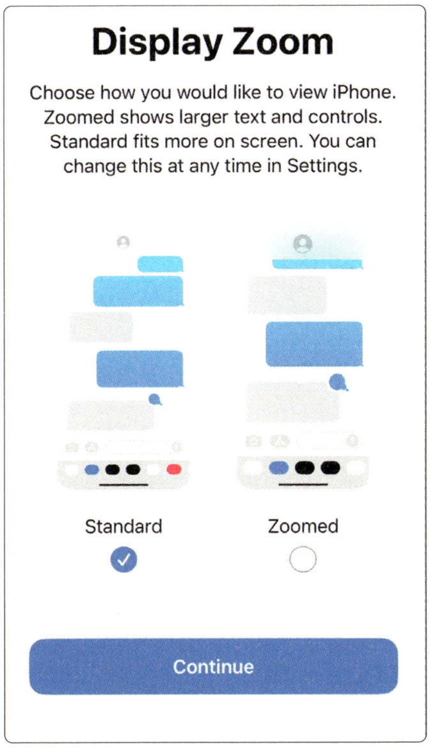

16 Do you prefer to have your display Zoomed, which shows larger text and controls, or Standard, for more on the screen? Decide here; you can change it later in Settings.

Erasing an iPhone

If you need to erase all previously used settings and data from your iPhone, you need to reset it to factory conditions then set it up using this tutorial.

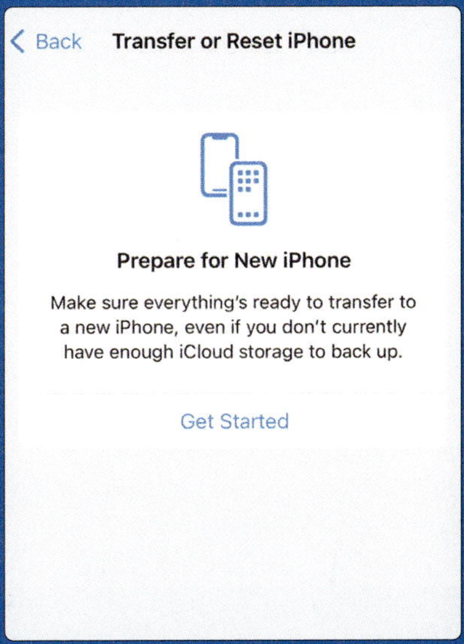

From the home screen, go to Settings > General. Tap Transfer or Reset iPhone at the bottom. Now tap Erase All Content and Settings. You're told what information will be safely deleted.

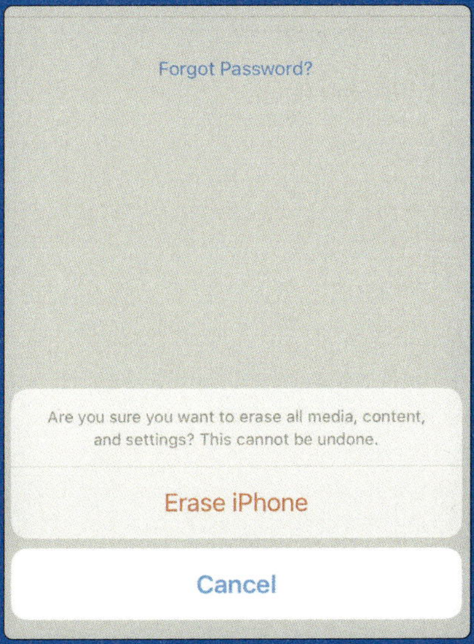

Tap Continue, then enter your passcode. Tap Erase iPhone, confirm it, and then enter the Apple ID. You might need to get these from the phone's previous owner. Your iPhone is then wiped.

Your Apple ID

If you don't already have a working Apple ID, and you didn't register one while setting up your iPhone, you should do so now. With it you can download applications from the App Store, use FaceTime, buy music and movies from iTunes and use many of the iPhone's features and services. Without an Apple ID, you won't come close to getting the most from your iPhone.

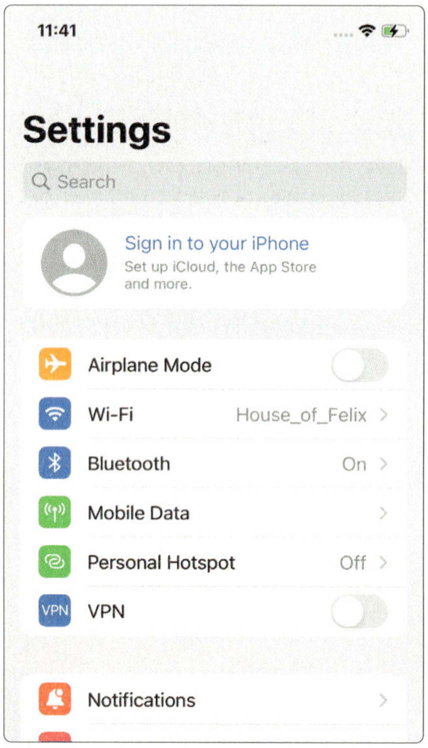

1 Open the Settings application from your iPhone's Home screen and scroll to the top of the screen. Tap the Sign in to your iPhone option right at the top of the list, then in the pop-up window, tap 'Don't have an Apple ID or forgot it?'.

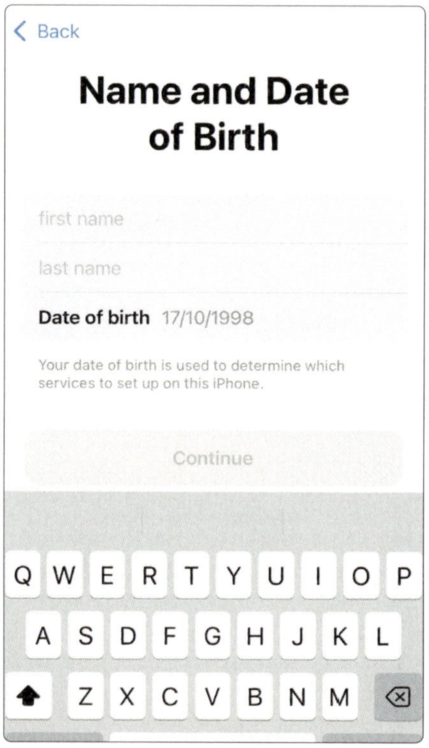

2 Tap Create Apple ID in the next window and, when instructed, enter your name in the fields provided. In the next field, Date of Birth, set your date with the wheels, and then tap Next to move on to the next step.

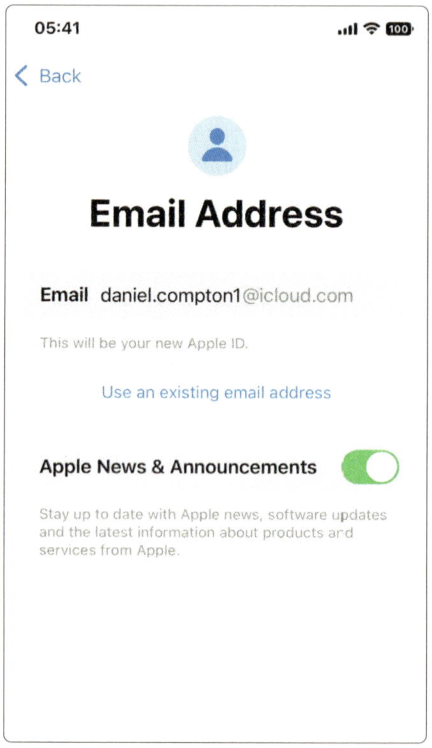

3 Then, you're asked whether you want to use your current email address (if you have one) for your Apple ID. Or use a free iCloud email address, which comes with your Apple ID. Accept the suggestion, or type your own.

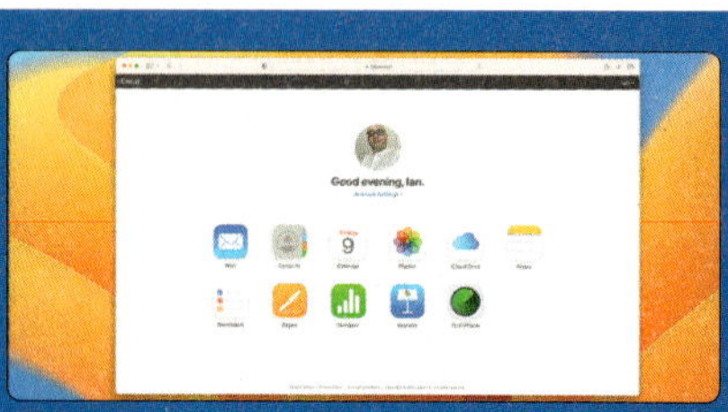

iCloud email

Your Apple ID gives you a free iCloud email address. You can use this email address on your iPhone and also on any other Internet devices you have, such as Macs, PCs or tablets, and through a browser at www.icloud.com. Best of all, you keep your iCloud address even if you change your Internet provider.

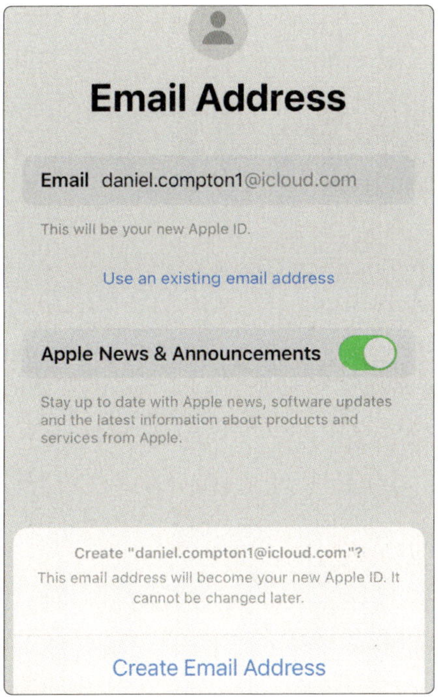

4 If you choose to use an iCloud address, you're asked to complete your email, which ends '@icloud.com'. If you're choosing a brand new iCloud address to use it may take a few tries before you find one that isn't already taken, but when you do, accept it by tapping Continue.

5 Now you must choose your password. As stated on the screen, it must be at least eight characters long and include at least one number, one upper case (capital) letter and one lower case letter. Make it something you can easily remember.

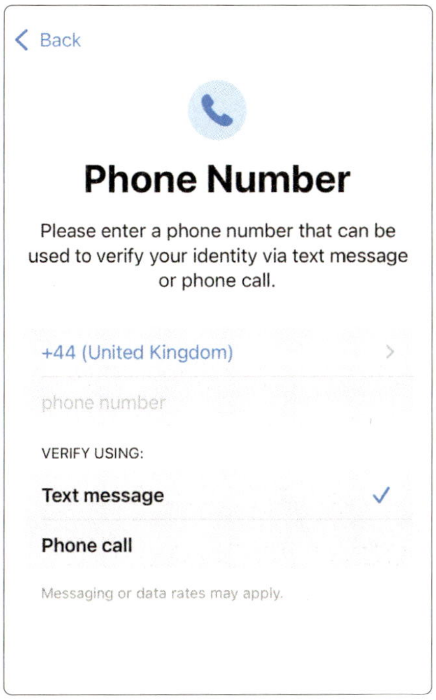

6 Apple needs your phone number so you can be contacted, via a call or text message, to confirm your identity. Use the number taken from your SIM card, or tap Use a different number, to choose another number for them to phone or message. Tap Continue.

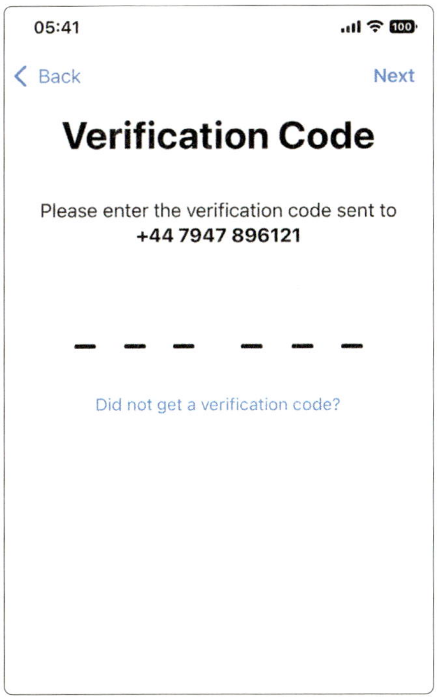

7 After tapping Next, you should enter the six-figure verification code that's just been sent to your device (or given to you in a call, if that was your preferred choice). When you enter the last digit, you automatically proceed to the next step.

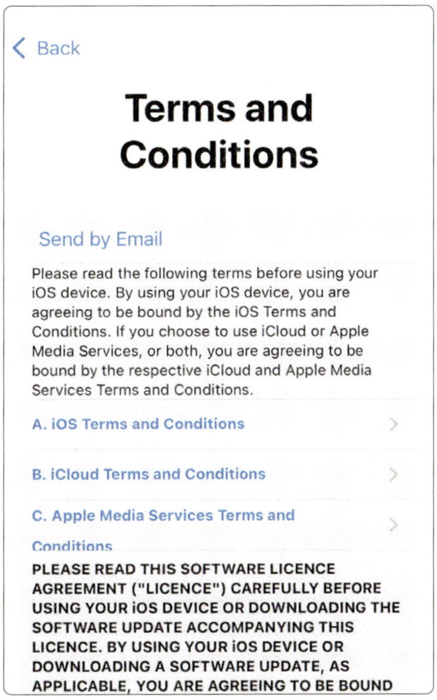

8 Agree to the terms and conditions and your iPhone signs into iCloud with your newly created Apple ID. When it's done, you must enter your iPhone's passcode, the one you use to unlock it on the lock screen, to complete the sign-in process.

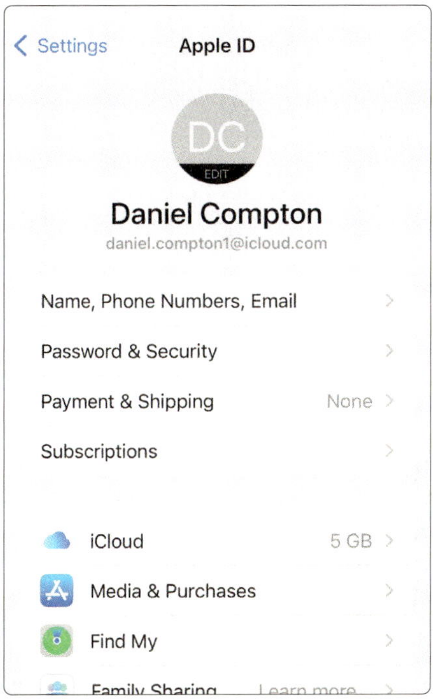

9 When the sign-in process is completed, you're shown your Apple ID screen. From here, you can tap the initials at the top of the screen to add a photo, tap iTunes & App Store, to set up media and purchases, and set up services like Family Sharing and iCloud.

Face & Touch ID

iPhones with a top-to-bottom screen have Face ID. Most iPhones with a Home button have Touch ID. You probably set up this service during the initial setup, but here's how to do it if you need help.

Setting up Face ID

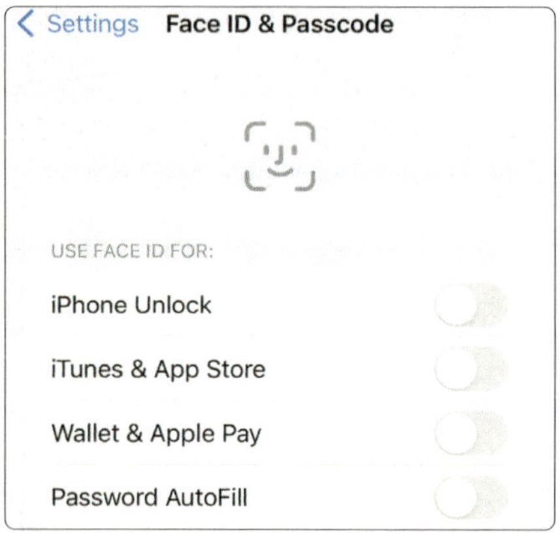

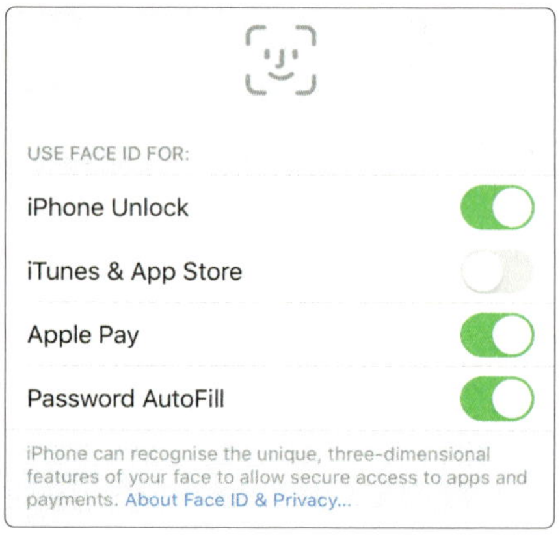

1 Go to Settings > Face ID & Passcode and enter your iPhone's passcode to continue. Tap Set Up Face ID or Set Up Alternative Appearance, or tap Reset Face ID to start afresh.

2 Position your face within the frame as instructed, then move your head in a circle until the small lines around your face are all green. Tap continue, then repeat for a second scan.

3 Your face is now registered with Face ID. Tap Done to return to the Settings screen, where you can configure your iPhone's Face ID feature to your own personal requirements.

Setting up Touch ID

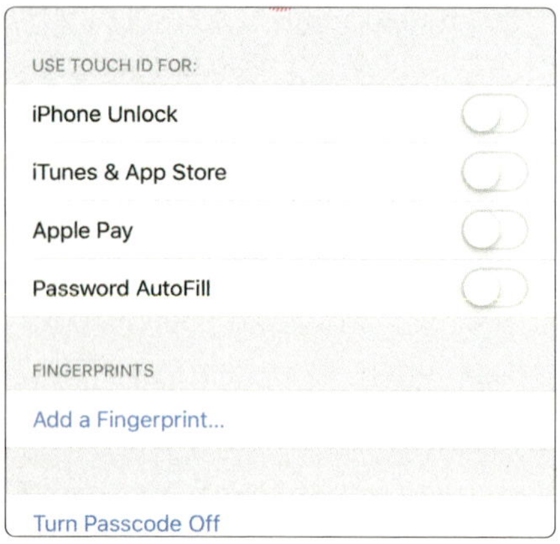

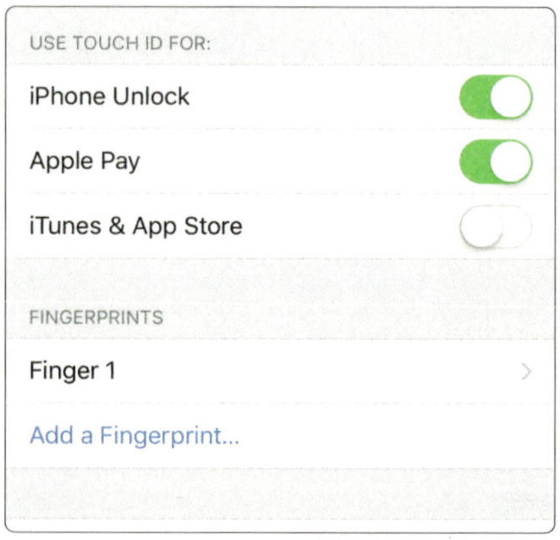

1 Go to Settings > Touch ID & Passcode and enter your iPhone's passcode when instructed. Tap the Add a Fingerprint link to start registering one of your fingerprints with Touch ID.

2 Place a finger on the Home button and follow the instructions, lifting and replacing your finger until the fingerprint is filled. Then do the same again with the edges of your fingertip.

3 When done, you return to the first screen, from where you can add another fingerprint if you wish. You can also choose which iPhone features can be activated using your Touch ID.

Using Face ID

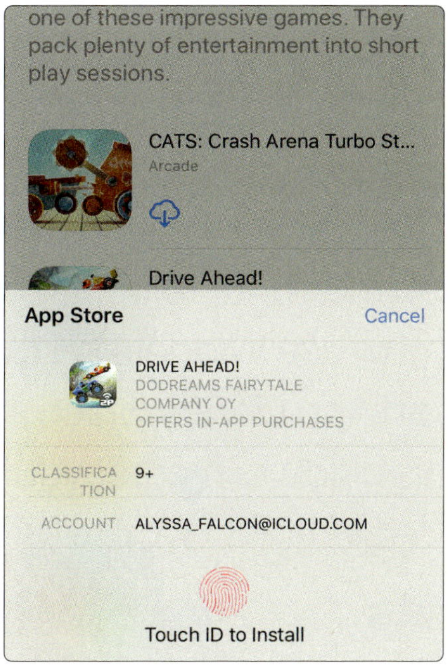

Unlocking your iPhone

1 With Face ID, simply look at your phone and the lock springs open, as you can see here. You can do it in any lighting conditions, even total darkness. If you have Touch ID, you can unlock your phone by pressing the Home button with a finger registered for Touch ID.

Making Purchases

2 Open the iTunes Store, App Store or Books Store and choose something you wish to purchase. When you're asked to pay, double-click the Side button and look at your iPhone. The purchase is made and a checkmark is displayed to show payment has been verified.

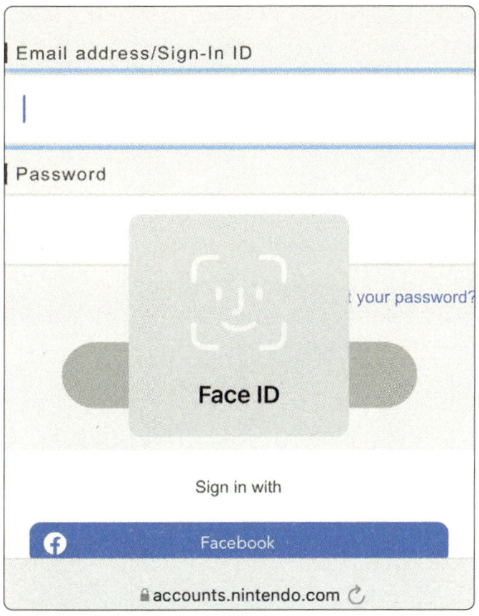

Giving Passwords

3 When logging on to a password-protected website, such as a forum or a store where you have an online account, tap the field where you have to give a name or password, and you're asked to use Face ID or Touch ID as applicable. Do so to fill these fields.

Using Apple Pay

4 Make sure Apple Pay is turned on in Settings > Face ID/Touch ID & Passcode and that you've already set up Apple Pay. To make a purchase, double click the Side button or place your finger on the Home button. Hold your phone near the reader.

Adding More Faces or Fingers

To add a new face to your Face ID, maybe so your partner or children can use your phone, open the Settings app and go to Face ID & Passcode. When instructed, type your passcode to proceed. On the next screen, which offers all sorts of customisation options for Face ID, look for a link that says 'Set Up an Alternative Appearance'. Tap it, and you're invited to set up Face ID again, just like you did when you set up your own face in Face ID. Tap the Get Started button and follow the tips for setting up Face ID offered earlier. You can have two registered faces with Face ID.

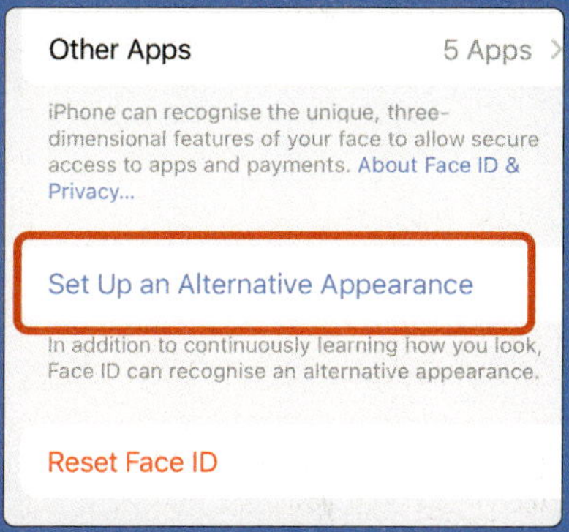

If you have a Touch ID iPhone, you can add more fingers; either your own, or someone else's whom you trust to open and use your phone. Go to Settings > Touch ID & Passcode, enter your passcode and on the next screen, tap Add a Finger. Follow the on-screen instructions to add your finger – the process is exactly the same as for the first finger you registered. When you're done, you have two fingers registered with Touch ID.

The Home Screen

The Home screen is at the heart of your iPhone. It's through this screen that you open apps, organise them into folders, edit and use Home screen widgets and more. You can now use Widgets on the Home screen, among your app icons, and there's an App Library which summarises your apps on one single screen. Follow this guide to master your iPhone's Home screen.

Home Screen Widgets

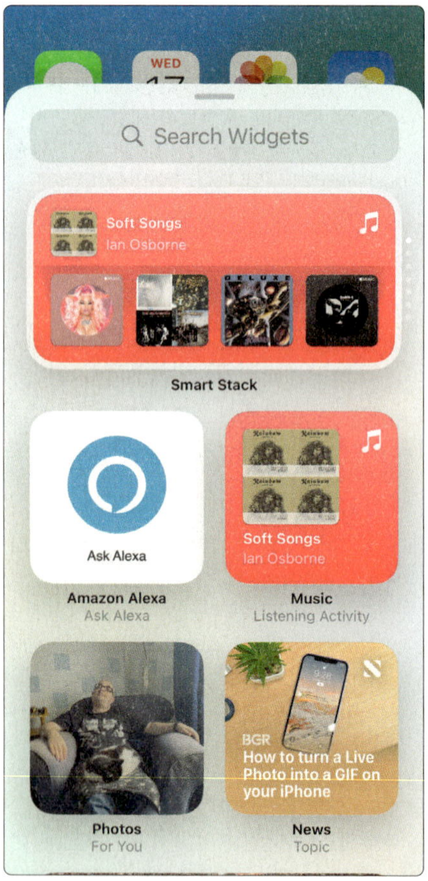

1 Widgets can sit on the Home screen. To add one, tap and hold an empty space until the icons start wobbling. Tap + (top-left) for a pop-up window, from where you can choose a Widget. They come in three sizes, based on the size of an app icon; 2x2, 2x4 and 4x4; Swipe the Widget left and right to see these sizes.

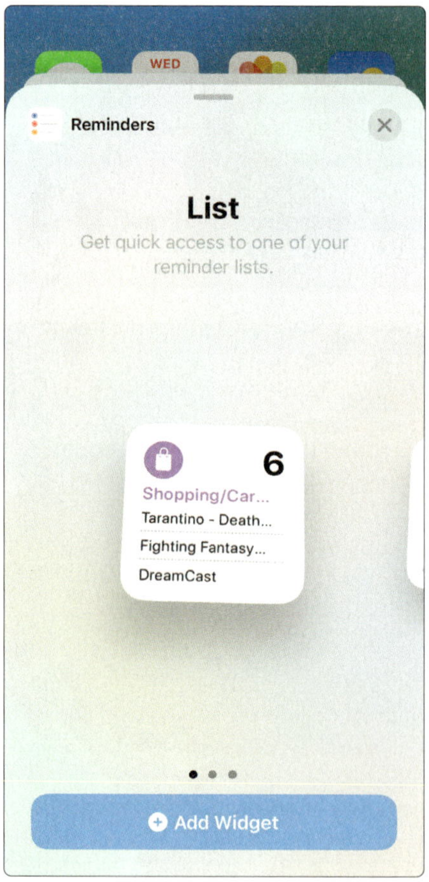

2 When you've chosen a size, tap Add Widget (bottom). You can drag and reposition it like an app icon. Tap a Widget on the Home screen to open its app. Tap and hold it for a pop-up menu that lets you edit the Widget. To remove a Widget, tap and hold it and select Remove Widget from the pop-up menu.

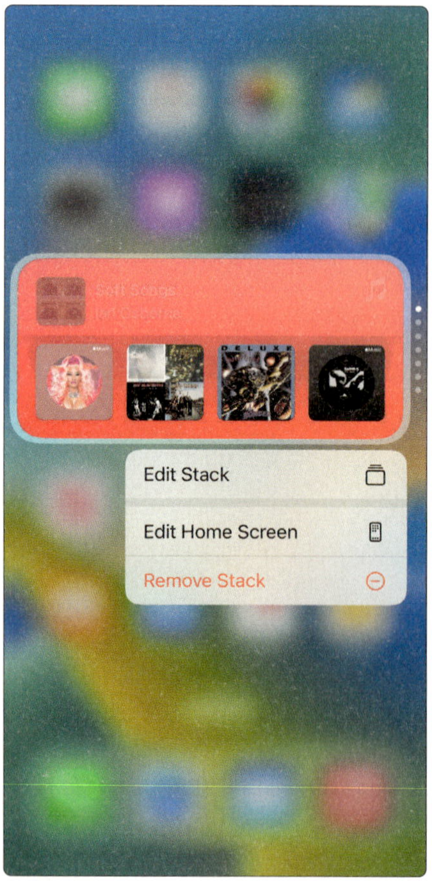

3 A Smart Stack is a series of Widgets that appear as a single Widget on the Home screen. it's at the top of the Widgets window. Drag it onto your Home screen to add it. To edit a Smart Stack, tap and hold it for a menu, then tap Edit Stack. To remove a widget, tap its minus sign, or tap Plus (top left) to add one.

The App Library

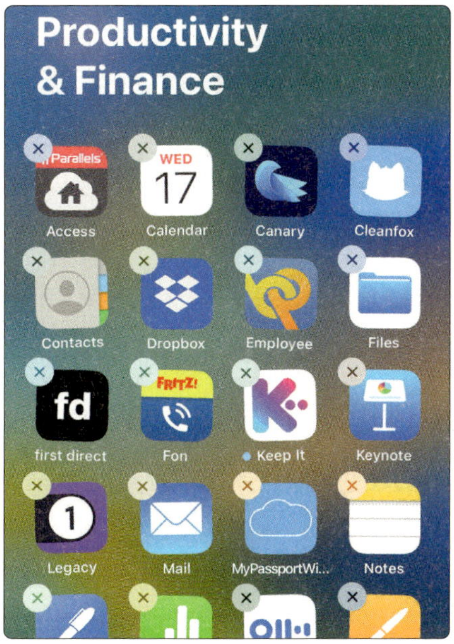

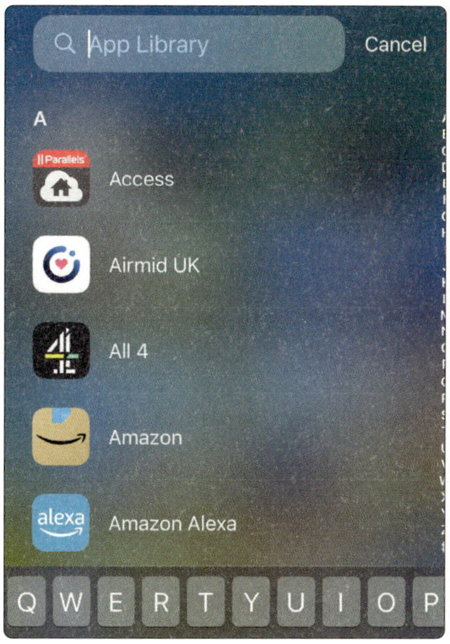

1 Scroll your Home screens all the way to the right for the App Library. Tap one of the larger app icons inside an App Library folder to open that app. Tap a group of four small icons to open the folder. Tap somewhere other than an app icon to get back to the App Library.

2 The App Library sorts apps into categories. You can hold a space between apps and make them wobble, then tap an X in the top-left corner of the app icon to delete it, and drag apps out of the folders too. Tap four small icons while wobbling to access that page; still wobbling.

3 Tap the Search field (top) for a list of your apps, which you can search. To hide pages on the Home Screen (not App Library), hold a space between icons to make them wobble. Tap the dots icon (bottom), then uncheck any pages you wish to hide or check them to show again.

Home Screen Folders

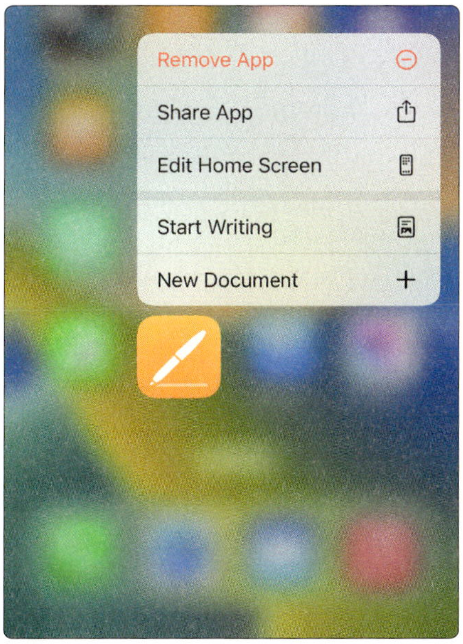

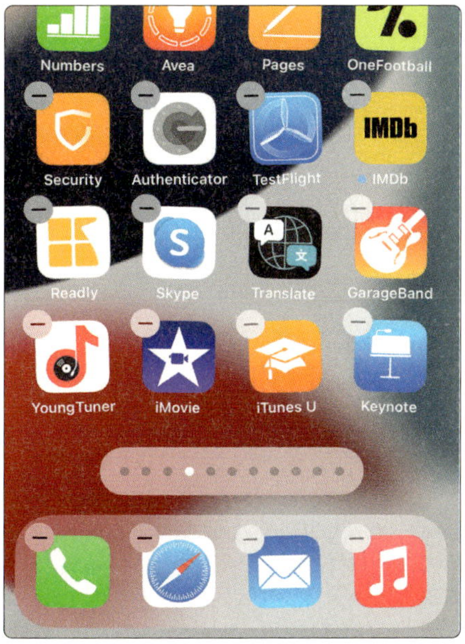

1 On this page, we have the iWork and iLife apps and also iTunes U. Let's make a folder. Tap and hold any app icon, then select Edit Home Screen from the menu. You return to the Home screen, but now the apps wobble and display a in the top left corner.

2 Find two apps you want in the folder and drag one of them onto the other. When a border appears around them, let go to form a new folder. Tap the new folder to open it. It's automatically given a name; change it if you wish. Just tap on it and edit it using the keyboard.

3 Tap outside the folder to get back to the Home screen. To add more apps to the folder, Tap and hold until they wobble, then drag an app onto the folder. To remove an app from the folder, open the folder, tap and hold until they wobble then drag the app off the folder.

Getting Online

The iPhone connects to the Internet automatically whenever you use the App Store, Mail, iTunes Store, Safari, YouTube or any other app that requires it. There are two ways of taking your iPhone online: via a Wi-Fi connection or a 3G/4G/5G mobile network. In this guide, we show you how to set up both, and also how to check your Wi-Fi signal strength.

Joining a Wi-Fi network

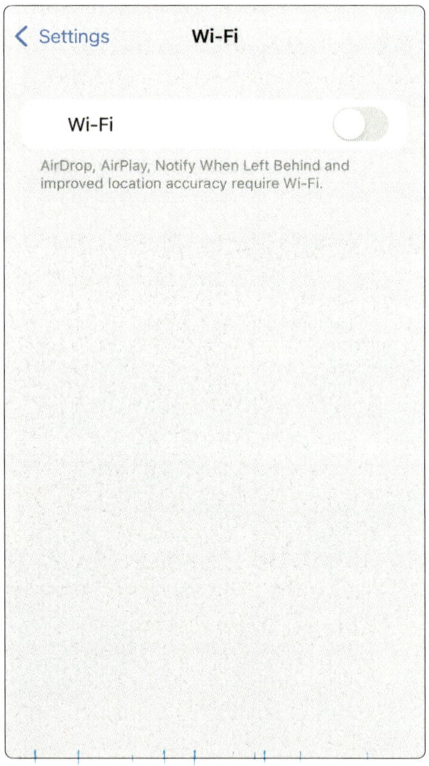

1 To activate Wi-Fi go to Settings > Wi-Fi and turn it on. The iPhone searches for all networks in range. If at home, pick your home network and enter the security details, the password should be supplied with your router.

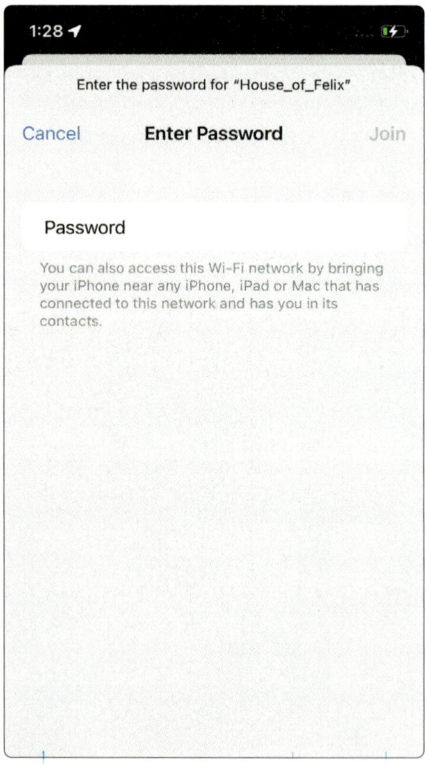

2 If you're at a public hotspot that has no security, you can just connect. If it's password protected, which is far more likely, you need to get the network name and the passcode from whoever is providing the Wi-Fi service.

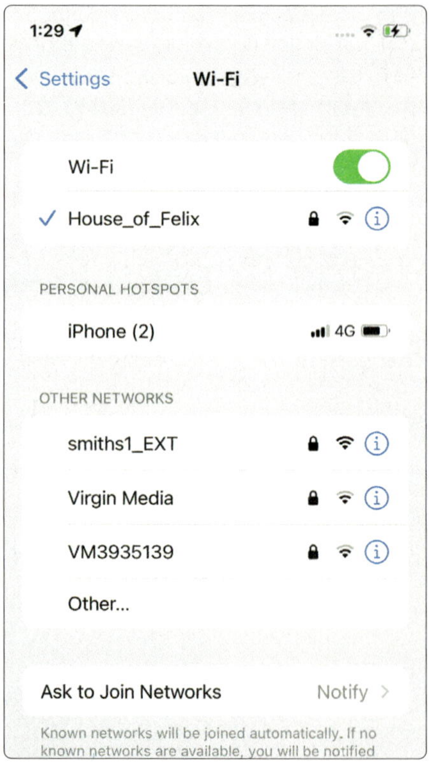

3 From now on, whenever you're in range of this Wi-Fi service the iPhone automatically connects without any prompting. If more than one is in range, the iPhone rejoins the last network it joined.

You can follow these tips for joining a public Wi-Fi service as well as for your home network. Ask the service provider for the Wi-Fi network's details, such as its name and password. You log on automatically next time you use this network but if the password has changed, you must enter the new one.

Joining a mobile 5G, 4G or 3G network

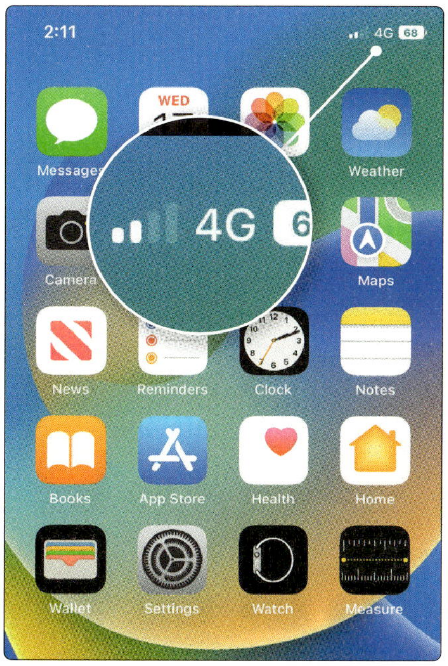

1 When the iPhone connects to the Internet using the mobile data network, you will see the 3G, 4G, 5G, EDGE or GPRS icon in the status bar at the top-right corner of the screen.

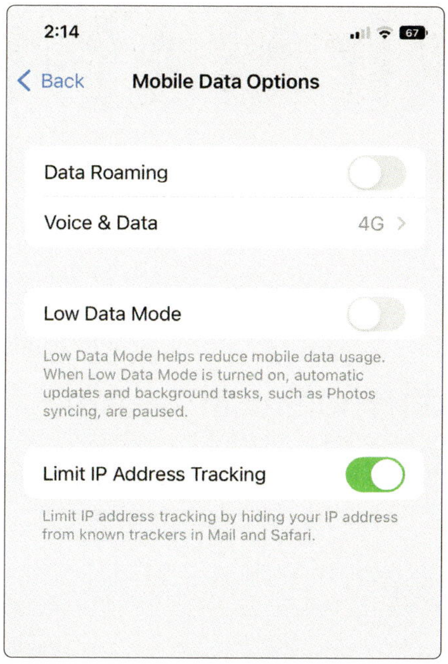

2 If you travel outside your usual mobile network coverage, you can still use 3G, 4G or 5G. To do this, turn Data Roaming on: Settings > Mobile Data > Mobile Data Options. Charges may apply.

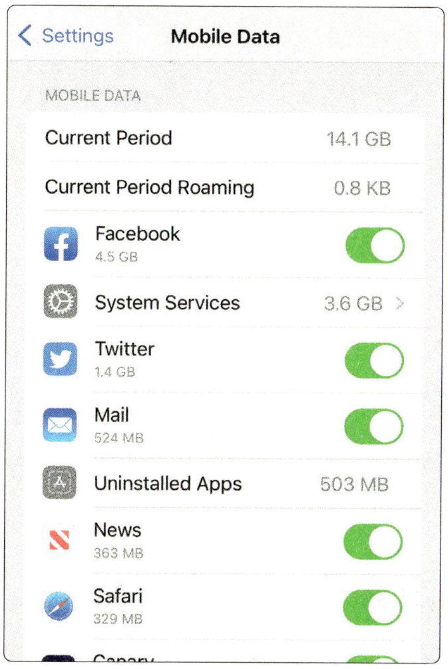

3 You can monitor your mobile network data usage by going to Settings > Mobile Data and then scrolling down to the Mobile Data section. The data settings vary depending on the carrier.

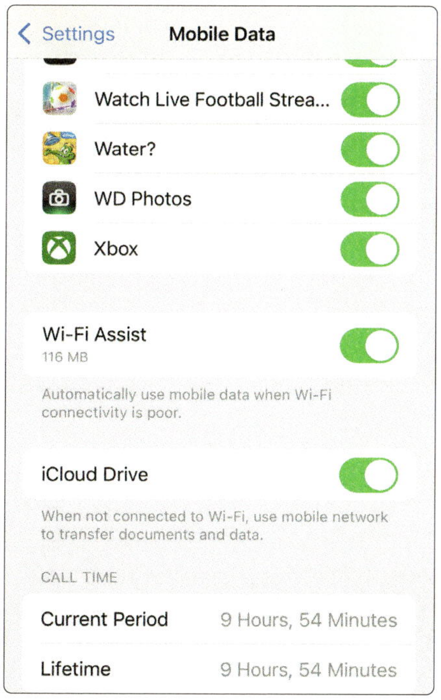

Wi-Fi Assist

Wi-Fi Assist switches to a mobile connection when Wi-Fi is unreliable. It's found in Settings > Mobile Data, and is on by default. To avoid large bills, it doesn't work when Data Roaming, and it won't work with some video apps.

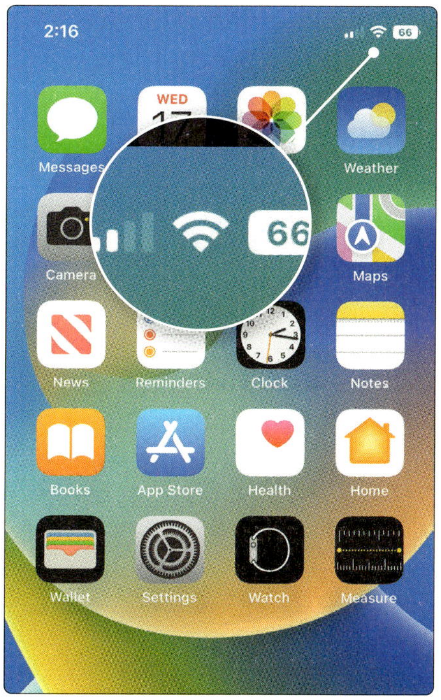

Signal Strength

To check the strength of your current Wi-Fi connection, look at the Wi-Fi icon found in the top right corner of the screen. The more bars that are solid, as opposed to being greyed out, the stronger the iPhone's Wi-Fi connection.

Password Sharing

You can share a Wi-Fi password from your Apple device with another Apple device that wants to join the same network. Both devices must have Wi-Fi and Bluetooth turned on, and neither should be running a Personal Hotspot. They need to be signed into their respective Apple IDs, and have the other person's email address in their Contacts app. They also must be within Bluetooth range, and be unlocked. When the new device tries to connect to the network, a pop-up invites the one that's already on there to share the password. Tap Share Password to do so.

Email Set-Up

Your iPhone's Mail app can send and receive emails from all of your email accounts. It's easy to set up and use with an iCloud, Gmail, Yahoo, AOL or Outlook email address. If you want to add your Internet Service Provider's own email account, it is a little more complicated. Here we take you through setting up each type of email account on your Apple smartphone.

Setting up accounts

For most of the popular web-based email services such as Gmail and Yahoo, the iPhone automatically enters most of the settings needed for you to access your account. We've put together these steps that cover each of the Internet's key email providers. Just follow this guide and you'll soon be emailing from your iPhone.

Setting up an iCloud email account

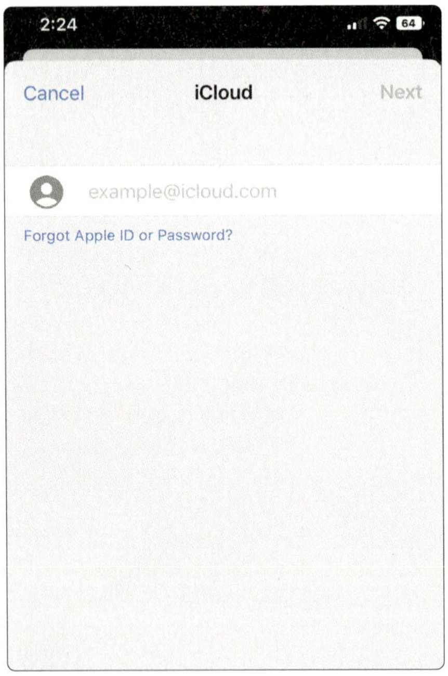

1 Tap the Settings icon and scroll down. Tap the Mail option, then Accounts. From here tap Add Account then tap the iCloud link and enter your Apple ID and Password. If you don't have an Apple ID, tap Create a New Apple ID instead and follow the instructions. Tap Next to automatically verify your details.

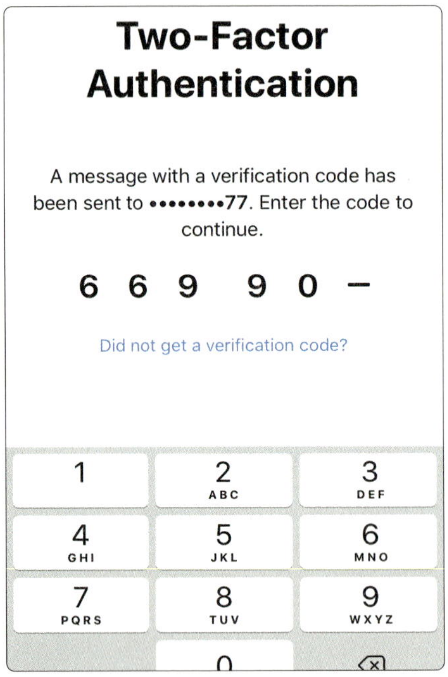

2 If you have Two-Factor Authentication on, you must authenticate now. Enter the verification code or tap the link and follow the instructions if you didn't get one. If you're asked whether you want to allow iCloud to access your location and use Find My iPhone, we suggest you agree.

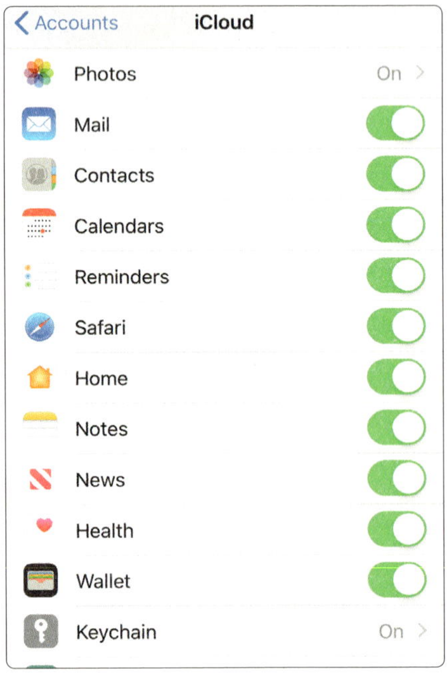

3 You're then taken to this screen, where you can select which of your iPhone's apps use the iCloud. Slide the Mail link to the On position. Deactivate any applications you don't want to sync with iCloud (you can always reactivate them later), and then tap Save in the top right corner to complete the setup.

Setting up Gmail, Yahoo, AOL and Hotmail accounts

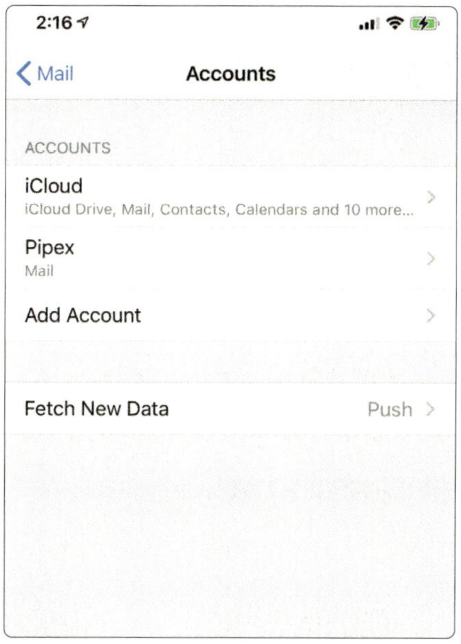

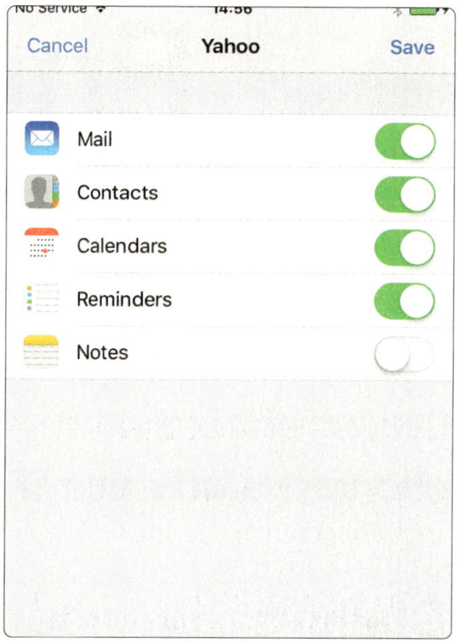

1 Tap the Settings icon on your iPhone's Home screen. Scroll down and click on Mail, then Accounts, then Add Account. This takes you to the list of email accounts that you can configure on your iPhone, such as iCloud or Google accounts.

2 From this screen, tap on either the Gmail, Yahoo, AOL or Microsoft Hotmail link (the process is the same). On this screen you need to enter your name, email address and your password for this account. Finally enter a description of the account. Click the Next link to continue.

3 From this screen, you can select which features of your email account you also wish to sync with your iPhone. When you have made your selections, and are happy to continue, all you have to do to complete the process is tap the Save link and you are ready to go.

Setting up other types of email account

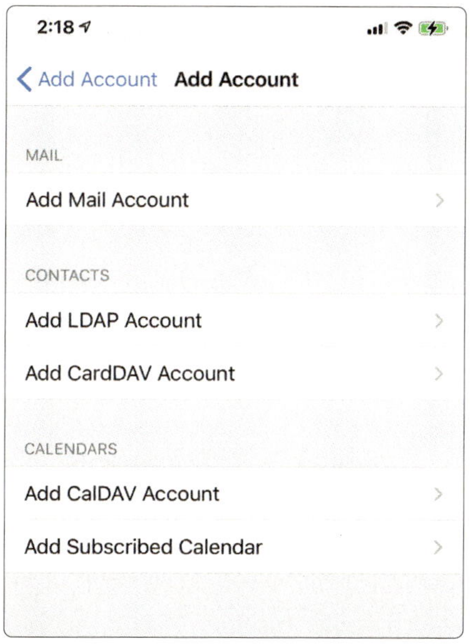

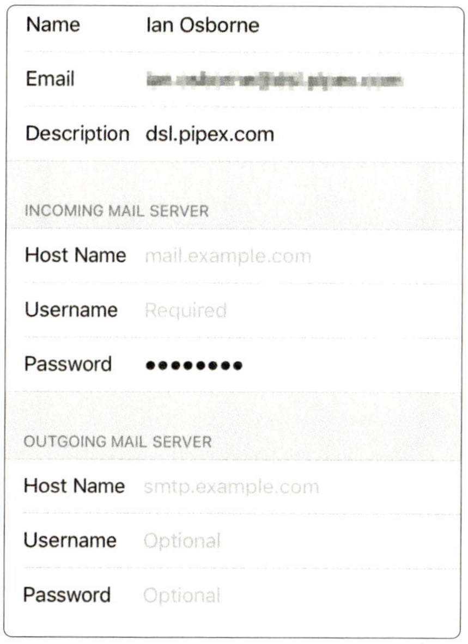

1 Go to Settings > Mail > Accounts > Add Account once more. If you wish to add a Microsoft Exchange account, tap the Exchange option on the screen shown above. If it's a service provided by your ISP (Internet Service Provider), tap Other at the bottom.

2 You will have to visit the support website of your email provider and seek out their help in setting up either a POP or IMAP email account on your iPhone. As these details are all different for each provider, we can, alas, only send you in their direction for help.

3 Once you have obtained all the required information from your email provider, you must then enter these details as requested. When complete, you are ready to go; your iPhone contacts the email server in question and downloads any emails you have for this account.

Phone Calls

With all the games, apps, videos, Internet browsing, email and photography available on your iPhone, one might be excused for forgetting it can also make and receive telephone calls. In this next section we take you through making and answering calls, and show you a few of the iPhone's clever phone-related features such as placing calls on hold and using voicemail.

Dialling a number from the keypad

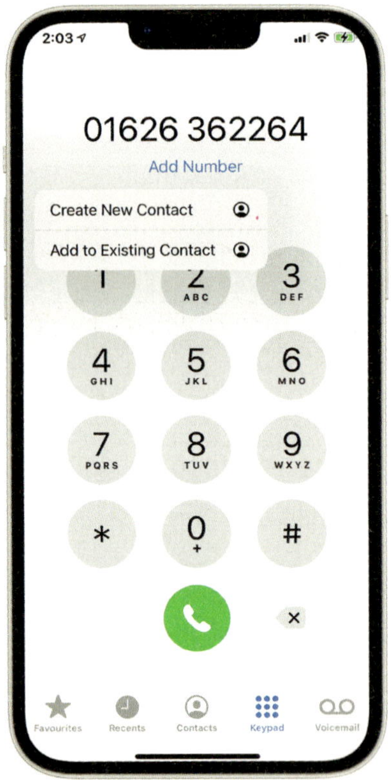

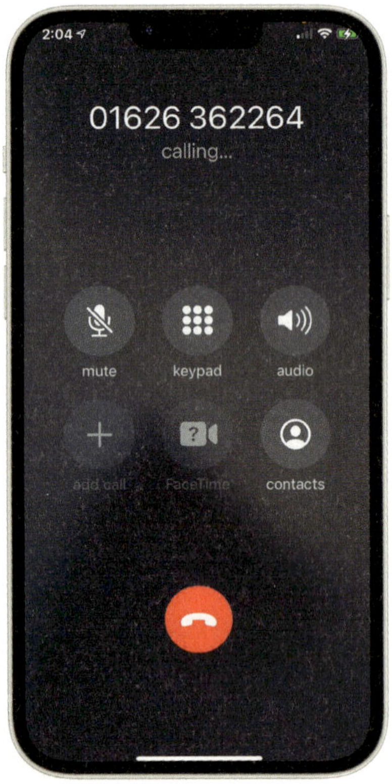

1 Tap the Phone app icon and then select the keypad link from the five options at the bottom of the screen. Enter the phone number by tapping the on-screen digits; the number is shown as you enter it at the top of the screen.

2 If this number is important and is likely to be used often, tap the Add Number link found under the phone number at the top of the screen to add it to your contacts list. If not, tap the green button to make the call.

3 The call automatically connects when your contact answers the phone at their end. To end the call, tap the End Call button, the red one; you're returned to the keypad screen and the call is terminated.

If you're ringing another Apple device, you can use the FaceTime app's audio mode to make a call over the Internet using Wi-Fi or 3G/4G/5G. There are no call costs, though mobile Internet costs might apply. See our tutorial on the FaceTime app later on for more information on making FaceTime Audio and Video calls.

Making a call from your contacts list

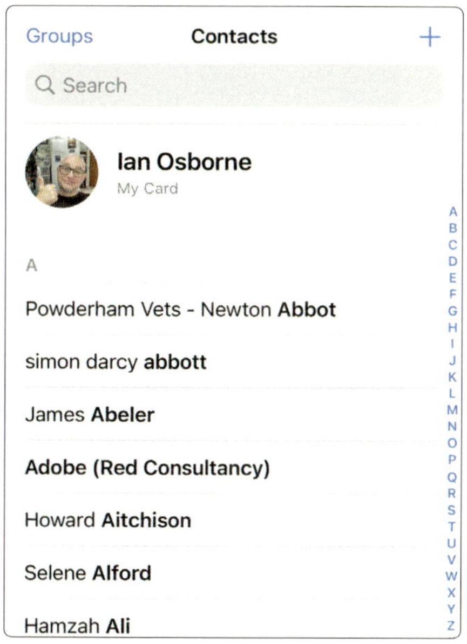

1 Tap the Phone icon and select Contacts. Scroll up and down until you find the number you wish to dial. Alternatively, enter the name of your contact into the Search bar.

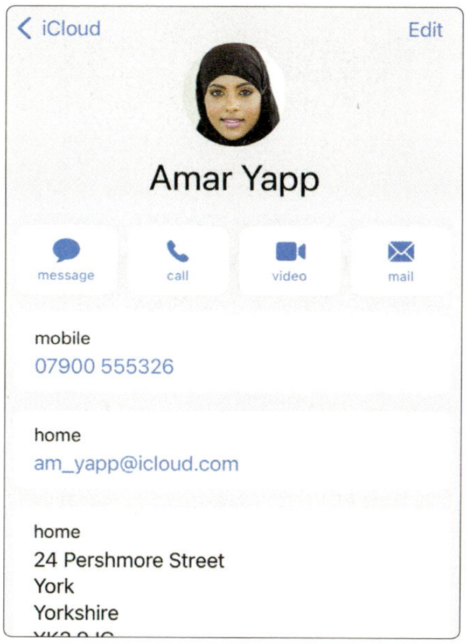

2 Once you've found the contact you wish to call, simply tap their name to be taken to their contact page. To dial them up, tap their phone number to place your call.

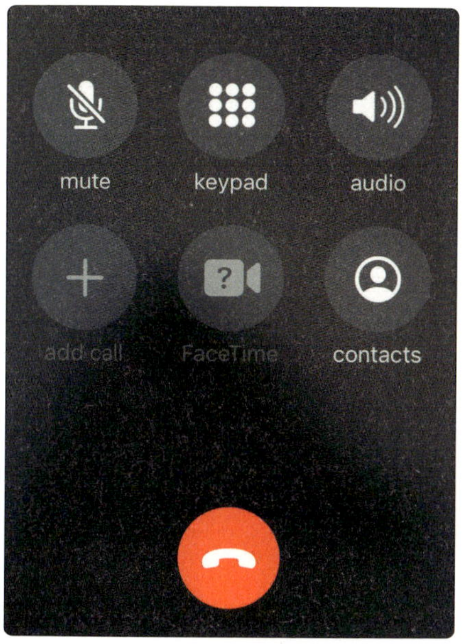

3 When you've finished your conversation, tap the End Call button, the red one showing the telephone receiver, to hang up; or wait for your contact to do the same.

Answering a call

1 Incoming calls appear as a notification at the top of the screen; you can accept or decline it. When you get a call you either see the name of the contact or the number displayed. If the number is withheld, the word "Blocked" appears.

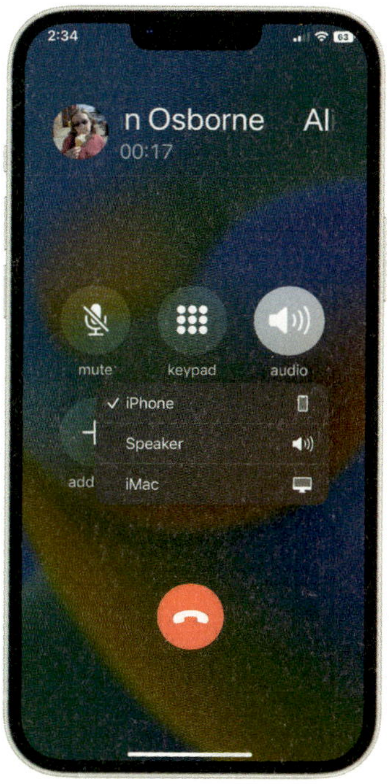

2 To answer the call, if your iPhone is in sleep mode, move the slider to the far right to accept the call. If you receive a call when you are using your iPhone, you can decline it by pressing the red button or accept via the green one.

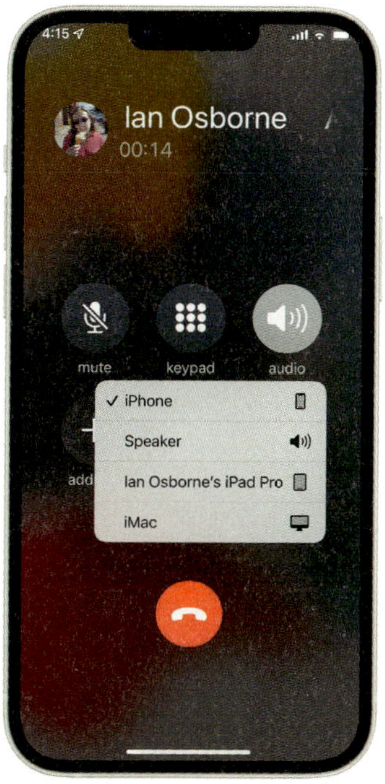

3 To go hands-free for the duration of this call, simply press the Speaker button on the upper right. This switches the outgoing sound to the main speakers, allowing you to talk without holding the phone.

Placing a call on hold

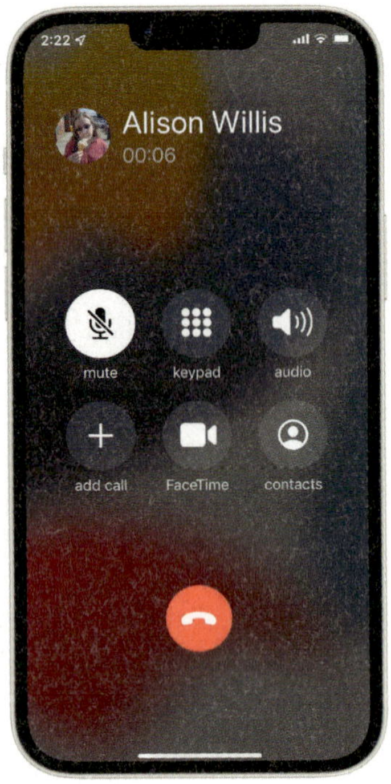

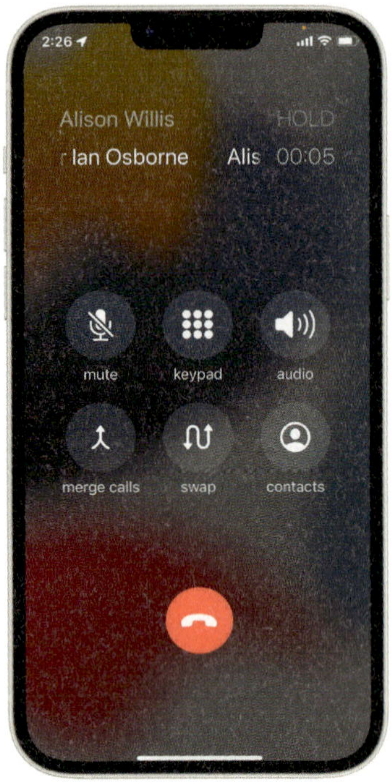

1 During a call, you can place the caller on hold by pressing Mute, pausing the conversation without actually hanging up the phone. To return to the call, tap Mute again.

2 Should a second caller ring when you're on a call, you have an option (the big red button) called Decline, which cuts off the second caller but lets them leave a voice message.

3 By selecting the Hold & Accept option, you place the original caller on hold, allowing you to answer the second call before returning to the first one by tapping swap.

Dialling a number from a secondary source

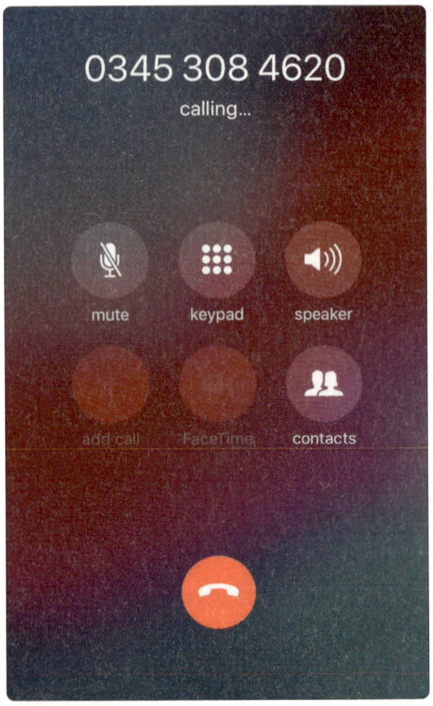

1 If you find a telephone number on a web page in Safari, the number is in a button. Tap on it to place the call.

2 You'll see a confirmation request. Tap Call to ring the desired number without having to use the number pad.

3 The call is placed, just as it would be if you'd typed it yourself or tapped a number found in your Contacts app.

Placing calls from a message or note

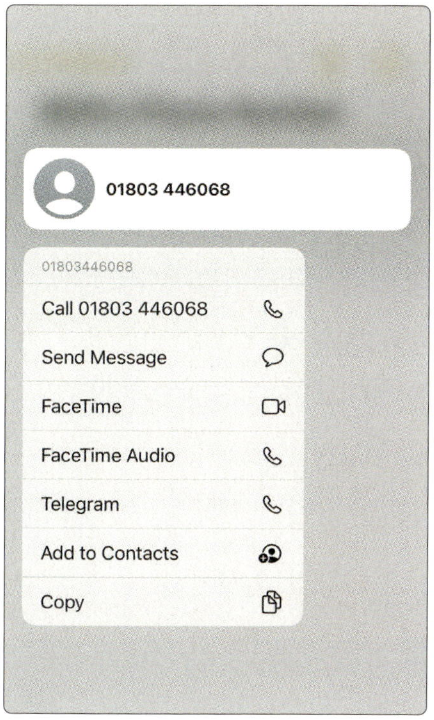

1 If you have a message, email, note, or document containing a phone number, you can place a call to it by tapping the highlighted, underlined number then tapping Call.

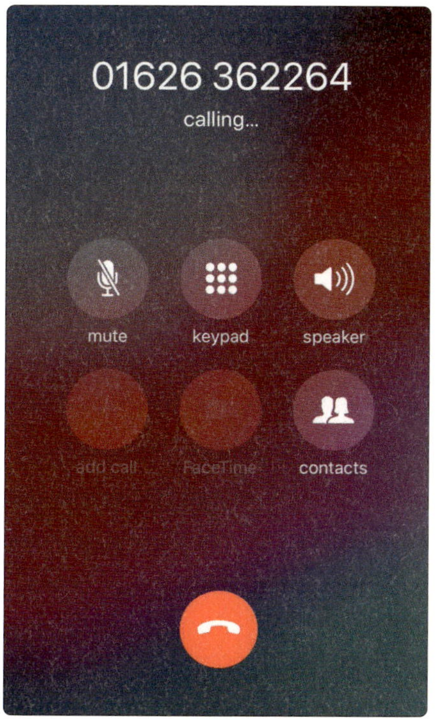

2 You will now place the call in the same manner as you have done previously. Please note that you receive no confirmation warning when you're using this method of calling.

Setting up and using your voicemail

1 To listen to your Voicemail messages, tap the Phone app and click Voicemail at the bottom of the screen, then tap Call Voicemail. A call is made to your voicemail service.

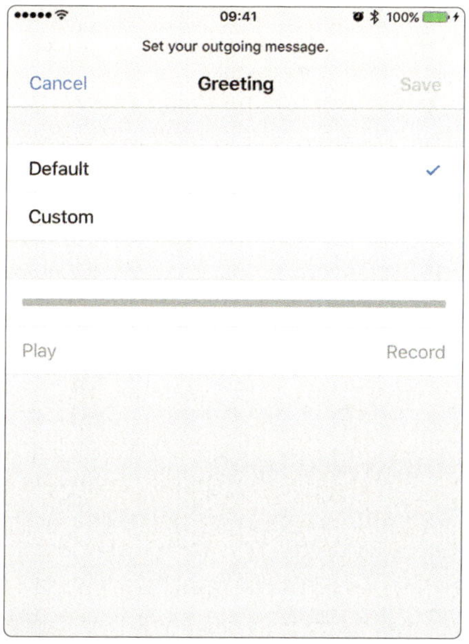

2 To customise your message, tap the Voicemail button. If there's a Greeting link on the next screen, follow it. If not, listen to your voice mails and follow the recorded instructions.

Blocking callers

Nuisance callers are the bane of every iPhone owner's life. It seems like hardly a day goes by when a call centre rings up asking if you want to change your energy supplier, consider life insurance or sign up for some service or another. Worse still are fraudulent calls claiming to be from your bank or the tax office, when it's really a criminal gang trying to get you to part with your money. Or maybe you're getting menacing or harassing calls from a stalker or an ex-partner? Thankfully, in iOS, you can block incoming phone numbers quickly and easily.

To block a number that has called your iPhone, in the Phone app, tap Recents and then tap the 'i' next to the caller you wish to block. Now tap Block this Caller, at the bottom of the screen. The phone number is added to your Blocked Contacts list, and can no longer contact you.

To view and edit your Blocked Contacts list, go to Settings > Phone > Blocked Contacts. You see a list of numbers you've blocked. Swipe a number left and tap Unblock to remove it from this list. If you want to call or send a message to a number on your list, tap the chevron to its right.

Another useful feature is sending unknown callers, that is, phone numbers that aren't in your Contacts app and with whom you haven't interacted in the past, directly to your voicemail so you don't have to deal with them there and then. This is a Settings option, so go to Settings > Phone > Silence Unknown Callers and turn it on. If you find it doesn't suit you, you can always turn it off again.

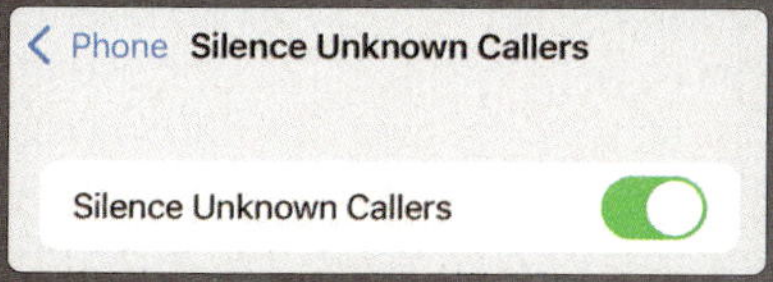

The Touchscreen

The iPhone's touchscreen supports more than one touch, that is, you can place more than one finger on it and the screen recognises their presence and movement. This allows for touchscreen gestures, which are achieved by placing one or more finger on the screen and swiping, pinching, spreading gesture and more. Here's a guide to gestures and what they do.

How to use Touchscreen actions

Touch

The iPhone has a capacitive touchscreen, which means it's sensitive to the tiny electrical charges in our bodies. With this type of screen, you only have to tap it, not press down hard with your finger. To activate items on the screen such as applications and settings icons, type letters and symbols using the on-screen keyboard or to press on-screen buttons, you simply (gently) touch them with your finger.

Touch and hold

Touch and hold is useful in a number of different situations. You touch and hold an item on the screen by touching it and not lifting your finger until an action occurs. The action in question depends on where you're using the gesture. For example, if you touch and hold a web link, you're presented with a menu giving you the chance to open it in Safari, add it to your Reading List, copy it or share it.

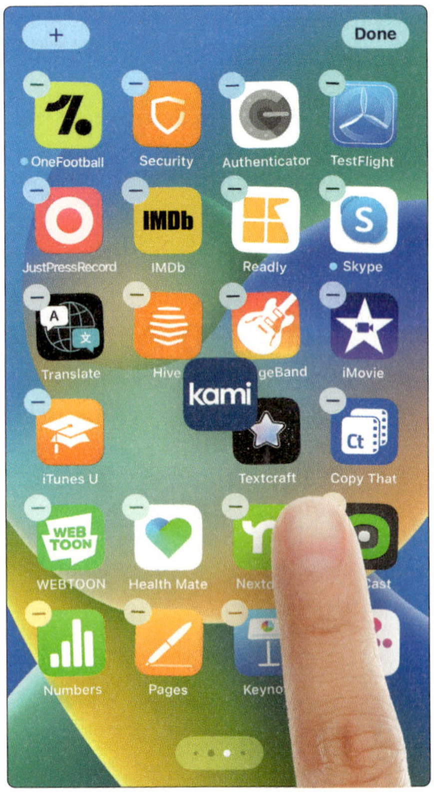

Drag

You can customise your iPhone's Home screen. To drag items around the screen and reorder them, hold an icon, and in the pop-up menu, tap Rearrange Apps. You can then put your finger on an app icon and, without lifting your finger, slide it across the screen until you reach the required position. Lift your finger off the screen and the item drops into that location (if it's free), moving the other icons out of the way.

Swipe or scroll

Many of the menus or web pages that you can access on the iPhone require you to scroll. To swipe or slide, quickly move your finger across the surface of the screen, without pausing when you first touch it. For example, the main Photos app lets you slide the screen left to right to scroll through your pics, and in some Calendar views you can swipe quickly across the screen to change the range of time visible.

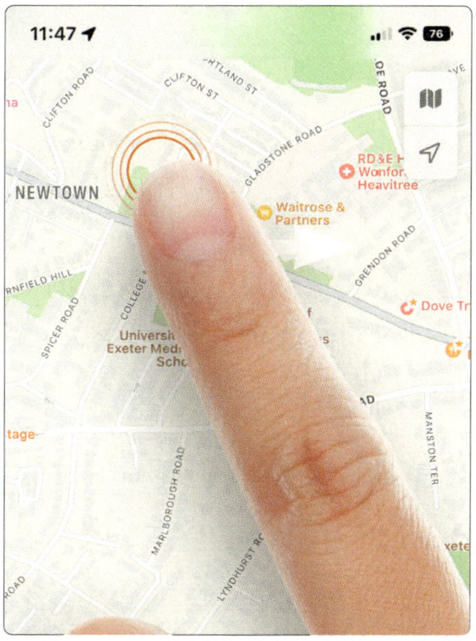

Double-tap

There are several places in apps where a double-tap is used. Tapping twice quickly on a web page, map or other screen will zoom in for easier viewing. You can double-tap a section of a web page in the browser to zoom it to fit the width of the screen. Double-tapping after pinching to zoom in some applications, such as the browser, reflows a column of text to fit the width of the screen.

Pinch to zoom

In some applications (such as Maps, Safari, and Photos), you can zoom in and out by placing two fingers on the screen at once and pinching them together (to zoom out) or spreading them apart (to zoom in). This also works to zoom in and out in the Camera app. Just use the gesture in the viewing area when you're ready to take a photo to give an optical zoom effect.

Swipe up for Home screen

On previous iPhones, you could get to the Home screen by pressing the Home button. As newer iPhones don't have a Home button, a new gesture is required. Simply swipe all the way up from the bottom of the screen and the Home page is revealed.

Swipe for the App Switcher

Previously achieved with a double-tap on the Home button, to get to the App Switcher, swipe up from the bottom of the screen and when your finger is halfway up, hold it steady until the other apps arrive, as seen here. You can then lift your finger.

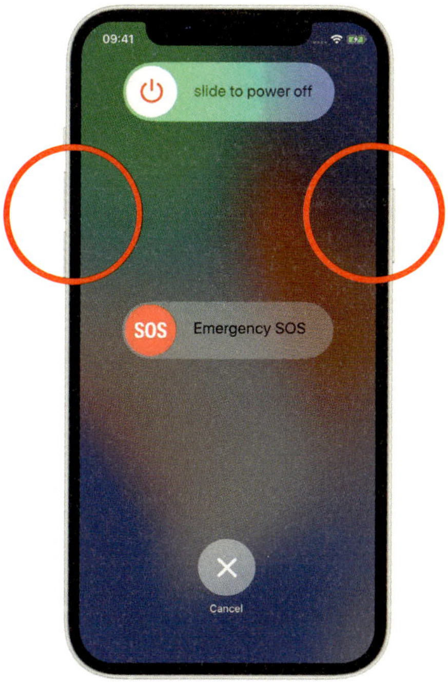

Restart your iPhone

To restart a newer iPhone with no Home button, press and hold both the Side button on the right and the Volume button on the left. On older iPhones, press and hold the side or top button. This screen appears, from where you shut down your iPhone with the slider.

The Keyboard

When it comes to using your iPhone, the keyboard is second only in importance to the touchscreen. If you familiarise yourself with the iPhone's virtual keyboard features, you can get so much more out of your Apple smartphone. This guide teaches you how to use the virtual keyboard, and its features such as voice input and additional languages.

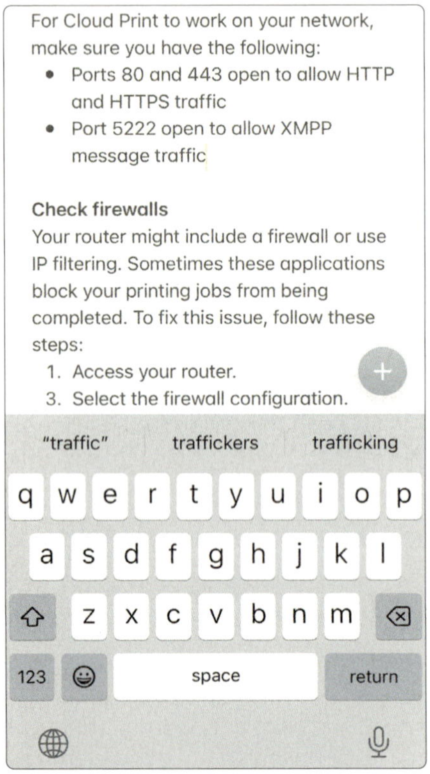

1 Once you've opened the on-screen keyboard, you can enter text by simply tapping on the keys as you would on any similar typing device. It's really easy and intuitive to use.

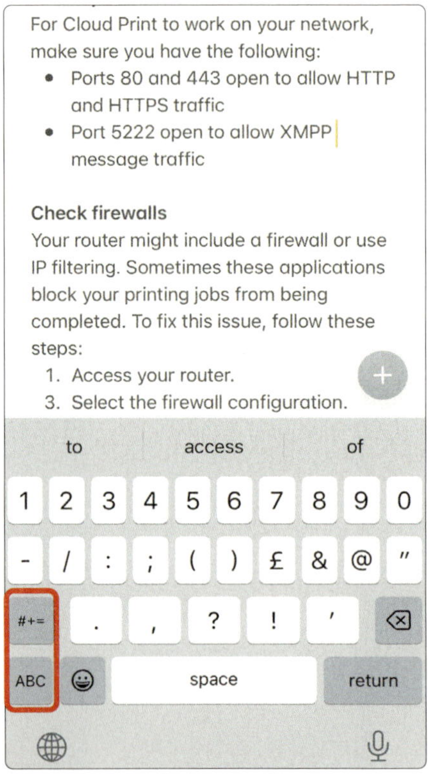

2 To add digits and punctuation, tap the 123 key on the lower-left side of the keyboard. A tap on the key above brings up more symbols. To return to letters, tap the ABC key.

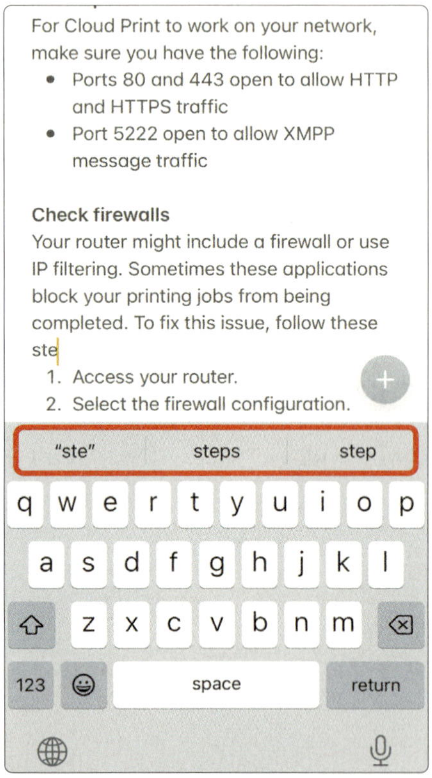

3 When you start to type a word, the iPhone tries to complete it for you and displays its predictions in a bar above the keyboard. Tap one of the suggestions to finish the word.

Shift key options

Tap the Shift key to switch to capital letters for the next key press only. Double-tap to lock it in caps mode, like a caps lock on a manual typewriter. In caps mode, tap the Shift key once to return to normal typing. The Shift key's graphic changes depending on whether it's in regular, caps-next or caps-lock mode.

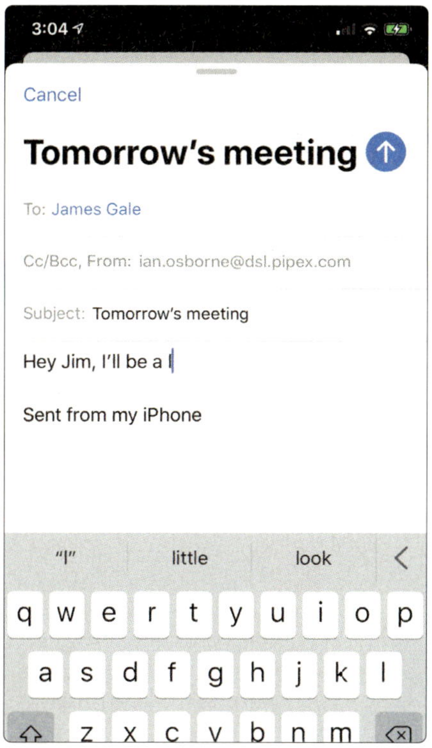

4 When sending messages or emails, predictive text learns your choice of language and suggests the correct word for the tone of what it is you're writing. Tap on the word to use it.

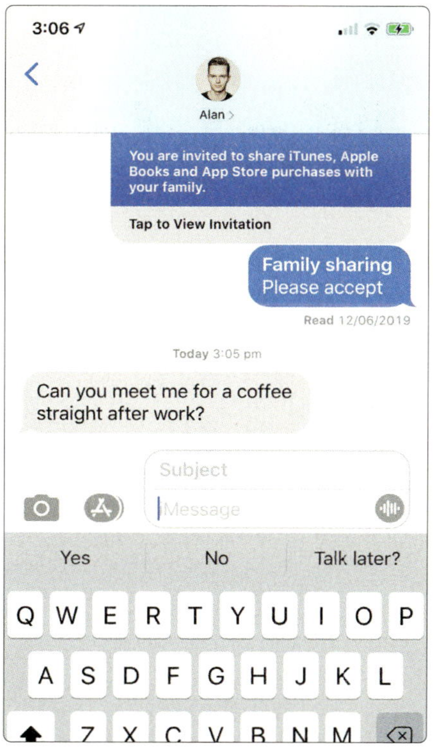

5 This predictive text feature also recognises if you are replying to a question that can be answered "Yes" or "No". As before, simply tap to select the answer that suits your reply.

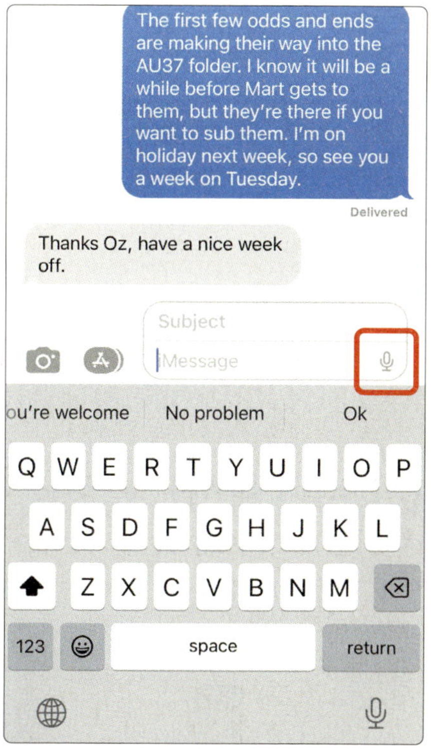

6 Notice the Microphone icon on or under the keyboard. This is the Voice Dictation key. Tap this and simply speak the text you wish to enter; it appears on-screen in real-time.

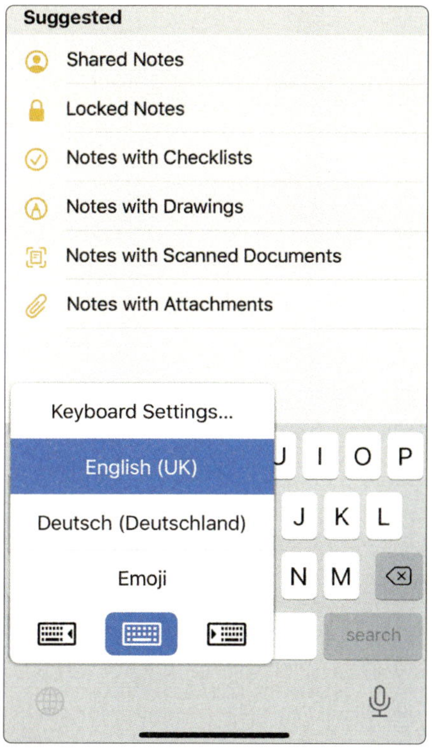

7 Additional keyboards can be accessed by tapping and holding the Globe icon and selecting an option. You can (de)activate predictive text from the Keyboard Settings link.

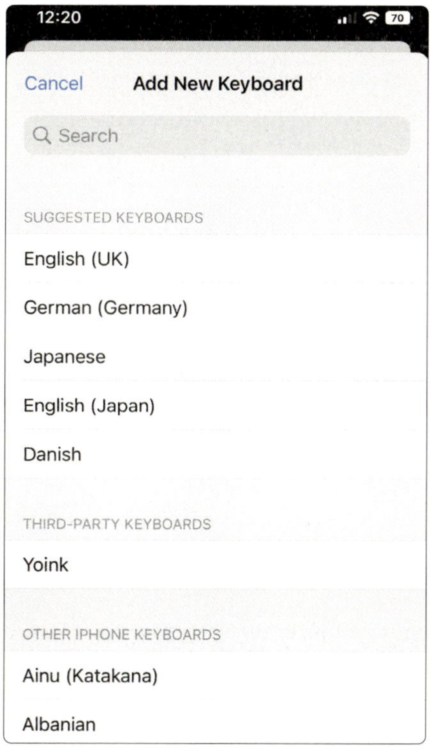

8 To add third-party keyboards, download the Keyboard app from the App Store. From Settings, go to: General > Keyboard > Keyboards > Add New Keyboard and select the app.

Swipe Keyboard

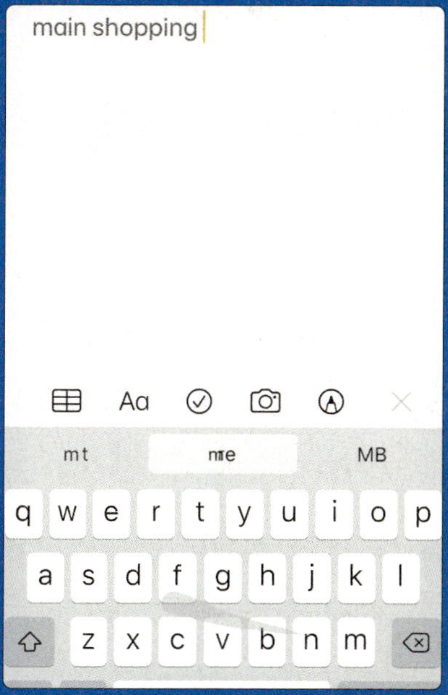

A new feature is the Swipe keyboard. Instead of tapping each key individually, you can drag your finger from letter to letter, without lifting it, until you get to the end of a word.

Control Centre

To access the Control Centre, swipe down from the top right corner, or if you have an older iPhone model, swipe up from the bottom of the screen. The iOS 16 Control Centre has some great features, which we look at here.

CONTROL CENTRE *in Focus*

1 In this box, you can turn on and off (clockwise, from top left) Airplane Mode, Mobile Data, Bluetooth and Wi-Fi. If you have 3D Touch, deep press the main box for more options.

2 This box shows what you're currently listening to. Here we're listening to the radio, so we can play/pause and skip forward or backward ten seconds. Deep press for more options, including volume control and external speakers.

3 Tap here to lock the screen in its current orientation, so it doesn't switch between landscape and portrait mode when you turn the iPhone. Tap it again to switch off the screen orientation lock.

4 Tap here to access the Screen Mirroring menu, which shows a list of devices to which you can mirror your iPhone's screen. Tap one of them and the iPhone screen is shown on that device.

5 This is the brightness control. Run your finger up and down it to raise or lower the brightness, or deep press for a bigger version of the slider and instant access to Night Shift Mode.

6 Your iPhone's volume control. Run your finger up and down the slider to adjust the sound. Do a deep press to open a bigger version of the volume control slider.

7 To mirror your screen, maybe to your Apple TV, tap here and select the target from the window.

8 Tap here to use the LED on the back of your iPhone as a torch. Deep press for a slider that lets you adjust the light's brightness.

9 Tap here to open the Clock app and go straight to its Timer feature. Deep press for access to an instant timer.

10 Tap here to open the Calculator app. Tap and hold to see, and if you wish, copy, the result of the last calculation you completed.

11 Tap this to access the Camera app. Deep press it to access photography options within the Camera app, such as selfies, video recording and the Slo-Mo function.

12 Tap here for the controls for your favourite HomeKit gadgets. It's a useful way to use Home controls without going through the app.

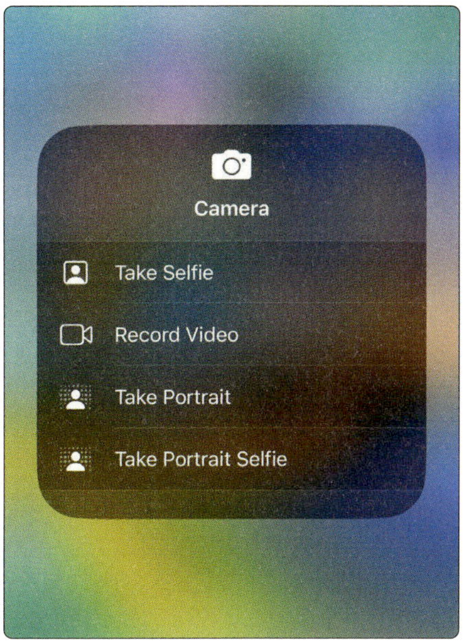

Deep press icons

If you tap and hold a Control Centre icon, it usually gives access to further functions. For example, the Camera icon provides the window shown here, and gives you instant access to selfies, video recording, and portrait photography.

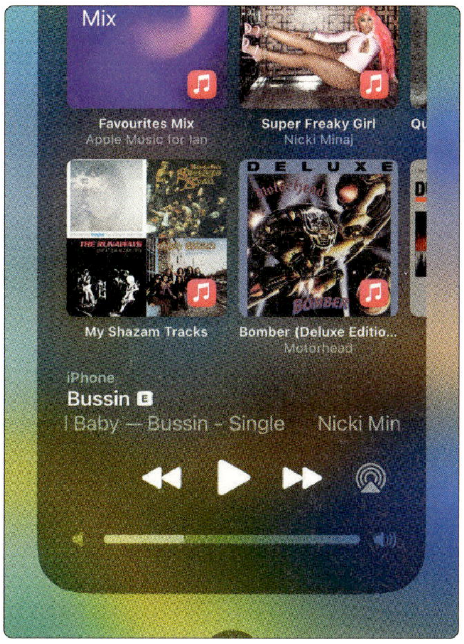

The music controls

Just like before, the music controls show you the currently playing song. You can skip forwards and backwards or play/pause from the Control Centre icon, but a long press gives access to more comprehensive controls and also the album art.

Access local Bluetooth & Wi-Fi

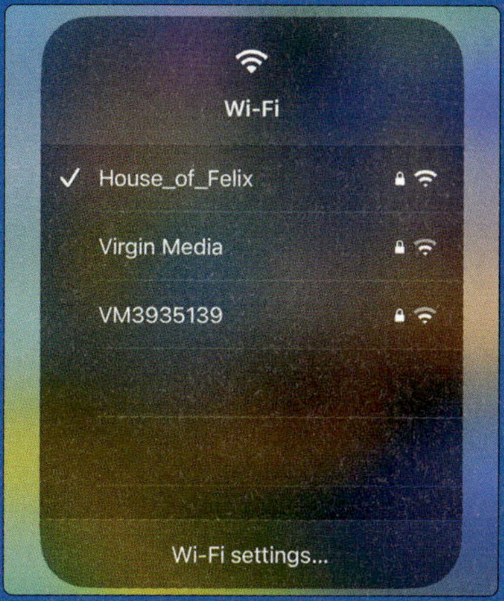

In Control Centre, tap and hold the top left box to open the larger window, then tap and hold the Wi-Fi or Bluetooth icon to switch between networks or BT devices. You can also access their Settings screens from these windows.

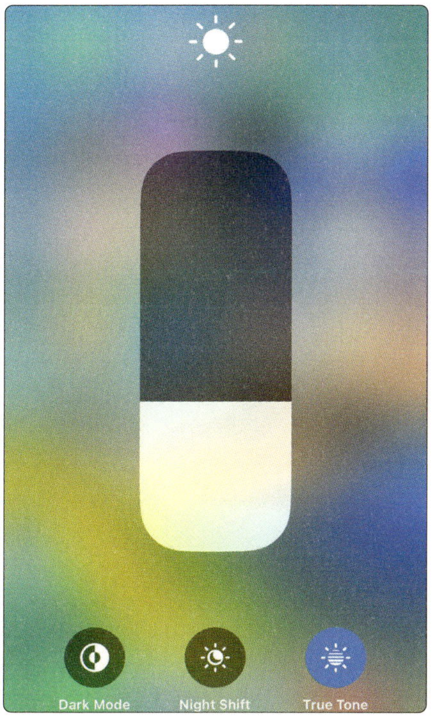

Night Shift mode

Tap and hold the brightness slider to access a larger version, and also three icons underneath. These are: (left to right) toggle between Light and Dark Mode, Night Shift (to reduce blue light) and toggle True Tone screen.

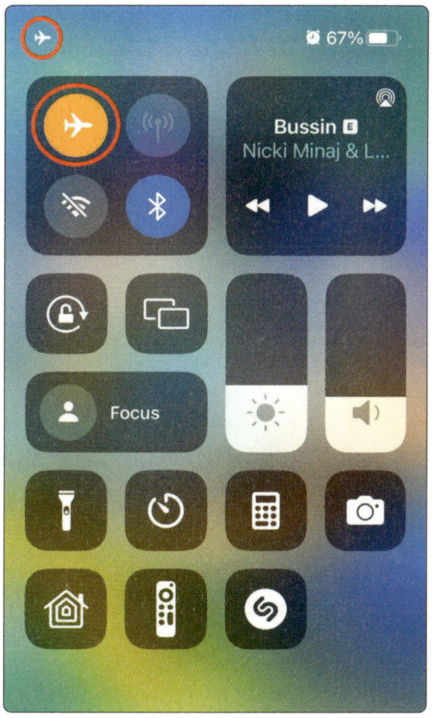

Airplane mode

The iPhone's Airplane Mode switches off its Wi-Fi and Bluetooth connections, as required by some airlines. It's also useful even if you're not flying: for example, if your battery is low and you're reading an iBook, Airplane Mode can save power.

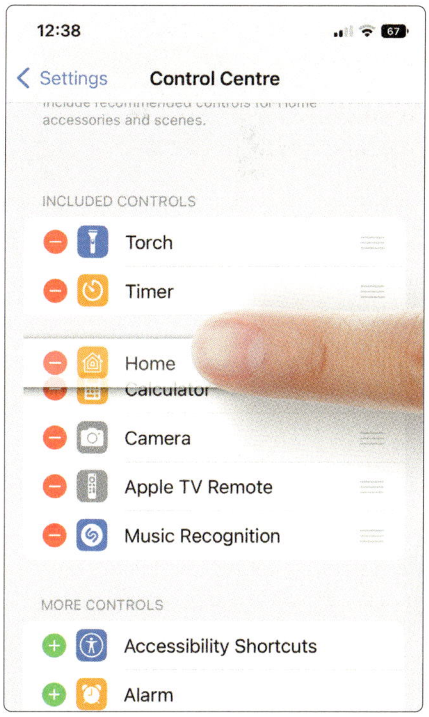

Customisation

Go to Settings > Control Centre and you can delete Control Centre icons you never use and add others, if you wish, using the '+' and '-' icons. You can also reorder the controls by tapping and holding their three-line icons and dragging.

Lock Screen

The lock screen has had a major overhaul in iOS 16. It now has a huge range of customisation options, with Widgets, animations and user-customisable time digits. Music controls now appear on the lock screen too. You can make multiple lock screen designs and switch between them as you please, and you can opt for a multi-layered wallpaper effect. Here's how to do it.

First steps with the lock screen

1 If your phone is unlocked, swipe the screen down to get to the lock screen. Deep press anywhere on the screen to get to the Collections screen, as seen here. Swipe the screen left and press the Plus icon to open a new lock screen.

2 A pop-up window invites you to choose a new wallpaper for your new lock screen. Slide the circular icons at the top to review the categories on offer. The rest of the screen shows samples; take a look to see what's on offer.

3 When you've chosen a wallpaper, you can add widgets. Tap the '+ Add Widgets' box for a pop-up window, from which you can choose them. They work a little like home screen widgets, but are available on the lock screen.

Choose and customise

When you've made several lock screens, you can choose between them by deep-tapping the lock screen and swiping left and right. To customise a screen you've already designed, tap the Customise button underneath.

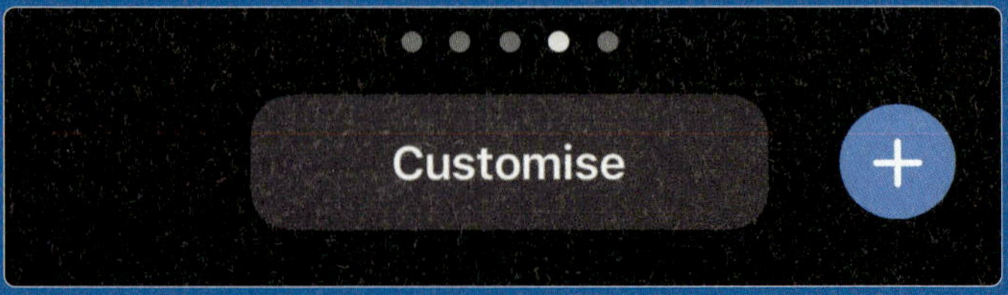

The wallpaper options

1 There are three categories of photo available at the top of the screen; Photos, People and Photo Shuffle. After choosing a photo for your wallpaper, you can swipe it left and right to choose from the various filters on offer.

2 Pinch and spread to fit the photo how you want it on the screen. Tap the three-dots icon for a pop-up, from which you can set the Depth Effect, where parts of an object appear on top of the time, on or off. Tap Done when you've finished.

3 If you choose an Emoji wallpaper, you can add up to six emojis. Tap them on the window. Swipe left and right for various patterns and designs made from those emojis. Tap the three dots icon to change the background colour.

4 Choose an Astronomy wallpaper and swipe left and right for options such as looking at the Earth, at your location on the Earth, the Moon, a detail of the Moon or the entire solar system. There are no specific customisation options.

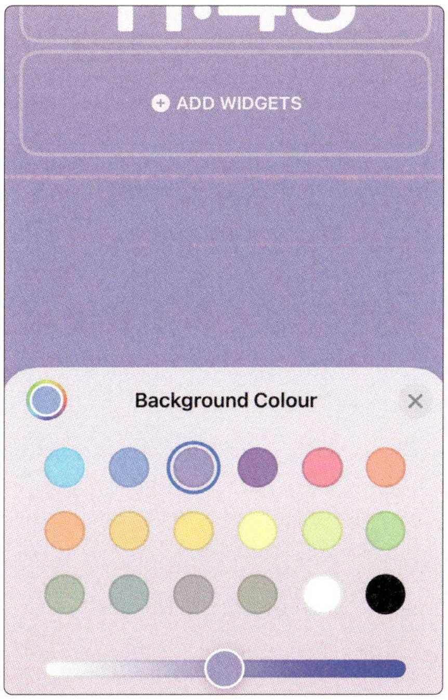

5 The Weather wallpaper shows the weather at your current location, and the Colour option sets a single colour for a lock screen. After setting a colour with the picker and the slider, swipe left and right for variations on the theme.

6 When you've finished customising a screen, tap Done and you're invited to set it as the Home screen as well (Set as Wallpaper Pair) or to set up the home screen separately (Customise Home Screen). It's entirely up to you.

Setting up your Widgets

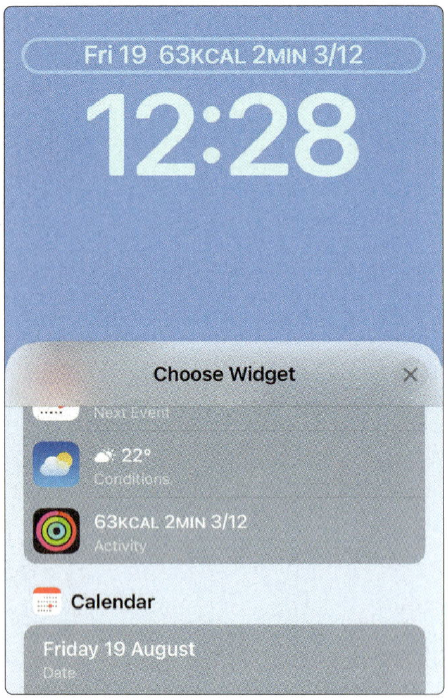

1 While customising a lock screen, you can change the widget above the clock. Tap the date and day strip. You can choose from a limited number of widgets here, gleaned from apps such as Weather, Calendar, Fitness and more.

2 To add a widget below the clock, tap the '+ Add Widget' box. You get a pop-up window showing the widgets on offer. They function like Today screen and home screen widgets, in that they glean and display information from apps.

3 The widgets at the top of the window are samples taken from the apps listed underneath. Tap them to add them to the widgets window. When it's filled, you have to delete a widget to add a new one – you can't start a second row.

4 Tap one of the apps listed lower down the widgets window and choose an app. You can then choose the size of widget you wish to use, and its contents, from those offered; swipe left and right to review them, and tap one to add it.

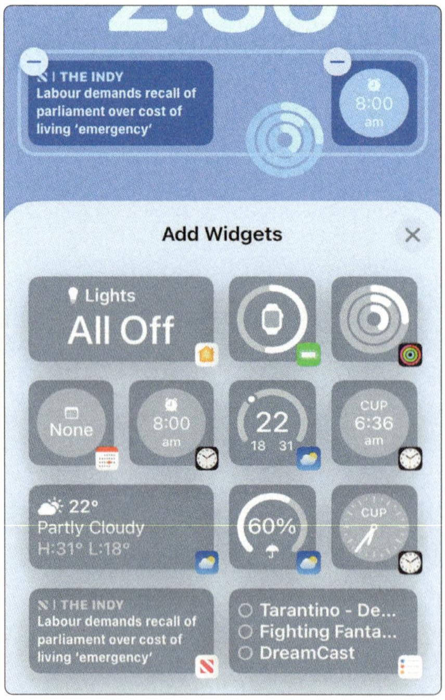

5 You can, to a limited extent, drag widgets back and forth in the box to reorder them. If you want to remove a widget, tap the minus sign in its top-left corner. Tap Done when you've chosen your widgets. You can change them later.

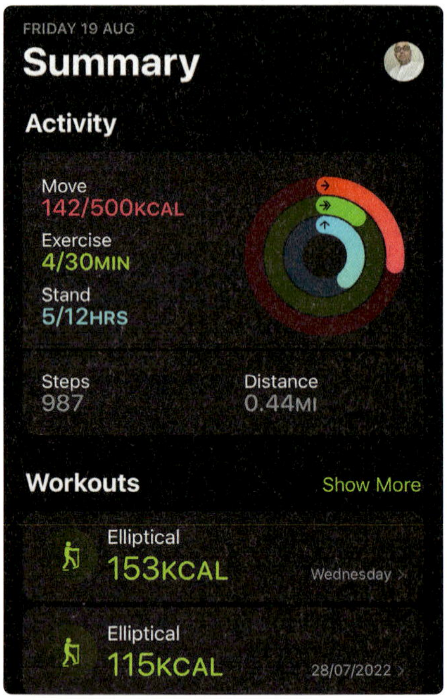

6 On the lock screen, you can tap a widget to open its app, on the 'page' from where the widget's information is from. To change your widgets, tap and hold the lock screen, tap Customise at the bottom then tap the widgets window.

Customising the time

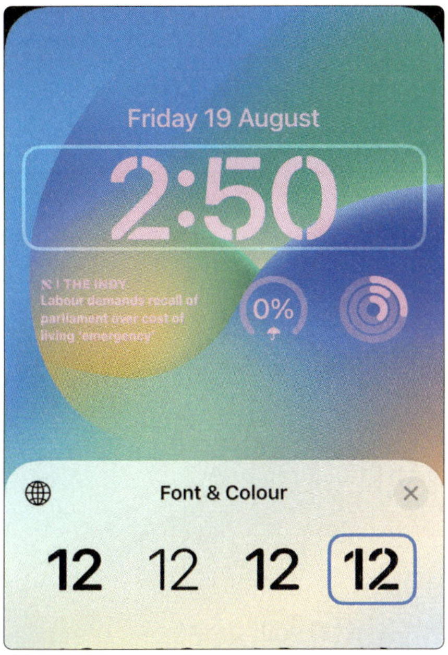

1 While customising your lock screen, you can tap the time to change the font and colour used for its numbers. You get a pop-up window showing various options for changing them. Tap a number style and a colour to do so.

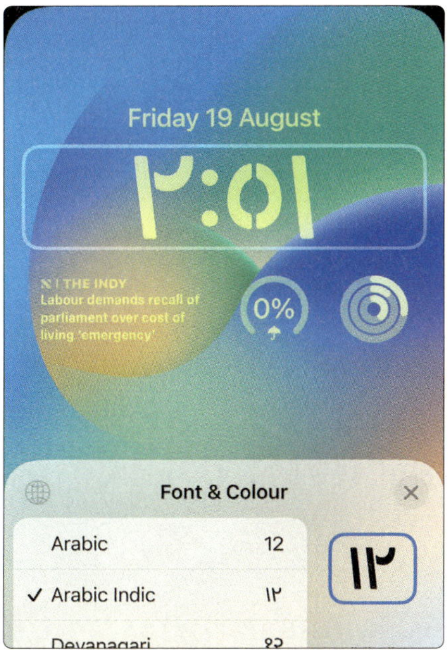

2 Tap the globe in the top-left corner of the window to opt between Arabic numerals (regular numbers), Arabic Indic (used in some Asian countries) and Devanagari (used for Sanskrit, Hindi, and other Indian languages).

Focus mode

1 Each lock screen you design can be linked to a different Focus mode. You can (for example) design one with work-related widgets and link it to your Work focus. Access the lock screen customisation screen as shown.

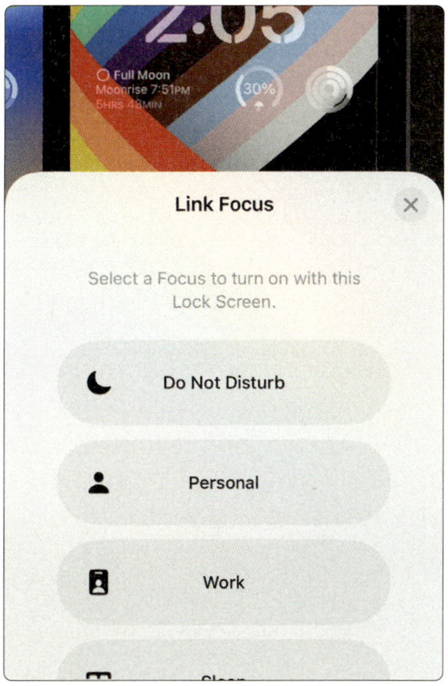

2 Scroll to the lock screen you want to link, and tap the Focus button at the foot of the screen. Choose one of your focuses, and then when you select the lock screen in question, you also turn on its linked Focus Mode.

Deleting lock screens

On the screen where you can swipe left and right to choose between a lock screen you've already created, if you come across one you no longer need, swipe it upwards and tap the dustbin icon at the foot of the screen to delete it.

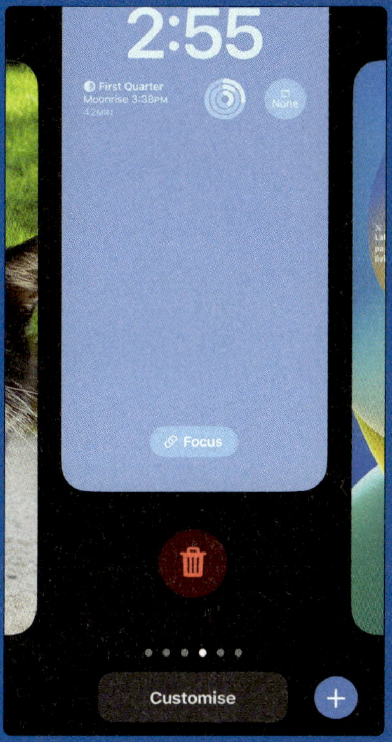

Live Activities

A feature that's coming soon is Live Activities, which is a new kind of notification that lets you watch something that updates in real-time, such as a sports game, a taxi driving to your location or a food delivery.

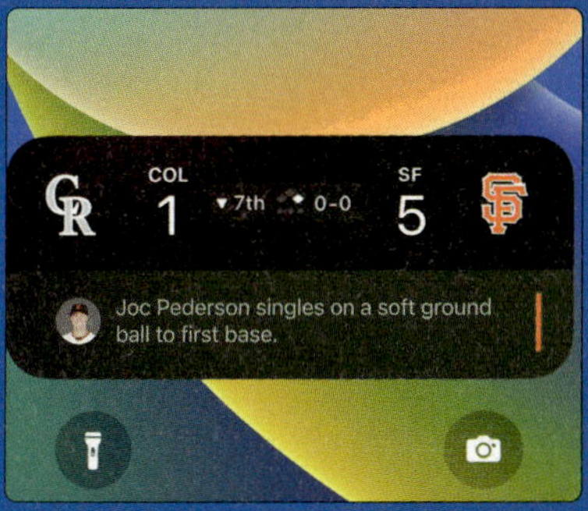

Your iPhone's Built-in Apps

iOS 16 comes with a host of bundled applications, for all sorts of tasks. Safari is your web browser, Mail lets you send and receive emails, Maps is great for finding your way around and more. In this section, we take a look at the iPhone's key apps, covering their basic functions and advanced features.

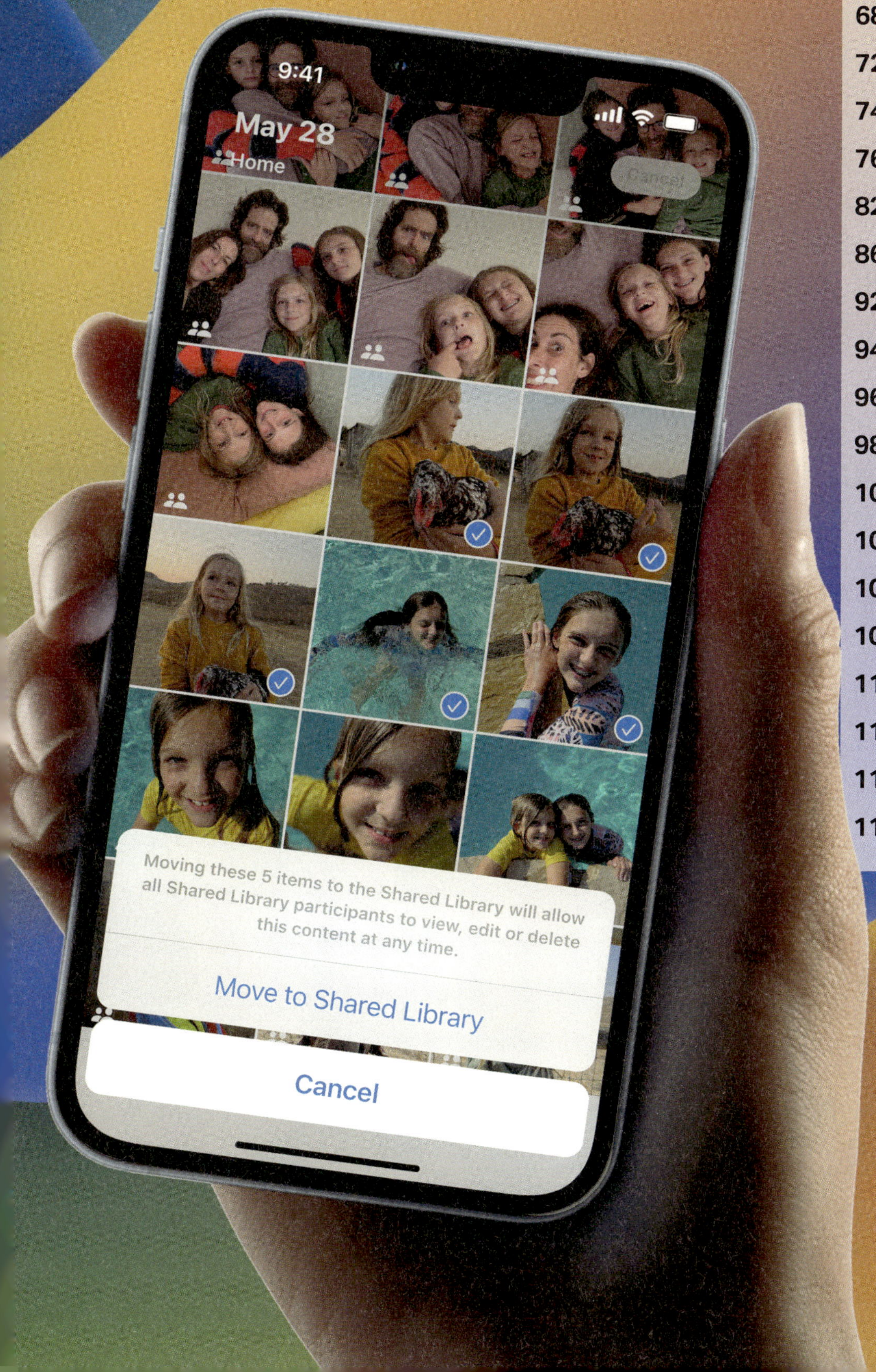
9:41
May 28
Home
Cancel
Moving these 5 items to the Shared Library will allow all Shared Library participants to view, edit or delete this content at any time.
Move to Shared Library
Cancel

The Mail App

The Mail app gets a significant boost with iOS 16. You can recall an email you sent in error, have the app remind you about an email you want to deal with later and schedule when an email is sent. Here's how to do it.

MAIL *in Focus*

1 This screen, in Mail, shows your Inbox. Tap the Mailbox link to go back and choose another mailbox, such as Drafts, Sent, Junk or VIP emails.

2 The Edit link puts an empty circle to the left of each email. You can tap these circles to add a tick, and then action multiple emails at once.

3 These are your emails, listed in the order they arrived. Tap on one to open and read it. Emails with blue dots to their left have not yet been opened and read. Pull down on the screen to get new mail.

4 Tap here to search your emails. You can type a name, a subject or something from the body of an email, and suggestions are offered as you type.

5 Drag an email to the left and you can tap one of the revealed icons labelled More, Flag or Delete. Drag it further to delete it immediately. Drag it right instead and you can mark the email as Read or Unread.

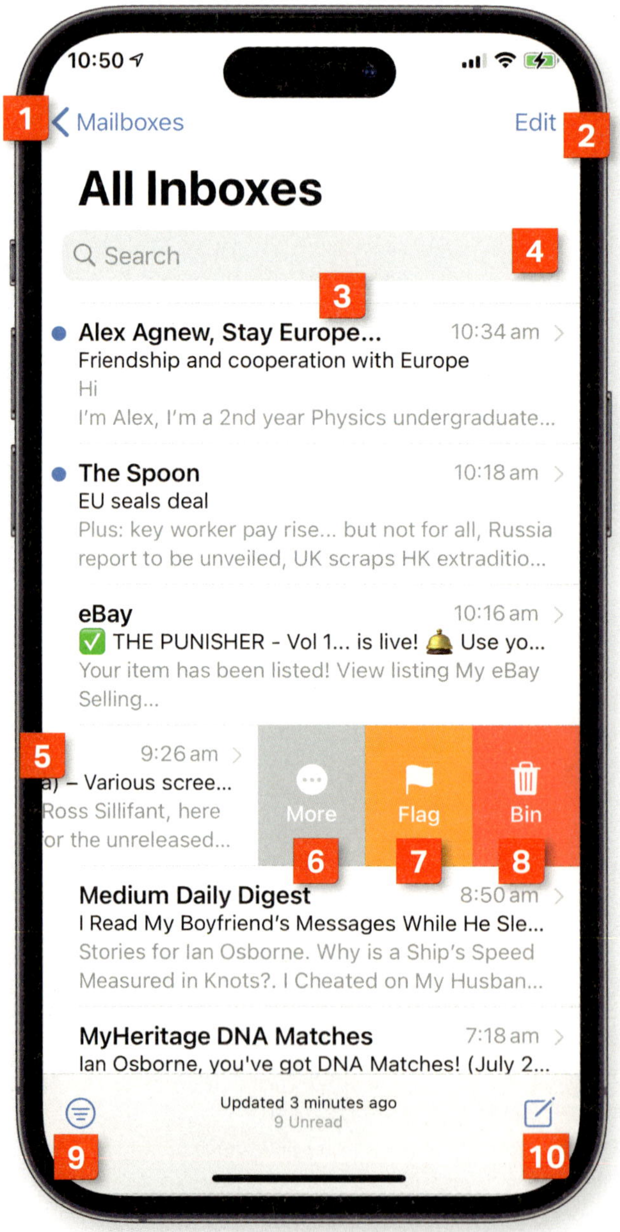

6 Tap More here for a pop-up window giving options to Reply to the email; Forward it; Mark it as read, unread, flagged or junk; get a notification when receiving replies to this email; and Move it to another mailbox.

7 Tap here to flag your email, that is, mark it for later reference. If you swipe left on an email that's already been flagged, this icon then reads 'Unflag'.

8 Tap here to delete an email, moving it to your Bin mailbox. If you do so by accident and want it back, tap the Mailboxes link, then Bin. Drag the email to the left again, then tap More and then in the pop-up window, tap Move so you can move it back to your inbox.

9 Tap this icon to show only unread emails and again to return to showing all emails, read and unread.

10 Tap this icon to open a new blank email for you to fill in and send. Tap and hold it for a list of draft emails, which you've started to type then saved for later.

Sending and scheduling emails

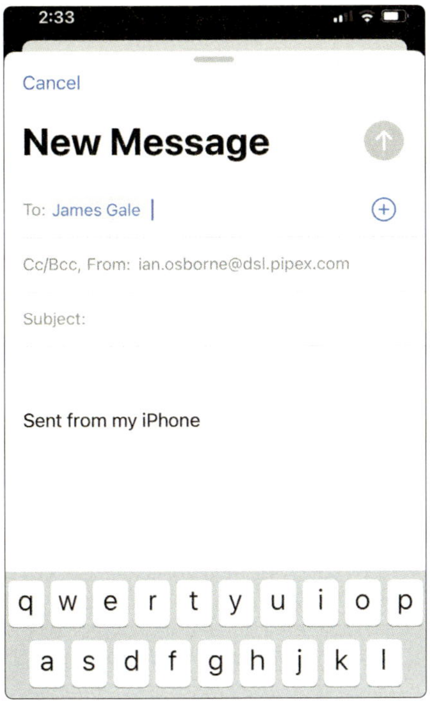

1 Tap the pen-and-paper icon (bottom right) for a new, blank email. Type the recipient's email address in the To field. If you've previously corresponded with them or they're in your contacts, you can type their name instead. Tap the Plus on the right of the To field to choose someone from your Contacts app.

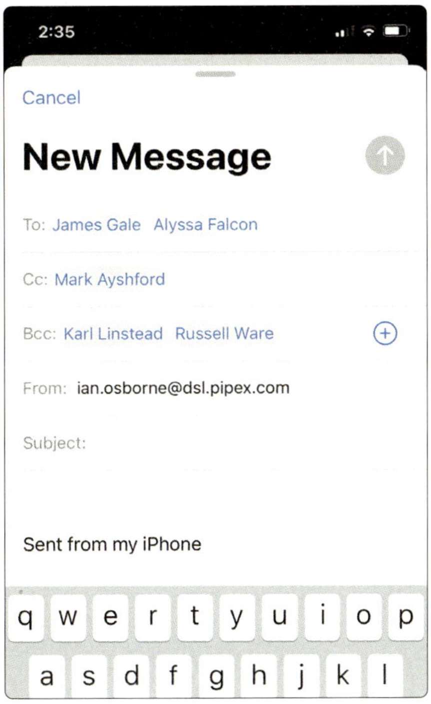

2 You can enter multiple email addresses in the To field. Tap the Cc/Bcc field and you can copy even more people in. Addresses in the To and Cc (carbon copy) field are visible to all recipients, but those in the Bcc (blind carbon copy) field are withheld. The Reply All function doesn't reply to bcc'd addresses.

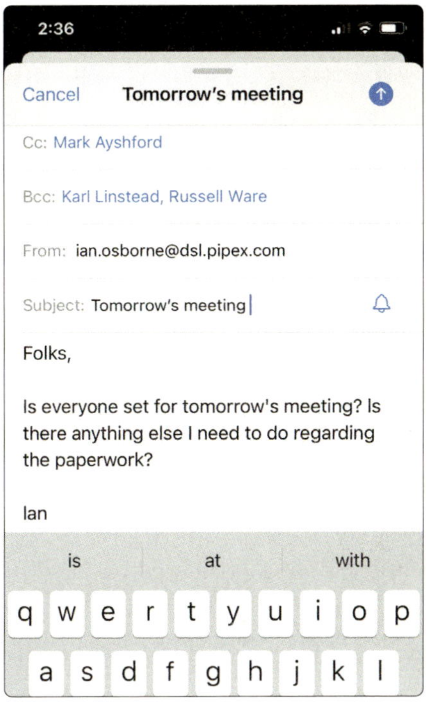

3 Type the email's subject; tap the bell icon to turn notifications of replies on and off. Enter the content of the message. Tap the up-pointing Arrow (top-right corner) to send. A progress bar shows it's on its way and when it's gone, you get a sound effect. You can see the sent email in the Sent folder.

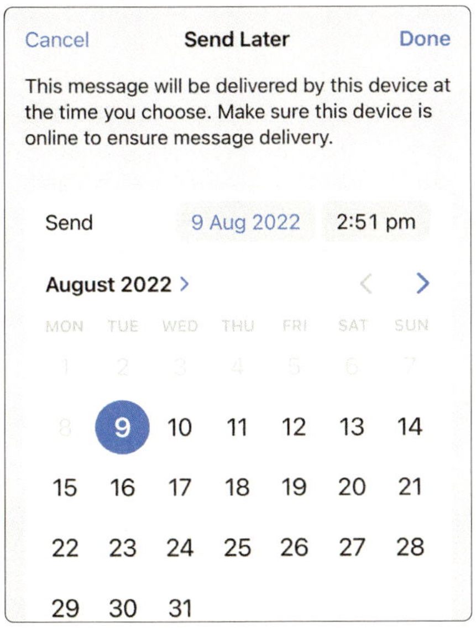

4 To schedule the email to send on a specific time and date, instead of tapping the Send icon (the arrow), long press it for a bubble with sending options. Tap Send Later... and tap a date to set the email to send on a certain day, and the time to schedule a specific time for it to go.

Replying to or forwarding an email

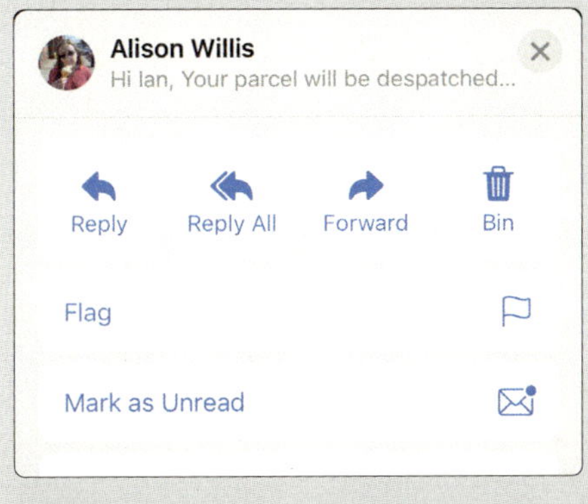

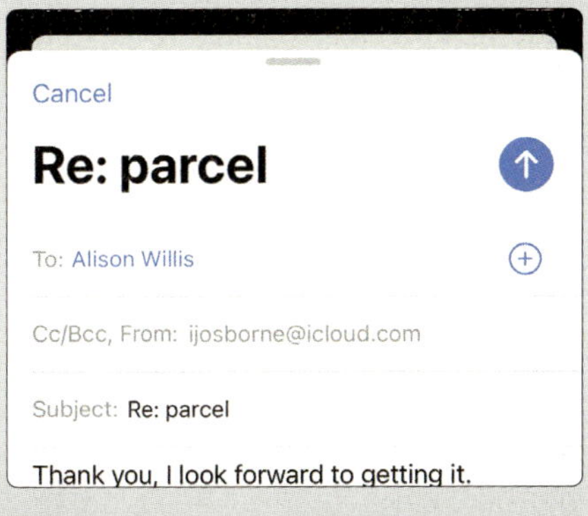

1 Open the email you want to reply to. Click the Arrow icon (bottom of the screen). A pop-up window appears, with a range of options; pull it up to see the full window. 'Reply' sends your response to the sender alone. 'Reply All' sends it to everyone who got the original email. 'Forward' sends it to a third party.

2 Tap the Cc/Bcc field and you can copy even more people in. Addresses in the To and Cc (carbon copy) field are visible to all recipients of the email but those in the Bcc (blind carbon copy) field are withheld. Type the email's subject and the content of the message and you're done. Tap the up-pointing Arrow icon to send it.

Deleting emails in the Mail app

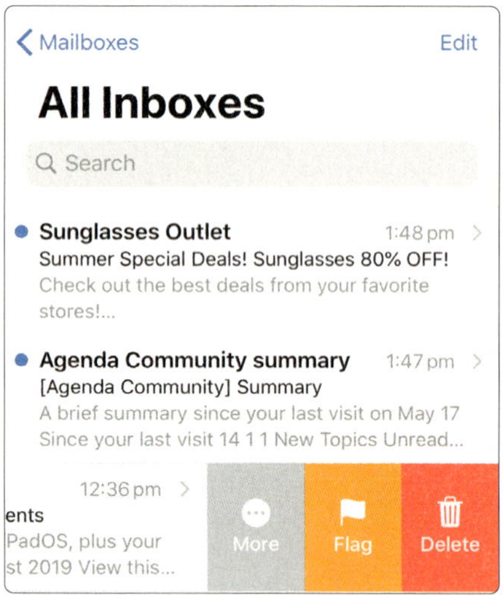

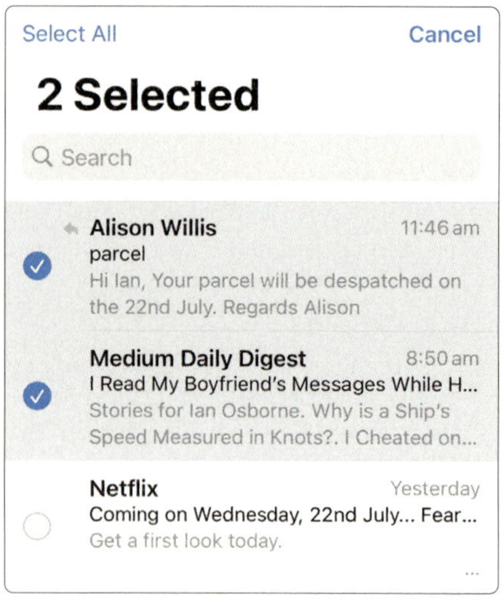

1 To delete an email swipe it left and tap Delete, or swipe it further to the left and delete it in one stroke. To delete multiple emails, tap the Edit link (top right). Circles appear next to the emails. Tap those you want to delete, or tap Select All in the top left to tick all the emails at once. Tap Bin.

2 Binned emails aren't immediately removed from your iPhone. Tap Mailboxes (top left), then tap the Bin icon to see emails you recently threw away. Tap Edit (top right), select emails you want to move or delete then choose the Move or Delete link as appropriate. Note the Select All link in the top left.

Mute thread

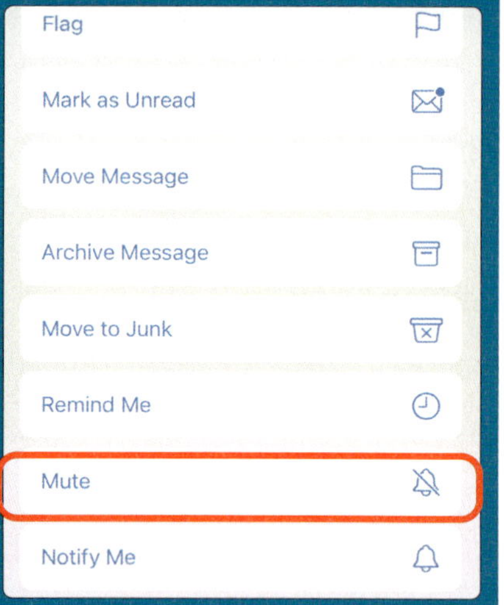

You can mute an email thread by opening the Reply menu, and tapping Mute. Alternatively, from your inbox, swipe the email left, tap More, and then tap Mute. To unmute, repeat these procedures and tap Unmute.

Sending attachments

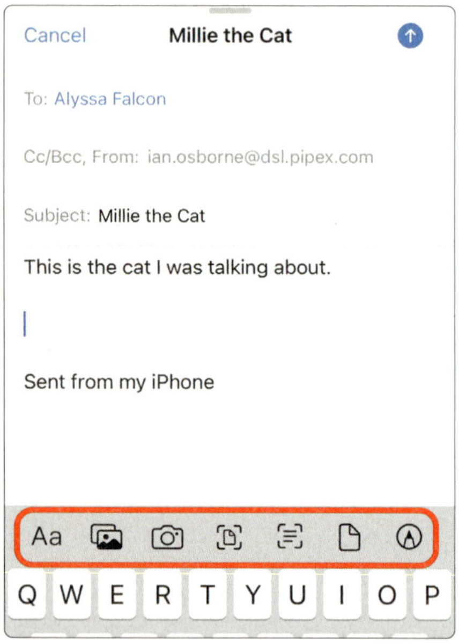

1 Tap the chevron (top right of the keyboard) for these icons. They are; Formatting, Attach Photo, Take & Attach Photo, Scan & Attach Document, Scan and Paste Live Text, Attach Document and Markup. Tap one. When sending a photo, a window pops up showing what's available. Tap all those you wish to send. Tap the 'X' to go back to the email.

2 If you're sending documents, you're taken to the Files app. Again, tap all those you want to send then tap 'X'. You can delete attachments you've added to an email before sending it; and add your message above or below the attachment too. If someone sends you an email with an attachment, you can tap it to open it and then tap Share for a range of options.

Formatting controls

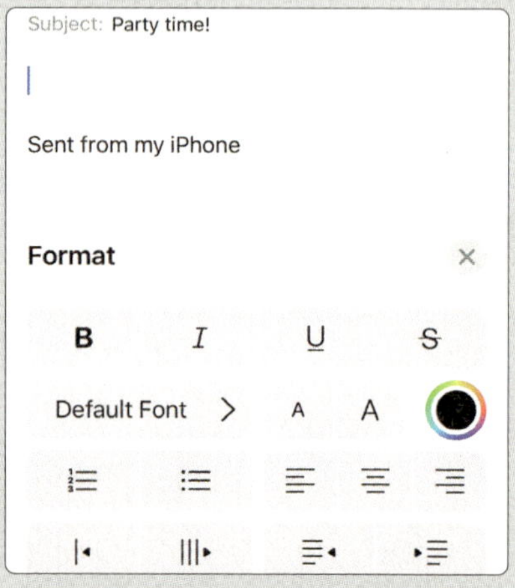

In the body of your email, tap the chevron (top right of keyboard) then tap the 'Aa' icon for formatting controls. Tap Default Font to change the font used in your email. Other formatting options change the size and colour of the text, justify it left, right and centre, make it bold, italic, underlined and/or crossed out, make a list or set an indent, or reduce/ increase the quote level.

Undo Send feature

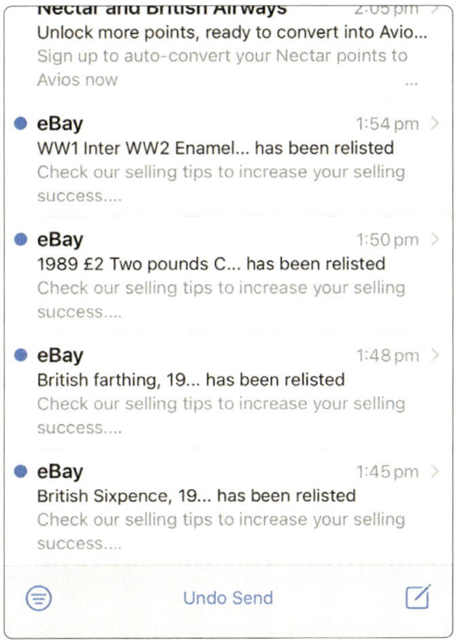

1 If you send an email by mistake, you have ten seconds to recall it. Simply tap 'Undo Send' at the foot of the email window. If the 'Undo Send' option isn't there, your ten seconds have expired and you can't unsend it.

2 After tapping Undo Send, the email is shown on the screen, just as it was before you sent it. You can now edit its contents and send it again by tapping the arrow, tap Cancel to delete it or long-tap the arrow to schedule it.

Downloading new emails

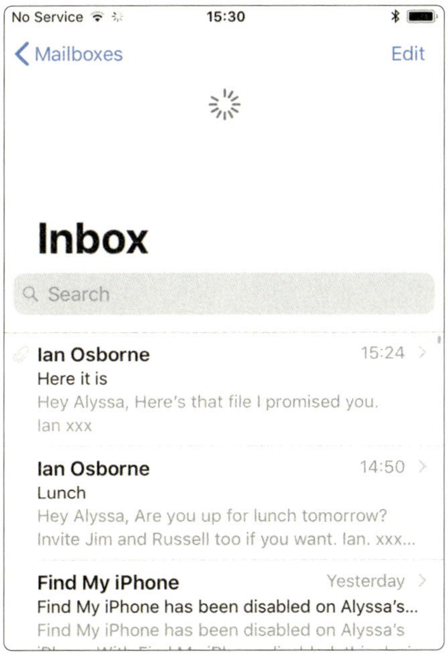

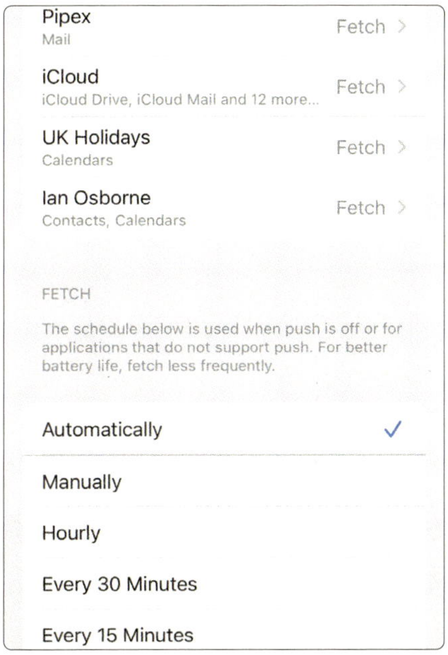

1 To manually refresh your inbox, pull the screen down until you see the swirl (seen here at the top). This shows the app is checking for emails. When it stops, the check is complete with all your new emails downloaded to your iPhone.

2 You can set Mail to check for new emails automatically. Go to Settings > Mail > Accounts > Fetch New Data. Set mail accounts to Push to have new emails sent straight to your phone, or Fetch to have Mail check at a set interval.

Adding VIP senders to Mail

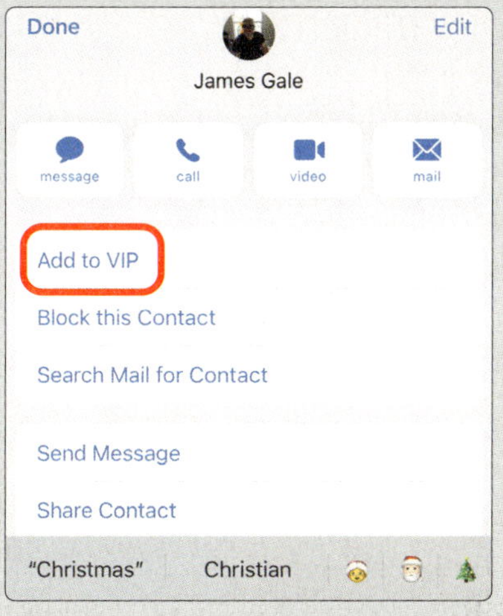

Find an email from the person you want to add to your VIP list, and open it. Tap the person's name atop the email, then on the next screen, scroll up until you see the 'Add to VIP' option. Tap it to add; it turns into 'Remove from VIP'. To view and edit your VIP list, go to Mailboxes, and tap the 'i' icon next to the VIP option.

Hide My Email

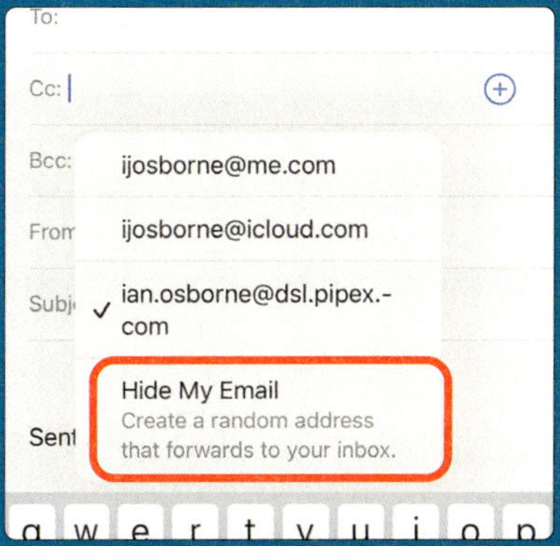

Before sending an email, you can tap the From email address (yours) to open the Cc and Bcc fields, then again for this pop-up. If you have more than one email account set up in Mail, you can choose which account to send it from, and if you don't want the recipient(s) to have your email address, tap Hide My Email to create a random address that forwards to your inbox.

Coloured flags

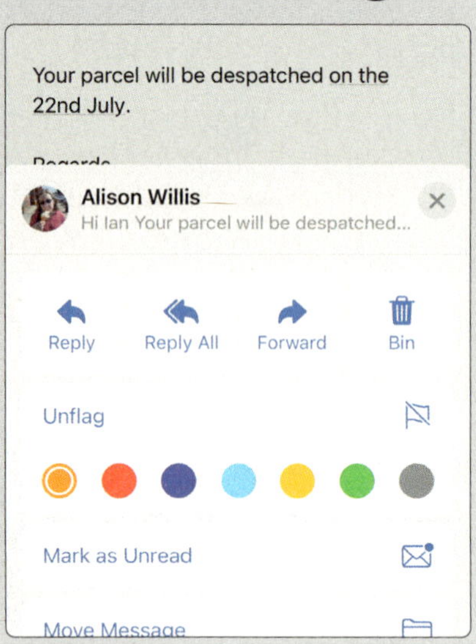

You can use a range of colours to flag your emails, which are synced across your devices. Open the email in question, tap the arrow icon at the foot of the screen, tap Flag, and choose a colour.

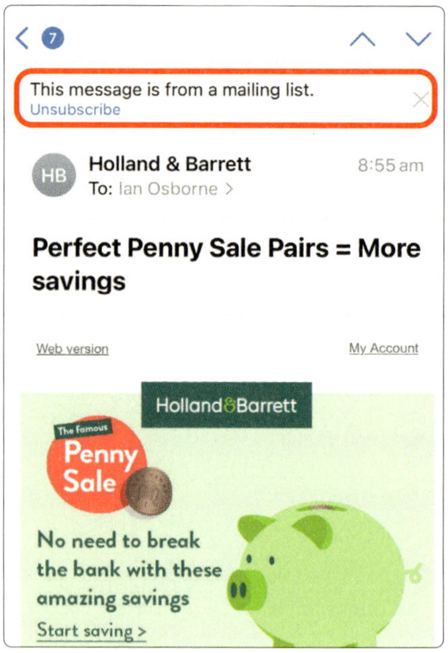

Email unsubscribe

If Mail sees that an email has been produced by a mailing list, it automatically adds an Unsubscribe link at the top of the email. Tap this link if you want to remove yourself from that particular mailing list.

Using signatures

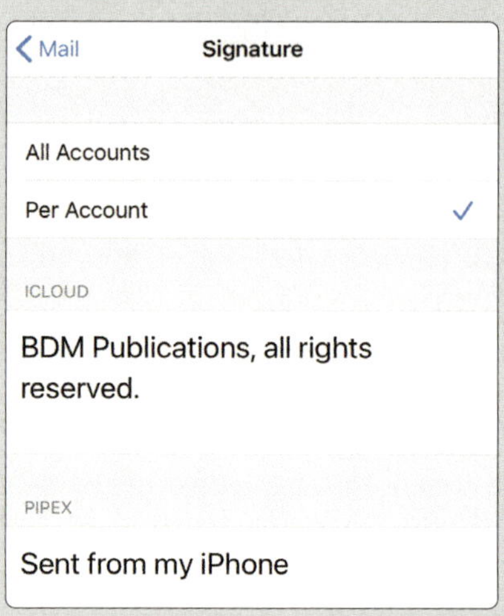

Go to Settings > Mail > Signature. By default, your signature reads, 'Sent from my iPhone'. Tap it and you can edit it to read whatever you like. If you have more than one email account, you can set separate signatures for each.

Block sender

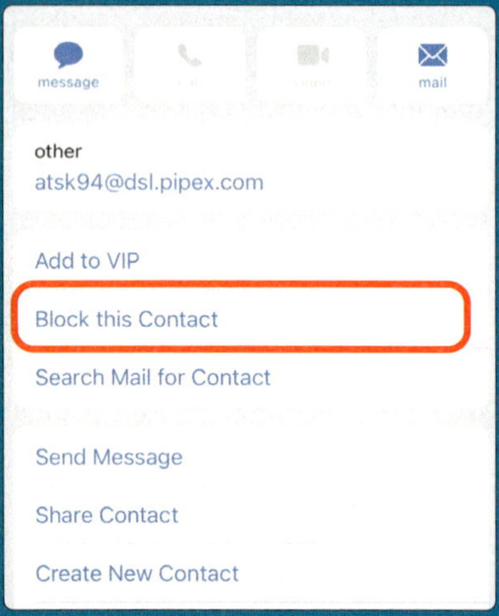

If you get an email from someone you want to block, tap their name at the top of the email and from the screen that pops up, tap Block this Contact (for people) or Block Sender (for mailing lists). Their email address is added to your blocked list. In Settings > Mail > Blocked Sender Options you can set what happens to them. In Settings > Mail > Blocked you can add new numbers or addresses, or unblock by swiping left.

Mail markup

1 Open a new email and add the attachment you wish to annotate. If the keyboard isn't up already, tap the body of the email, then the chevron in the top right to bring up the tools. Tap Markup at the end of the row.

2 You can then use the tools to mark up the picture. Tap and hold a tool for customisation options, tap the colour wheel to change colours and tap the arrows in the top left for undo-redo. The + icon gives more tools.

The Remind Me feature

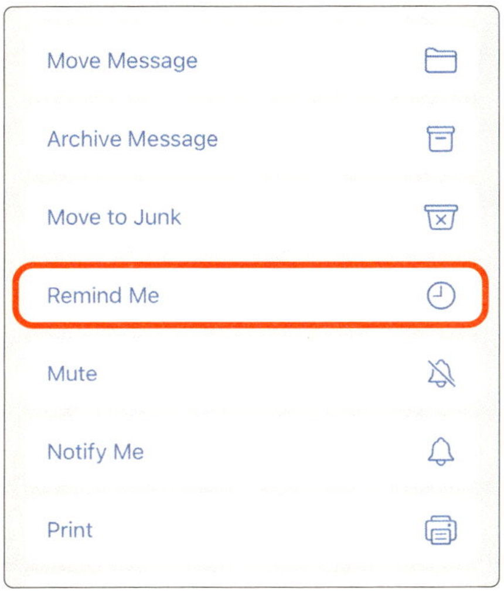

1 If you get an email which you want to be reminded about so you can read or reply to it later, with the mail open tap the Reply icon (curly arrow). In the option list that pops up, tap Remind Me. Alternatively, in the mailbox slide it right and tap Remind Me.

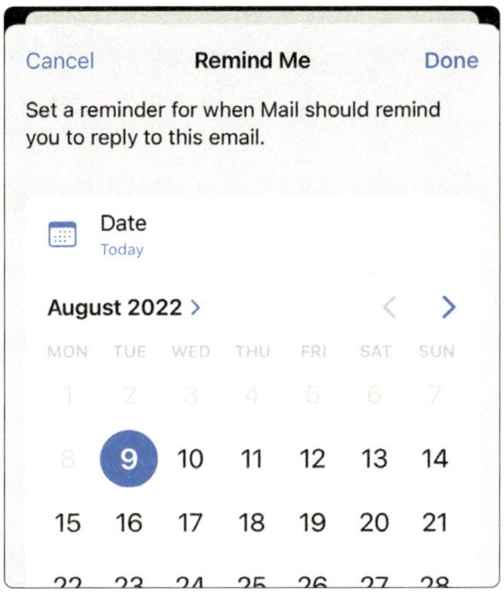

2 A window appears where you can opt to be reminded in an hour, tonight, tomorrow or later. Tap the Remind Me Later option to choose a date and specific time. At the time of your choosing, the email is moved to the top of your inbox with a Remind Me label.

Long press on email

In your Mail app's inbox, tap and hold an email for a pop-up menu. Slide this menu upwards to see all the options it offers, which includes reply, forward, notify, mute, move, or delete it altogether. Tap Mark.. and you can flag it, mark it as read/ unread, or move it to junk.

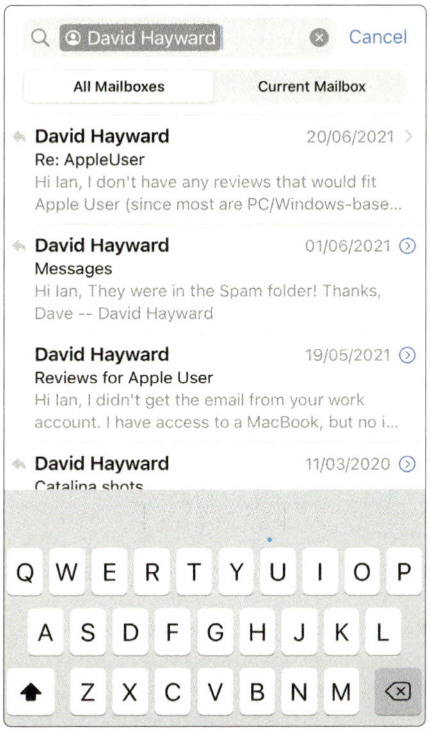

Searching emails

Using the search field at the top of the screen, you can search your emails. You can search all mailboxes or just one. If you look for a person, you can search for emails from, to, or mentioning that person. There are more features than ever in the Mail app's search.

Privacy features

According to Apple, emails sent to you may include hidden pixels that give the email's sender information about you. Merely opening the email allows information to be collected by the sender, including your IP address, how many times you opened the email, whether you forwarded it and more. This data can be collated, and ultimately creates a profile of your online behaviour and might even identify your location.

The Mail Privacy Protection feature stops this happening. When it's switched on, email senders, including Apple, cannot glean this information from your email activities. As Apple puts it, "When you receive an email in the Mail app, rather than downloading remote content when you open an email, Mail Privacy Protection downloads remote content in the background by default regardless of how you engage with the email. Apple does not learn any information about the content." All remote content is downloaded through proxy servers too, so the sender can never see your IP address.

To activate Mail Privacy Protection, go to Settings > Mail > Privacy Protection and switch it on.

If you subscribe to iCloud you also get a feature called Hide My Email, which isn't available to those who only have a free iCloud account. With this feature, you can send an email without the recipient ever knowing your actual email address. To use it, go to Settings > [Your Name] > iCloud > Hide My Email. Tap '+ Create New Address' and you can get a unique email address that forwards emails to your own email inbox, but can be deleted at any time. So, for example, if you want to enter a competition without giving your 'real' email address, use Hide My Email to create a new one, and if the organiser sends you endless spam, you can delete the spoof email address and get rid of them in one go. Easy!

The Safari App

Safari is awesome for navigating the worldwide web, and in iOS 16, it gains some great new features. You can give a tab group its own Start page or share them with your friends, translate on-site text and more.

SAFARI *in Focus*

1 A web page can contain words, pictures, videos, icons and more. Tap a link on a web page, such as the pictures here and icons atop the page, to go to a new page or open a menu. You can also scroll the screen up and down by dragging it up and down with one finger.

2 This controls window hides when not in use; tap it to open again. Swipe the window left and right to cycle through open tabs. Tap it to type a new URL or get to the Start page, and deep press it for more options.

3 Tap here for a pop-up window offering a long list of options such as opening the site in a different app, turning Reader View on and off, translate the website and Request Desktop Website.

4 This is the URL (Uniform Resource Locator; the web address) of the page you're currently viewing. A lock icon next to it means the website is secure. Safari has verified its ownership with a certificate, and any information you enter on that website is encrypted. Long press it for an options window such as copy the URL, paste one in and more.

5 Tapping the curly arrow here reloads the web page you're currently looking at. It's useful if it hasn't loaded correctly or if it needs updating, such as a news or live sports page.

6 These chevrons let you move forwards and backwards through your browsing history. They only appear when needed; if either or both are greyed, there's nothing to navigate forwards and/or backwards to.

7 This is the Sharing icon. Tap here for a range of options, including sending the page by AirDrop, Messages, Mail and more; saving to Bookmarks, Reading List or Favourites; searching on the page, and more.

8 The open-book icon gives quick and easy access to your Bookmarks, your Reading List and your browsing History.

9 A quick tap on this icon takes you to the Tabs screen. The tabs you have open in Safari are arranged as thumbnails. There you can close tabs by tapping the X in its corner, open a new tab and more. Tap and hold it to give you a pop-up menu offering various useful options.

First steps with Safari

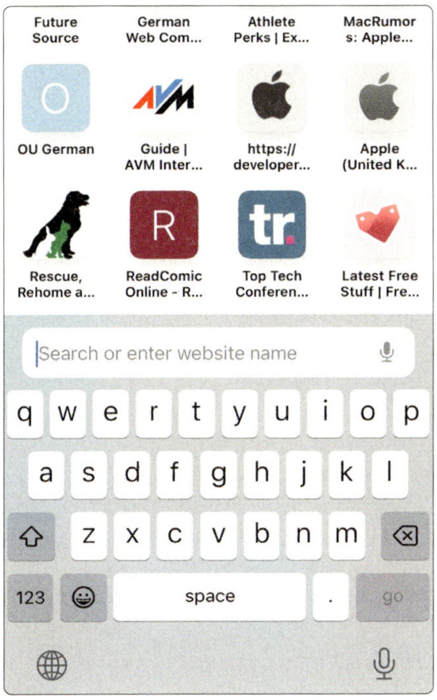

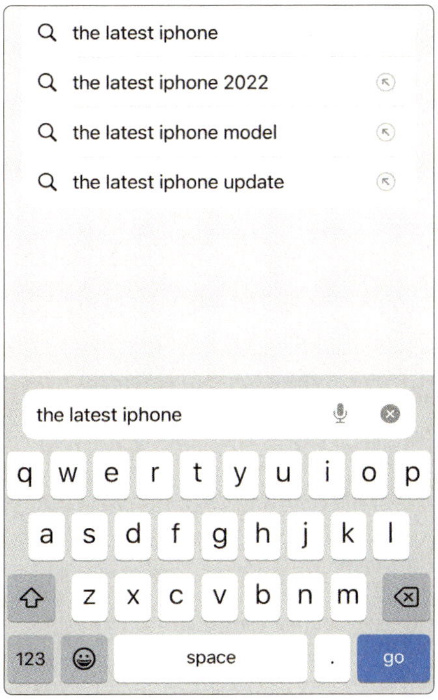

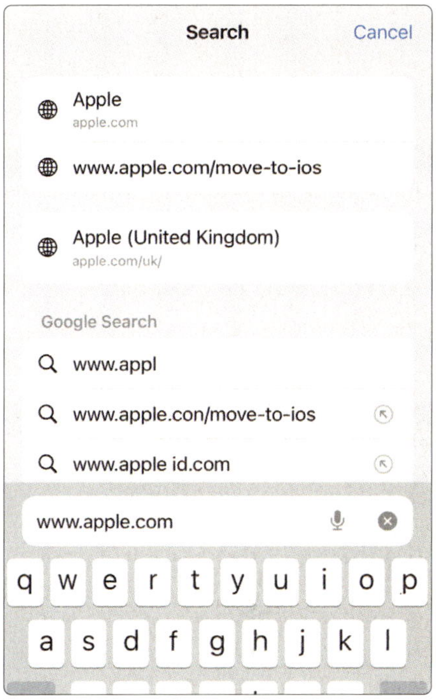

1 When you first open the Safari app, you see your Favourites page, which might be empty if you've never used Safari before. Tap the window at the bottom of the screen to bring up the keyboard and the search/URL field as shown.

2 To search the web, type your search term here. Options are offered as you type; tap one to search for that term immediately, or tap the arrow to its right to enter it into the field without searching yet. When you're done typing, tap Go.

3 If you know the URL you want to visit, you can type it here directly. An auto-complete option is offered as you type. Instead of typing, you can tap the mic in the Search/URL field to speak the search term or URL instead.

Using Bookmarks

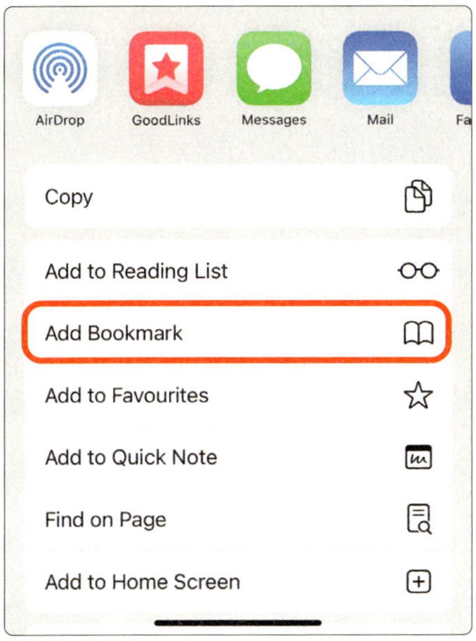

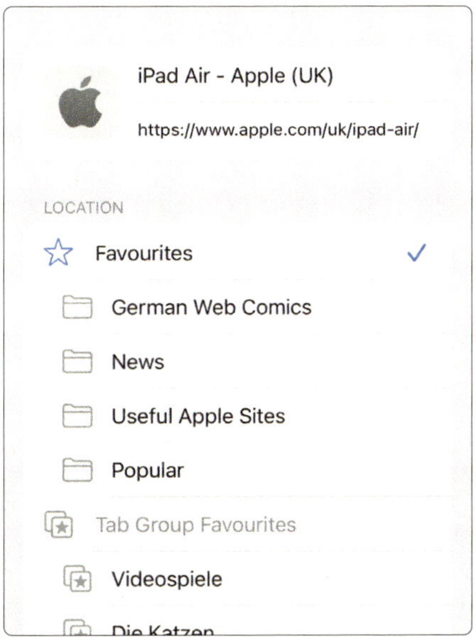

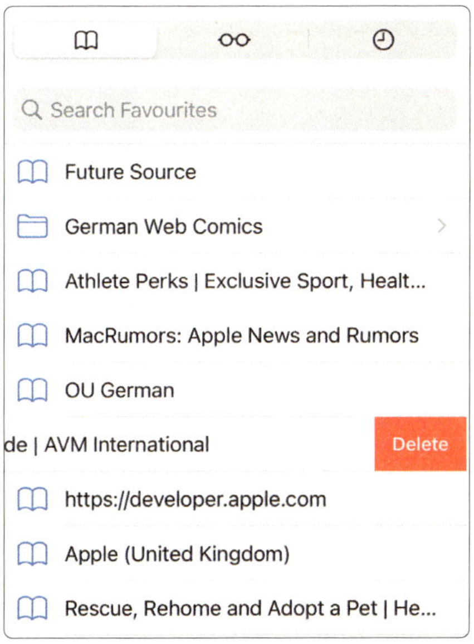

1 To bookmark a website for later use, tap the Sharing icon, scroll up the pop-up menu and tap the Add Bookmark option. You're taken to a new screen, which is titled 'Add Bookmark'.

2 Here you can edit the title by which the site is bookmarked, and tap Favourites to choose a different folder to save it to. When you're done, tap Save (in the top-right corner).

3 To access a bookmarked page, and tap the book icon in the tools at the foot of the screen. Navigate to the site you want, and tap it. To delete a bookmark, swipe it left and tap Delete.

History and Reading List

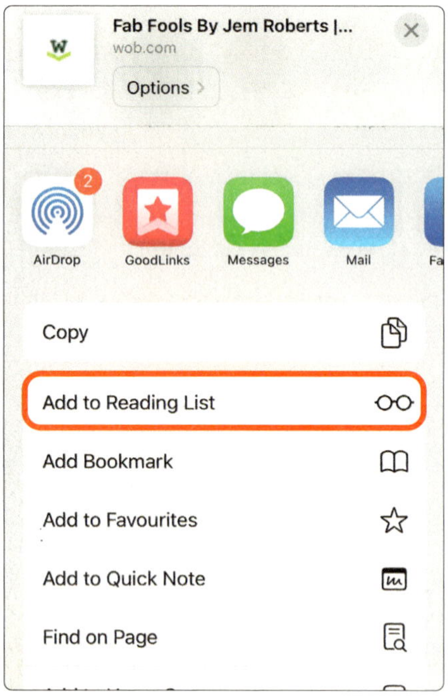

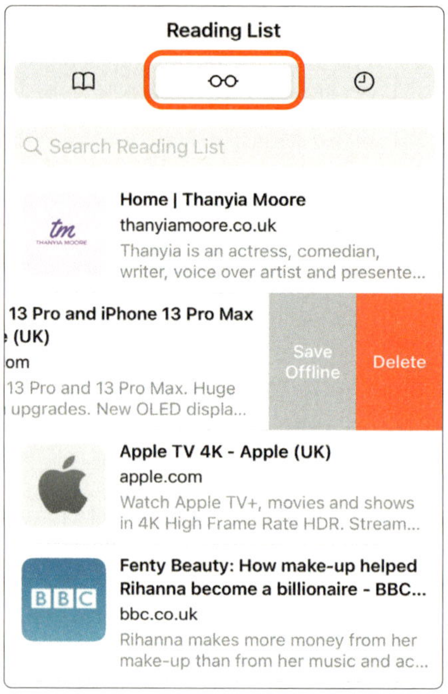

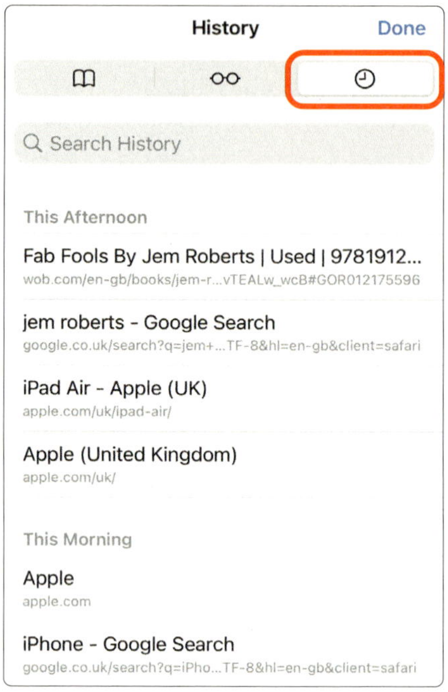

1 If you come across an interesting site that you don't have time to read right now, add it to your Reading List. Tap the Sharing icon, and scroll up to Add to Reading List; then tap it.

2 To open a Reading List site, tap the Book icon, then tap the 'glasses' icon. Scroll to find the site, then tap it to open. Swipe a site left to remove it or save it for offline reading.

3 To access recently viewed sites, tap the Book icon, then tap the clock icon as shown. Here, and also in Bookmarks and Reading List, you can tap and hold a listed site to get a preview of it.

Rotate screen

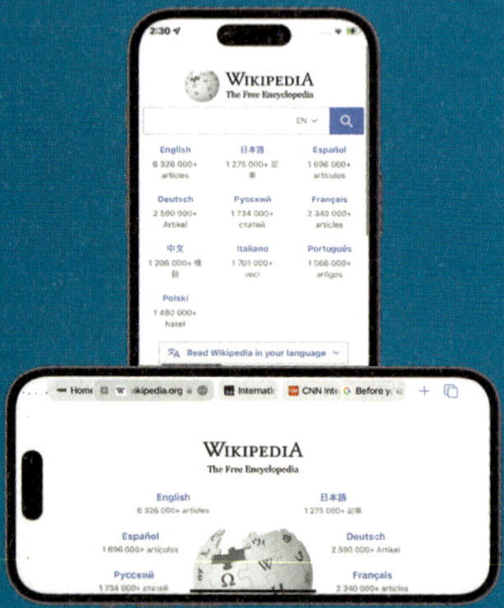

Pages can be oriented landscape or portrait by rotating the iPhone. Most of the time, you'll probably use the regular portrait view, but if the website is very text heavy, it might be more comfortable to read it in landscape. In Landscape Mode, the tabs and tools appear at the top of the screen.

Safari Extensions

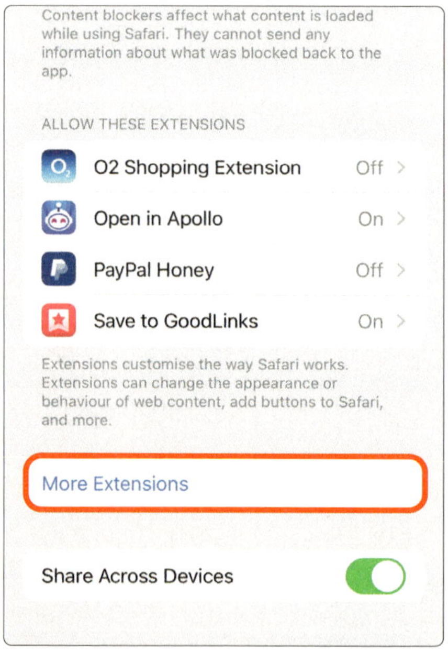

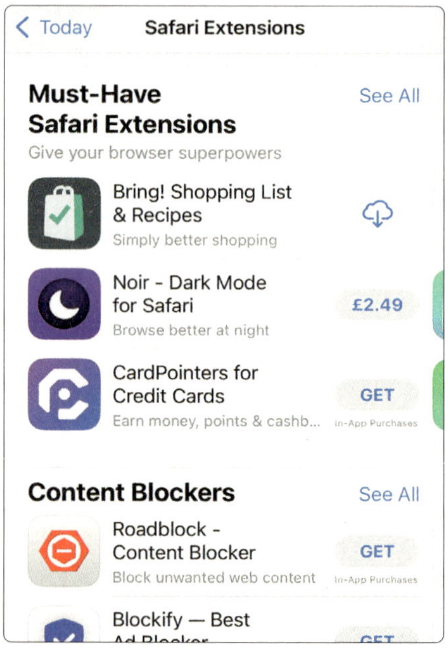

1 Extensions add functionality to your Safari app, including add blocking, shopping and more. Open Settings > Safari > Extensions. To install a new extension, tap More Extensions.

2 You're taken to the Safari Extensions section of the App Store. Find one you like and add it. To turn off an extension, go back to the screen from the previous step and tap the switch.

Tab Groups and Tab Group Sharing

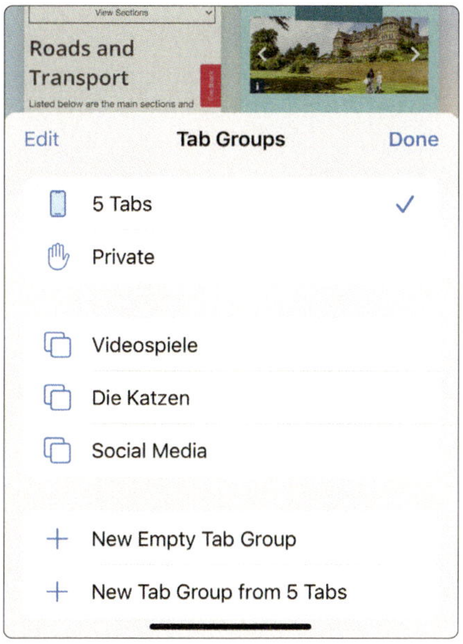

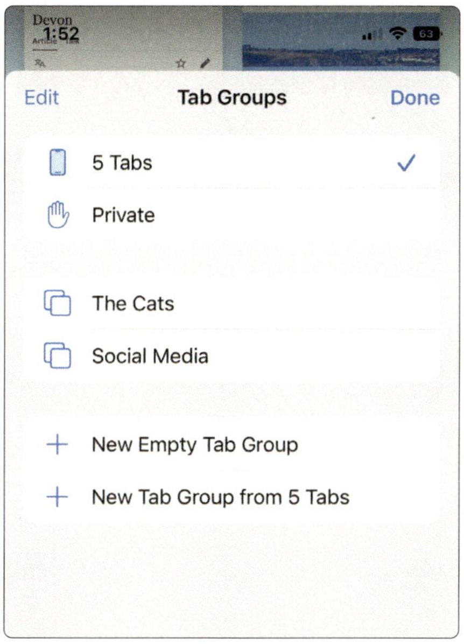

1 You can save a group of tabs, and then open or close them as a group. To save all your open tabs as a group, tap the tabs icon in the URL bubble at the foot of the screen, tap the word 'Tabs' in the middle of the controls to open this menu and tap New Tab Group from X Tabs and give it a name.

2 The other way of making a Tab Group is, on the screen in the previous step, tap New Empty Tab Group, then name. When you wish to save a website to this Tab Group, tap the tabs icon, then deep press the thumbnail for the site. Choose Move to Tab Group, then tap the name of the group to add it.

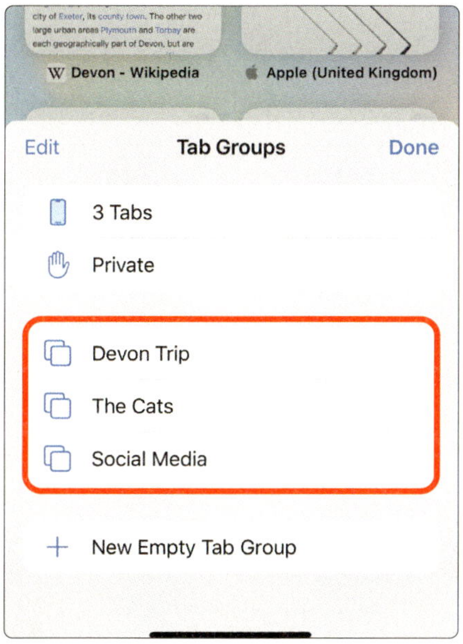

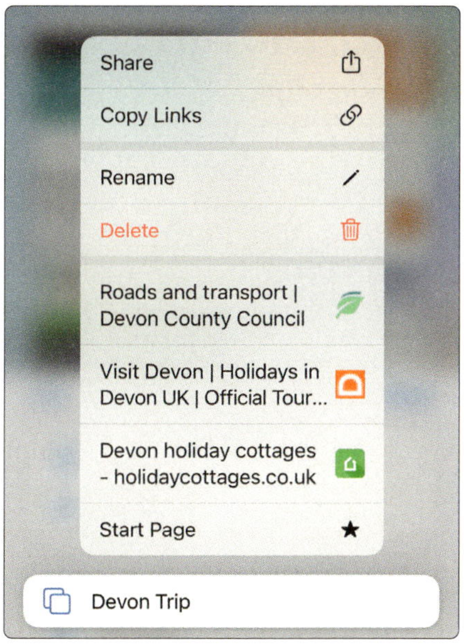

3 To open a group of tabs, tap the tabs icon in the controls at the foot of the screen, then tap the description in the bottom-middle. Tap one of your Tab Groups to open every tab in that group. To go back to the tabs you had open before opening your Tab Group, repeat and tap 'X Tabs' further up the menu.

4 Each Tab Group can have its own Start page if you wish. Tap the Tabs icon, then the Plus sign on the left to open a new Start page for that group. Scroll down and tap Edit to customise it. You can also long tap a tab group and select Share to share the entire tab group via messages.

Privacy Report

Safari works very hard on looking after your privacy. For a report on how the browser has recently taken action to protect your privacy, tap aA/jigsaw icon and scroll to Privacy Report. Tap it and you get all sorts of information on trackers that have been prevented from profiling you and a list of websites that have been involved in tracking.

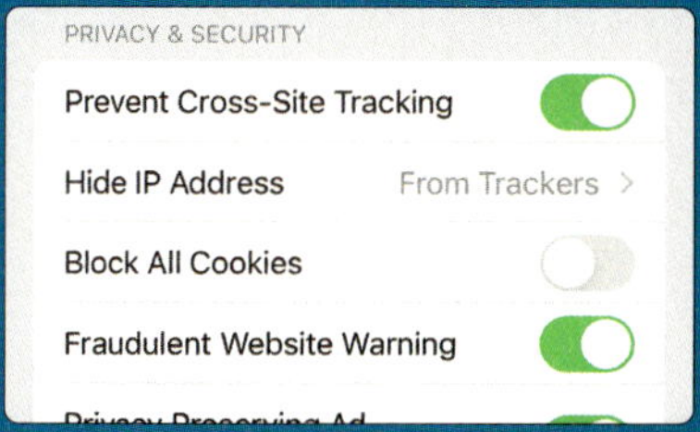

Return to Old Layout

If you dislike the new Safari layout, with the URL and toolbar at the bottom of the screen, open the Settings app and tap the Safari option. Scroll to the Tabs section, showing two line drawings of an iPhone, marked Tab Bar and Single Tab. Tab Bar is selected by default, but if you tap Single Tab, you return Safari to its old layout.

Password monitoring

If you're using a password that has been compromised by a data breach, that is, it has turned up when a website was hacked, Safari warns you and advises you to change it. Your saved passwords are regularly checked against a list of breached passwords, and the whole process is secure and private. Even Apple doesn't see your password information.

Searching for and Copying Text

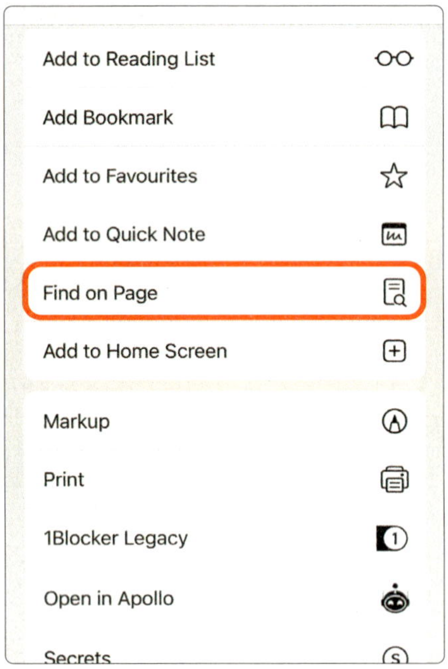

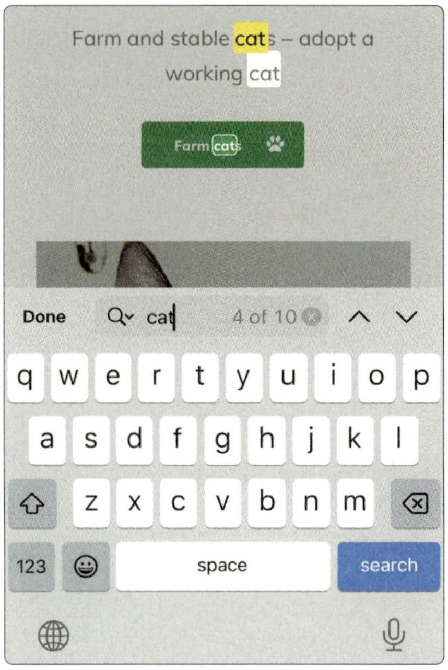

1 You can search a web page for text. Tap the Sharing icon in the controls, and tap Find on Page. Enter the word or phrase you wish to look for on the open web page. To the right of the Search field, you're shown how many instances of the word or term are found on the page.

2 Tap the chevrons next to the Search field to cycle through the instances where the word or phrase appears. To copy selected text, highlight it and if a bubble menu doesn't appear, tap it. You can then tap Copy to copy it to your clipboard, ready to paste elsewhere.

AutoFill

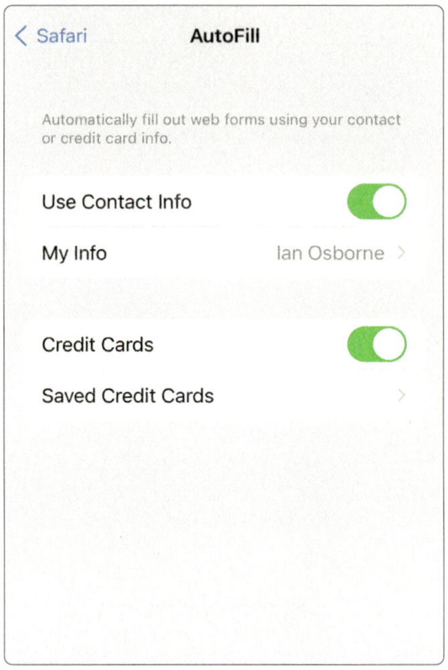

Go to Settings > Safari > AutoFill > My Info, and select your own Contacts card from the list. From now on, when filling in a web form, the AutoFill option is available; tap it and fill in the form from your Contacts card. You can save credit cards too, but not the security number on the reverse.

Translate web pages & in-picture text

1 To translate a foreign-language website into your native language, tap the aA/Jigsaw icon and select Translate Website... On the next screen, you're shown a list of languages you can translate it into. Choose one, or tap Preferred Languages... to add more.

2 Harnessing the power of Live Text, you can even translate words found in a photograph or illustration. Highlight the text in question, then tap it for an options bubble. Navigate the options using the chevrons at either end of the bubble, then tap Translate.

Private Browsing

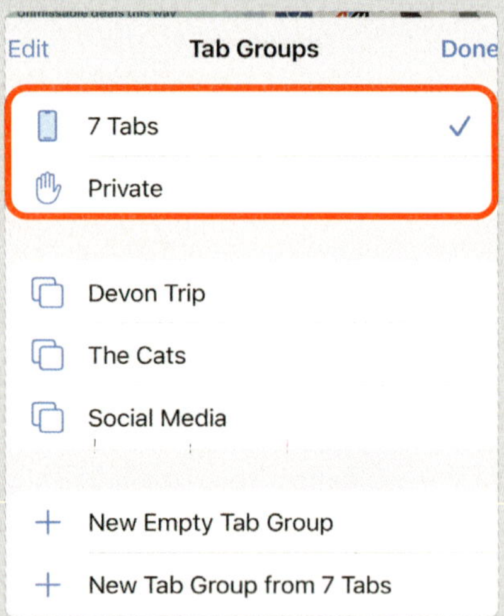

Private Browsing leaves no trace of where you've been in your history. To switch between regular and private modes, tap the Tabs icon, then tap the Tabs chevron at the foot of the screen. You can switch between modes using the menu that pops up.

Reader view

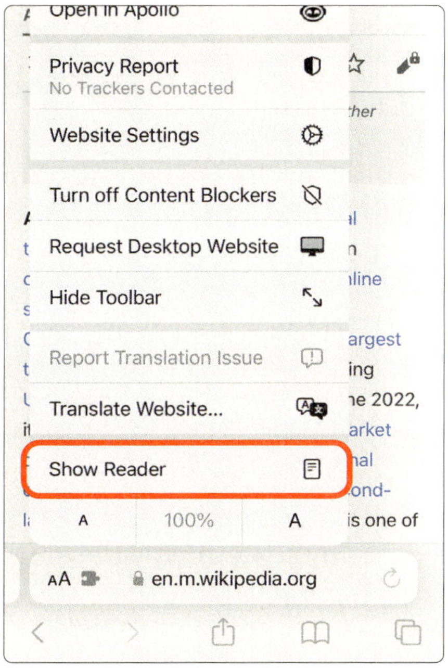

In Reader View, a website is cut back to the bare minimum, so you can read or print it without distractions. Not all sites support Reader View. To switch to it (if available), tap the aA/Jigsaw icon and choose Show Reader. To switch back to normal viewing, tap the icon again (it's now black) and select Hide Reader.

Edit passwords

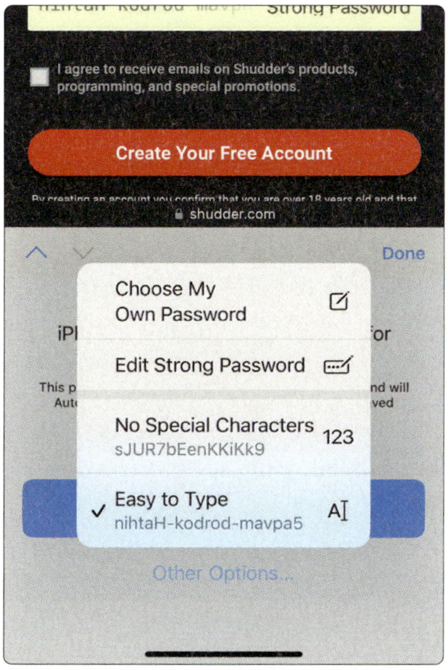

When you register with a website, Safari suggests a strong password. If it doesn't fit the site's requirements, you can edit it. Tap the password field, and in the pop-up, tap Other Options... at the bottom. Choose 'Edit Strong Password' from the window that appears, and customise it to the site's requirements.

Play a video

Some websites offer videos that can be played within the website itself, instead of sending you to a video hosting site like YouTube. Tap the Play icon to watch the video. Tap the video and the controls are shown. Typical controls include pause/play, scrub through the video and open in full screen mode.

Add to Home Screen

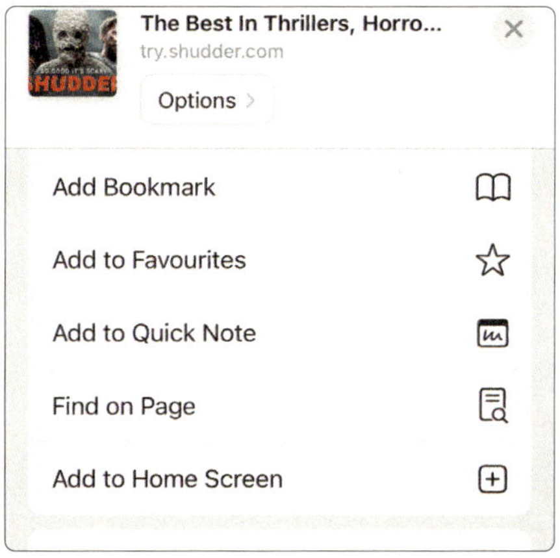

You can add a website to your Home screen, so it appears as an icon. When you tap that icon, the website opens in Safari. To save a website to your Home Screen, tap the Sharing icon and then select Add to Home Screen. You're then allowed to edit the name of the page if you wish. Tap Add to add it.

Safari settings

Here are some other things you can change in Settings > Safari.

Page Zoom: Set your browser to be zoomed in or out of a website.

Request Desktop Site: Switch it on and Safari always shows the desktop version of a website, not the mobile one.

Reader: Switch it on to automatically use the Reader View on websites.

Camera/Microphone/Location: Do you want websites to have access to these things? By default they have to ask, but you can change this to Deny or Allow.

Language: You can switch to another language for Safari if you wish.

Downloads: Set where documents and data downloaded in Safari is saved. By default, it's your Downloads folder in your iCloud Drive.

Search Engine: By default, Safari uses Google as a search engine. This setting lets you change this to DuckDuck Go, Yahoo or Bing and more.

Block Pop-Ups: Find the Block Pop-Ups setting and tap the switch to turn off those irritating pop-ups that appear over websites.

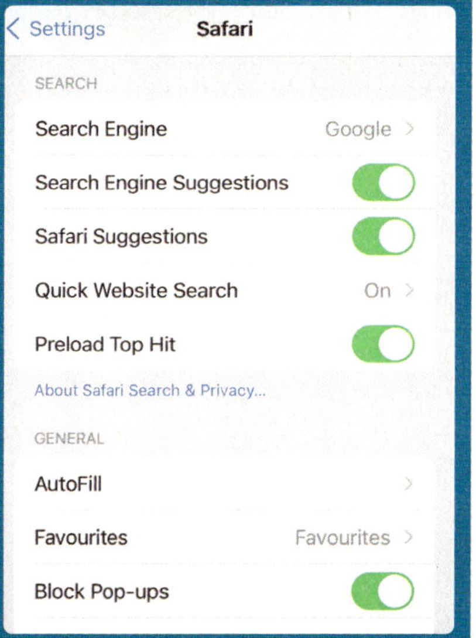

Block All Cookies: Sites can no longer leave cookies on your phone.

Clear History and Website Data: Tap this link and you can wipe your website history, cookies and other browsing data; for the sake of your privacy.

The Reminders App

With the Reminders app you can set up reminders, assign them to lists and trigger notifications at a specific time and date or when you arrive at or depart from a specific location. Here's how to get more from it.

REMINDERS *in Focus*

1 Use the Search field to search your reminders. Titles, notes, people, locations and more are searched.

2 Tap this link and you can edit your lists; delete them with the minus sign, reorder by dragging the Three-line icon up and down and tap the 'i' icon to rename a list, change its colour and choose a new icon.

3 Smart lists. 'Today' is reminders scheduled for that day, 'Scheduled' shows all scheduled items, 'All' lists all reminders, and 'Flagged' shows those to which you've added a flag. 'Completed' shows reminders you've checked as done.

4 These are your lists. They can be called anything you like. Tap one to open it and see the individual reminders you've added, mark reminders you've done as complete, and add new ones.

5 You can share a Reminders list with someone else, as long as they have a Mac or iOS device. The list then appears in their own Reminders app, and any edits you make are also made on their list, and vice versa.

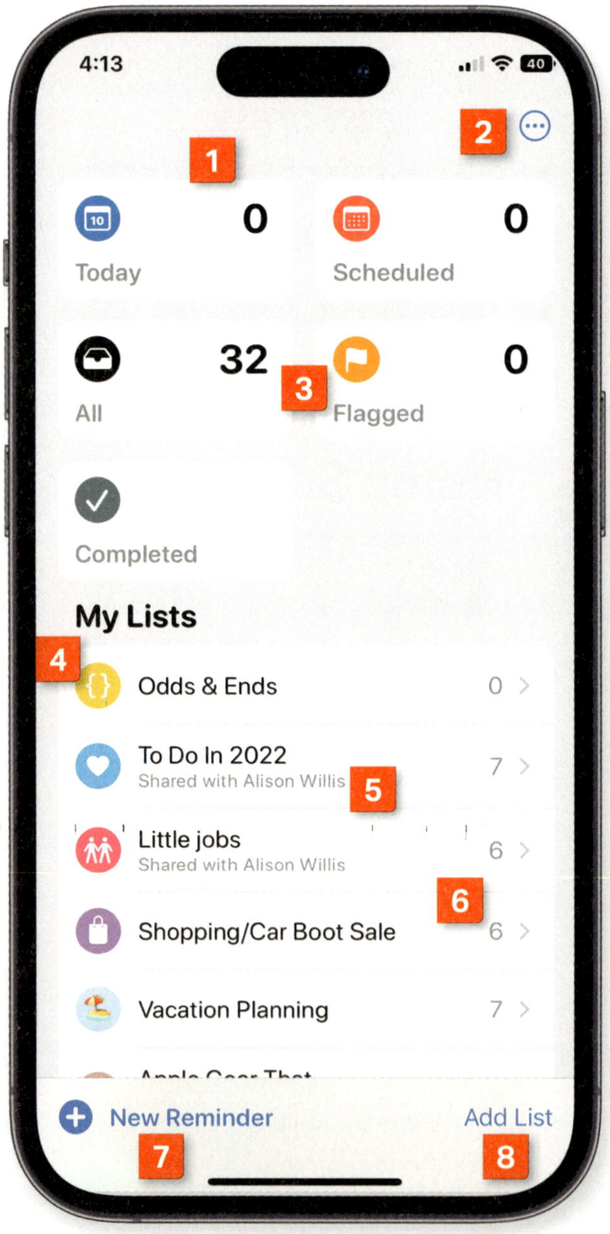

6 Numbers on the right of each list represent the amount of outstanding reminders that are contained in it. When you mark one as done, it's removed.

7 You can now create a reminder directly from the app's front page, instead of having to open a list first. Just tap to create a new one and assign it to a list.

8 Tap here to create a new list, which appears in the My Lists section of the Reminders home page. You can move 'individual reminders to another list.

Pinned Reminder lists

You can pin a Reminder list to the top of the screen. Just swipe the list you want to pin to the right, and tap the pin icon. It then appears as a thumbnail along with the smart reminders. To unpin, long tap and select Unpin.

Creating and using Reminders

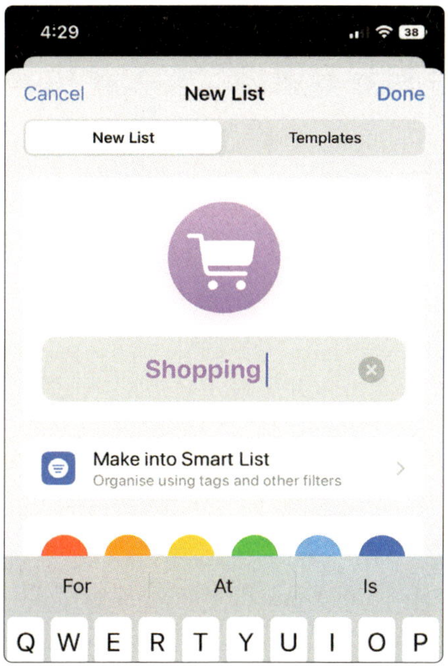

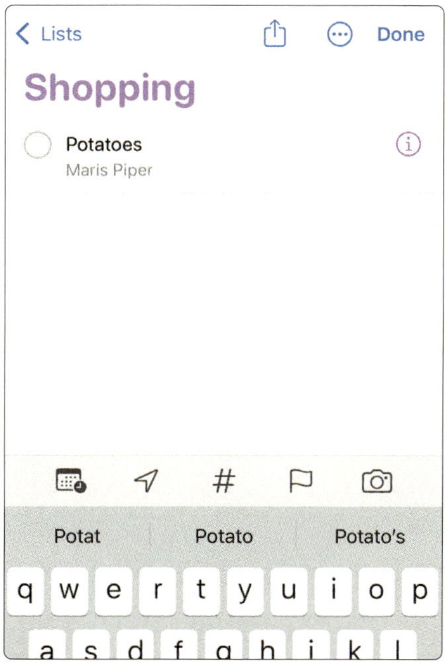

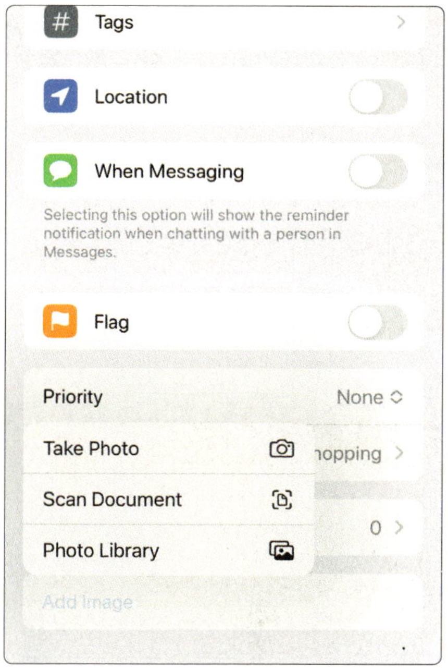

1 To create a new list, on the home page tap Add List (bottom right). Add a title (anything you like) and scroll up to choose a colour and icon for it. You can make it a Smart List if you like – tap Make into Smart List and set the filters. Tap Done when finished.

2 To add a reminder to a list, open it then tap New Reminder. Add a name and, if you wish, tap the 'i' icon next to it to add notes, a URL, or a flag, set a priority, Date and Time to schedule a reminder and more. When you've carried out the task, tap the circle to its left.

3 Tap the Add Image link near the bottom of the Details screen (tap 'i') and you can add a photo from your Photos app, take a new one, or scan a document. This picture appears in your list, associated with that particular reminder. Tap to enlarge it.

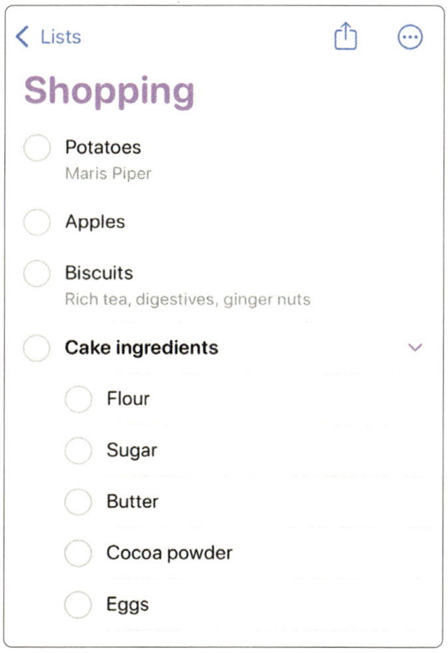

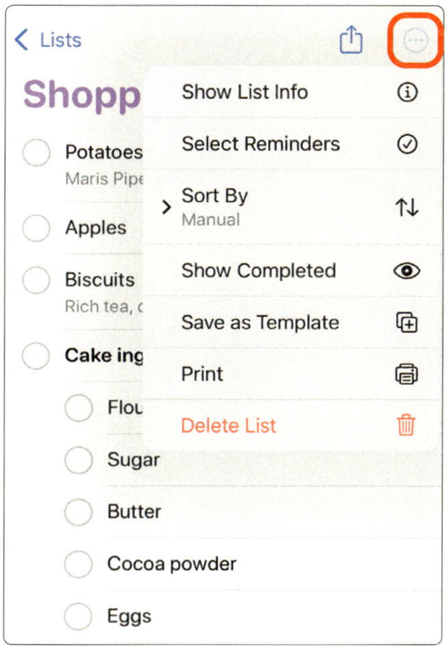

4 From the Details screen you can add Subtasks to a reminder, breaking down the item of which you need reminding into smaller tasks. In your reminders list, they appear in a collapsible list under the reminder in question, and can also be marked completed.

5 If you open a Reminders list and tap the three-dots icon, you can choose Save as Template from the pop-up menu. You can then open templates from the three-dots menu on the home page, choose one to use and create a new list based on it.

User Tags

Tap the # icon above the keyboard and type a word, and it becomes a hashtag. These are used to help organise your reminders. On the front page, scroll up and there's a section called Tags. Tap one of your tags to see all the reminders you've tagged with that word.

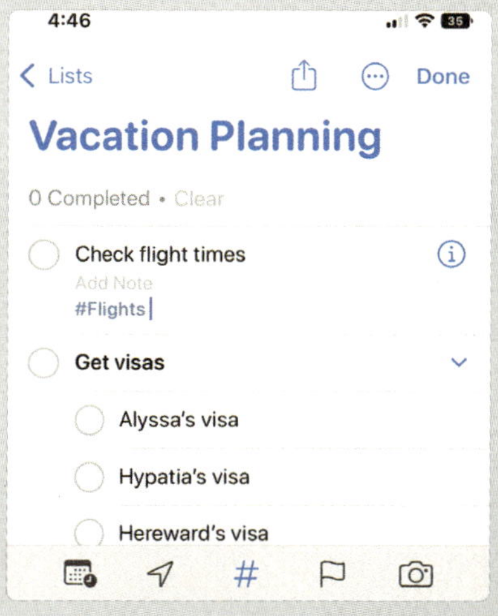

The Messages App

Messages is one of the most popular apps on your iPhone. You can use it to send regular text messages, or free iMessages to others with an Apple device; and also to send pictures, videos and audio messages.

MESSAGES *in Focus*

1 Tap here to take you back to the list of message conversations. Tap one of them to open, and if you wish, continue that conversation; such as the chat you see here.

2 This is the person you're chatting to. The picture is drawn from your Contacts app and is replaced by an initial if it's not available. Tap this pic for more options, including sharing your location, making a call or video call, send an email and more.

3 Tap the video camera icon here for a pop-up menu, offering FaceTime Audio and FaceTime Video calls. Tap one to make that call.

4 Your outgoing messages are on the right, incoming ones on the left. Received messages are grey. Sent messages are blue if sent to another Apple device using the free iMessage service, and green if they're sent to non-Apple devices as regular SMS messages.

5 Messages can contain attachments such as photos, videos or small pictures called emojis, such as smiley faces or the coffee cup picture seen within the message here.

6 When an outgoing message has reached its reader, it's labelled 'Delivered'. After it has been opened, this is replaced by the date or, if more recent, the time it was read.

7 Tap the camera icon to open the Camera app. Take a new picture and add it to your message.

8 This icon toggles between the App Drawer, which is seen below, and the predictive text bar found over the keyboard in a number of apps.

9 Type your message in this field. When you're ready to send, tap the blue arrow that appears at the right-hand side of the text field when you've typed something in here.

10 Tap the mic and speak a message, and it's converted into text.

11 If you want to send an emoji, such as a smiling face or an object like the coffee cup seen above, tap and hold this key and then choose the emoji keyboard from the pop-up.

12 Tap here to dictate your message instead of typing it. Your words are converted to text as you speak.

Sending a new message

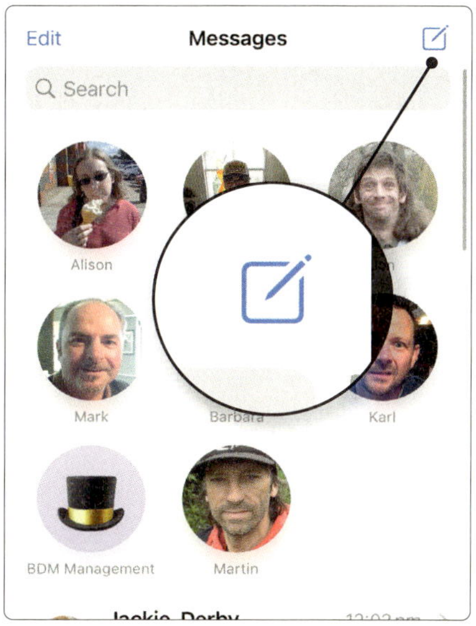

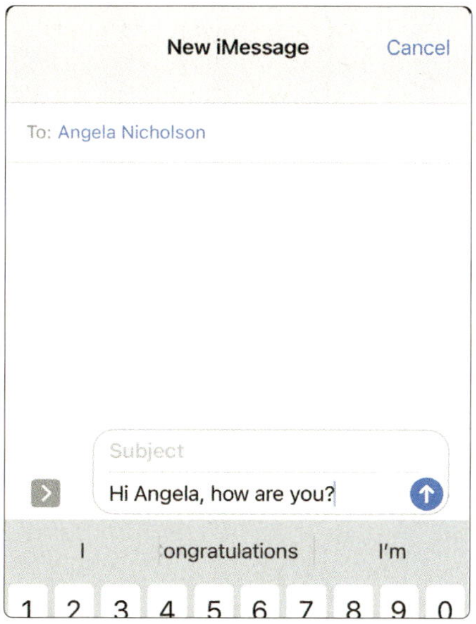

1 Tap the Pen and paper icon in the top right corner to open a new message. In the To field, type the mobile number or email address of the person you want to message. If that person is in your Contacts app, type their name instead, or use the + icon on the left.

2 If the To field turns blue, it can be sent through iMessage (free). If it turns green, it's sent as a regular text message. If it turns red, the device you entered can't receive a message. When the other person is typing a reply, three dots in a speech bubble appear.

Voice and video messages

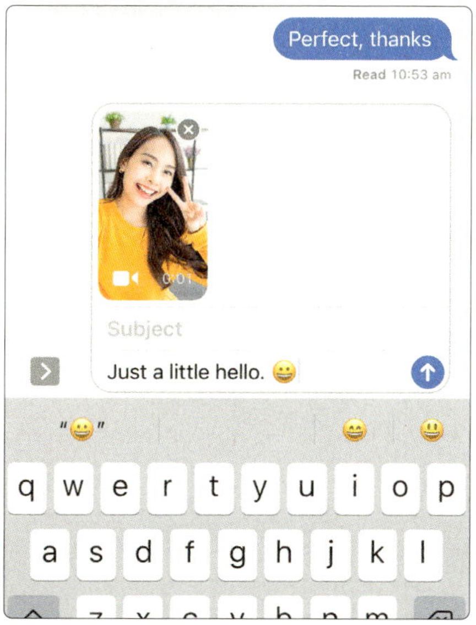

1 To send a voice message, tap the Audio icon in the App Drawer. The keyboard turns into a mic. Tap it, record your message and then tap again to stop. There's now a wave form in the message field. Tap the blue arrow to send the recording, or the 'X' on the left of it to delete it without sending.

2 To send video messages, tap the Camera icon to open the Camera app, from where you can select Video and record your movie in the usual way. When you're finished, tap Play to review it, Retake to try again or the blue arrow to add it to your message. The blue arrow sends it straight away.

Photo Management

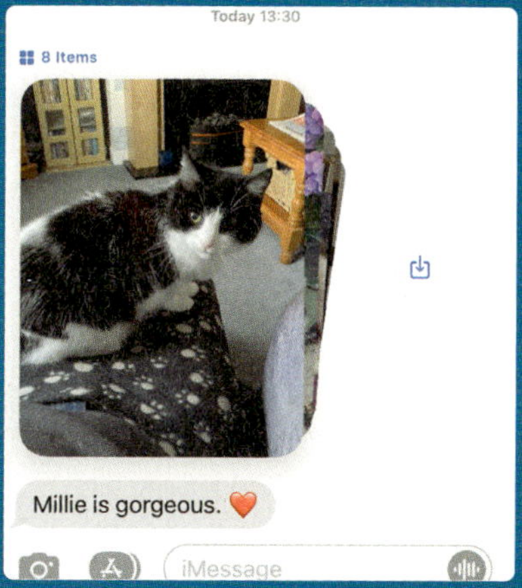

The Messages app is very efficient and user-friendly when it comes to dealing with photo attachments.

To send a photo, tap the Photos App icon at the bottom of a Messages conversation and you see a grid of photographs from your Photos App. Tap as many as you like to select them. You can now choose which order their placed in your message. Just tap them in your chosen order, and they're numbered instead of ticked. To unselect a photograph, simply tap it a second time and the number disappears. When you're ready, tap Add in the top-right corner and the photos are added to your outgoing message. Here, you can scroll the pictures left and right to review them. Each has a cross in the top-right corner – tap it to remove that particular picture. You can then add your text message in the comment field. Press the up-pointing arrow to send it, as always.

Attachments that are sent by or received by you appear in your Messages conversation as a stack. Above this stack is a small icon followed by the number of items in that stack; and for received items, to the right of the stack is an icon that looks like the the Sharing icon upside down. To flick through the items in your stack, tap the stack and swipe them left and right. Tap the icon and number of items above the stack to see them all as a grid. Tap the inverted Sharing icon to download the photos to your Photos app.

Group Messages

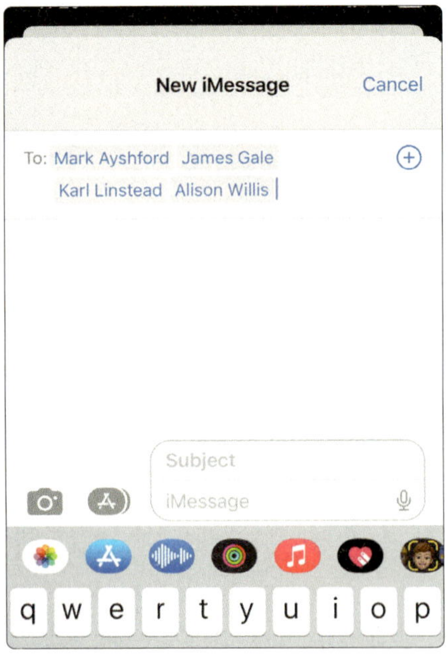

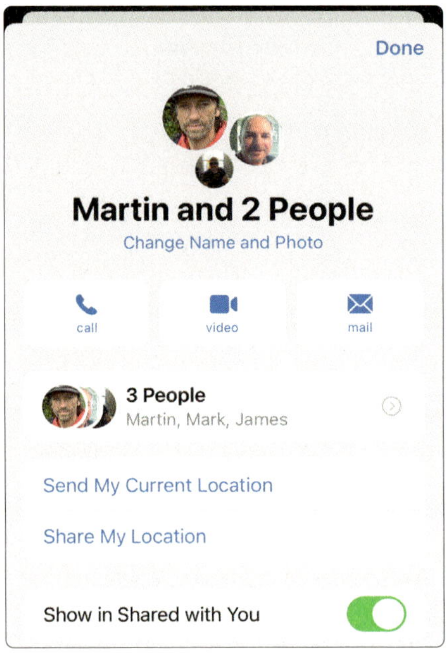

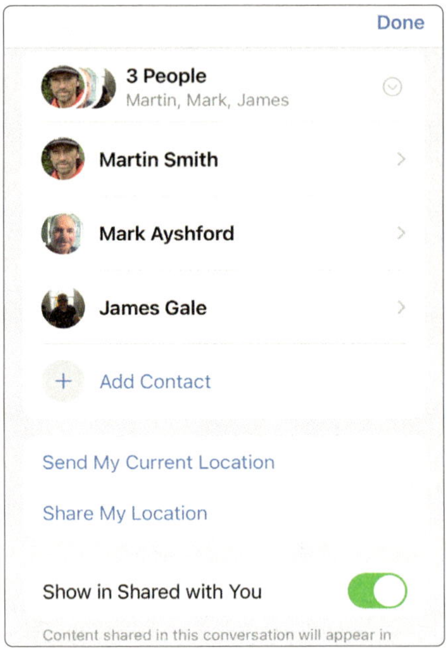

1 You can add multiple recipients to start a group conversation, just by typing more than one person's name or number in the To field of a new message. When group messaging, the name of the sender appears above each message so you can see who said what.

2 When looking at a group conversation, access unique controls by tapping the People icons at the top of the screen. Tap Change Name and Photo under the icons to rename the group, and give it a single picture. The 'Leave this Conversation' link removes you from the group.

3 Tap People and then tap Add Contact to add someone to the group. Use the location links to let everyone know where you are. Type a name of someone in the group to send the message to that person alone. Long tap a message to reply directly to that specific message.

Using Memoji and Animoji (requires Face ID iPhone)

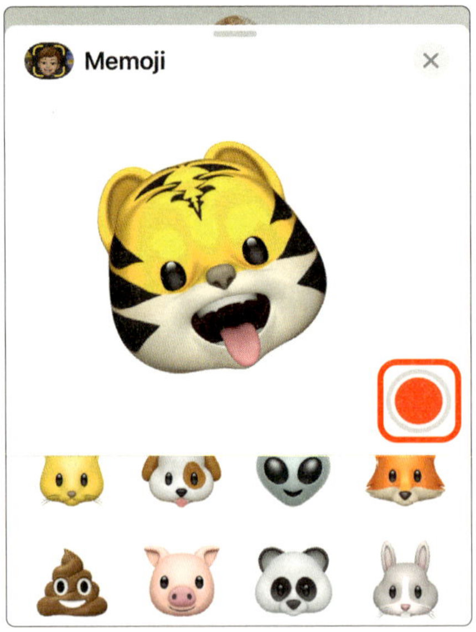

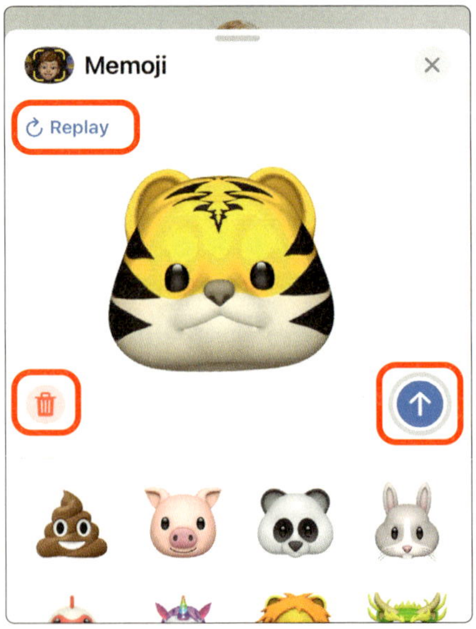

1 In Messages, open the App Drawer (tap the 'A' icon) and tap the Memoji icon. Slide left and right to cycle through your Memojis and Animojis, or swipe the window up to view the full range. Tap '+' to create a new Memoji.

2 Hold the phone in front of you. Turn your head, open and close your mouth, blink or stick out your tongue, and the emoji's animations do so too. To record your animated message, tap the red circular button. Tap it again to stop.

3 When you've finished, send it with the blue arrow, play it with Replay or bin it with the red trash can. Recording and sending animojis is exclusive to iPhones with Face ID, but you can receive them on other Apple gear.

Pinned Messages

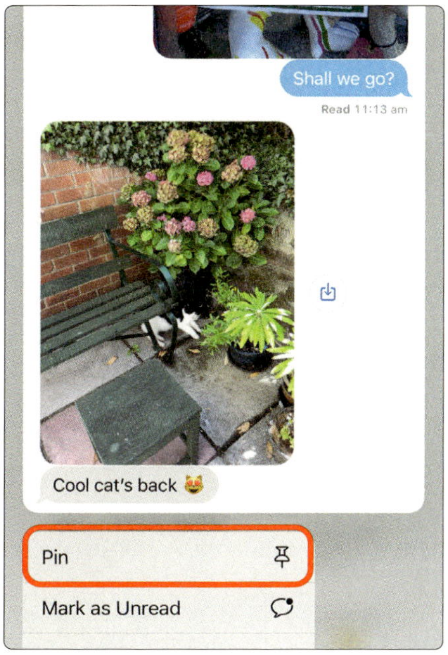

To pin a conversation to the top of your screen, tap and hold it to bring up this options window. Tap Pin, and the person or group appears atop the Messages screen. Up to nine can be pinned in this way. To unpin, tap and hold a pinned conversation and tap Unpin.

Details Window

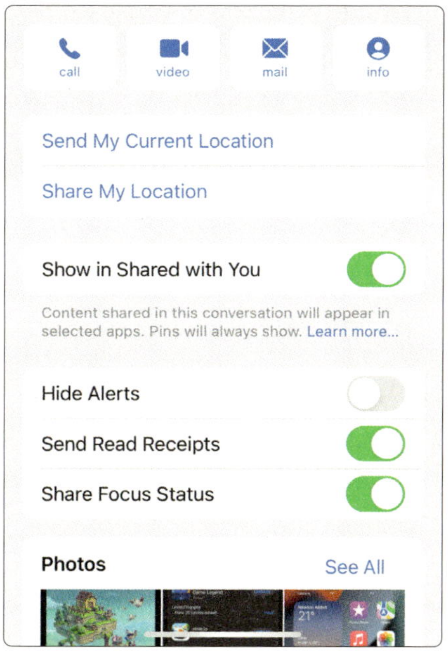

Open a message and tap the icon pic at the top for the details screen. From here, you can initiate an audio or video call, send an email, access that persons Contacts card (info), send or share your location and more. Scroll up for attachments to and from that person.

Messages Profiles

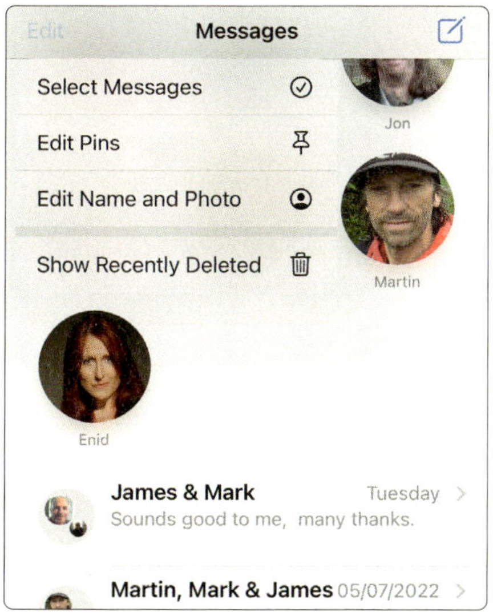

On the Messages screen, tap Edit (top-left) for a pop-up. Tap Edit Name and Photo. Tap your initials to choose a photo or a memoji, and set your display name. You can then turn on Name and Photo Sharing, so this name and photo are shared when messaging.

Shared with You

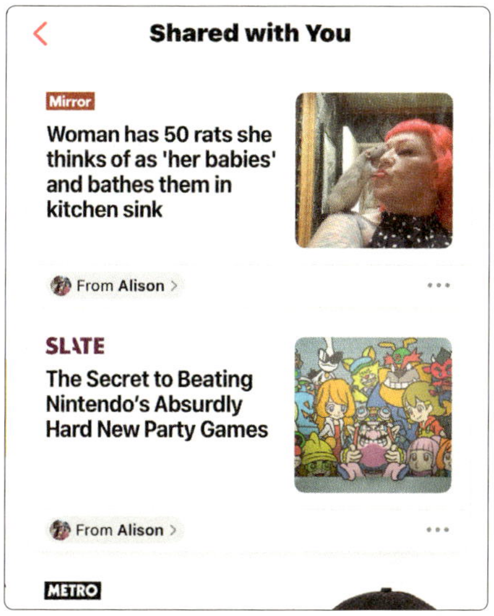

If someone sends you a photo, video, web link, Apple TV link, Apple Music track, News link or a Podcast using the Messages app, that item is also listed in its native app, eg. a news item is in the News app. Look for the Shared with You section in the relevant apps.

The App Drawer

Tap the 'Apps' icon to the left of the Message field to toggle between having the App Drawer and Predictive Text Bar over the keyboard. The functions of the various icons in the App Drawer are as follows.

Photos: Opens a window showing pictures and videos from your Photos app, which you can add to your messages.

Store: Tap this to open the App Store's section on goodies for your Messages app.

Audio: Record an audio clip and send it as a message.

Fitness: Stickers and graphics relating to your Fitness app.

Music: Share something you've listened to using Apple Music. If the recipient also subscribes, they can play it from your message.

Digital Touch: Draw and sketch, then send your creation as a picture or video in a message.

Memoji: Opens your Memojis and Animojis, so you can record as an animated character or drag one into your message as a sticker.

Stickers: Drag a sticker into your message to send it as a picture.

Images : Choose from a range of animated pictures, or GIFs, to send with your message.

...And More
After these standard App Drawer icons, those you've bought or are associated with an app you've installed, are shown.

What's new in iOS 16 Messages?

Delete and Recover Messages, and Report Junk

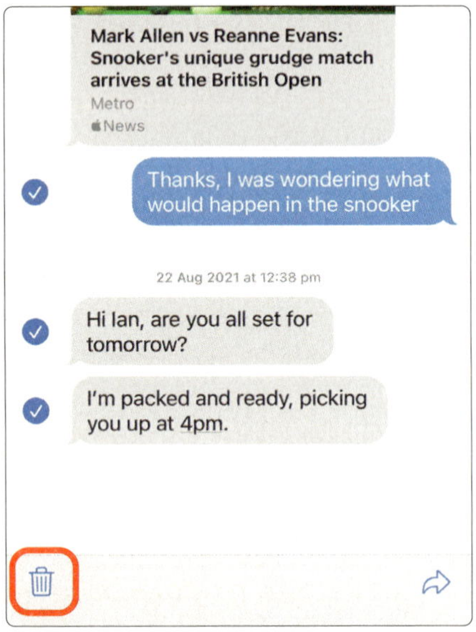

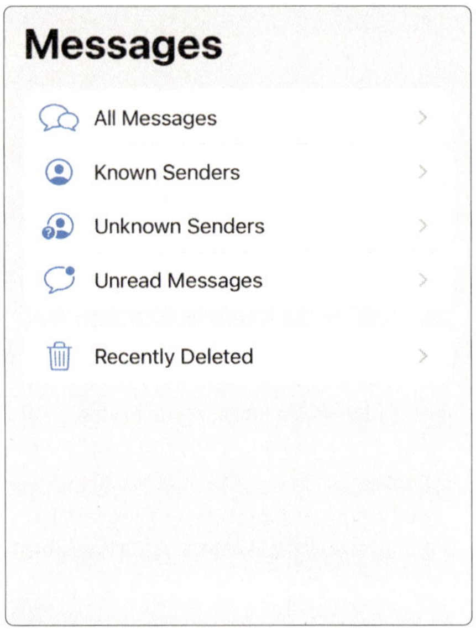

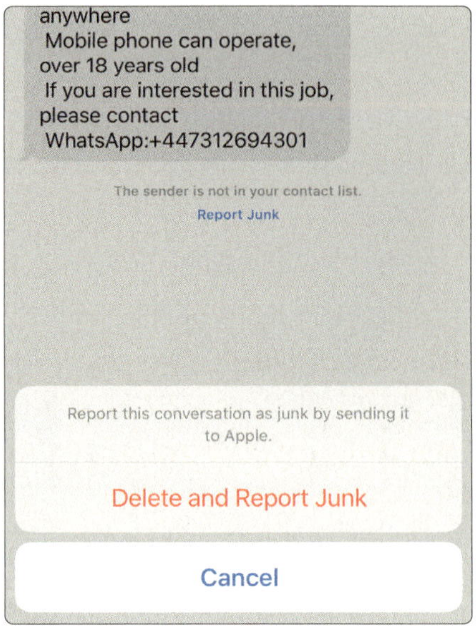

1 To delete messages, open the conversation and long-tap on a message, and tap More in the options window that pops up. Tick bubbles are shown next to the messages. Tick the messages you want to delete, then tap the dustbin icon (bottom left).

2 To recover deleted messages, go to Settings > Messages and turn on Filter Unknown Senders. On the conversation list, tap Filters in the top-left. Open Recently Deleted, tick anything you want to recover then tap the Recover All option.

3 To recover a conversation individually, long-tap and tap Recover. If you open a message that might be spam, tap the Report Junk link that appears under it, then tap Delete and Report Junk to alert Apple and your network provider.

Unsend and Edit Sent Messages

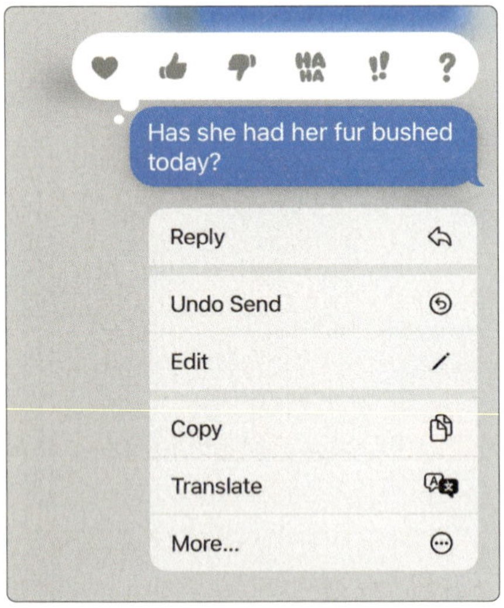

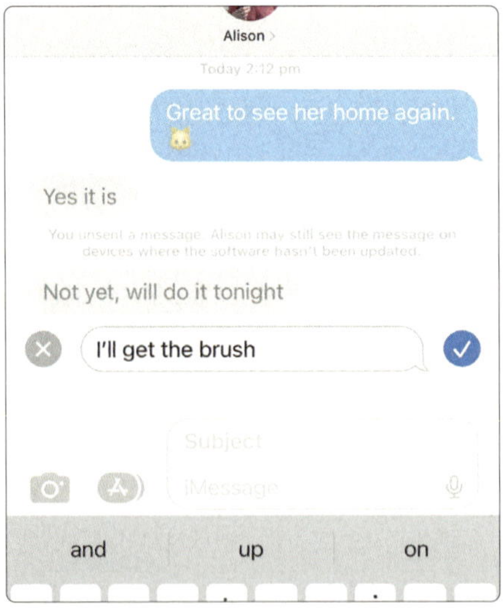

1 You can recall a message up to two minutes after sending it. Simply long-tap the message in question, then tap Undo Send. It disappears from your screen, but unless you're sending to an iOS 16 device, the recipient still has it.

2 You can edit a message for up to 15 minutes, but again, unless you sent it to an iOS 16 device the recipient can see both the old and the new one. Long-tap the message, then select Edit, and make changes then tap the tick.

Mark Unread

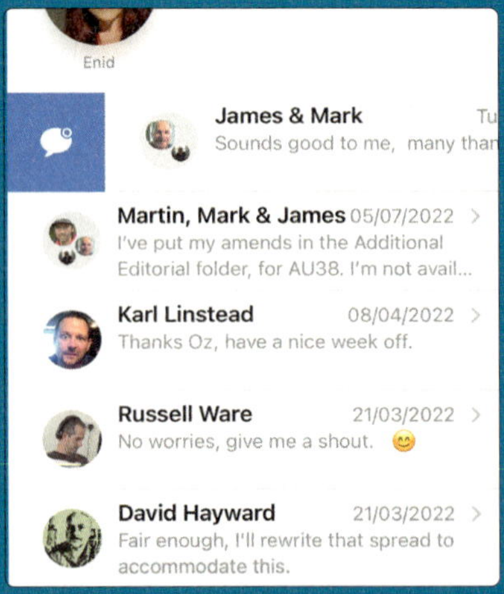

To mark a message as unread, either swipe the conversation to the right and tap the speech bubble icon, or long-tap the conversation and in the options window that appears, select the Mark as Unread option. A blue dot appears next to the message.

More great Messages features

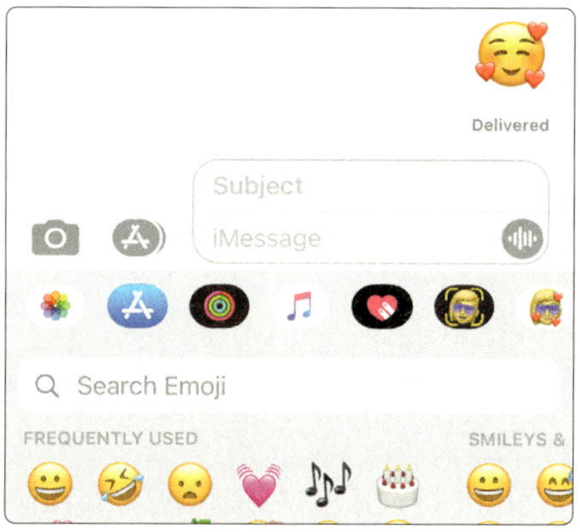

Using emojis

Emojis, including smiley faces, can be found by tapping and holding the keyboard's Globe icon and selecting Emoji. Slide them right and left for more. An emoji sent on its own is shown larger.

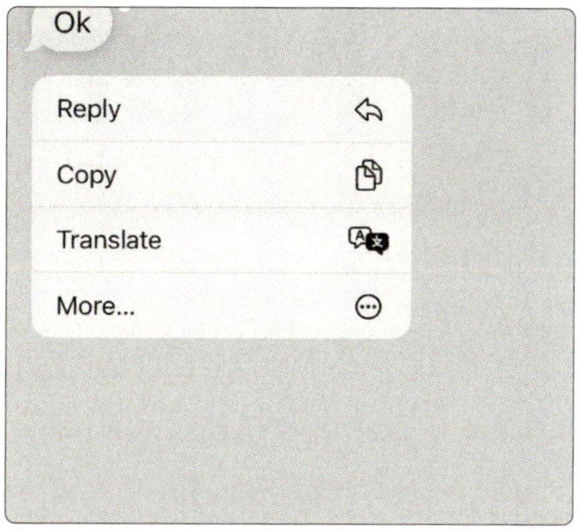

The hold bubble

Tap and hold on a message you've received and a bubble appears above it. This bubble offers a range of options. You can like or unlike the message with a thumb icon, send a heart, a laugh or question mark and more.

Rich links

When someone sends you a web link in a Messages conversation, you get a preview of the website, right there in the message. All you have to do is tap the link to go straight to the linked site in Safari.

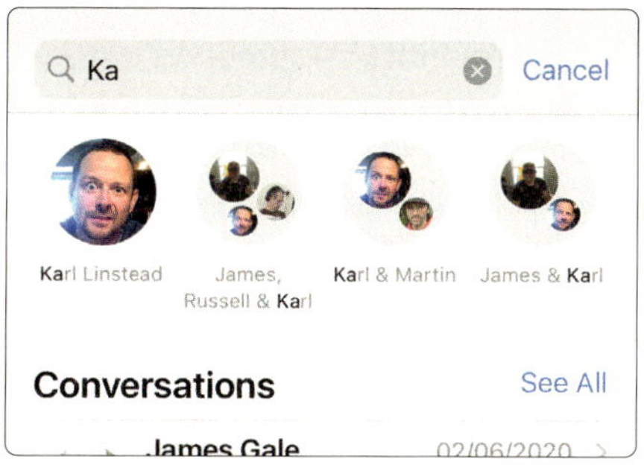

Search features

Pull down the Messages screen to see the Messages app's search field. Tap it, and you're offered recent people, links, photos, and locations. Start to type, and these suggestions are streamlined, and conversations are added.

Scribble and draw

Turn the iPhone into landscape orientation and on the virtual keyboard, tap the 'squiggle' key in the bottom right. You get a pad on which you can make finger drawings or write scribbled messages. Tap Done to put it in your message.

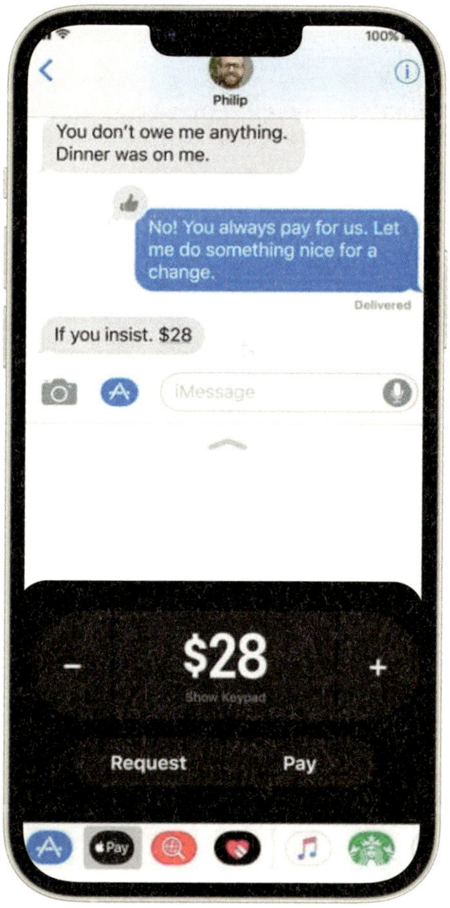

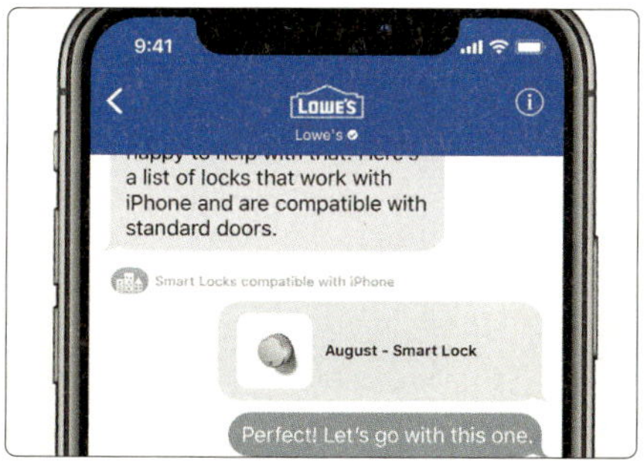

Business chat

Business Chat lets businesses connect with customers using Messages. You can chat to a salesperson or customer services, schedule an appointment or make purchases. Start a Business Chat conversation from Safari, Maps, Spotlight and Siri.

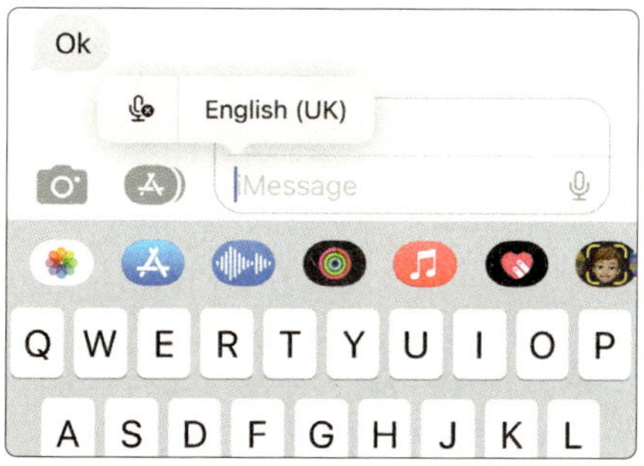

Dictation

If you're tired of typing, you can use the keyboard's microphone key to dictate your message instead. Tap it, then speak what you want to say and it appears in the text field. The more you use it, the more accurate the text-to-speech function gets.

Apple Pay

You can send money through Apple Pay in Messages, assuming your iPhone is capable of using this feature. Tap the Apple Pay icon and follow the instructions to send money. This feature is not yet available in every territory.

Using Memoji

A Memoji is a cartoon representation of you, created on your iPhone. You can design them to look like you and use them as both stickers and Animojis. New emojis are added with iOS 16; look out for a troll, a battery low symbol, a pouring glass, an empty jar, a person wearing a crown and more. As Memojis need a TrueDepth camera, only iPhones with Face ID can use them.

How to make a new Memoji

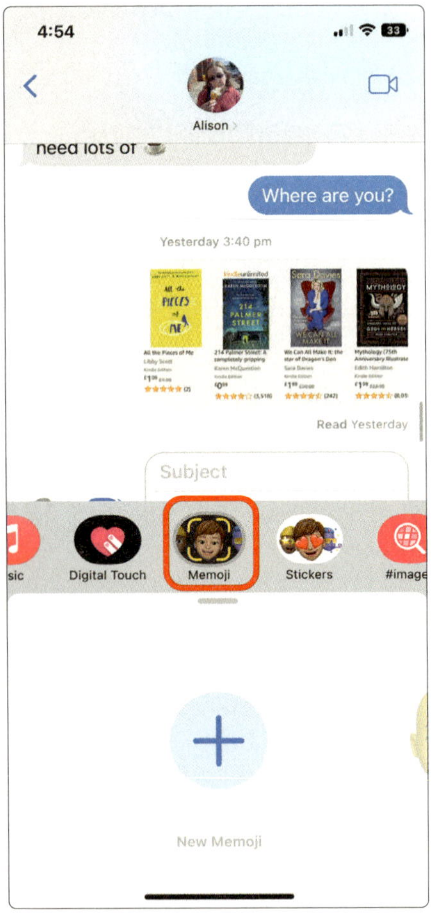

1 Open the Messages app. Tap the Memoji icon in the app drawer and scroll all the way to the right until you see the Plus icon. Tap it to start your Memoji. Note: if the Memoji icon isn't there, your iPhone is likely too old and cannot use Memojis.

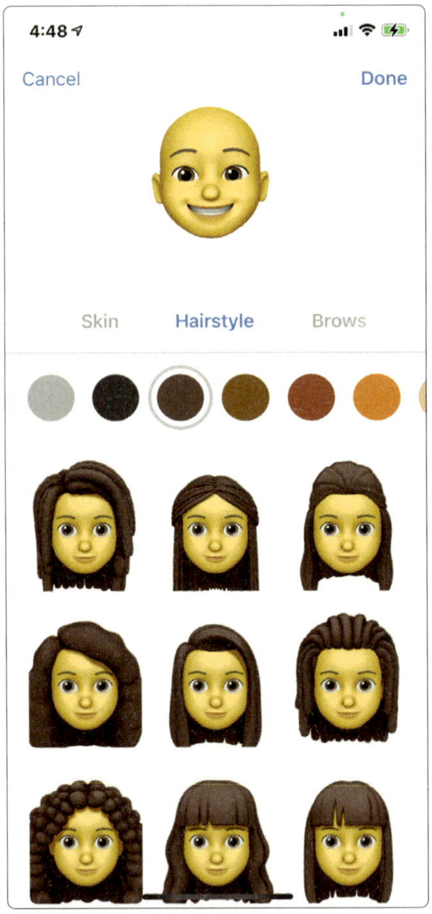

2 Under a blank face you see a slider. Using this slider, the colour options and diagrams, build your Memoji any way you wish. Choose a hairstyle and colour, add glasses if you wear them, and more. You can make as many Memojis as you like so have fun and get creative.

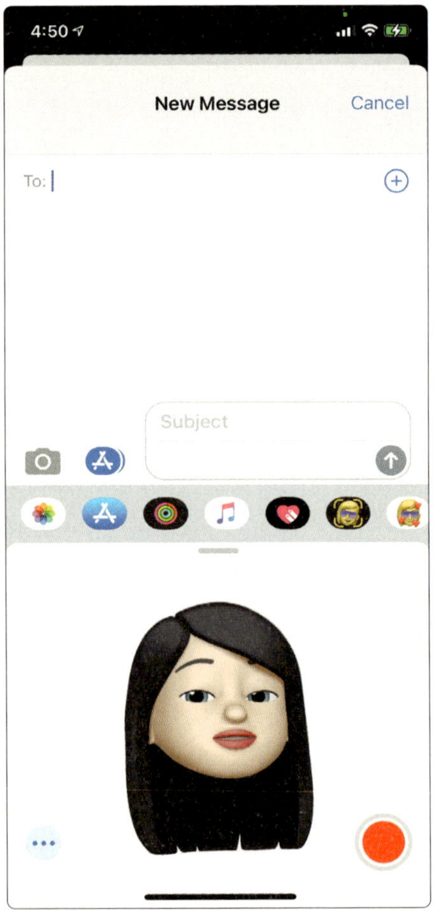

3 When you're finished, tap Done. Your Memoji is added to your Animoji collection, from where it can be used in the usual way, just as if it was a regular Animoji. You can use it as a sticker, an animated emoji or in the FaceTime app for video chat.

How to use your new Memoji

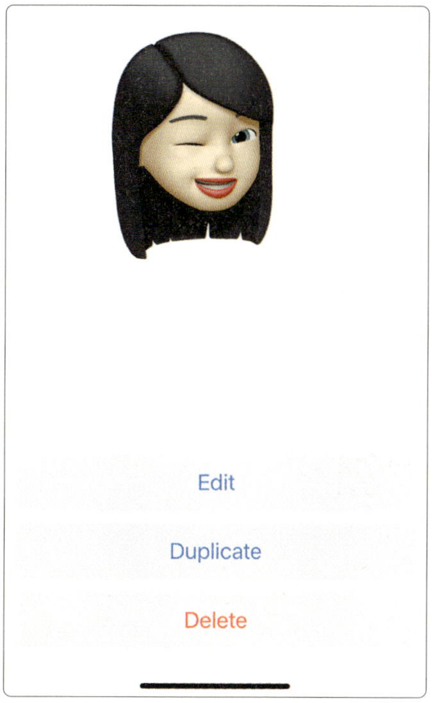

1 Next to the Memoji, on the left, is an icon showing three dots. Tap it and you can edit your Memoji, duplicate it so you can edit it while keeping the original or delete it if you no longer want it.

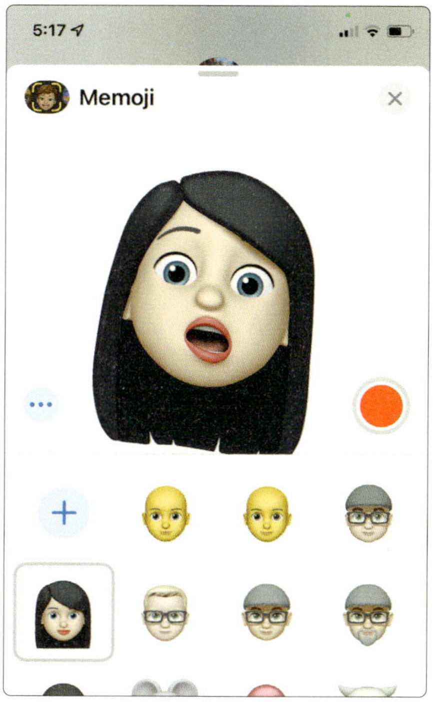

2 You record with a Memoji in exactly the same way as you do with an Animoji. First of all, select your Memoji and tap the red record button to the bottom right of the Memoji.

3 Record up to 30 seconds of speech, with the Memoji following your expressions. When you're done, tap the blue arrow to use the message or the bin to delete it.

4 You can use a Memoji (or indeed an Animoji) as a sticker too. Just navigate to your Memoji, pull the required face and then tap it to add it to your regular text message.

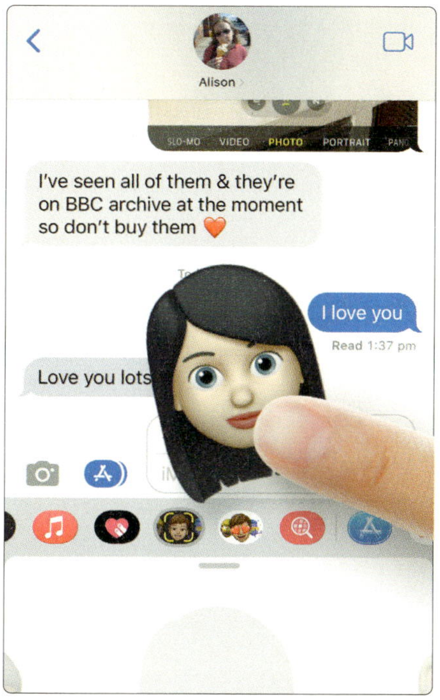

5 Alternatively, tap and hold your Memoji and drag it onto your message. While it's stuck to your finger, you can resize and rotate it before attaching it to your message.

6 Both the FaceTime app and the Messages camera feature have a star-shaped icon (bottom left) that lets you add effects, including your Memojis, to your pics and videos.

The Notes App

Notes is great. Not only can you store your scribblings, you can also create checklists and tables, add videos and pics, share notes with others and even collaborate on a note. You can password-protect a note for privacy too.

NOTES *in Focus*

1 Tap this link to go back to the folder containing the currently open note. As you can see, that's the iCloud folder, which is synced across your Apple devices, including your iPhone. You can then tap another folder on the Folders screen to open it, and look at the notes inside.

2 At the top of a note, you can see the date and time when the note in question was last edited. Drag the note down to get this information.

3 The sharing icon opens the sharing, collaboration options, and more. The three-dots icon opens a window containing a lot of options, including searching within the note, moving it, pinning or locking, adding lines and grids and more.

4 Various typographic options are available. You can underline, bold and italicise text, turn it into a title or heading, justify it right, left or centre, make a list using numbers or bullet points, and more.

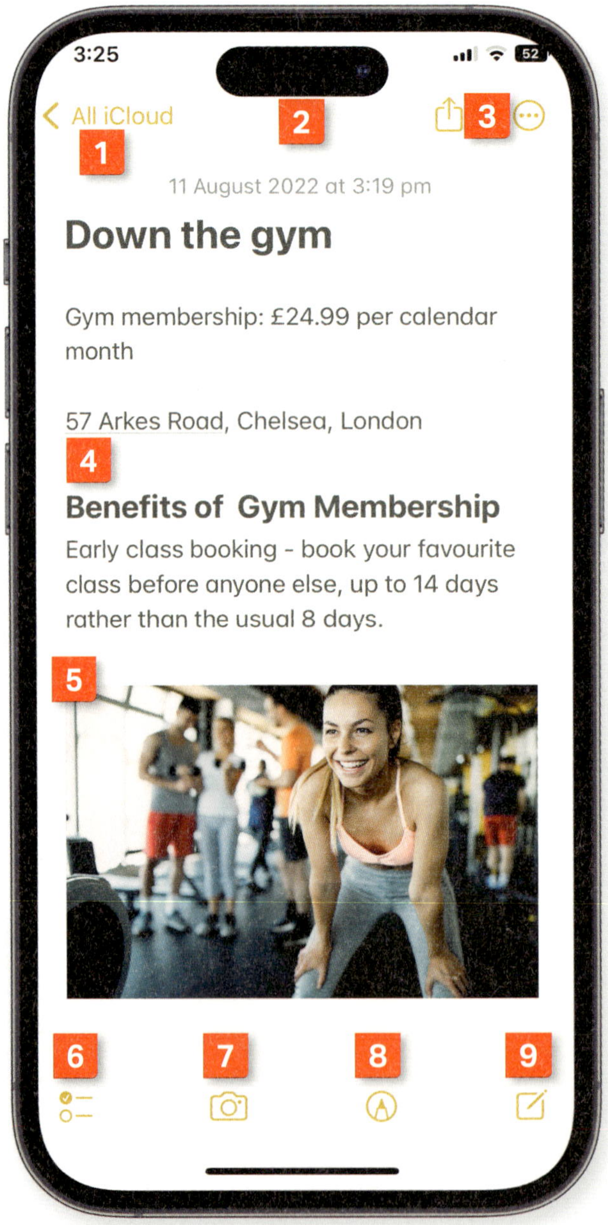

5 A note can contain both text and attachments such as the photo seen here. A video attachment can also be used and you can save a location from the Maps app to a note. Tapping a location attachment opens it in the Maps app.

6 Highlight a list of items in your note and then tap this icon here to turn it into a handy checklist.

7 This icon gives you access to a range of attachment-related options, namely Scan Documents, Take Photo or Video, and Choose Photo or Video from those already stored on your iPhone.

8 The Markup icon. Tap it to open an art toolbar that lets you make simple sketches and drawings on a note or its attachments. You can scribble or sketch on an existing note, or on a blank one, as you wish.

9 Tap here to open a new, blank note for you to fill in and save.

Getting started with the Notes app

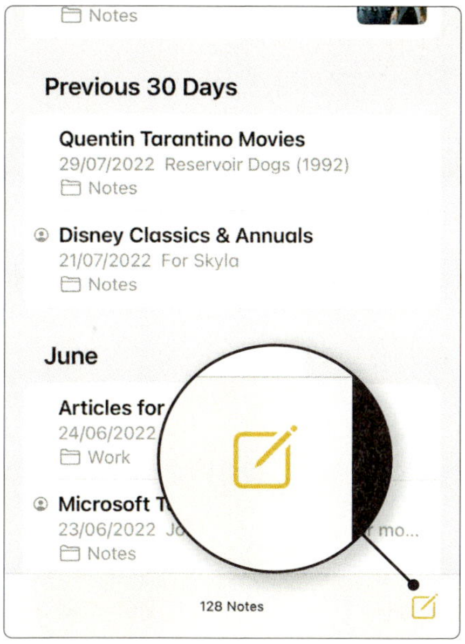

1 When you first open Notes, you see a list of previously saved notes. If you haven't made any yet, this list is, of course, empty. To create a new note, tap the pen-and-paper icon in the bottom right corner.

2 Tap on the note and the keyboard appears. The first line you type appears as a header. The icons shown above the keyboard are: Add a Grid, Format, Make a Checklist, Add an Attachment and Markup respectively.

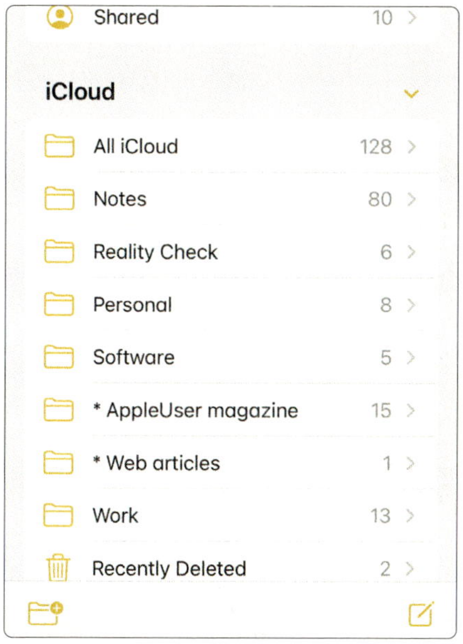

3 Tap the chevron in the top left corner for a list of the folders in which your notes are stored. If you want to sync notes via iCloud, they have to be in the iCloud section. Tap the folder icon (bottom left) to create a new folder.

More features of the Notes app

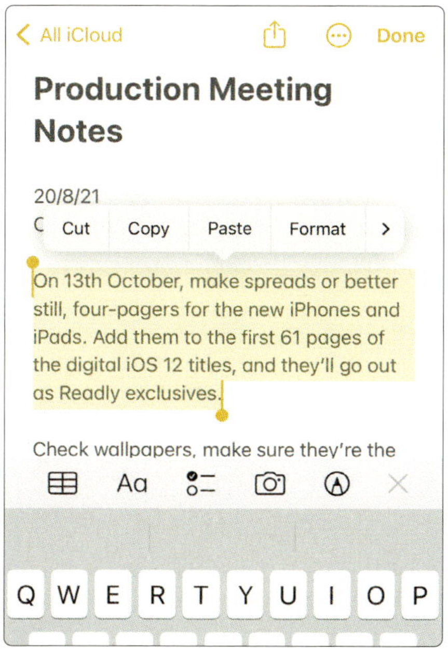

1 Double-tap to select a word or triple-tap to highlight a paragraph and drag the handles to select more or less text if necessary. You bring up a contextual menu offering formatting and attachment options too.

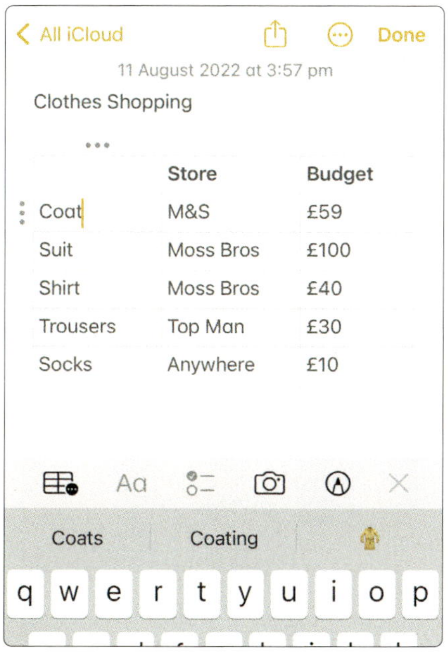

2 The first icon in the tools above the keyboard sets up a table. You can type in every cell and double-tap the three-dot icons for a pop-up menu to add or delete rows and columns. You can drag rows and columns after tapping this too.

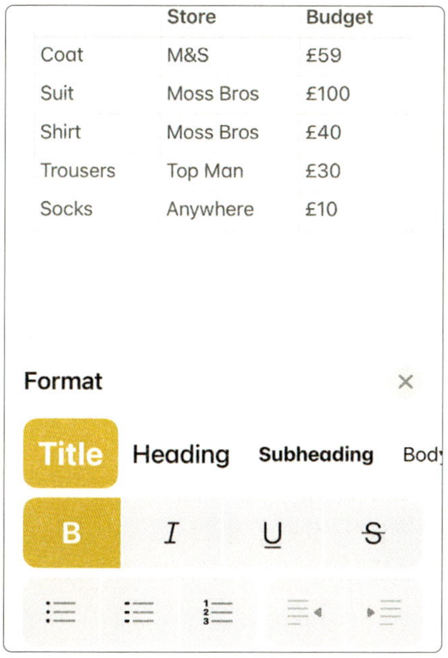

3 Highlight some text then tap the 'Aa' icon for the formatting options. You can justify it right, left or centred, turn it into a title or a heading, make it bold, italicised, underlined or crossed out and more. Tap 'x' to go back to the note.

4 Highlight a list and tap the tick icon to turn make a checklist. Tap a circle to tick it, and again to untick. Tap and hold an item to drag it up and down. Tap and hold for a contextual menu, then tap Checklist and you can opt to tick/untick all, delete ticked items, or send them to the bottom.

5 The camera icon brings up a sub-menu about attachments. You can add a photo or video from your Photos app, scan a document and add it to the note, take a new photo or video or scan text using your iPhone's camera, harnessing the power of Live Text.

6 Tap the pen in a circle icon to add a sketch to your note. It brings up drawing tools, which you use to draw and colour. Tap the circle on the right to change pen colour and opacity. Note the Undo and Redo tools above the sketch.

7 Tap a photo or attachment in a note, then tap the pen icon in the top-right and you can draw on the attachment using the markup tools as seen in the last step. Tap the Plus sign for extra annotation tools, as shown here.

Quick Notes

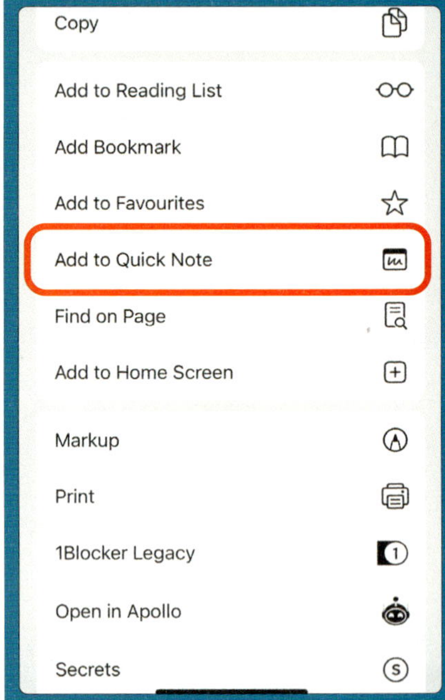

Quick notes let you copy whatever you're looking at in an app into a note. To use it, in most iPhone apps, just find the Sharing icon, tap it and tap Add to Quick Note in the pop-up window. Add text if you want, then tap Save.

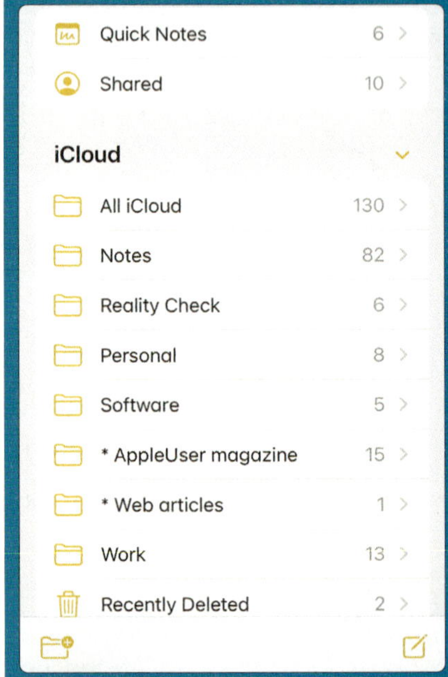

To review your Quick Notes (which are synced using iCloud), open the Notes app and navigate to the Folders screen. Tap Quick Notes. Tap a note to open it. If you deep tap a note icon and you can move it to a regular Notes folder.

The Action and Share menus

Tap on the three-dots icon found at the top of the screen for the action menu, or the Sharing icon for the share menu. These guides show you what you see if you do so with a note open in the app.

The Action Menu

1 Scan: Tap here to scan a document with your camera, and add it to a note.

2 Pin: Pin a note to the top of the notes list. If the note you have open is already pinned, this option turns into Unpin, which does the opposite.

3 Lock: Lock a note so it can only be opened with a password. You can set a password yourself, or use your device passcode and/or Face ID/Touch ID. If the note is already lock-protected, the option here is to remove the lock.

4 Find in Note: If you've a note with a lot of text, this is a useful option that lets you search it for a particular word or phrase. You're told how many times that word or phrase appears in a note, and can use the chevrons next to the search field to cycle through them.

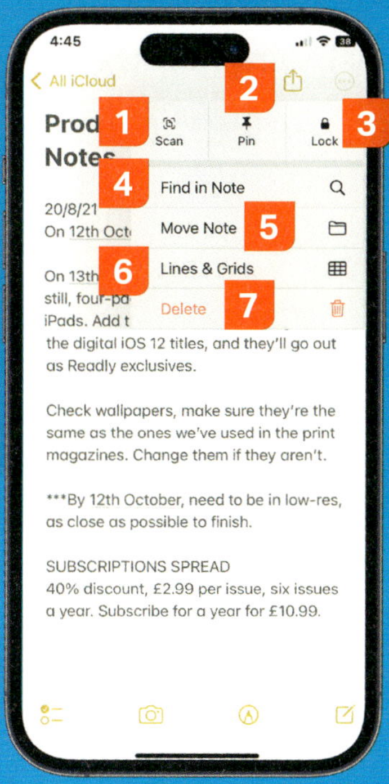

5 Move Note: You can arrange your notes in folders, and move an open note between them using this option. You can also move a note out of the Quick Notes section into one of your regular folders.

6 Lines & Grids: Adds lines or a grid to the note, to make it easier to use the Markup feature for handwritten notes or sketches. It's only for Markup; if you type something onto the note, it appears above or below the lines or grid.

7 Delete: This option removes a note from your Notes app. If you delete something by mistake, go to the Folders screen and tap Recently Deleted, open the note and tap the folder in the bottom bar to move it. Deleted notes are kept for 30 days before being erased permanently.

The Sharing Menu

1 Pull-Down Menu: If you're planning to share a note you can tap here to choose between offering to Collaborate on a note (so edits made by either of you are shared with the other party), or Send Copy, whereby they get an identical copy of your note, but edits made afterwards are independent.

2 Favourites: A row of contacts, badged with a method of sending a shared note. Tap one to send the note to that person, using the method offered. These favourites are compiled automatically from your previous interactions.

3 Methods of Sending: Choose one of these and tap it to share the note using the app in question. You then add the contact details of the person you wish to send it to.

4 Copy: Copy the contents of the open note, so you can paste it elsewhere. You can paste this pretty-much anywhere where text can be written. Just the thing if, for example, you want to paste a note into the body of an email.

5 Markup: You can arrange your notes in folders, and move an open note between them using this option. You can also move a note out of the Quick Notes section into one of your regular folders.

6 Print: If you have a printer on your wireless network, you can use AirPrint to print out the open note. Tap here to do so.

7 Third Party Apps: A lot of third-party apps also have sharing options, the specifics of which depend on the app in question. These options are listed at the foot of the Sharing menu here.

The Calendar App

Calendar is great for organising your life. You can add events and appointments, schedule alerts, invite contacts to events and sync Calendar with other calendar apps. It can remind you about upcoming events too.

CALENDAR *in Focus*

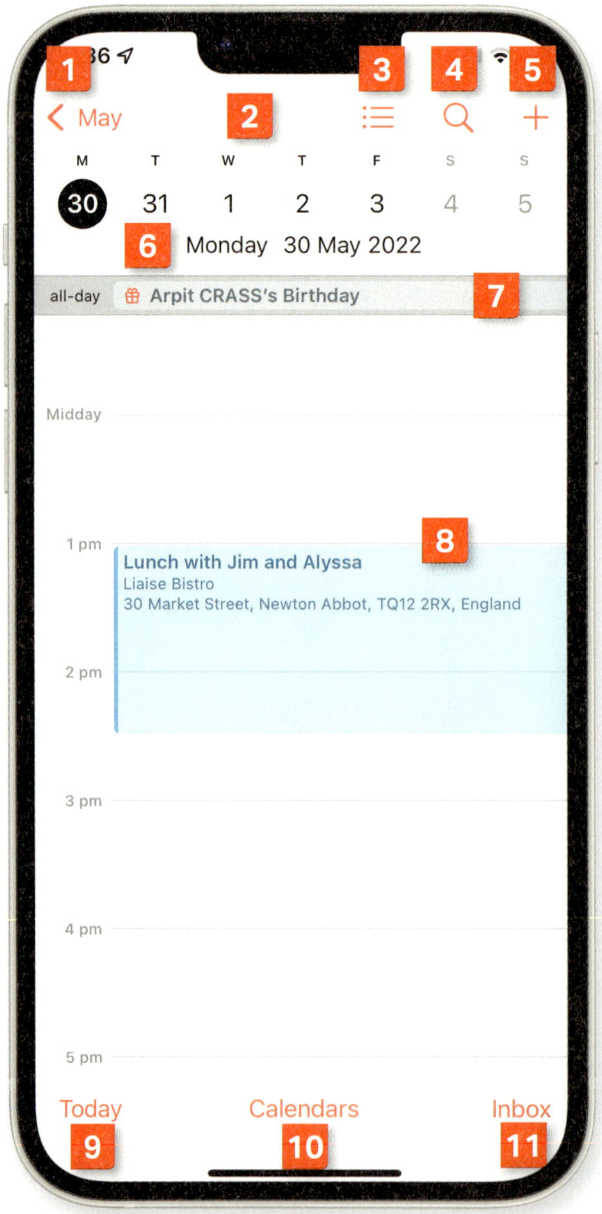

1 Tap this link to go back to the month view, showing the whole of the month.

2 Here you see the days of the month, with the currently displayed day highlighted. So here we're looking at 12th November.

3 This icon gives you a list of upcoming events, displayed according to their date and time.

4 Tap here to search the Calendar app, looking at titles and content in your calendar entries.

5 Tap here to create a new calendar event, setting the date, time and title, as well as whether it repeats (for example, with birthdays and anniversaries), which calendar it's in, when it starts and ends and more.

6 The day, date, month and year currently open are shown here for easy reference.

7 All-day events such as public holidays and birthdays are listed at the top of a day's list of calendar events. You can tap this all-day entry for more information.

8 This event is to take place between 1pm and 3pm on the date in question. Tap the event for more details and options.

9 Wherever you are in the Calendar app, tapping the Today link takes you back to the current day's entries, as seen here.

10 You can set up more than one calendar, so your events can be sorted into categories such as work, home and whatever else you choose. Tap here for a list of your calendars.

11 Invitations to join shared calendars arrive in your inbox, which you can reach by tapping the link found in the bottom right corner here.

Emailing events

To send an event from a Mac, drag it off your Calendar app onto your desktop (this doesn't delete the event from the Calendar app), where it appears as a .ics file, then send it by email.

Exploring the Calendar app

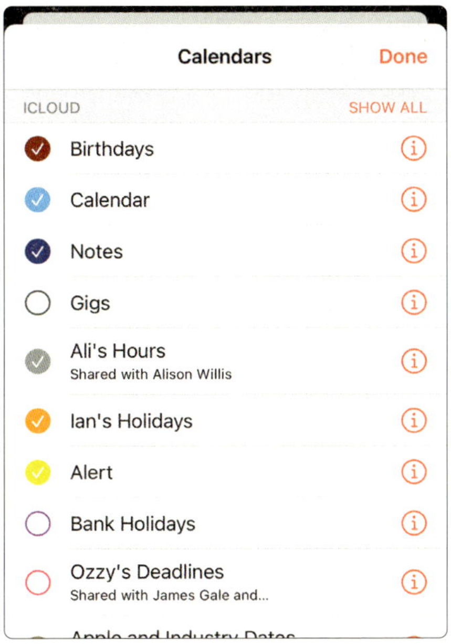

1 Tap the Calendars link at the bottom of the screen to see a list of all your calendars set up on your iPhone. Each has a circle next to it. Tap this circle to turn a calendar on and off, showing and hiding their entries on the main screen. This is useful if your Calendar app is getting crowded and difficult to navigate.

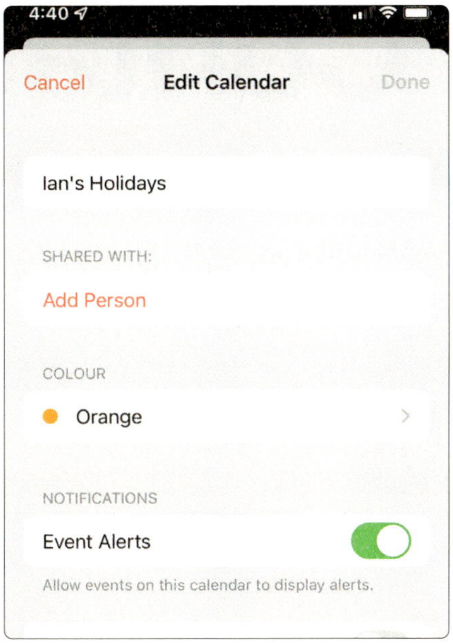

2 Tap the 'i' to the right of a calendar for this screen, where you can edit the calendar's name, change its colour, choose whether it produces alerts and whether it should be made public. Tap the Add Person link to share it with someone, after which you can add and edit events on that particular calendar.

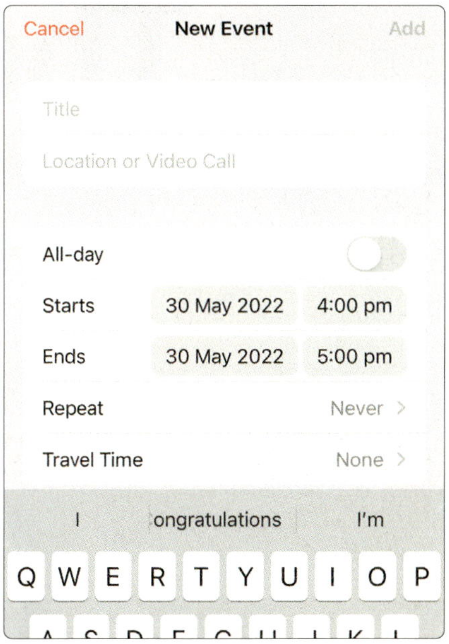

3 To add an event, tap the plus symbol to the top right of the screen. Enter a title and location for the event in the field provided, choose a start and end date and time, set whether the event is to repeat either daily, weekly, every two weeks, monthly or yearly and decide whether you want an alert.

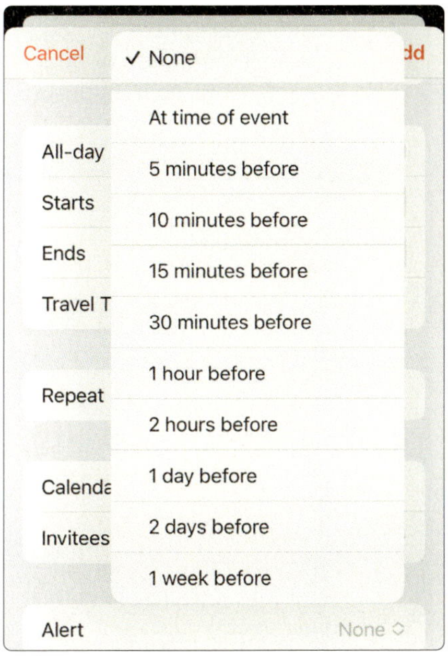

4 If you choose to receive an alert, you can set when you want it to trigger. You can also enter notes or details in the bottom field, which is useful as the Calendar app's search facility can find text in these notes. When all details have been confirmed, tap Done to finish.

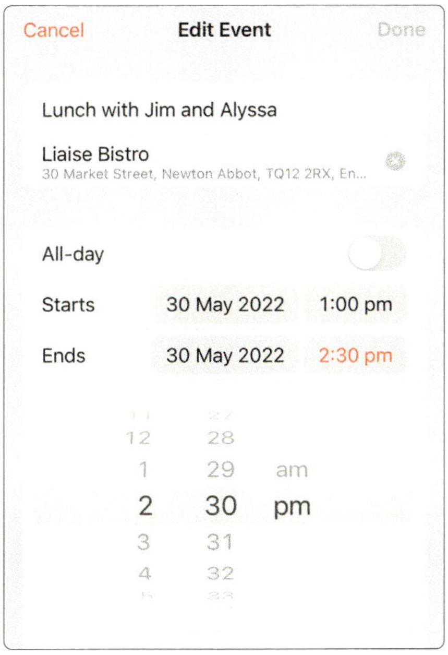

5 To edit an event, tap the event and then tap the Edit button that appears at the top right of the screen. From here you can tap on any of the fields to change the details. To delete an event, tap it, tap the Edit button then the red Delete Event button at the bottom of the screen.

6 To invite other people to this event, tap Edit, then Invitees. Tap the + icon and navigate your contacts, or just type in their details in the To field. Enter as many as you like, then tap Done and they're all contacted. If they accept, the event is added to their own calendar.

The Contacts App

The Contacts app is your iPhone's versatile digital address book. You can use it to store all your family, personal and professional contacts; and with iCloud, so their details are synced between all of your Apple devices.

CONTACTS *in Focus*

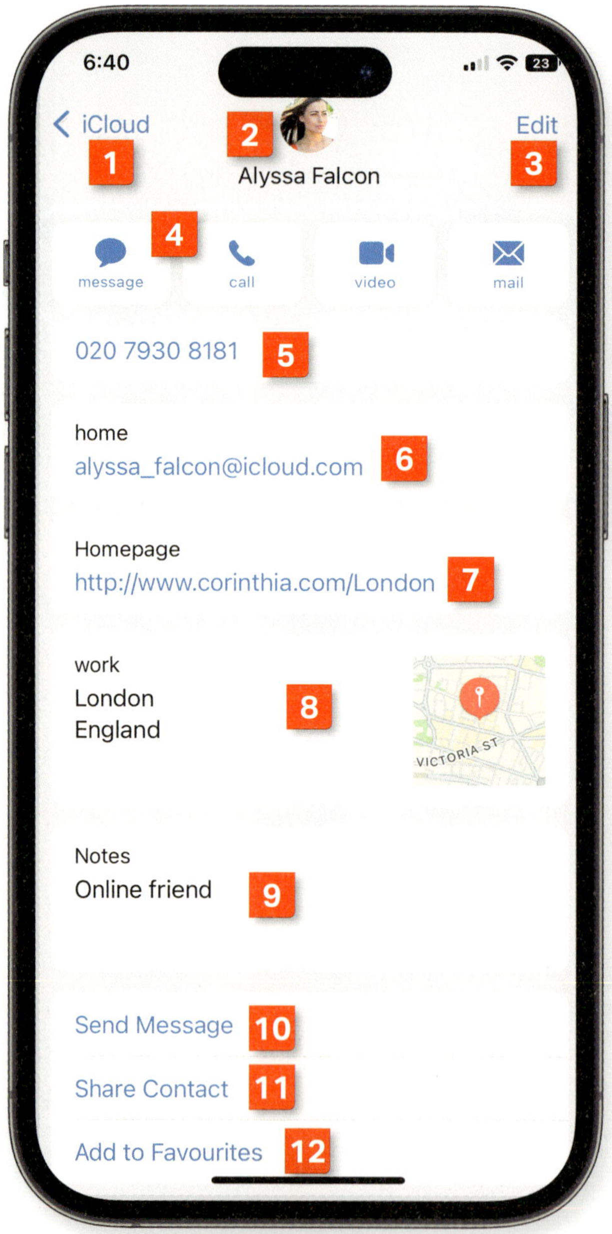

1 Tap here to go back to the previous page; maybe a contacts group, or search.

2 The name and picture of your currently open contact. If you don't yet have a picture here, the person's initials are shown on a grey background.

3 Tap Edit to add, remove or change information on the contact card. You can add things like birthdays and social media addresses as well phone numbers, street addresses and more.

4 These icons let you communicate with your contact directly from the Contacts app. Tap to send a message, make a call, make a video call or send an email. A greyed icon means the feature is unavailable.

5 Phone numbers for the contact. You can add numbers for home, work, mobile and more. Tap a number to make a call to it.

6 You can add as many email addresses as you need to a contact (for home, work and more). Tap an email address to open a blank email, with that address already in the To field.

7 If your contact has a home page, whether a personal or business site, you can add it here. Tap to open it in Safari.

8 You can add addresses for home, work and more. A preview from the Maps app is shown. Tap it to open the Maps app at the location of that address.

9 You can write anything you like in the Notes section found here. The notes are searched when using the Search Field, so it's a useful way of keeping yourself more organised.

10 Tap here to send a message to your contact using the iPhone's Messages app.

11 The Share Contact feature lets you send your contact's details to a third party, by email, messages, AirDrop and more. The recipient can then open and save that contact card to their device.

12 Add your contact's message details, phone number, email addresses, and/or other details to your list of favourites found in the Phone app.

Adding new contacts

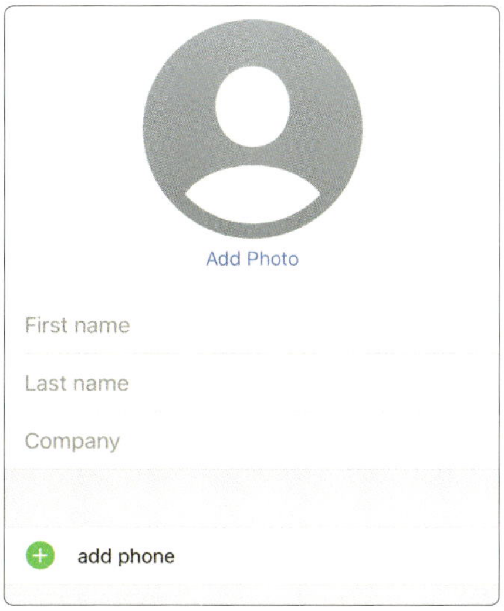

To add a new contact, press the Plus icon in the top right corner. Enter details such as the name, phone number and address by tapping the green plus icons in the contact card. Tap the silhouette to add a photo, or emoji if you prefer. If you want to enter something that isn't on the card, scroll to the bottom and tap Add Field.

Game Center profile

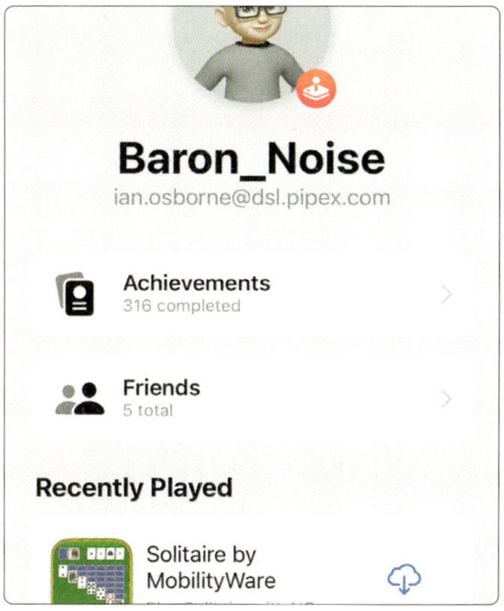

A feature coming soon to the Contacts app is Game Center integration. You will soon be able to access your friends' Game Center profiles from their card in your Contacts app, letting you see what they're playing, what achievements they've done and more. Just the thing for competitive gamers who have to beat their chums.

Assign a ringtone

You can assign an individual ringtone or text alert to a specific contact, so you always know when that person calls or texts. Open their contact card, tap Edit (top right) and scroll to Ringtone and Text Tone. If you haven't changed them already, they're set at 'Default'.

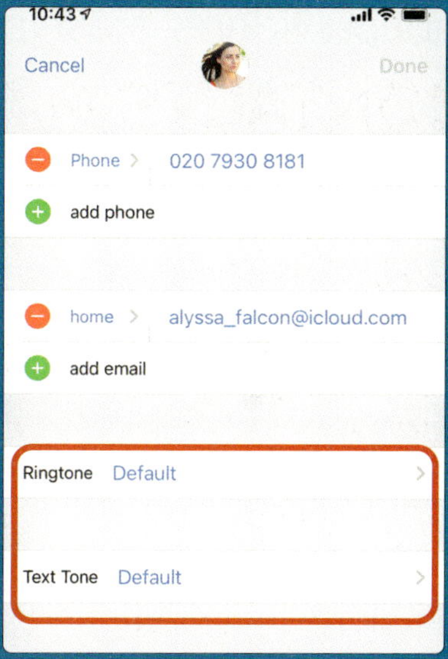

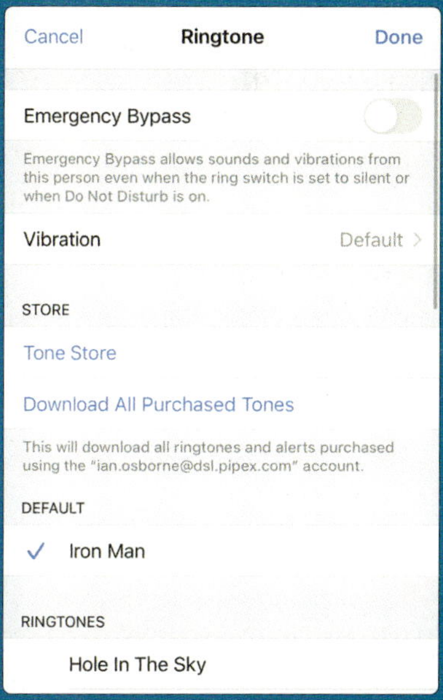

Tap the one you want to change and select a new one. This tone is now used for incoming calls or messages from that contact. You can also turn on Emergency Bypass, which lets that contact get through to you even when your phone is on Do Not Disturb.

Merging duplicates

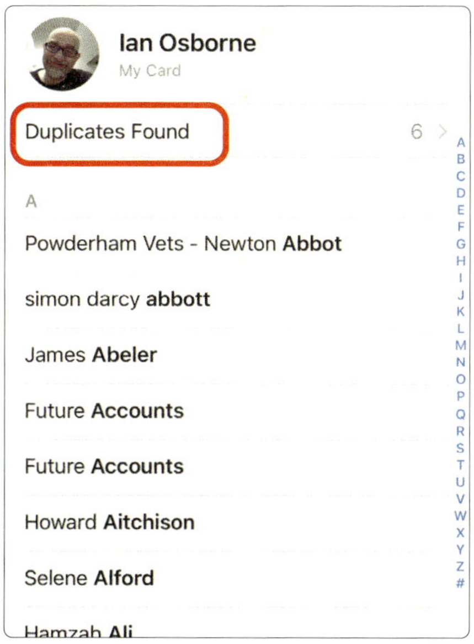

1 Open the Contacts app, and tap your main list, which holds all your contact cards. If there are duplicates, at the top of the list is an option called Duplicates Found, with the number of duplicates to its right. Tap this option.

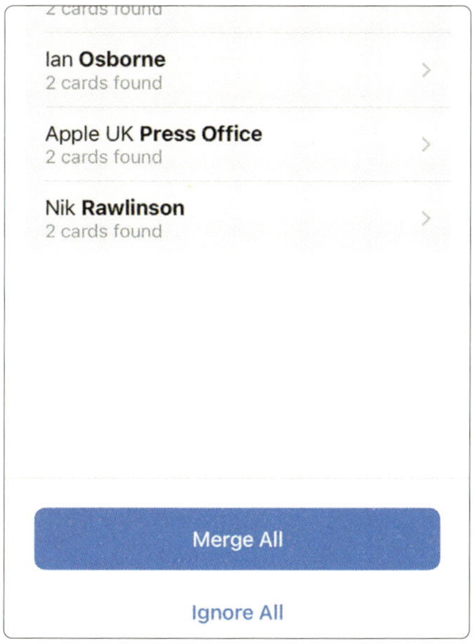

2 On the next screen you're shown what the duplicates are, and invited to merge or ignore them all. Alternatively, tap an individual duplicate and merge or ignore it individually. The contacts are merged, and their details combined.

The Camera App

Here we show you how to make the most of the iPhone's cameras. With the Camera app, you can take amazing still pictures, record regular and slow-motion videos, make panoramic shots, take live photos and more.

CAMERA *in Focus* (older iPhone's interfaces may vary)

1 Tap the flash icon to turn it on or off, to suit current lighting conditions.

2 Tap this to change the Night Mode setting. A slider lets you switch from Auto to manually setting the time length of the photo, but there's no real need to do so.

3 Tap the inverted 'V' icon to open a row of control icons under the picture. These give greater control over things like the flash and HDR feature.

4 HDR stands for High Dynamic Range. It averages the exposure by taking photos at different exposures in a short burst and then combining them into a single image. This icon turns it on or off.

5 A Live Photo adds a few seconds of video to the still picture, giving it a mildly animated feel. Tap this icon to toggle it on and off.

6 Tap the screen to set a focal point. The camera focuses on whatever's in this part of the picture. Move your finger up and down the screen to adjust the brightness slider to its right.

7 If your iPhone has the feature, tap here to choose from wide angled (0.5x) regular (1x) and zoom (2x) pictures.

8 Use this slider to switch between the various picture settings offered by the Camera app.

9 Tap here to open the last photo or video you took. You can delete it straight away if it wasn't what you want.

10 Tap here to take a photo or to start a video recording. You can use the Volume buttons instead too.

11 This icon switches between using the front and rear cameras.

More Controls

Tap the chevron (3) for a row of icons that give you greater control over some of the camera's functions. These are (left to right); Flash; Night Mode; Live Photos; Aspect Ratio; Change Exposure; Shutter Timer; Camera Filters; High Dynamic Range.

Capturing still photographs and video explained

1 Open the Camera app. To flip between the front and back cameras, tap the circular icon (bottom right). To switch between video and stills, use the slider under the image; moving between Time-lapse, Slo-Mo, Video, Photo, Portrait and Pano.

2 Zoom in and out using pinch and spread gestures on the screen. To take a photo, tap the big white button or a Volume button. For Burst Mode, (multiple images at once), on older iPhones tap and hold the Shutter button. See the next section for newer iPhones' Burst Mode.

3 To record a video, set the slider to the Video option. Tap the red on-screen button to start recording. While recording, tap the white button (bottom left or right, depending on iPhone) to take a still photo. Tap the red button (now a square) to stop recording.

4 You can also shoot video footage in Slo-Mo (slow motion). It's shot in exactly the same way as regular video, as explained in Step 3, but with the Slo-Mo option chosen using the slider, as shown here.

5 The final option available on the slider is the Time-lapse feature. Tap the shutter and you can now take frame-long videos at set time intervals, showing the passing of time. It's a really great feature to use.

6 To take a square photo, move the slider to the Photo option and tap the chevron atop the screen. Tap the ratio in the controls that appear (4:3 by default), and change to 1:1 for a square photograph. Ideal for Instagram and profile photos.

7 The Pano option is for the panoramic camera feature. Tap the shutter and move the iPhone along the on-screen marker, you can take a continuous horizontal image. Tap the arrow to reverse its direction.

8 You can access real-time filters for your photos and videos, giving them various effects. Tap the icon (top right corner) and select a filter. Used correctly, these filters can really add to your digital photography.

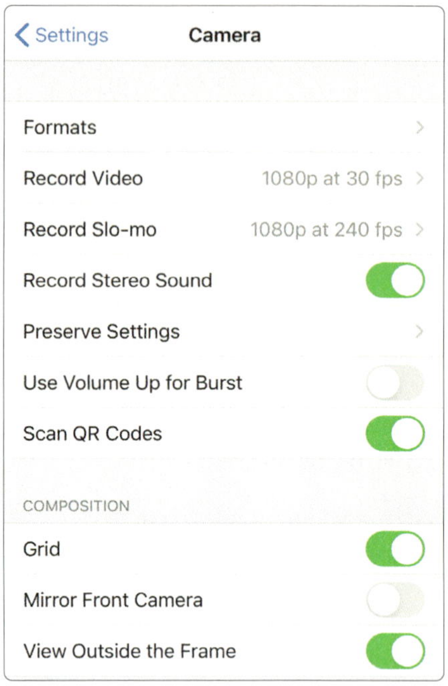

9 For additional features, return to the Settings app. From this link select Photos & Camera. You can then access facilities that greatly assist you in your composition, such as an overlay grid and video settings.

Taking and editing Live Photos

1 Live Photos capture a few seconds of video and sound from before and after the still is taken, for an animated photo. To turn it on and off, turn the slider below the image to Photo, then tap the circles icon in the top bar.

2 You can touch any part of a Live Photo and it comes alive, showing you the few seconds of video captured either side of the still image. It works like this if you use your Live Photo as a Lock screen picture too.

3 To edit a Live Photo, open it in Photos, tap Edit and on newer iPhones, tap the Live Photos icon at the bottom. You can drag in the ends of the slider, cutting off superfluous frames, and tap a frame and set it as the key image.

More Great Camera Features

Reading QR codes

You can read a QR code with the Camera app. A QR code is a machine-readable pattern made up of black and white squares that typically opens a URL. To scan one, hover the camera over the code. There's no need to press the Shutter button. In the latest versions of the Camera app, Apple has added a frame around the code, making it easier to scan. When you get a notification, tap it to activate the QR code.

Manual focus

While taking a photo, tap the screen. The yellow box that appears is the focal point of the picture, where the iPhone focuses when you press the Shutter button. If you want to move the yellow box and focus on another part of the photo, simply tap that area of the screen. The box moves to this section, making it the new focal point.

With the focus box on the screen, you can also alter the brightness of the photo by dragging a finger up to increase the exposure or down to decrease it.

Optical zoom

The optical zoom works on any iPhone with at least two cameras on the rear. When lining up your photo, there's an icon at the foot of the viewer which lets you choose between '1x', '2x' and in some cases, '0.5x'. The '1x' setting is normal size, with no zoom. '2x' is twice as close, using an optical zoom; there's no loss of quality. Tap this icon and a wheel appears, allowing you to zoom in up to 10x, but anything over 2x is digital zoom, that is, the pixels are blown up with an inevitable loss of quality. If you have a '0.5x' setting, that's a wide-angled lens that makes things look further away.

Portrait Lighting #1

Set the slider to Portrait, and choose from Natural Light, Studio Light, Contour Light, Stage Light, Stage Light Mono or High Key Light Mono on the wheel that appears. These settings recreate the sort of lighting setup a professional studio photographer might use. When you turn the wheel, the lighting is applied in real-time, so you can see immediately what affect the changes have on your portrait. Find one you like or if you don't want to apply Portrait Lighting yet, choose Natural Light. Now shoot the picture in the usual way. Note, you can't hold the button for multiple pics in Burst Mode whilst taking a Portrait Lighting shot.

You can apply lighting effects to your picture after it's been taken, as long as it was taken in the Portrait option. Open the picture in Photos and tap Edit. Tap the icon at the foot of the photo and choose an option from the lighting wheel.

Portrait Lighting #2

The Portrait Lighting modes allow you to adjust the intensity of a Portrait Lighting effect. Choose a Portrait mode and drag your finger up and down the screen. High intensity shots smooth out the skin and sharpen the details, while low intensities are subtler.

Look out to for High-Key Mono, a new Portrait Lighting effect found on the far right of the effects wheel. This gives a very striking black and white image, overlaid on a plain white background. The look is sophisticated; just the thing for arty photos.

Something else to play with when using Portrait Lighting is focal range. Tap the 'f' in a circle in the top-right corner, and you can use the slider that appears to change the amount of the picture that's in focus. You can, for example, have the subject of your picture sharply in focus and the background blurred, for some great effects.

Camera Features on the Latest iPhones

The latest high-end iPhones have excellent cameras, and a revised interface for the Camera app to help you make the most of them. The Zoom function is implemented a little differently; there's a QuickTake feature to let you quickly film a video without changing modes and the Burst Mode needs a new gesture too. There are extra controls, including the famous Night Mode, and you can take a wider image using Capture Outside the Frame. While most of the Camera app is just like it is on other iPhones running iOS 13 or later, these are the new features and interface changes and how to use them.

Action Mode

The iPhone 14 series offers a new Action Mode for recording video. When active, this new feature automatically steadies the shot, so it doesn't move and jerk with the camera. It's like using a gimbal, but without the extra gadget.

Portrait Photos and Cinematic Mode

On the iPhone 13 or later, Portrait Mode lets you blur objects in the foreground, giving a better depth-of-field effect. Also, when recording Cinematic Mode videos, the depth-of-field effect has been improved on these models of the iPhone.

Prioritise Faster Shooting

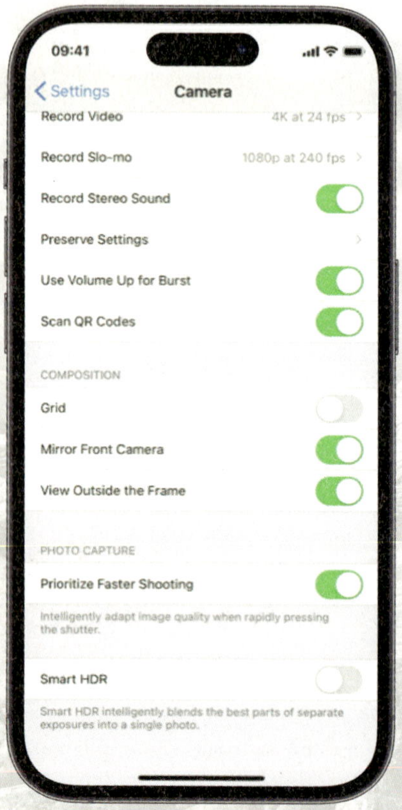

You can have the Camera app prioritise taking pictures faster over quality.

To take one snap after another without a pause, you can set your Camera app to prioritise faster shooting over better pictures, so the iPhone spends less time processing the picture you just took in order to get ready for the next shot. Go to Settings > Camera and flick the Prioritise Faster Shooting switch. This feature works intelligently, so if you're not taking rapid photos, the iPhone still prioritises processing the picture.

Wide Angle and Zoom

Open the Camera app, and at the foot or side of the viewfinder (depending on how you're holding your phone), you'll find zoom controls. On the iPhone 11, there are two buttons: 0.5x and 1x. The iPhone 11 Pro and Pro Max add a third button: 2x. Tap '.5' for 0.5x, wide-angled photography. Tap '2' for 2x, zoom photos. Tap and hold any of these buttons for a control wheel.

If you want to take a wide-angled shot, simply choose a number lower than '1' on the zoom wheel as shown.

Choose a zoom of up to 2x optical, or 10x digital using the zoom wheel.

Burst Photos

There's a different way of taking 'burst' photos, that is, a series of pictures, one after another. Instead of simply holding down the Shutter button, as was the case for older iPhones, you now tap the Shutter button and drag your finger towards the thumbnail of the previous picture you took. Lift your finger to stop taking pictures. If you decide to delete one, you're asked whether you want to erase just the one photo or the entire burst.

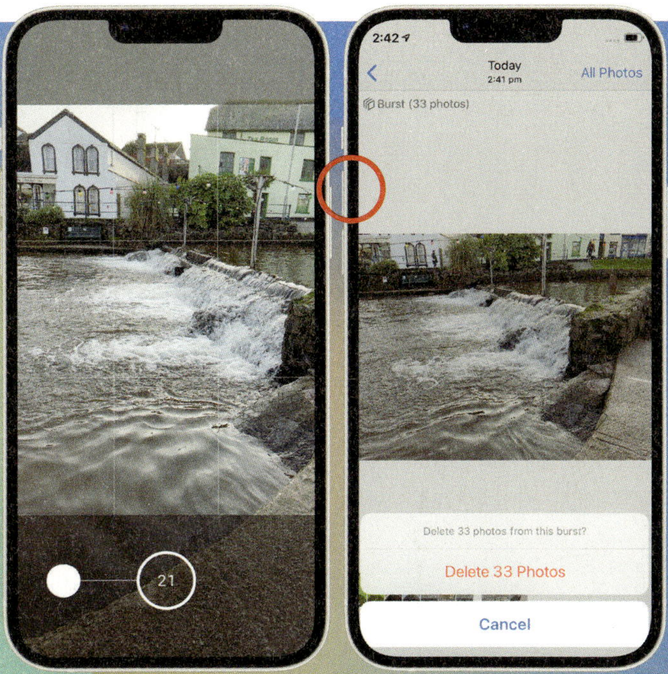

A 'burst' of photos is a series of snaps taken one after the other, in quick succession.

You can use the Volume Up button to take 'burst' photos, that is, a series of snaps taken in quick succession by holding down the button. Activate this option in Settings > Camera, by turning on the Use Volume Up for Bursts switch.

You can delete an entire burst of pictures at once; tap the thumbnail for the option.

QuickTake Videos

To take a QuickTake video, hold the Shutter button (or the physical Volume control button) and you record a video, even in photo mode. To stop recording, lift your finger. To continue recording without holding your finger on the screen, slide it towards the Lock icon and release. You then stop recording by tapping the Shutter button again.

There's offer an easy way of taking videos without changing your camera settings. It's great for taking a video quickly.

Night Mode

When taking a photo in the dark, and the iPhone's camera decides your picture needs a longer exposure than usual, a moon icon appears in the top left corner. Tap it to activate Night Mode. If it's really dark, it might activate automatically. When enabled, the Night Mode icon has a yellow background and the exposure time is shown. Increase or decrease this by dragging the slider under the picture, from 'Off' to a maximum time (in seconds) determined by how dark it is. When you're ready, tap the Shutter button to take your photo.

Here, Night Mode is switched off.

The yellow icon shows Night Mode is on. Tap it to set a longer or shorter exposure time with the wheel found above (portrait) or to the right of (landscape) the shutter button.

Slofies: Slow-Motion Selfies

Switch to the front-facing camera, and use the selection wheel to select Slo-mo. The slofie video is recorded at 120 frames per second and is automatically in wide-angle, so you can capture far more of what's around you.

The Photos App

The Photos app is more than just a photo manager. It's also a very powerful image editor, where you can colour correct, enhance, crop and generally improve your snaps. Here we take you through its various tools.

PHOTOS *in Focus*

1 This is the name of the Photos album you have open (or in this case, where the pics were taken, as we're looking at all the photos and not a single album), and the dates between which the photos contained in that album were all taken.

2 Tap here to select photos. You can pick out as many as you like, and dragging your finger will select multiple photos more easily.

3 Tap the three-dots icon for a pop-up that lets you zoom in and out, set the thumbnails, filter pictures, show them on a map and more.

4 These are your pictures. Tap the Select link, then tap photos to select and unselect them. Tap and hold a picture for a pop-up that lets you Copy, Share, Favourite or Delete it.

5 The total number of photos and videos you have in your Photos app.

6 View your photos according to the year, month, or day they were taken, or look at all your photos.

7 Tap the Photos icon in the bar at the foot of the screen for the page shown here, which displays all the pictures and videos in your Photos app as thumbnails.

8 The For You icon takes you to a screen offering a selection of pics as Featured Photos, a summary of pictures you've shared (Shared Album Activity), and suggestions on photos you should share.

9 This gives access to your photo albums, including ones you've created yourself and standard albums, such as People, which groups photos according to the folks in them and Places, showing where the pics were taken. Scroll to the foot of the screen for smart albums showing media according to type, Imports, Hidden photos, Recently Deleted and more.

10 Searching has been greatly improved in the newer releases of Photos, with multiple search terms catered for. You can search for items and themes such as 'Christmas' and 'cat' and find photos containing those objects or items.

Editing techniques made easy

1 Open a photo. To bring up the key editing tools, tap Edit (top right). If the image can't be edited for any reason, you can duplicate it and edit the copy, as shown here. Tap the 'Duplicate and Edit' link to proceed.

2 Tap the wand to freshen up your shot, using the Photos app's editing algorithms. The three-dots icon next to it lets you use Markup, and the curly arrows let you move forwards and backwards through edits.

3 The various tools available let you set the brightness, contrast and saturation of the photo, crop or rotate it, set a filter to give it a whole new look and more. Experiment with them and you'll soon master the editing tools.

4 You can use the Photo app's editing tools on videos taken on your iPhone, as well as photos. You can also trim the start and end of the footage; tap and drag the handles at the start and/or end of the video.

General tips for the Photos app

Open a photo by tapping it. Zoom in and out using the pinch and slide gestures. Drag a zoomed picture to move it around. Swipe through your photos by dragging the open image left or right to move to the next one.

To delete a single photo or video, open it and tap the trash icon. If it's not there, the photo was added to your iPhone through syncing and cannot be deleted in this way. Tap the arrow-in-a-box icon for sharing options.

Creating new albums

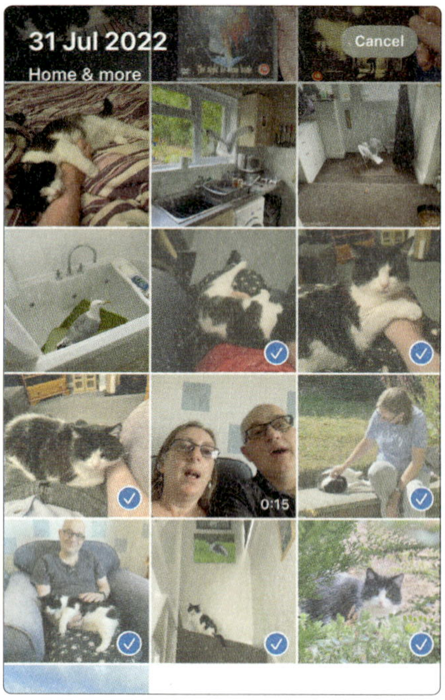

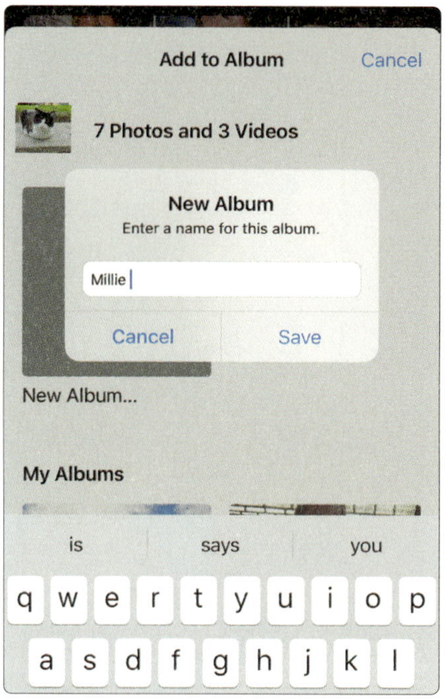

1 To create a new photo album, on the main Photos page, tap Select (top right). Select the images you want to add to the new album by tapping individually or dragging your finger over them.

2 Tap the Share icon, then select Add to Album or Add to Shared Album. You can then add them to an existing album, if you have any made or make a new one, give it a name and then save it.

Record your location

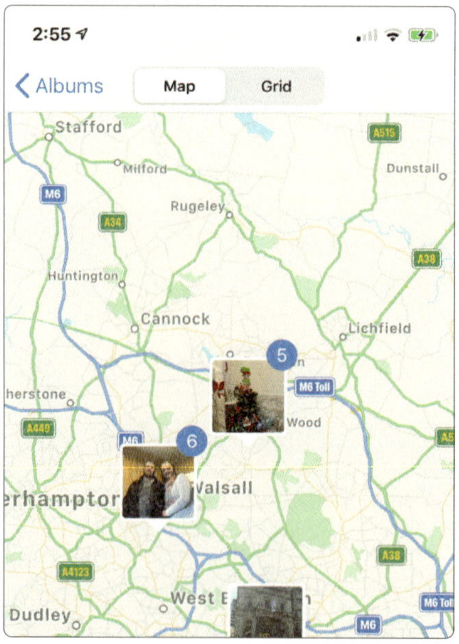

1 In Settings Privacy > Location Services turn Location Services on. Take a picture in the Camera app and you're asked to allow it to use your location. Tap Allow and the location in which it was taken is recorded.

2 Close the Camera app, open the Photos app and tap Albums at the bottom of the screen; then tap Places. You're shown all the locations where you have taken photos. Tap each location to see the images you have taken there.

iCloud photos

You can upload photo albums to your iCloud online storage space and invite others to take a look at them.

- iCloud Photos feature must be turned on. Go to > Settings > [your name] > iCloud > Photos and make sure iCloud Photo Sharing is on. You don't need to have Photo Stream on.
- In the Photos library, tap Select and tick the images you wish to share. When all your images are ticked, tap the Sharing icon.
- Tap Add to Shared Album for a pop-up. Tap Shared Album at the foot of the pop-up to choose whether to add it to an existing album or start a new one. Give it a name.
- If you're starting a new shared album, you're then invited to add people with whom you want to share it. If they're in your Contacts, just type their names.
- Tap Next and you can comment on your new shared album. Then tap Post (top right). An alert is sent to those you've invited to see it; they can accept or decline.
- To make changes to that album, in Photos, tap Albums then find it under Shared Albums. Manage your photos here or tap the silhouette (top-right) to change its settings and/or invite more people.

iCloud Shared Photos Library

If you have Family Sharing switched on, you can share family photos in a separate iCloud library. Everyone in the shared album can add, edit and delete photos. You can even set smart rules to choose to share existing photos, or add them straight from the camera app. Go to Settings > Photos to set up a Shared Library.

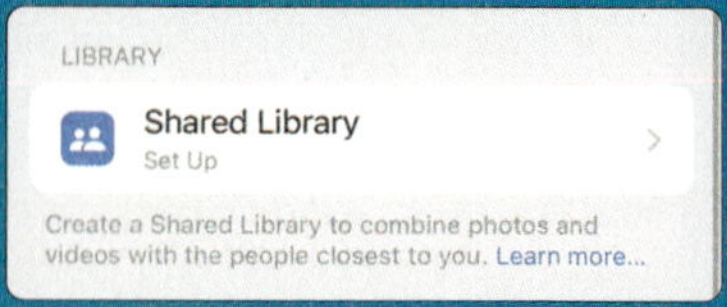

More features of the Photos app

Add captions

You can add a caption to a photo. Open it and swipe up to reveal the caption field, where you can type whatever you like. It's a great way of reminding yourself who or what's in the picture, what you were up to when you took it and other such comments and ideas.

Flexible Photo Viewing

You can filter photos when you view an album or the All Photos screen. To do so, tap the three-dots icon. For an album, tap Sort to view the pictures in a custom order, or for All Photos, tap filters to restrict your viewing to Favourites, Edited, Photos only, Videos only or All Items.

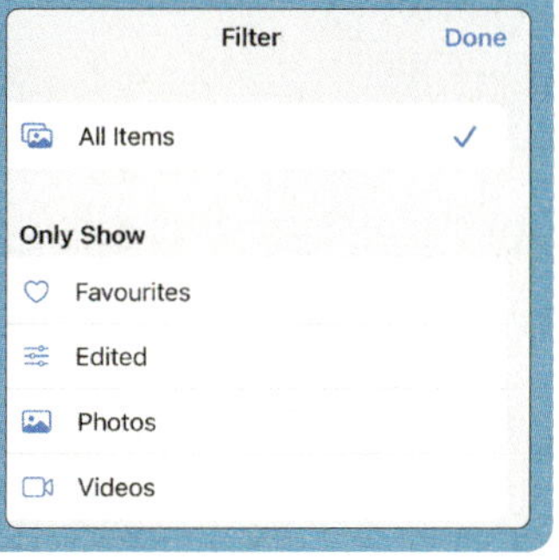

The image picker

When you access the Photos app from elsewhere in iOS, such as when adding a photo to a message or email, you use the image picker. You can find the picture you want with smart searches and tap it to select that picture or pictures.

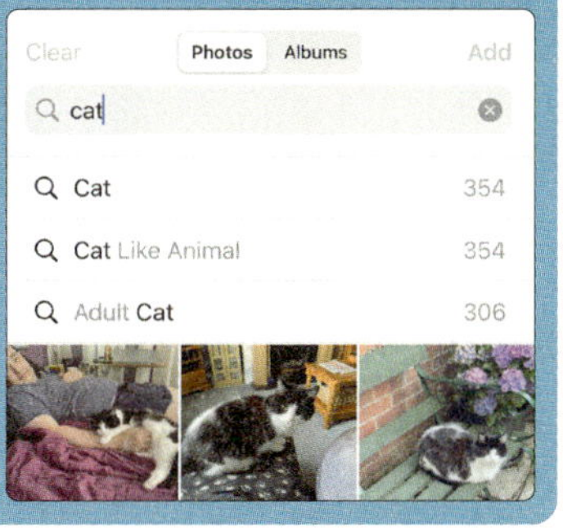

Detect Duplicates

To detect and manage duplicate photos, tap the Albums icon and scroll all the way to the bottom. There's a Duplicates option; tap it, and you're shown the pictures and videos that might be duplicated. Tap the Merge button next to the ones you'd like to merge.

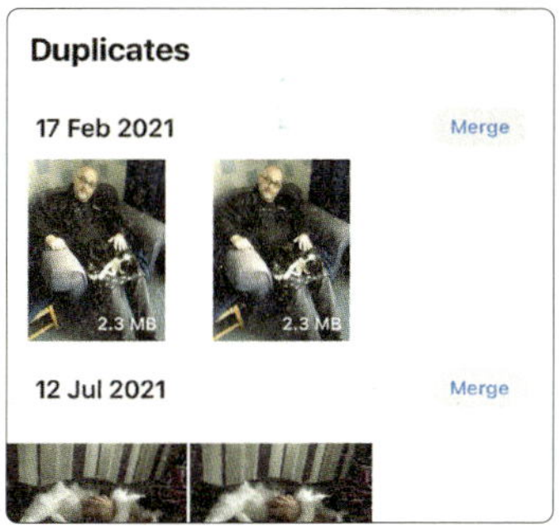

Hidden & Recently Deleted

Two app-created albums, Hidden and Recently Deleted, are locked by default. Tap Albums and scroll to the bottom to find them. They show a lock icon. Tap one and use Face ID or Touch ID to open it. Photos you've recently (last 30 days) deleted or have hidden can be restored.

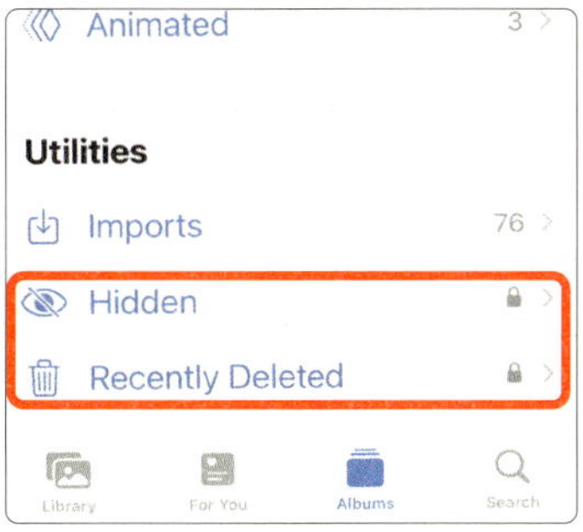

Live Photos

Live Photos offer a few seconds of video before reaching the still picture. To find your Live Photos, tap Albums at the foot of the screen, and under Media Types, you'll find a link for Live Photos. To see a Live Photo in motion, open it then tap and hold.

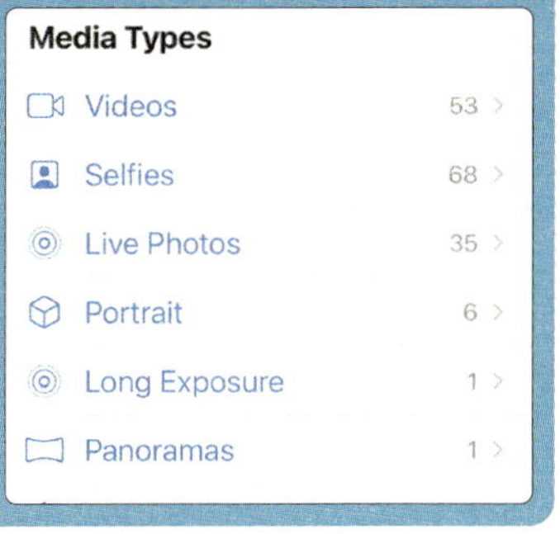

Copy & Paste Edits

After you've edited a photo, you might want to reproduce these edits on one or more further photos. After editing, tap the three-dots icon and choose Copy Edits. Now on the main Library page, select one or more pictures, tap the three-dots icon and select Paste Edits.

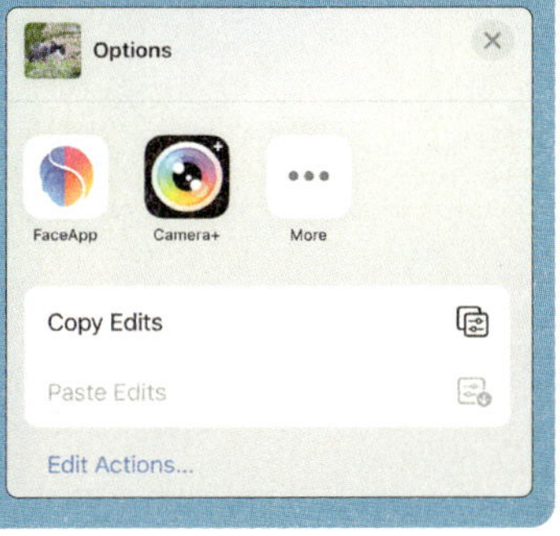

New Memory Features

Under For You, tap an item listed in Memories for a slideshow. You can now swipe back to previous pictures without interrupting the music. You can also stop Memories appearing in the Photos widget; in Settings, go to Photos and turn off Show Featured Content.

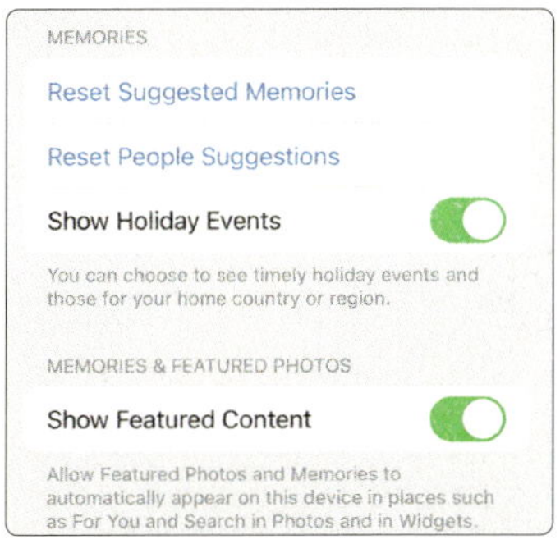

The Maps App

Maps is a superb navigational tool. Making great use of the iPhone's location awareness, it gives an accurate map of your location, shows directions to where you want to go and helps you find local amenities.

MAPS *in Focus*

1 Tap the folded map icon for a pop-up window, where you can switch between four map types; Explore, Driving, Public Transport and Satellite view.

2 Tap this arrow icon to focus the map on your current location. Tap it again and the map rotates as you move, so the direction your travelling is always 'up'. A third tap returns it to its default function.

3 The blue dot shows your current location on the map and the direction you're facing. The smaller the blue circle around it, the more accurate the location is.

4 Use the search bar found here to look for a location or nearby feature; we looked for Fast Food. Tap the Search field without typing anything for a list of recent searches and popular search options such as Petrol Stations, Restaurants, Shops and Bars.

5 Current weather information is shown here. Go to Settings > Maps and turn on Air Quality Index and this is then shown here too. Deep press on this data for a window showing more weather information, drawn from the Weather app.

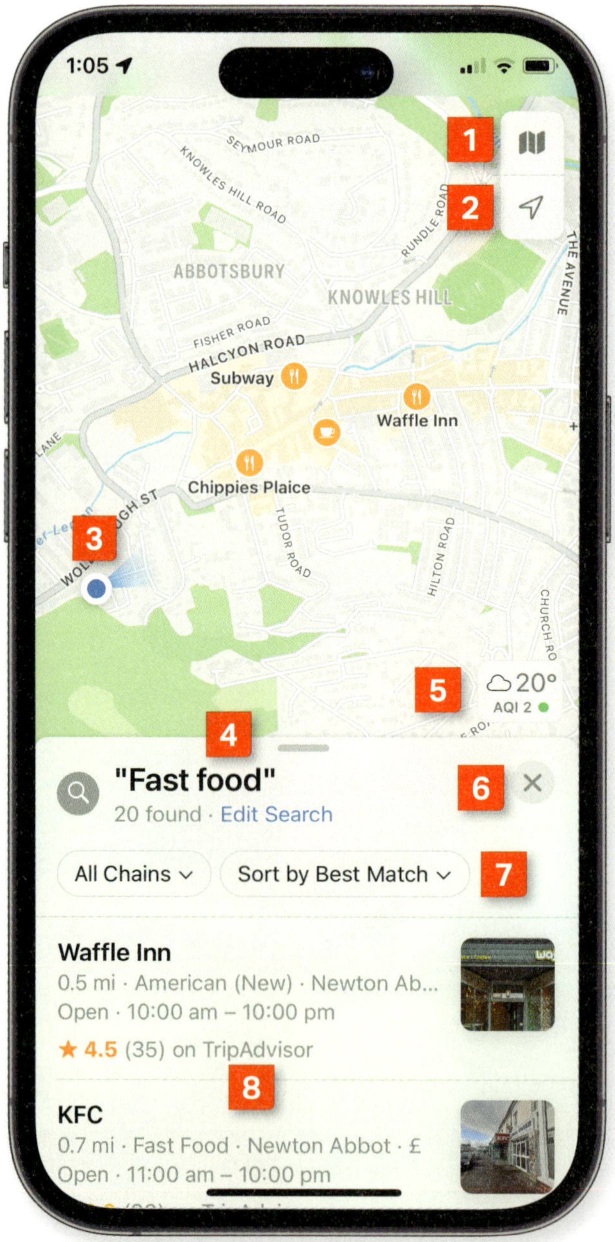

6 The 'X' icon collapses the bottom window panel, giving you a better look at the main map screen; or you can simply swipe it down.

7 Use these buttons to filter and fine-tune your search, for example, restricting a search to specific fast food outlets, and changing how they're sorted.

8 We're looking for fast food, so nearby chip shops, burger cafes and sandwiches are shown here. The list offers information on the establishments shown on the map. Tap one, on the panel orthe map for more details.

A word of warning

Like any sat-nav, Maps is not infallible. It's up to you to make sure you follow road signs and the road laws. By all means follow the Maps app but don't neglect your basic road skills.

Using route planning and navigation

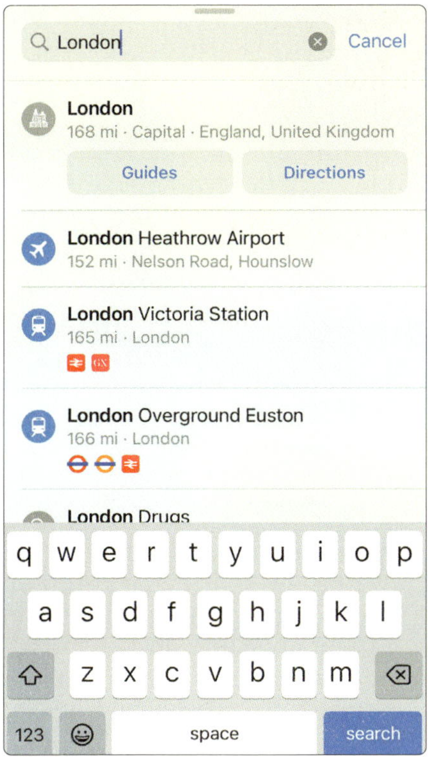

1 Enter the name of the place you want to go to, in the Search field at the foot of the screen. Choose the destination option you're looking for if necessary, and then tap the blue button showing an estimated journey time. Alternative routes are then shown as lighter blue lines: switch between routes by tapping one.

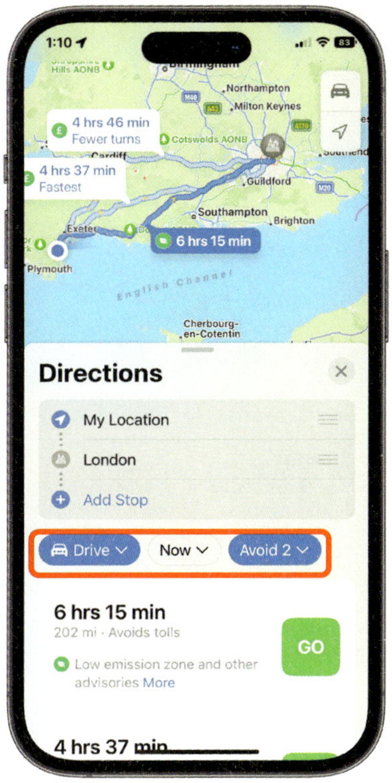

2 Alternative routes are shown as lighter blue lines; tap one to change. The Add Stop option lets you add up to 15 mid-journey stopping points to your route. The highlighted buttons (left to right) let you; choose method of transport; set departure time/date; choose options based on travel mode. When ready, tap its green Go button.

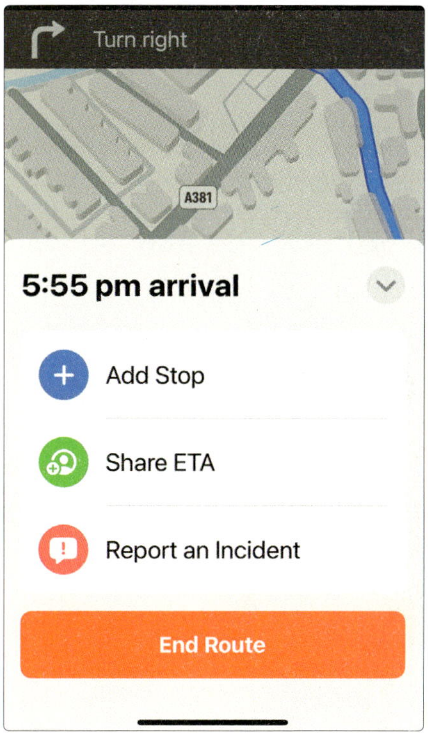

3 If you need to break your journey, lift up the bottom panel and type Add a Stop. A list of options appears; Lunch, Petrol Stations, Coffee, Parking, Corner Shops and Banks. Tap the option you wish to stop for, and a list of nearby amenities appears. Choose one, and tap Go next to it.

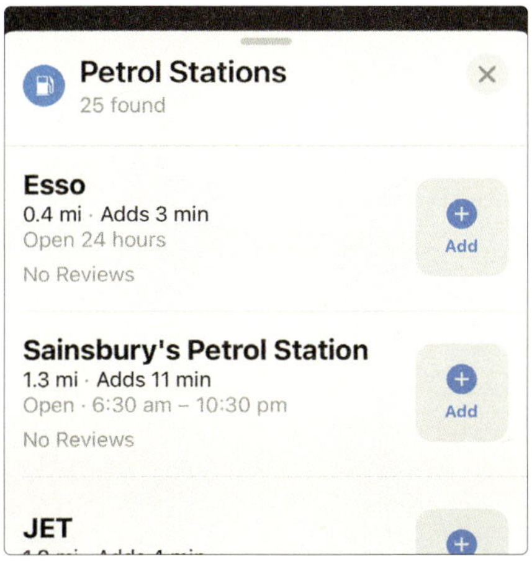

4 A list of available facilities in the category chosen is shown. Find one that suits your needs, and tap the '+ Add' button next to it. Your route is revised, with the en route stop you just chose added to it. Information about that facility, such as what payment types they take, is also shown.

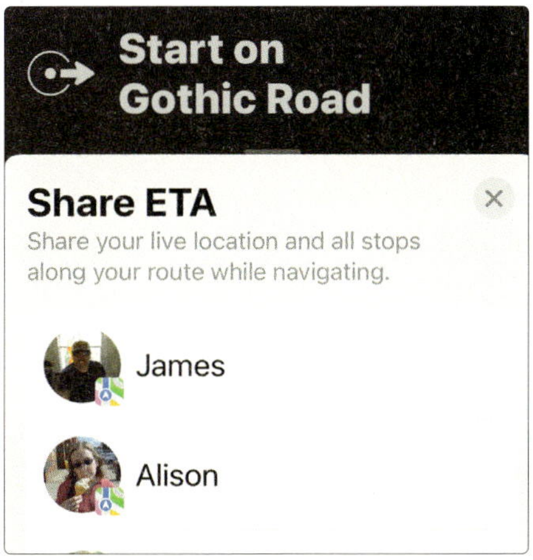

5 When you've done what it is you stopped for, on the Maps screen, tap the blue strip at the top labelled 'Resume Route to [Destination]'. The originally planned route is resumed. Another option available on the bottom panel is Share ETA. Tap it to share your expected time of arrival with friends and contacts.

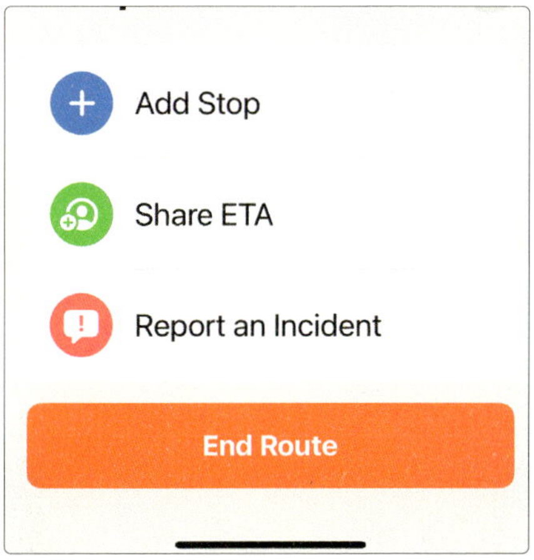

6 If there's a problem and you need to change your route on the fly, tap the chevron on the left of the bottom panel for the options, and tap the End Route button. You can then tap Directions to your destination again on the next screen and choose an alternative route when Maps recalculates your journey.

Cycling and Electric Cars

Two features that are gradually being rolled out in Maps, but aren't yet available in all territories, are travelling by bicycle and driving an electric car.

For cyclists, choosing a bike as your mode of transport gives you route planning that takes account of dedicated cycle paths and road elevations. If there's a dedicated cycling route available, your route plan will take you down it as an alternative to using the road. And you're warned about big hills too, so there are no nasty surprises on the way.

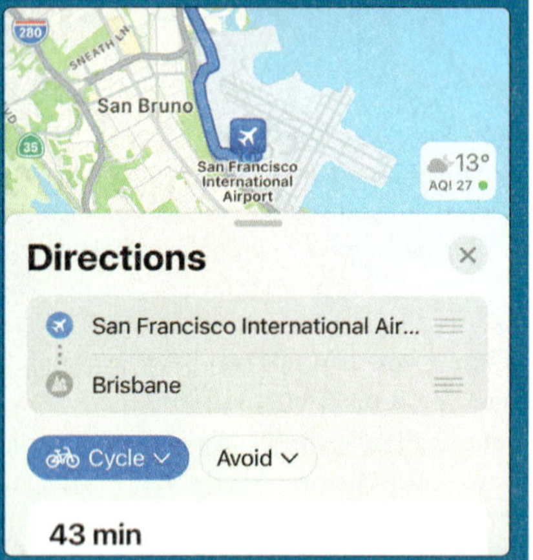

For those who drive an electric car, the route planning features are largely the same as they are for petrol cars, but for fuel stops you're shown recharging stations along your journey instead of petrol stations.

Unfortunately, both of these features are limited to certain locations and journeys at the moment, but they'll roll out in other territories with time.

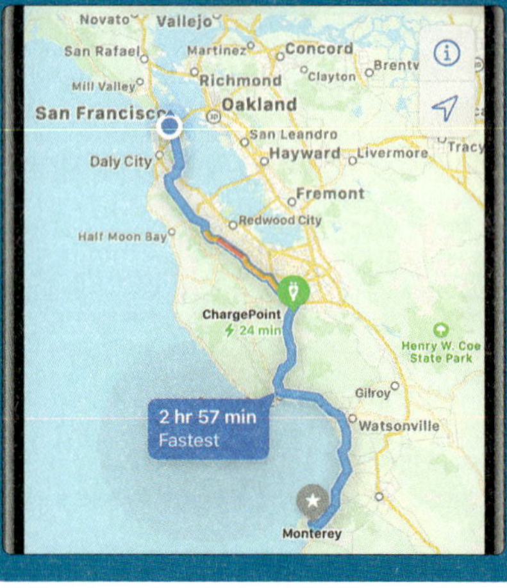

The public transport feature

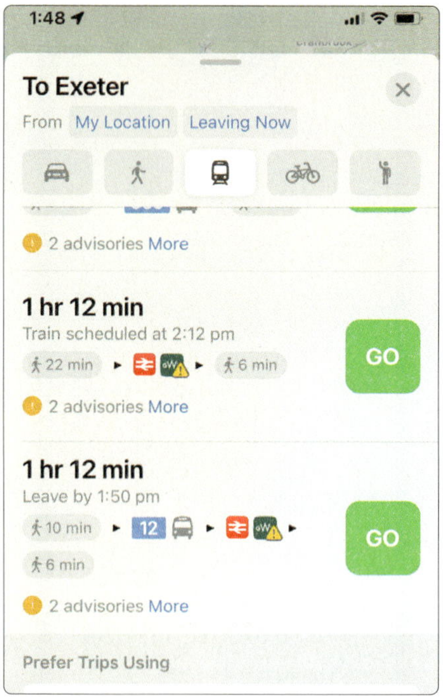

1 Choose a destination, and tap the train icon for public transport routes. You can journey using more than one method of public transport. Scroll the window up and untick anything you'd rather not use. Find the route you want and tap its Go button.

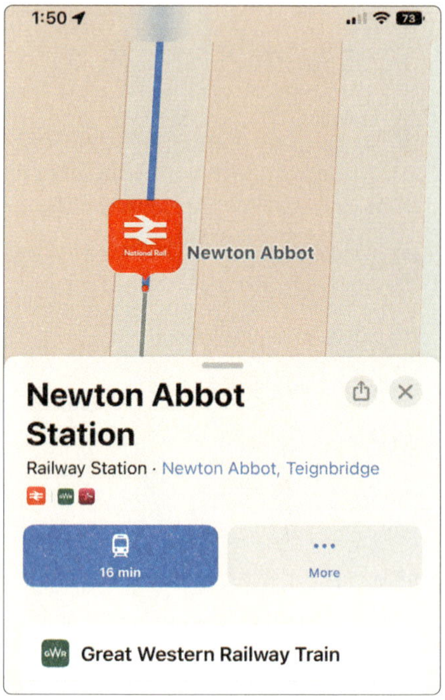

2 Tap on a train or subway station on the map for a pop-up showing a list of forthcoming departures from that station. Tap on a service for more information. Transit and flight information is now updated in real time, so check back often for the latest information.

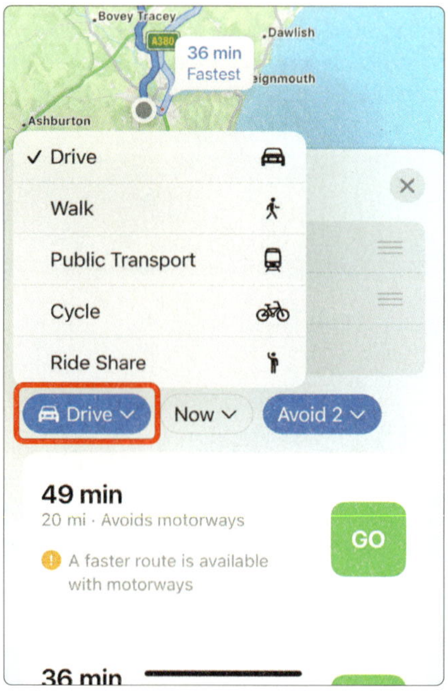

3 Set your destination, then tap the options menu indicated for a pop-up. Choose Public Transport. Tap the third pulldown, now labelled 'Prefer', and uncheck any transports you'd rather not use. Choose a route and tap 'Go'.

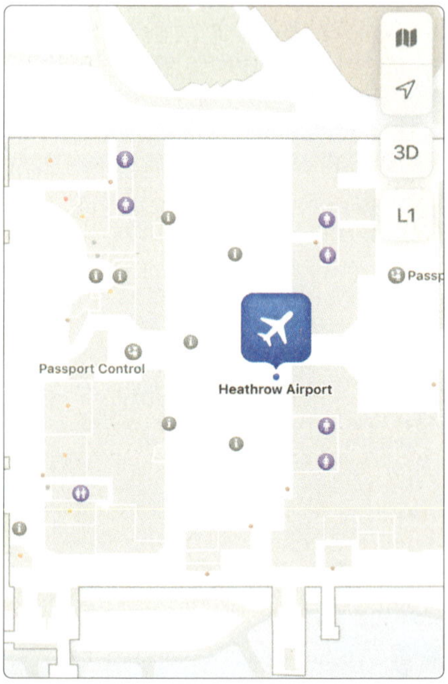

4 Buildings such as subway stations have been carefully surveyed, so Maps shows not only their location but also all the entrances and exits to that station. It can even show maps of their indoor areas and features as well.

More great Maps features

Traffic information

When following a driving route, traffic information is incorporated into the route information, so you know what to expect. For example, sections of your route where traffic jams are expected are coloured red. Workman signs means there are scheduled roadworks happening. Tap a workman icon and then tap the information icon for more details.

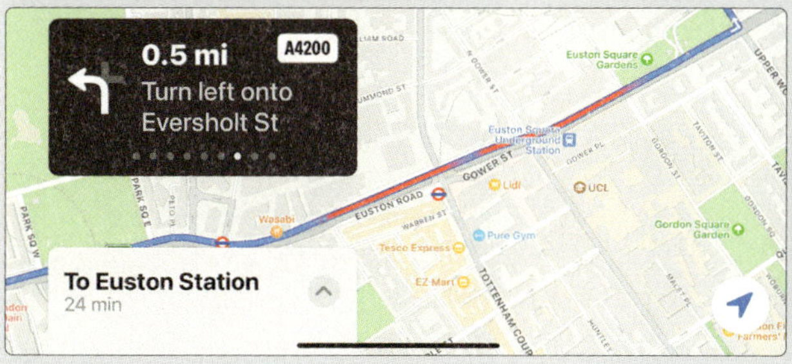

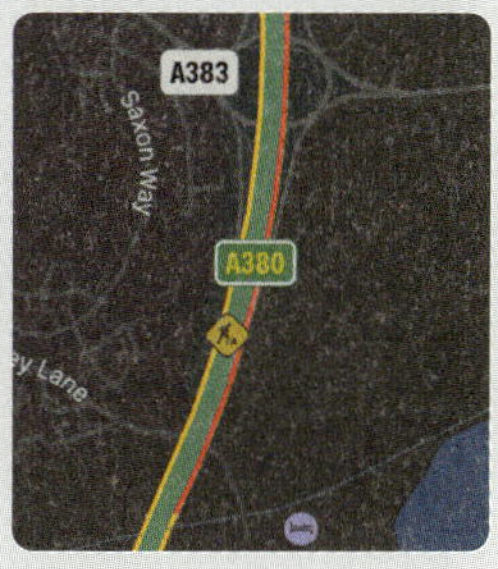

3D features

In Satellite view, tap the 3D icon (top right) to switch to a 3D perspective. Zoom in and out, and twist to explore, tap 2D to return to a flat map. Also, after accessing a city's details, if there's a button marked 'Flyover', you can tap it and watch a 3D flyover tour.

Guides

Swipe up the information panel to see My Guides; groups of favourite places you've saved for later use. By default, you have a Guide called My Places. Tap New Guide to start a new one. Type a name for your Guide, then tap Create. You can then search for and add as many locations as you like. Tap the Share icon and you can share the entire collection with someone else too.

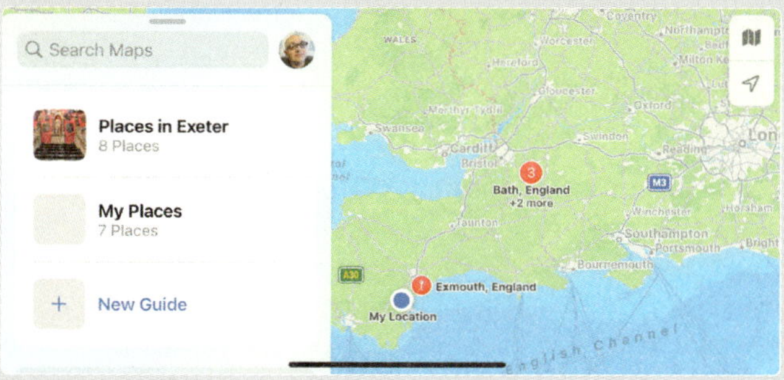

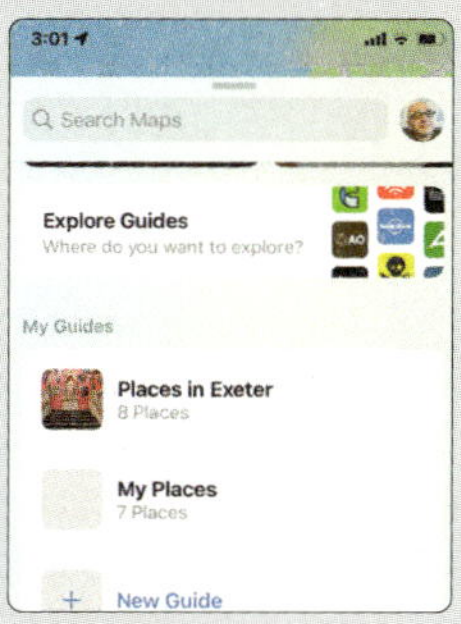

Features and Favourites

Type a location in the search field to find it. This can be a town or city to which you wish to travel, an address or postcode you're looking for, or a local service or facility like a train station or a museum. When looking for the latter, a list of nearby establishments is given and they're located on the map.

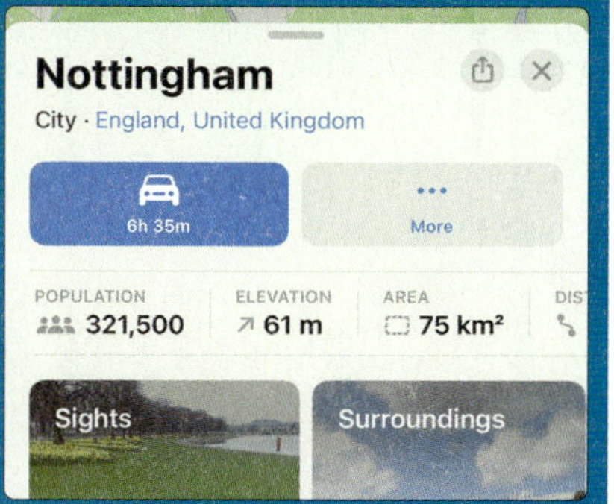

Favourite locations are listed under the search field. If you've identified your home address in Contacts, that's already there, and you can add your work too. Tap Add to add more locations to your favourites, where they're always to hand and easily selected when using the Maps app. To add a location or feature to your Favourites, tap the three-dots icon near the top of the guide, next to the blue button, and choose Add to Favourites.

Alternatively, scroll the guide all the way to the bottom and tap Add to Favourites there.

Enhanced details

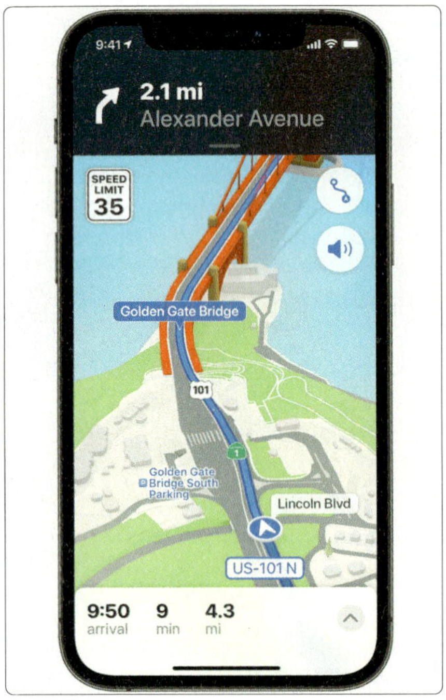

When using Maps on your iPhone or on CarPlay, the 3D city maps have been enhanced. New on-screen details make things like turnings, bike lanes and pedestrian crossings more apparent. On public transport, nearby stations are made clearer, and Maps lets you know when you've arrived at your station.

AR walking instructions

1 If you have an iPhone with at least an A12 chip (XS/XS Max/XR or later), and are in a city where the service is available, you can use augmented reality to find your way around. After inputting where you want to go, in the application's Street View, scan local buildings with your iPhone.

2 Maps works out where you are and superimposes walking directions onto the screen as shown. This feature will roll out in London, Los Angeles, New York, Philadelphia, San Diego, San Francisco Bay Area and Washington DC by the end of 2021, with other territories following.

Leave and arrive times

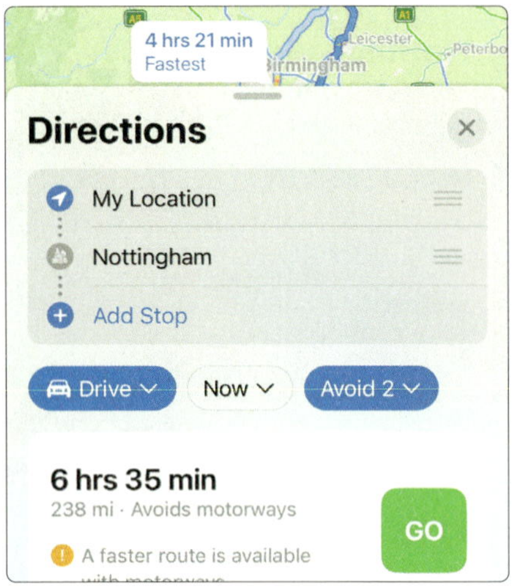

1 When planning a journey, it's possible to set it up for a future date. After entering your destination and mapping the routes, tap the small button labelled 'Now', found to the right of the blue method-of-transport button.

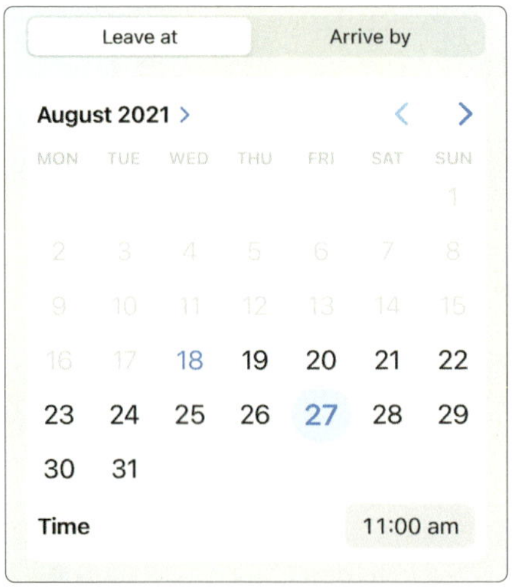

2 You're shown a calendar and a time. You can tap a new date on the calendar, using the chevrons at the top to change the month if necessary. Tap the time and you can set it to a departure time of your choosing.

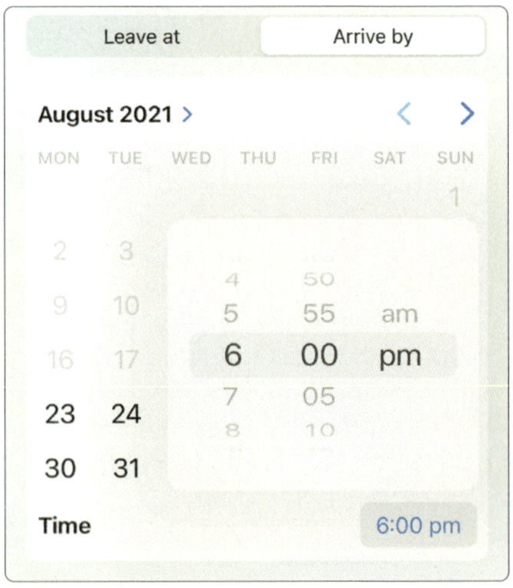

3 Tap the Arrive By tab at the top of the screen, and you can set a time by which you must arrive at your destination. Tap Done when you've finished, and your chosen Leave or Arrive Time is incorporated into the route timings.

User accounts

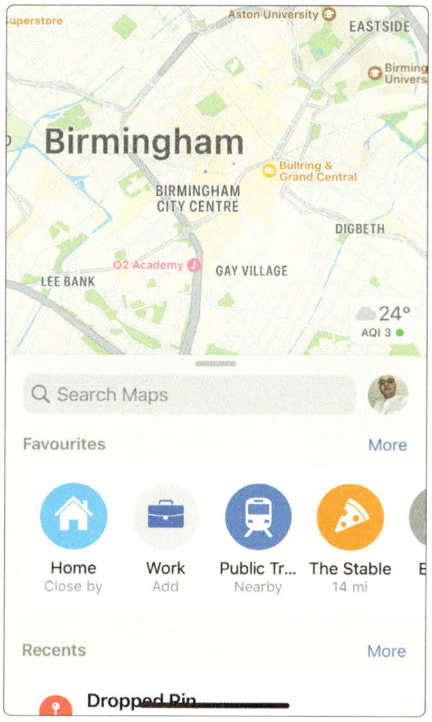

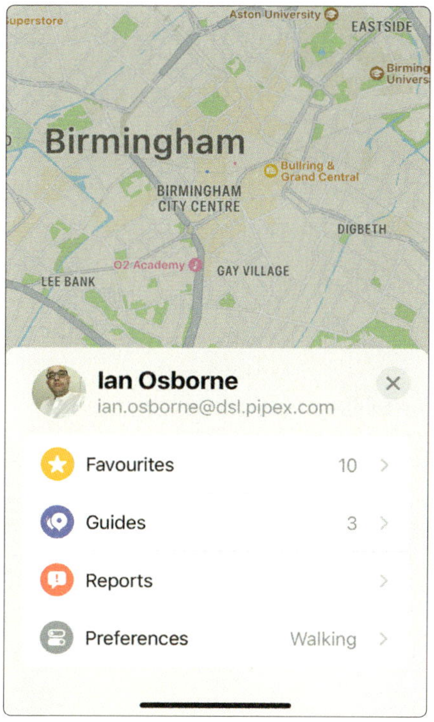

1 You can store your Maps settings and preferences in your user account. It's easy to do. First of all, tap the circular icon, which might be your initials or a picture, which is found to the right of the Maps app's Search field.

2 On the next screen, you can look at your Favourites, Guides, Reports and Preferences; just choose one of the options. You can, of course, edit these details, make reports and set preferences, all of which are saved.

Weather warnings

With climate change and global warning, flash floods are becoming more common. Thankfully, the Maps app warns you of adverse weather conditions such as this. If your route is likely to take you through an area where a flood is current or imminent, for example, you get a weather warning and an alternative route that avoids the problem. Tap one of these on-screen warnings for more details of what the issue is, and you're shown the warning on the route on which it occurs. Tap More on this warning, and more information is offered. If you want to learn even more about the problem, this screen will offer a link to The Weather Channel.

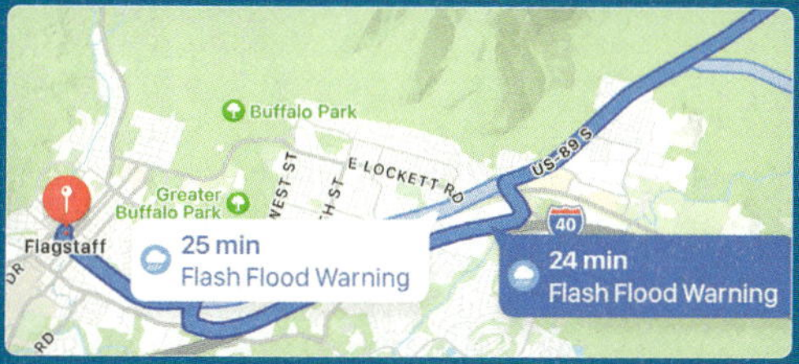

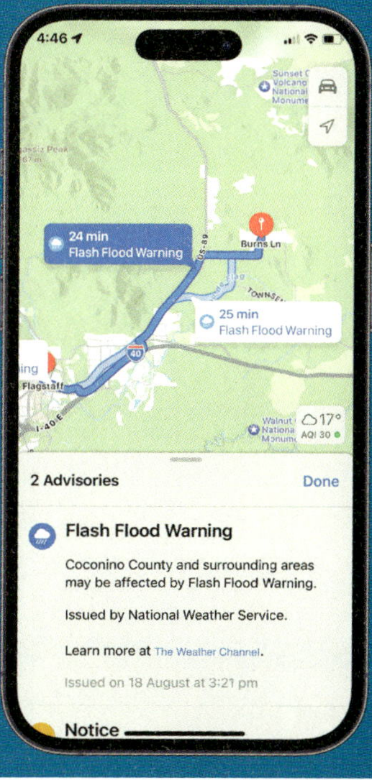

All Around the World

The Maps app includes a beautiful interactive globe which you can spin, explore and zoom into on your iPhone. To access the globe, simply open the Maps app, and pinch until the map zooms out so far that you can see the Earth as a whole. Drag your finger around it to rotate the globe in 360 degrees.

Find a piece of the world you'd like to explore, and you can zoom in by placing two fingers on the screen and moving them apart. As you fall closer and closer to the Earth, the planet's natural features are highlighted as well as cities and countries. Mountains, for example, are located on the map. Tap one and you're shown information such as its elevation above sea level and how long it is from the bottom of the mountain to its summit.

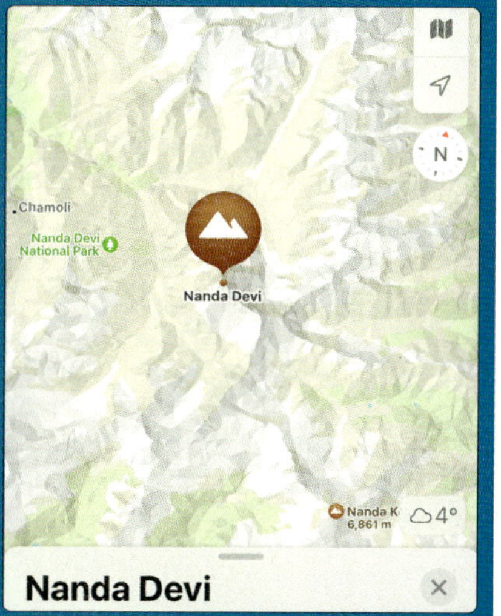

The Translate App

The Translate app lets you translate foreign languages into your native tongue on the fly and also translate your own language into something else. It's fast, private and a great boon to holidaymakers and business travellers.

TRANSLATE *in Focus*

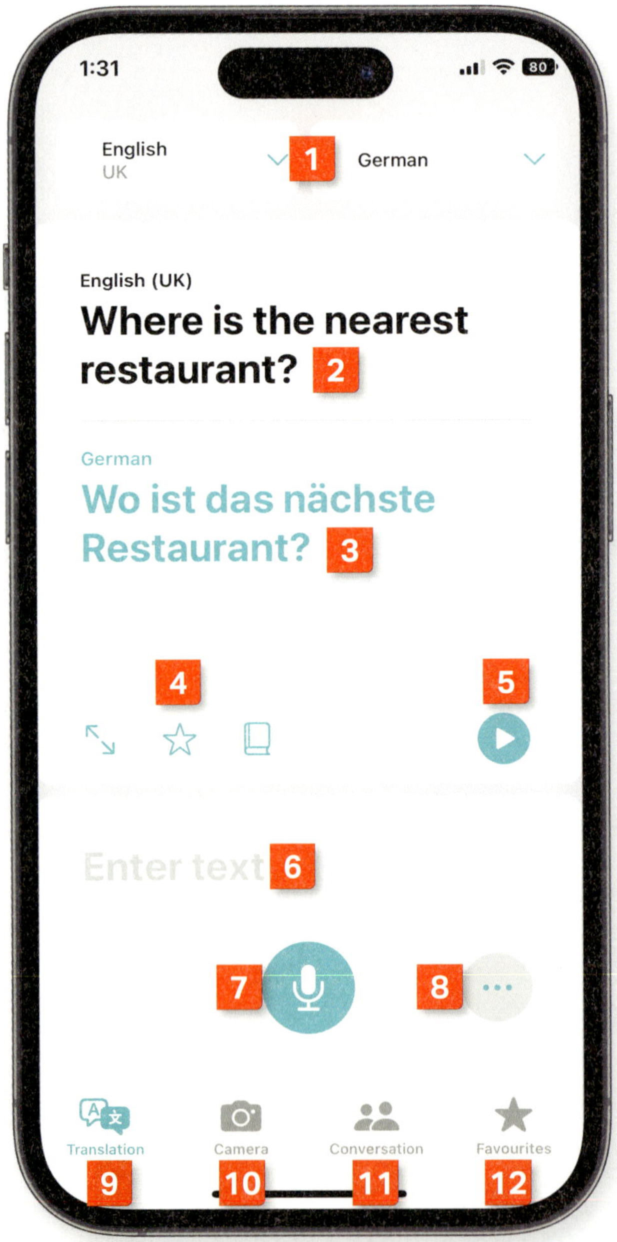

1 These are the languages you're currently translating out of (left) and into (right). Tap the down-pointing chevrons to choose another language.

2 This is the last thing you typed into Translate.

3 This is the translation of the English you typed in. As you selected German at the top of the screen, it's translated into German.

4 These icons are; Switch to full-screen mode for the translation; save the translation as a favourite; and look up a highlighted word in the dictionary.

5 Tap Play to read the translation out loud.

6 This is where you type the text you wish to be translated. Tap here to bring up the virtual keyboard.

7 Tap here and speak what you want to be translated instead of typing it. The app listens, and when you stop speaking, translates.

8 Tap this action button for options to automatically Play Translations, and/or Detect Language.

9 Tap here to get to the main Translation screen

10 You can use your iPhone's camera to translate words found in the environment, such as books or signs.

11 Tap here for the Conversation mode, in which two people can take it in turns to speak

12 Favourites gives access to translations previously saved for later use, and also recent translations. Swipe them left for various options.

Attention Mode

In landscape mode, there's an icon in the bottom-left corner showing outward-pointing arrows. Tap it and you're shown translated text in Attention Mode, with larger words. Tap the speech bubbles (right) to go back to Conversation Mode and the Play icon (left) to speak the translation out loud.

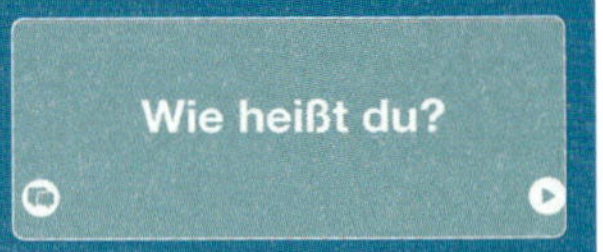

Using the Translate app

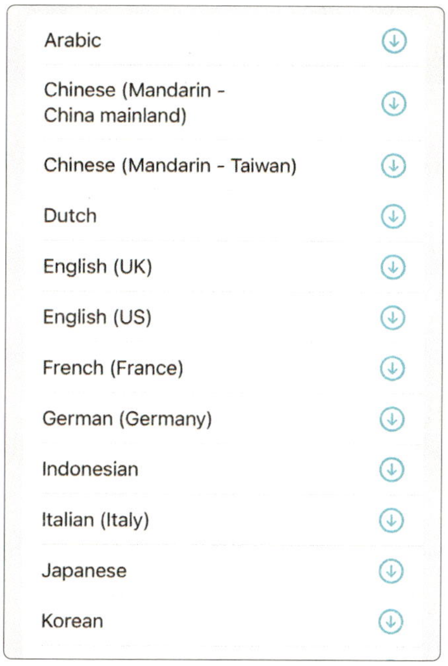

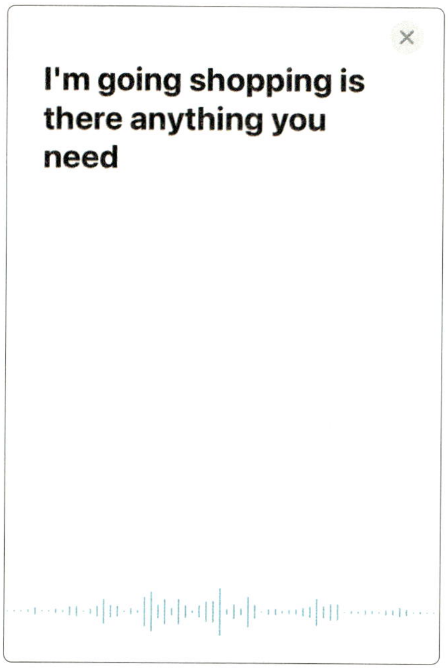

1 Tap one of the buttons atop the screen to choose one of the languages you wish to use, then do the same with the other. They're arranged in alphabetical order, and the currently chosen language is ticked.

2 If you need to work offline, for privacy or because of Internet connection issues, while you're online tap one of the language buttons and at the bottom of the list, tap Manage Languages. To download one, tap its arrow icon.

3 Having chosen your languages, tap the large microphone icon and speak. The app listens to what you say, then offers a translation. Alternatively, tap 'Enter Text' and type something. This is also translated as text and spoken.

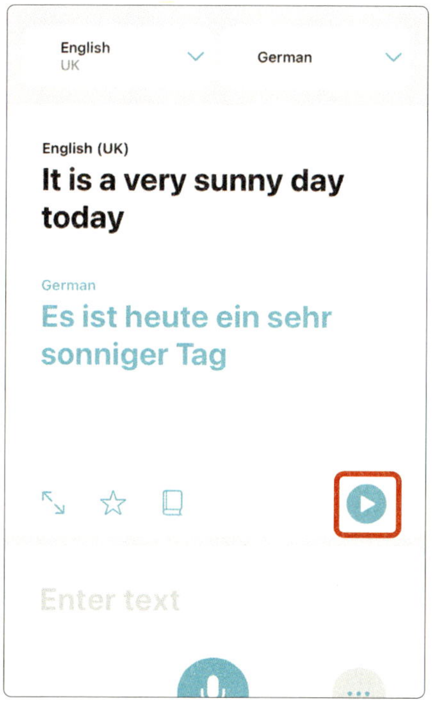

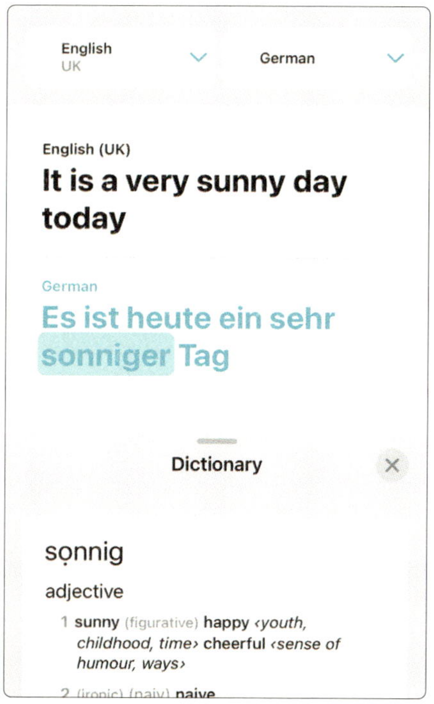

4 In the translation window, tap the Play icon to have it read out again or tap the star outline to add it to your favourite phrases. Tap the Favourites icon at the foot of the screen to review recent translations and your favourites.

5 Tap the book icon under a translation for the dictionary. Now tap on a word in your translation to have it defined and its grammar and usage explained. This is very useful if you're trying to learn a new language.

Using the Camera

You can also translate text using the iPhone's camera. Tap the camera icon at the foot of the screen, and frame the text you want to have translated in the screen. Tap the button underneath and the text is translated.

The Health App

The Health app is great for keeping all of your personal medical information in one place; and for tracking your exercise and fitness regimes. You can store clinical documents too. If you have an Apple Watch, the Health app really comes into its own with fitness tracking in Activity, but it has plenty to offer even if you don't use Apple's amazing smartwatch.

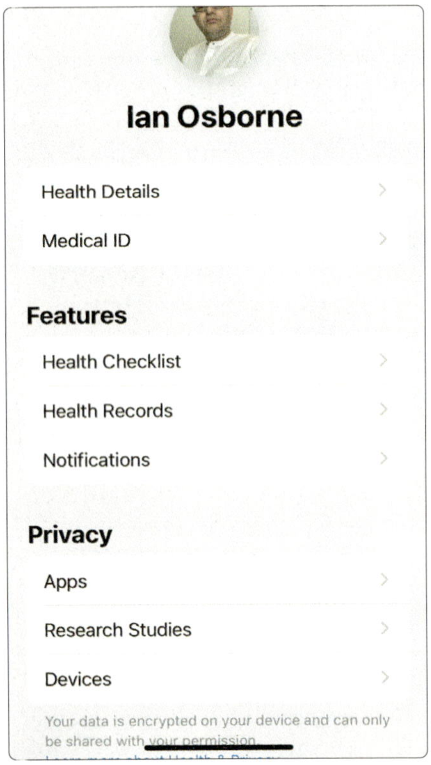

1 Set up your Health Profile. It should appear the first time you open the app, but if not, tap the icon in the top right corner of the Summary screen. Tap Health Details, then Edit and add your information. Do the same for Medical ID too.

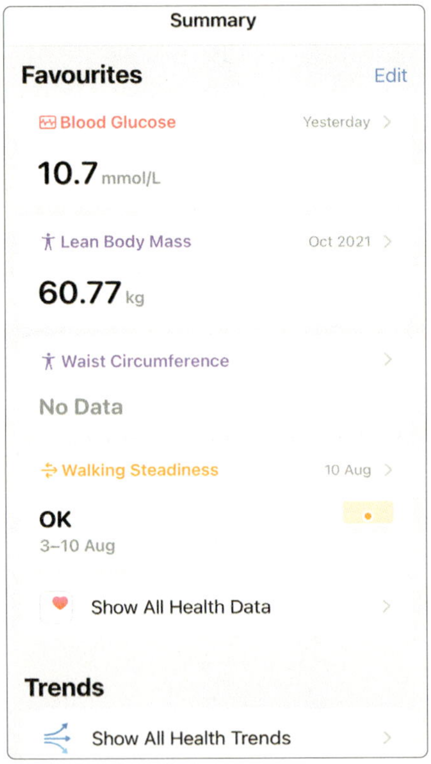

2 The main Summary screen, accessed by tapping the Summary icon at the bottom, starts with your Favourites. To configure, tap the Edit link and choose the items you want to use. Note the Existing and All tabs.

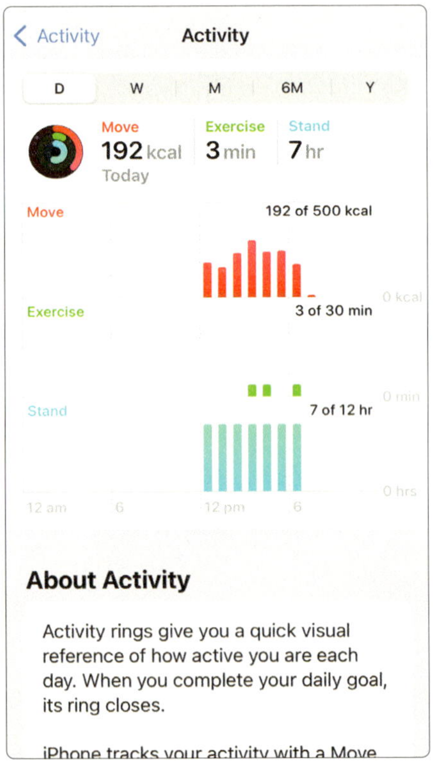

3 In the Browse tab, tap Activity and then Activity again for your Activity data, which is taken from your Apple Watch. It shows how you're getting on filling your rings today, and how your activity level compares over the last week, month and year.

Medical ID

The Medical ID option, found by tapping the top-right icon on the Summary screen then tapping Medical ID, is a great way of storing useful private medical information that might be used in an emergency. It can be accessed from the iPhone's emergency dialler when the phone is locked, so a doctor or an ambulance crew can always retrieve it.

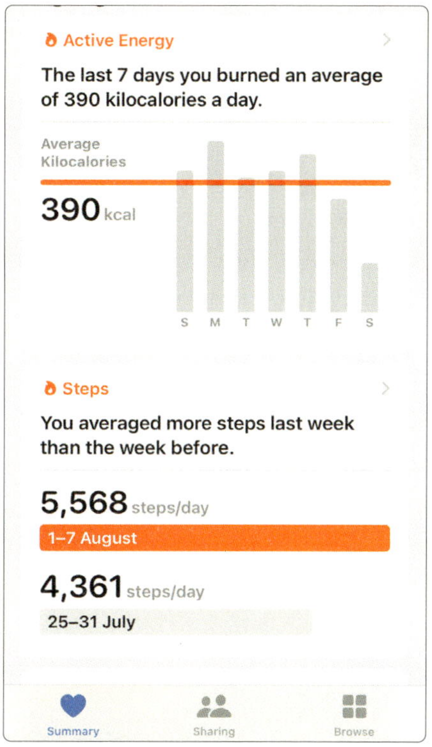

4 Scroll down the Summary and highlights are offered, such as how many calories you've burned exercising, and how many flights of stairs you've climbed. Tap one for a more detailed analysis. The data for these pages can be added manually or by other apps.

Sharing Tab

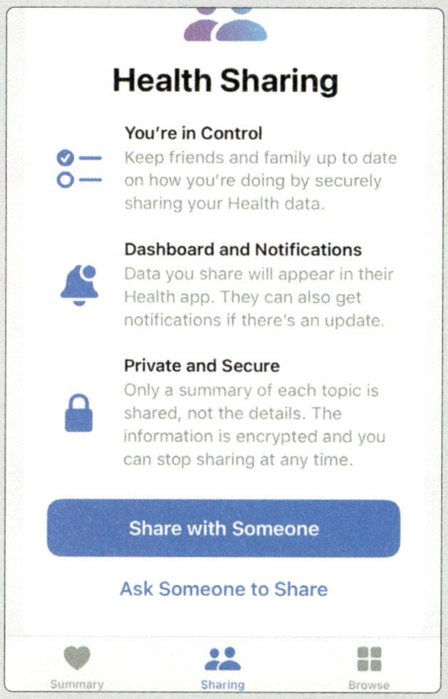

The Sharing tab, introduced with iOS 15, lets you share your health data with family, caregivers or a care team. Tap Sharing at the foot of the screen, then tap Share with Someone and choose who to share with. Tap Apps and you can choose which apps are shared.

More Features of the Health App

Apps: At the foot of the Summary screen is a list of apps that have relevance to, and can interact with, the Health app. Tap one to be taken to its page on the App Store, from where you can purchase it and download it to your iPhone.

Browse: Tap the Browse icon at the foot of the screen for more health information and data. They're arranged into categories, so you can easily find what you're looking for. There's also a search field available too.

Hardware: If you have health peripherals such as smart scales, they might be compatible with the Health app. Open the device's own app, and see if Health is listed. If it is, configure what information the apps can share.

Health Records: At the foot of the Browse window is a category called Health Records. If your healthcare provider makes such data available, you can add them to the Health app here. This feature isn't yet available in all territories.

Cycle Tracking: This feature found under the Browse tab lets women analyse their menstrual health and predict the date of their next period. The app can send notifications, and also predict fertile times too.

Sleep Monitoring: Under Summary, look for Set Up Sleep. If you wear a compatible sleep monitor, you can have its information sent to your Health app, where your sleep patterns can be recorded.

Articles: Scroll the Summary tab to near the bottom and you find a series of articles about health. Tap one to read it. They're a useful way of learning about the relevance of some of the information offered in the Health app.

Health Records: If your healthcare provider has compatible healthcare records, they can be shared with the Health app. Under Browse, scroll up and under Health Records, tap Add Account and follow the on-screen instructions.

Organising your Medications

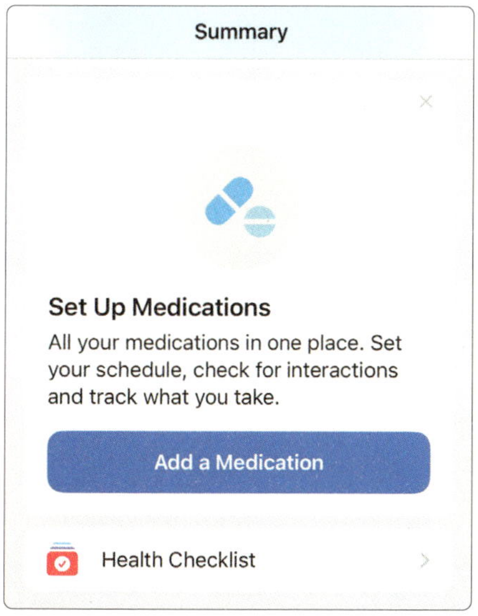

1 In the Summary section (see icons at the foot of the screen), scroll down to Set Up Medications. Tap Add a Medication, and take a look at this section. Tap the Add a Medication button, and enter any medications you take regularly.

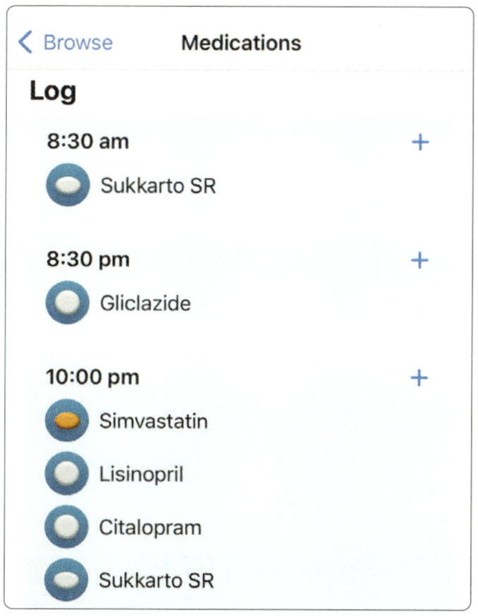

2 When you've logged all the medicines you regularly take into the Health app, along with vitamins, supplements and anything you take 'as needed', you get a warning if anything you're taking clashes with other medications.

The Wallet App

With Apple Pay, you can leave your wallet at home and shop with your iPhone! Instead of picking through your purse or wallet trying to find the correct credit card, you can store your payment cards on your iPhone 6 or later versions and use them to make payments at the tills. Here's how to set up and use this exciting new Apple easy payment service.

How to store credit and debit card information

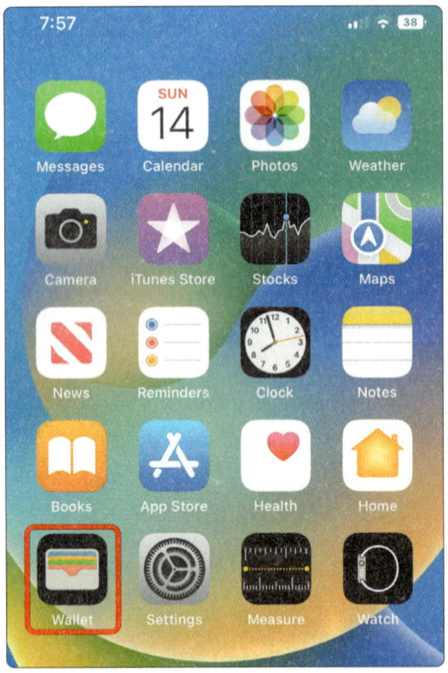

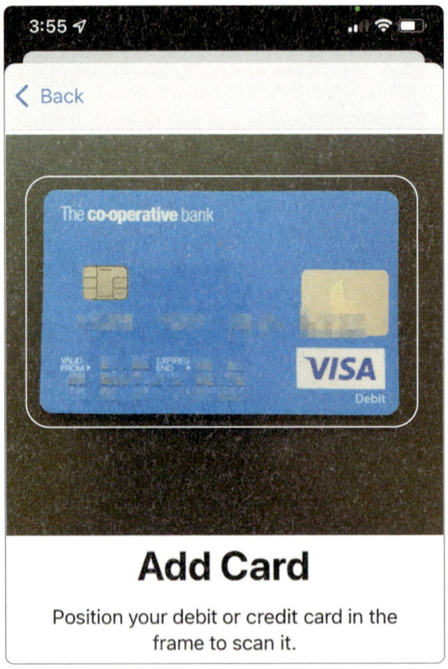

1 To use Apple Pay, you need at least an iPhone 6, 6 Plus or SE; or an Apple Watch connected to a compatible iOS device. Apple Watches are compatible with the iPhone 5 or later, including the iPhone SE and require at least iOS 8. You can make Apple Pay payments online with an iPad Pro, Air 2, Mini 3 or later.

2 Credit or debit cards are added to Apple Pay through the Wallet app. To add a new card, use your iPhone's rear camera to take a photograph of the card in question. Just keep it in the frame as advised on screen, and the card is photographed and its information stored. Or type the information in manually.

3 Your credit and debit cards are then stored in Wallet, ready to use with Apple Pay. You can add the credit or debit card from your iTunes account simply by typing in the card's security code. The first card you enter becomes the default payment card, but you can change this in Settings if you wish.

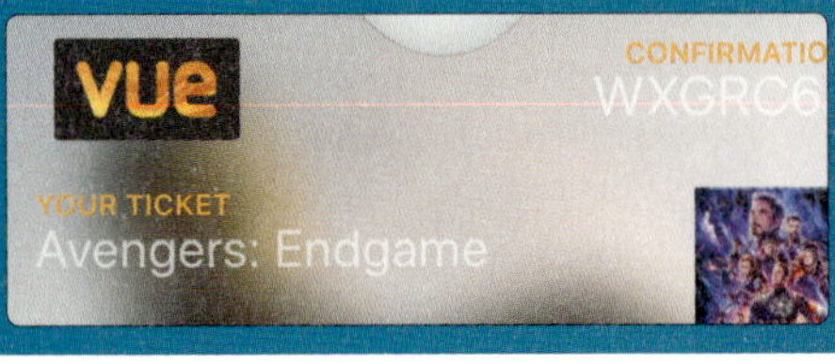

e-Tickets

Some places, like airlines and movie theatres, offer e-tickets. Order your tickets online and they can be emailed directly to you and stored in the Wallet app. When you arrive, you simply open the app and your e-ticket can be scanned, just like a paper ticket.

Using Apple Pay on the iPhone

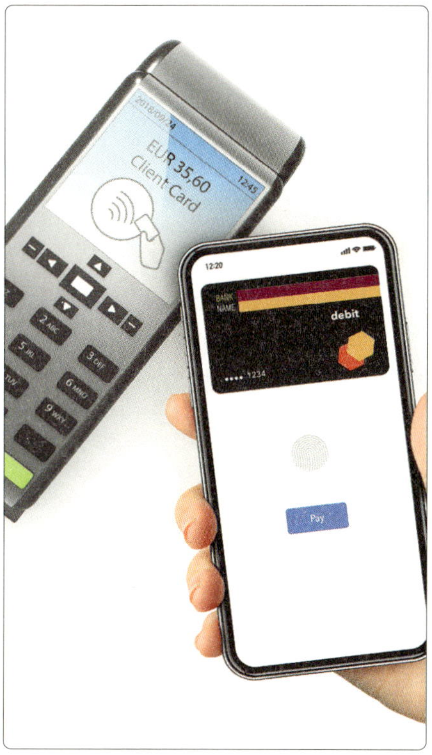

1 After you've registered your payment cards, to use Apple Pay, wave your iPhone over the contactless payments reader. On an X-series iPhone, use Face ID to confirm your identity, but with earlier iPhones, hold your finger on the Home button so your identity can be confirmed using the fingerprint scanner.

2 There's no need to open the Wallet app to use Apple Pay. You don't even have to unlock your iPhone; the service works even if it's in sleep mode and the display is blank. You do not have to look at your screen to know the payment has been accepted either. It's confirmed with a vibration and a beep.

Order Tracking

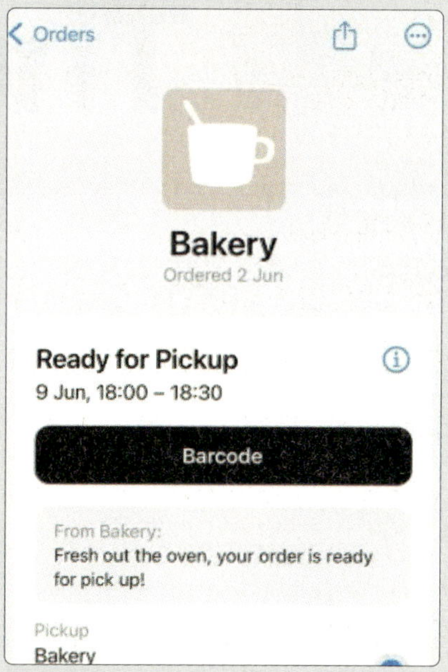

If you make a purchase using Apple Pay, and the merchant participates in the scheme, you can use the Wallet app to track your order. On the opening screen, tap the box icon (top right) to trace delivery or pickup times.

More Wallet features

Transactions

Tap a card, and transactions you've made with that card are listed underneath. Not every bank issues this information, but if yours does, you can see both what you've spent and where, using the Apple Pay service.

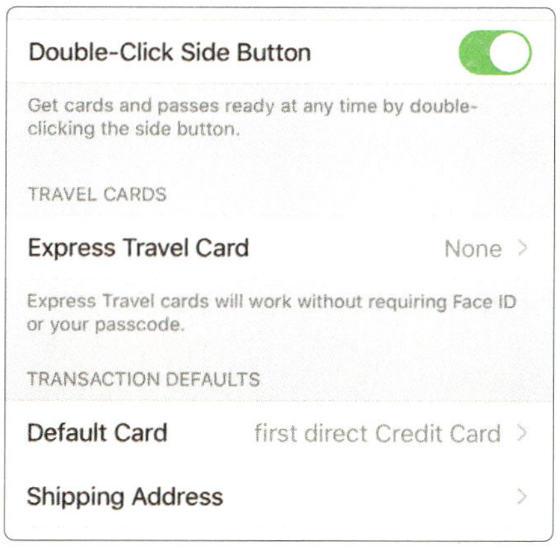

Settings

In Settings > Wallet & Apple Pay, you can configure the feature to suit your needs. Set up an Express Travel Card for travel terminals, choose your default card, change your shipping address and more.

Keys & IDs

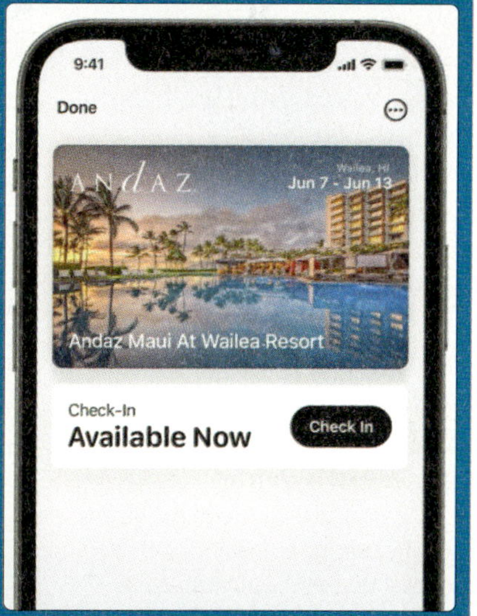

Digital keys and identification options are gradually emerging, with more and more vendors getting on board. You can unlock a hotel room, office, your house or car and more, and even share these keys using Messages, Mail, WhatsApp and other apps. A Wallet ID can be used for age verification too.

The Music App

With the Music app and a subscription to Apple Music, you can stream tunes over the Internet to your iPhone. Choose from an amazing library of over 50 million songs, with no limit to how many you listen to.

MUSIC *in Focus*

1 This is the main page of the Apple Music streaming service, where albums, artists and playlists tailored to your tastes are suggested for your listening.

2 Tap here to see your account details. You can change your username to a specific Music app nickname, choose more of your favourite artists, replace the silhouette with a photo and add some personal details.

3 Top Picks is a range of playlists from bands and artists curated by the Music app to match your tastes, gleaned from what you've listened to. Tap one to play the tracks.

4 The mini-player shows the track you're currently playing. You can tap it to expand it to full-screen size, with all the usual audio controls available to use.

5 You can use the skip track and pause/play controls here without having to open the mini-player first.

6 The Listen Now page is accessed here. This is your gateway to the Apple Music streaming service. It's this page we're looking at in this annotation, which is why it's coloured red.

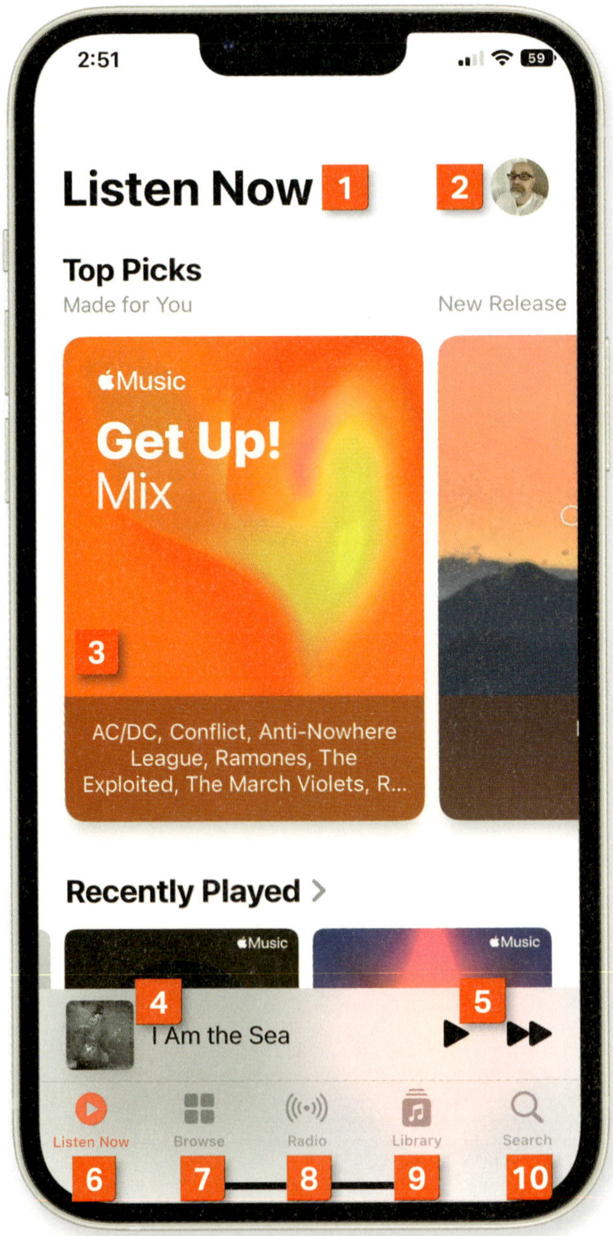

7 Tap this icon to get to Apple Music's Browse page, where you can check out the songs and albums that have recently been added to the Apple Music service.

8 Tap here to access Apple Music's radio stations, including Apple's exclusive Beats 1 station. Radio programmes are streamed over the Internet.

9 Your own music library. Music you've bought from iTunes, ripped from your CD collection or downloaded using the Apple music streaming service is found here.

10 The useful search facility. Look for artists, albums and songs. It searches both your own music library and the Apple Music service.

Equaliser

If you want to fine-tune your sound according to what you're playing, go to Settings > Music and tap the EQ option.

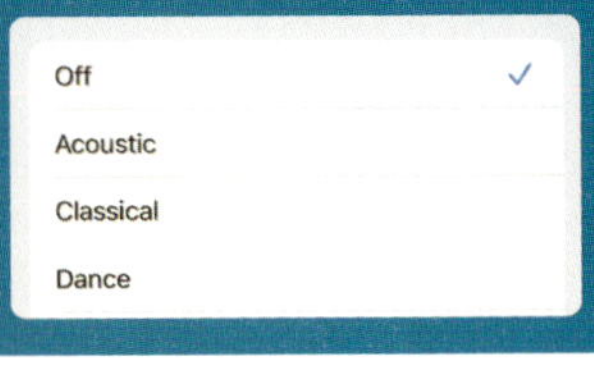

Getting started with Apple Music

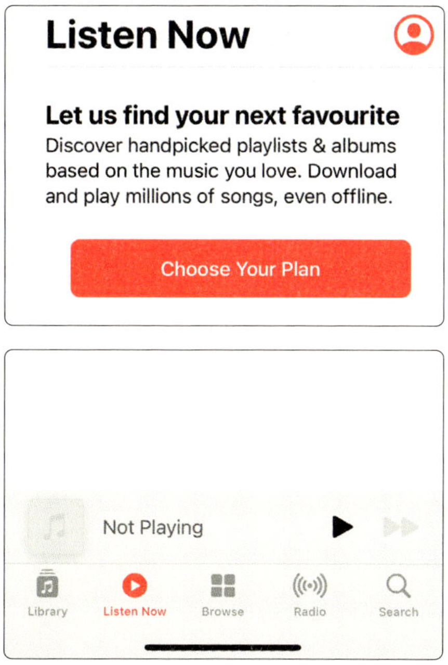

1 Tap the Listen Now icon found at the bottom of the screen and tap the Choose Your Plan to begin the sign-up process for the Apple Music service. You get your first three months of Apple Music for free but if you decide to remain a member after this initial trial period, you're charged a set monthly fee.

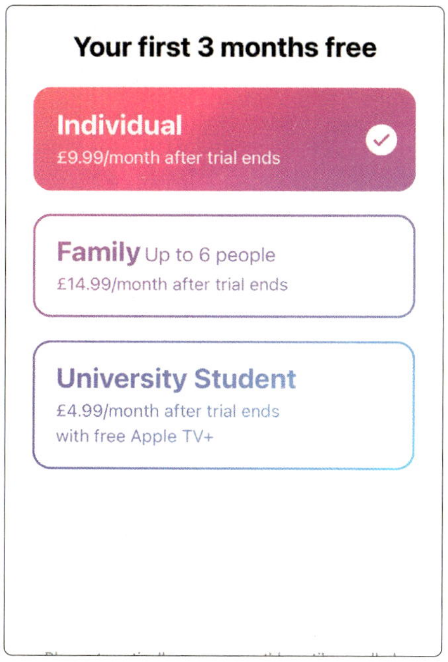

2 You must then choose a plan. You can take out an Individual Apple Music Membership for £9.99/$9.99/9.99 €, a Family membership for up to six members of your household for £14.99/$14.99/14.99 € or a Student account for £4.99/$4.99/4.99. The Family memberships can use Apple's Family Sharing feature.

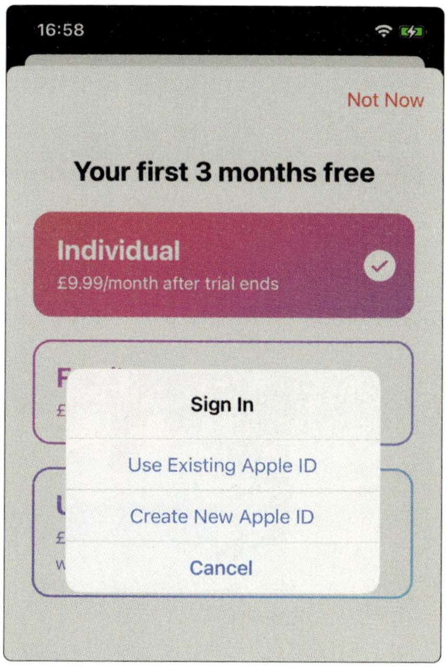

3 If you're not already signed in with your Apple ID, you must do so now. Type your details as instructed, then tap the OK link. You must then verify your payment details. Again, follow the on-screen instructions and do so, then when requested, confirm your purchase of an Apple Music subscription.

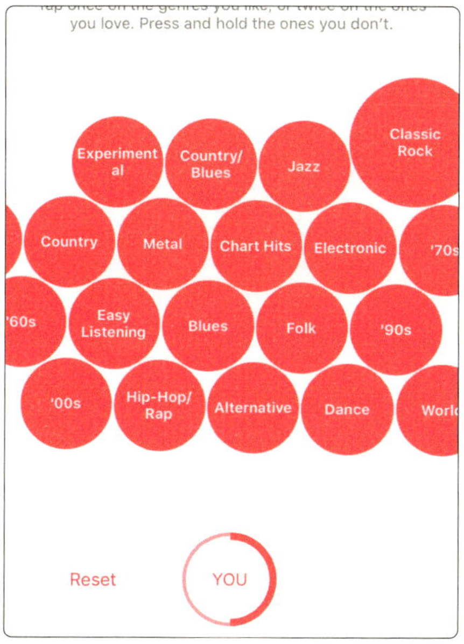

4 You see this screen, where you can identify musical genres that you like. Tap on the dots representing your favourite types of music. Tap twice for genres you especially like. When you're done, click Next and repeat the process for bands and artists as offered. Tap Done.

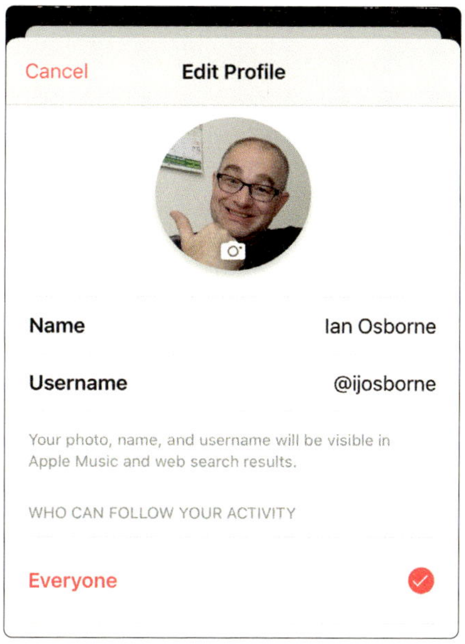

5 If you want to register a unique Apple Music nickname, first tap the silhouette icon in the top right to get to your account. Tap on your own name at the top of this screen and on the next one, tap Edit and enter the nickname of your choice. When finished, tap Done in the top right.

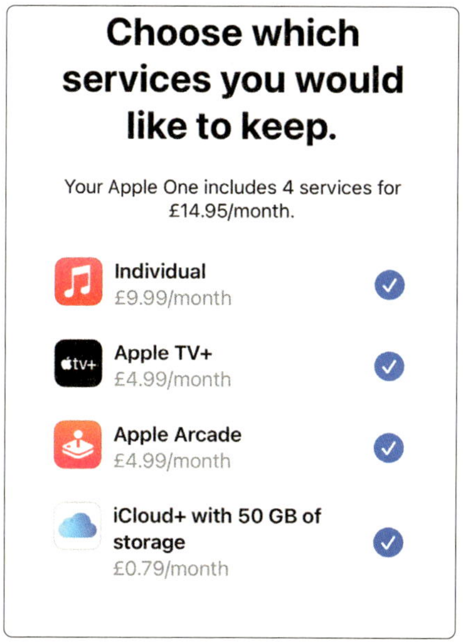

6 To cancel your subscription, open Apple Music and tap the account icon (top right) for your account details. Tap Manage Subscriptions, and choose your options from there. If you have an Apple One subscription, you can cancel it and choose to retain individual services.

Using Apple Music and the Music app

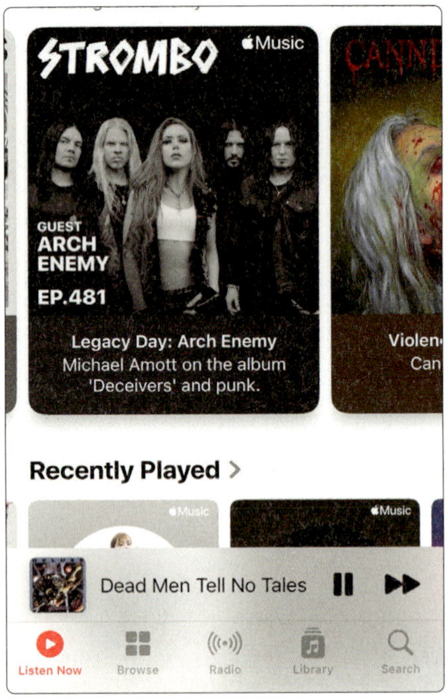

1 Tap the Listen Now icon, in the bottom-left corner, to get to a screen offering suggestions of bands and albums based on the choices you made whilst setting up Apple Music. These suggestions are playlists and albums. Tap one, then choose a track or an album to play. The music is then streamed to your iPhone.

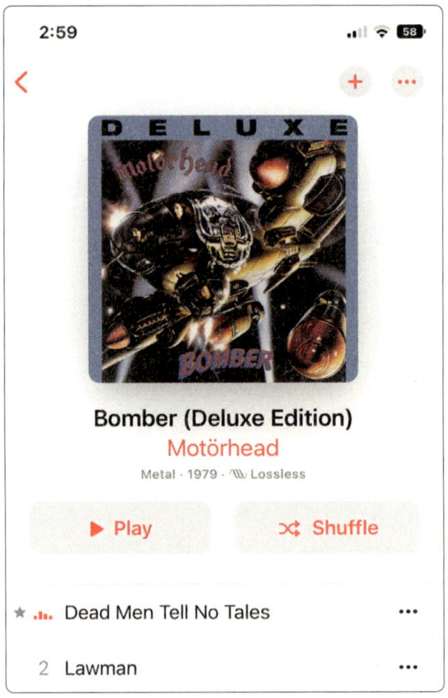

2 Having chosen an album or a playlist, tap a track to play it. When it's finished, the next track plays, in the order shown on the list. Use Shuffle to play them in a random order. Tap the three dots icon and then the heart icon to identify it as one of your favourites. This improves the Music app's later suggestions.

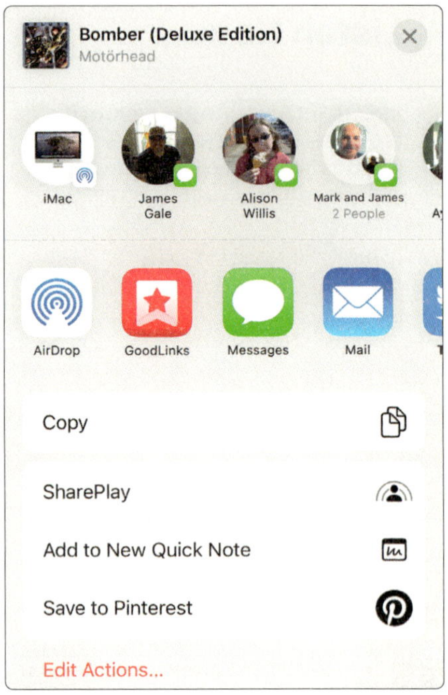

3 The ubiquitous Share button is also found by tapping the three-dots icon. Use it and you're given the opportunity to share a link by AirDrop, Message, Twitter, Facebook, Mail and more. You can tap the track currently playing and then the three-dots icon to share an individual song too.

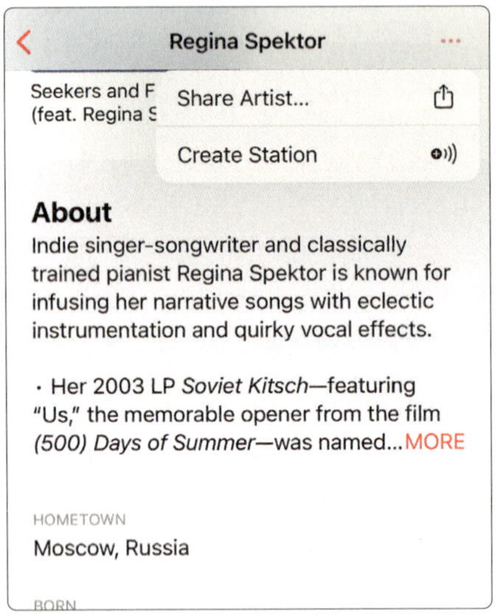

4 Tap on the name of an artist to get to their home page, which offers access to more of their work and also some information on the artist in question. Use the Three-dots icon on this page to get to this pop-up window, from which you can share the artist or make a station based on their music.

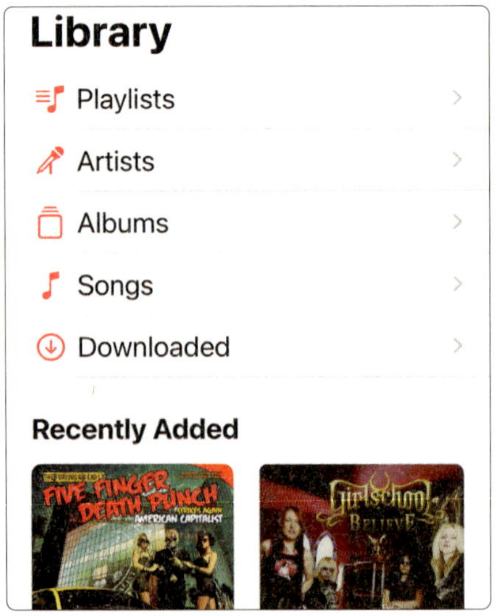

5 All your own music, whether ripped from your CD collection, bought from iTunes or downloaded through Apple Music, is found in the Library section. Tap the Library icon to access it. You can have your music collection ordered according to artists, albums, songs and more. Just follow the links.

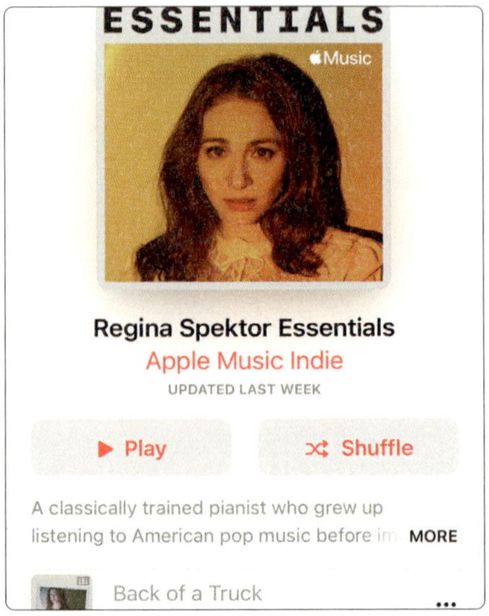

6 To add an album to your library, tap the Add icon, or tap the three-dots icon, then Add to Library. To download it to your iPhone too, tap the down-pointing arrow (top right). To play it tap Library, then Downloaded Music. If you cancel your Apple Music subscription, this music is lost and can no longer be played.

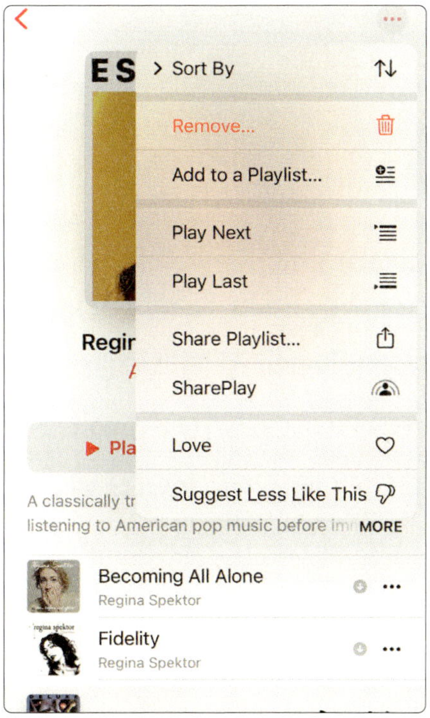

7 The tracks are downloaded to your iPhone as shown. To remove them, go to Library > Downloaded and open the album or track in question. Tap the three-dots icon. At the top of the pop-up window is the Remove... link. Tap it and the songs are deleted from your iPhone.

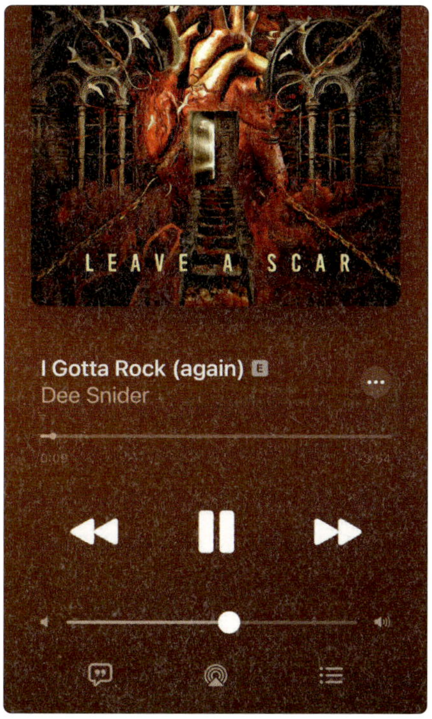

8 Throughout the app, the mini-player sits above the icons at the foot of the screen. Tap it to open this full-sized play screen. The three icons at the bottom are for displaying the song's lyrics if available, changing the output source and a list of what songs are playing next.

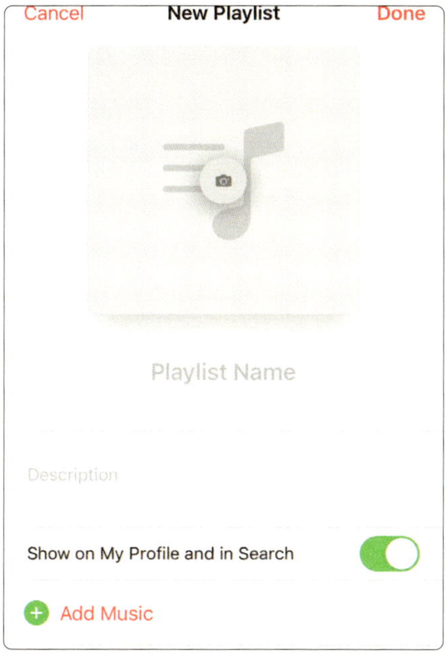

9 To create a playlist, go to Library and tap Playlists at the top of the screen. Tap New Playlist, then add a title and description; if you wish, add a picture by tapping the camera icon. You can then add songs from your library by tapping the Add Songs link. Then use the plus sign next to tracks you want to add.

10 To change the output source for your music (that is, what you're listening to it through), open the Control Centre and tap and hold the audio controls. Tap the icon in the top right of the next window. You can choose between your iPhone's speakers and connected headphones or speakers.

More Music Features

Duplicate song warning

If you attempt to add a song to a playlist when the song in question is already there, you now get a warning. You can add them again if you really want to, there's no need to do so by accident now.

Sort playlists

You can now organise your playlists according to Title, Artist, Album or Release Date. To do so, open the playlist, tap the three-dots icon (top right) and tap Sort By.

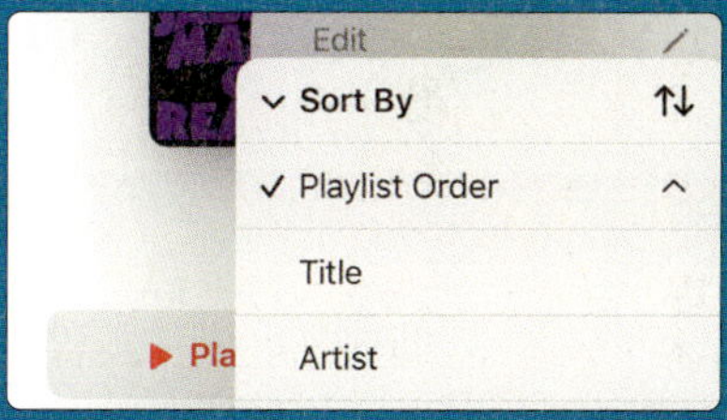

New Favourite option

On a band or artist's profile page, there's a star icon next to the three-dots icon in the top-right. Tap it for improved recommendations and alerts about new music from that performer.

Music's time-synced lyrics

When listening to a song, tap the mini-player to get the full-screen player, and then tap the bottom left icon, the quote marks in a speech bubble. You get the lyrics, synced with the song. This feature isn't available on every track, but it's great fun for those that have it.

Did you think that it would end?

The TV App

The TV app brings your viewing into one app, making it easier and more convenient to subscribe to third-party TV channels and enjoy all your movies and TV shows under a single app. It also gives access to Apple's TV+ subscription service for exclusive Apple-created content. Here we take a look at the new app and how to watch shows on your iPhone.

Finding and viewing TV shows

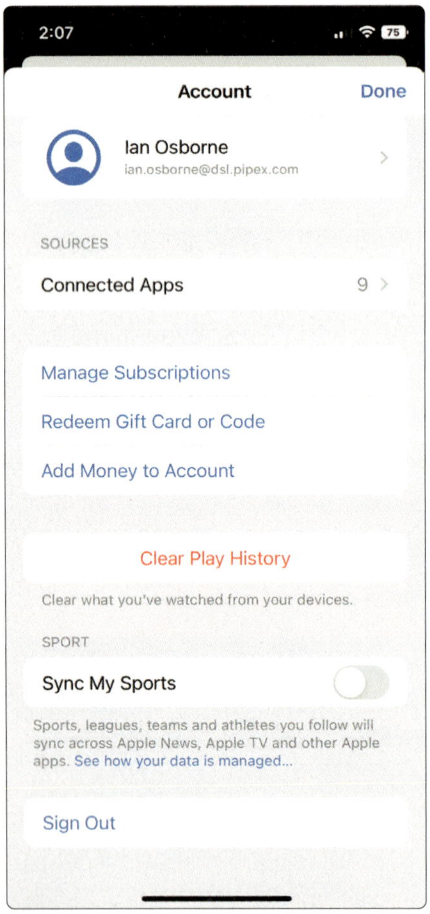

1 From the main screen, tap the top right icon (silhouette or your photo) for this window, from where you can manage your account (tap your name), manage services to which you've subscribed, or add funds or gift cards to your Apple account, to spend on apps and media.

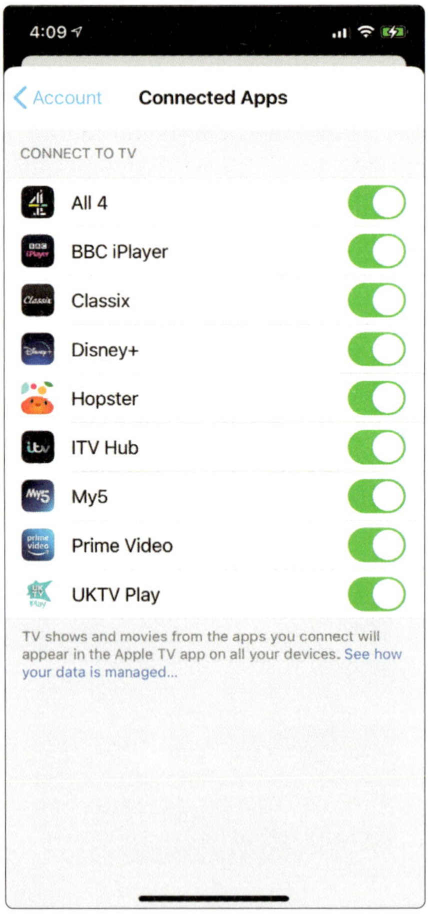

2 Tapping Connected Apps shows the TV and catch-up apps you downloaded from the App Store, and that are linked to your TV app. Tap the switch to unlink an app and stop its content appearing in your TV app. If you don't have any, download some now.

3 Tap Account in the top left corner to go back to the previous window. Then tap Done, in the top right corner, to get to here. This is Watch Now, the TV app's main page. Scroll up for more categories, including shows that have been shared with you via Messages.

4 On the Watch Now screen, shows are arranged in rows. Scroll them left and right for more. Up Next, offers programmes and series you're part way through watching and content you've recently bought. What to Watch, is suggestions based on past viewings.

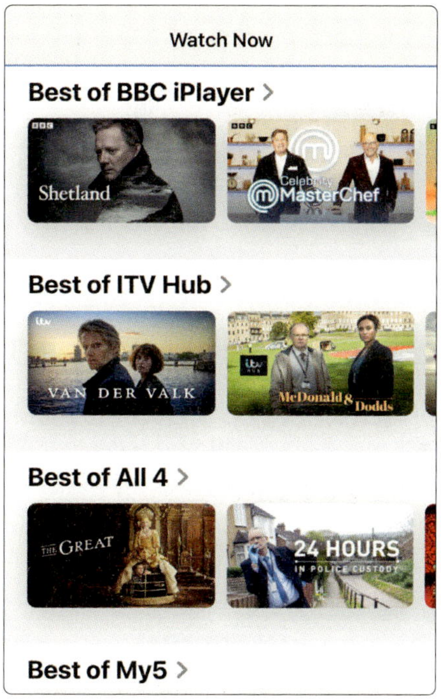

5 Scroll the Watch Now page further up for content deemed the best of the apps you have linked to your TV app. You can watch them here instead of closing TV and opening the app in question. Scroll up still further for more suggestions, arranged in categories.

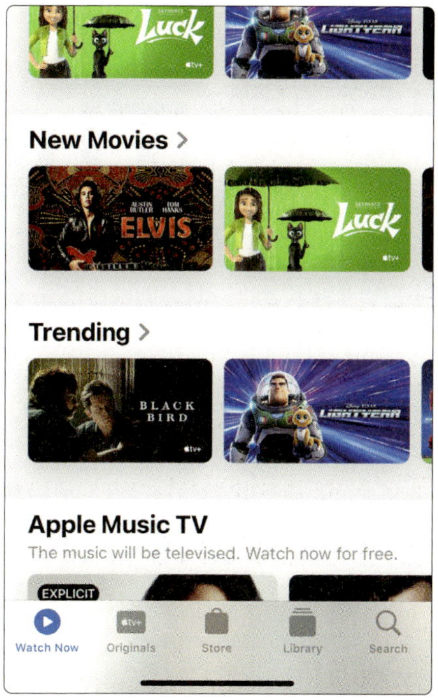

6 At the foot of the screen, you can find icons labelled Originals, Store and Library. Originals takes you to programmes offered on the the Apple TV+ subscription service, Store is for buying media and Library is for shows you've already bought and/or downloaded.

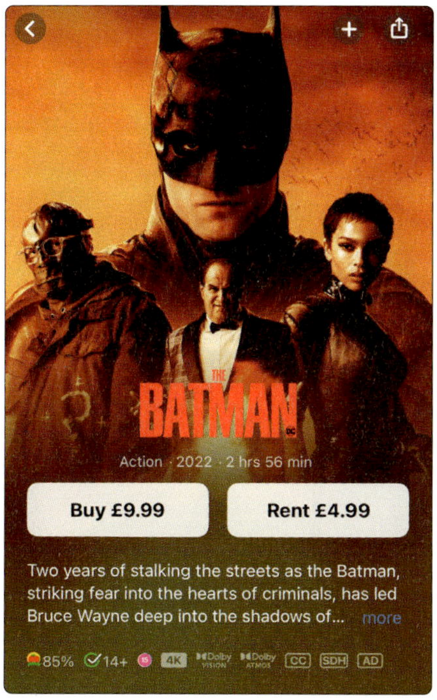

7 You can buy or rent a show or movie, directly from the TV app. Just tap Store, find something you're interested in and choose whether to buy or rent it, paying from your Apple ID account. Scroll up for more information, including trailers you can watch for free.

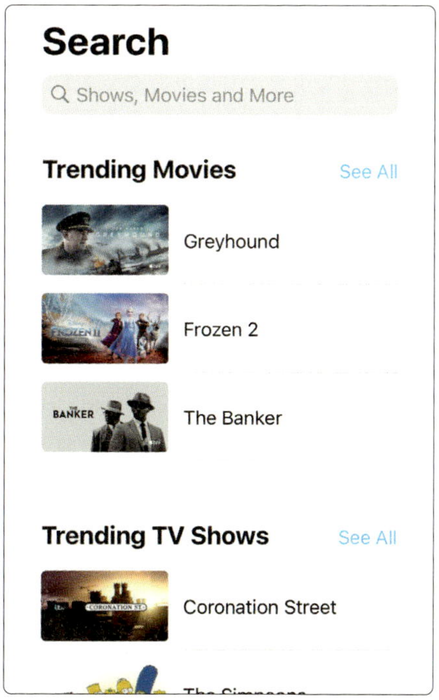

8 Naturally, you can use the Search feature, found in the bottom right corner, to look for content you own or that's available to buy/rent. Just type a search term. Possible results are offered as you go, so you should soon find what you're looking for.

9 When watching a show or movie, tap the screen to bring up the controls. The X in the top left corner closes the video; top right lets you set the volume. On the screen are controls for play/pause and to skip ten seconds forward or backward.

The Books App

The Books app turns your iPhone into a fully featured eBook reader. You can buy new eBooks directly from the Books app, read them on your iPhone, bookmark pages, make notes and even add PDF documents.

BOOKS *in Focus*

1 See how many pages are left in the chapter here.

2 Read your book here. Tap anywhere around here to see how many pages you have left to read (see 14).

3 Tap here or slide right to go to the previous page.

4 Tap here or slide left to go to the next page.

5 This shows how much of the book you've already read. Tap it for a chapter list.

6 Tap here to see bookmarks and highlights you've added to the book as you read.

7 Search the book for a word or phrase.

8 Tap here for a controller that lets you change the brightness, font, text size and other option.

9 The Sharing icon. Tap it for iOS sharing options.

10 This icon lets you lock the screen to its current orientation, so it doesn't change between portrait and landscape when your rotate the screen.

11 Tap here to bookmark the current page. To add a highlight, select the text you want to highlight in the usual way, then select 'Highlight' in the contextual menu.

12 Tap the cross icon here to close the book you're currently reading.

13 The total number of pages in the book, and the page you're on appear when you tap the screen. After a few seconds, it reverts to just showing the page you're on.

14 Tap this icon to open the options window seen in the main screen here.

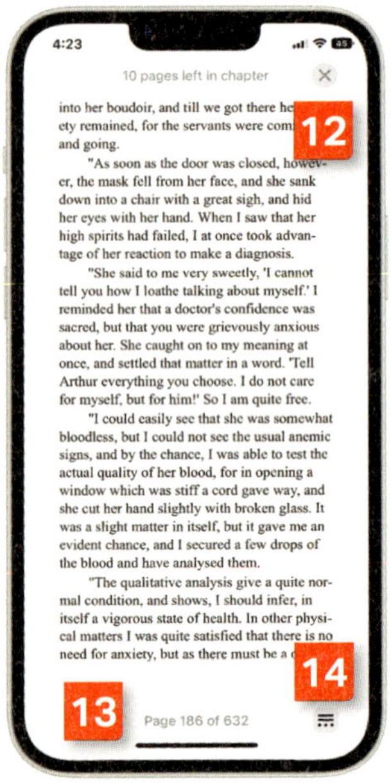

Buying books

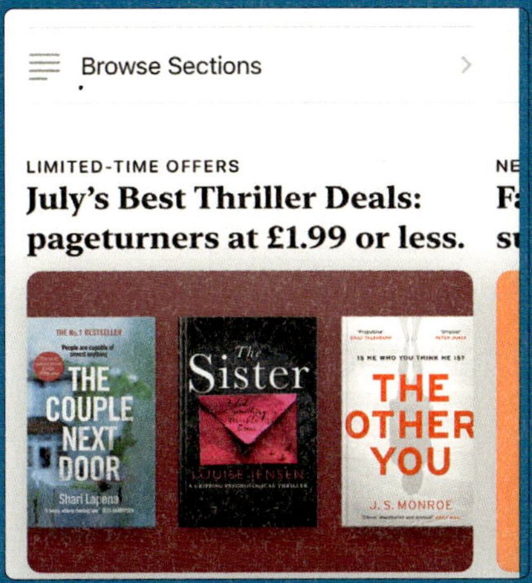

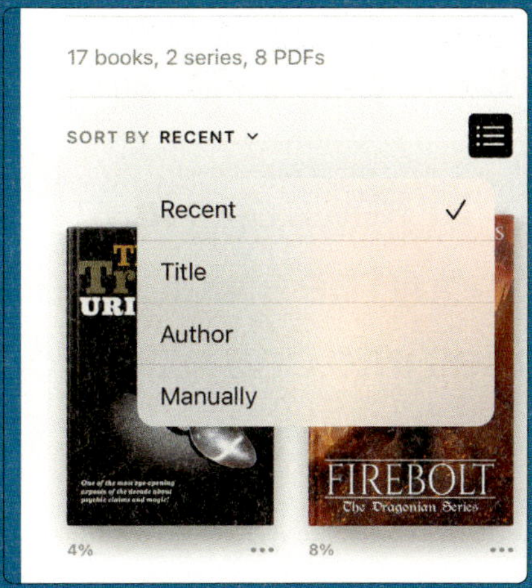

To buy digital books, tap Book Store at the foot of the screen to see titles listed under categories such as Staff Picks, recommendations For You, New & Trending and more. Tap Browse Sections at the top to look at specific genres. To buy a book, tap on it, then the price, then Buy Book. Tap Sample for a free taster. Sign into iTunes if requested.

Tap Library to see your books. Open one by tapping on it. Tap Collections for filter options. The icon on the right above the books switches between list and cover view. To remove books, tap Edit (top right), tap a book or books, then tap the dustbin. Books you bought but aren't on your iPhone are marked by a cloud. Tap it to download again; you won't pay twice.

More Books features

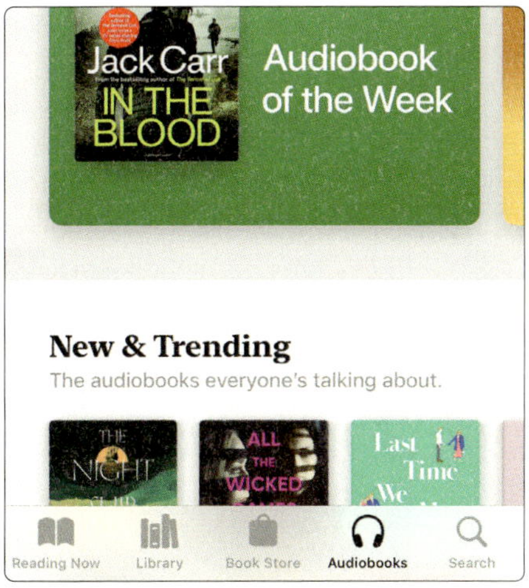

Audiobooks

The Books app has its own Audiobooks tab. On the main Books screen, tap it to be taken to the Audiobooks store. Tap the icon in the top right corner to be taken to a new screen, from where you can browse audiobooks according to genre, charts, bestsellers and more. Tap on an audiobook for an in-depth description, the opportunity to buy it or add it to your wish list, or listen to a free sample.

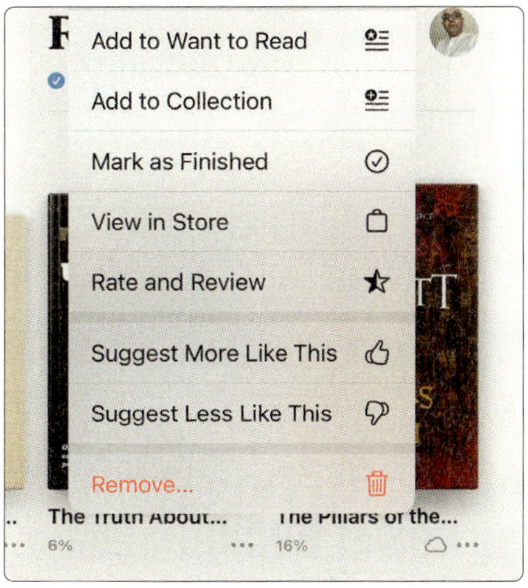

The Three-dots Icon

In several places in the app, you see an icon showing three dots beneath a book cover. Tap this for a range of options. Tap the Remove icon to hide a book you've purchased, or delete a downloaded book, so it appears but with a cloud in the corner (you can download it again later). On a document, you can delete it from your iPhone or from all your connected devices.

Adding PDFs

You can add PDFs to the Books app. Email it to yourself as an attachment, open the email and tap the PDF. Tap the Share icon in the bottom left corner, and then tap More > Books. On a Mac, you add them by opening Books, going to File > Add to Library and navigating to the document. It can then be opened on any device using the same Apple ID.

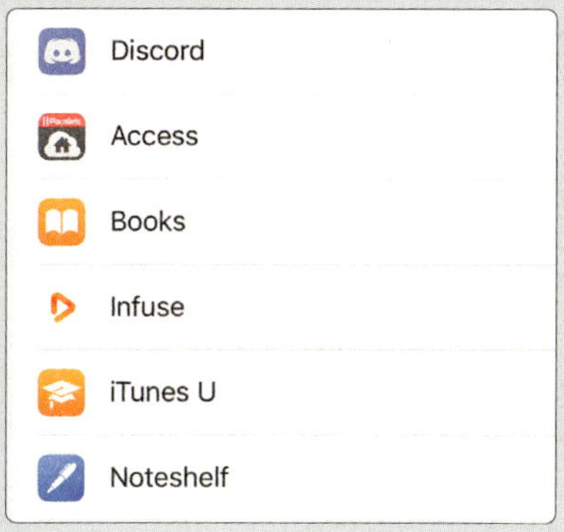

Having a book read to you

Have your books read to you using a feature called VoiceOver. Go to Settings > Accessibility > VoiceOver and switch VoiceOver on. Go back to Accessibility (tap once to highlight, then double-tap to go back) and tap scroll with three fingers to find Accessibility Shortcut. Select the VoiceOver option, which can then be switched on or off by triple-pressing the Home button. Not every book is VoiceOver compatible.

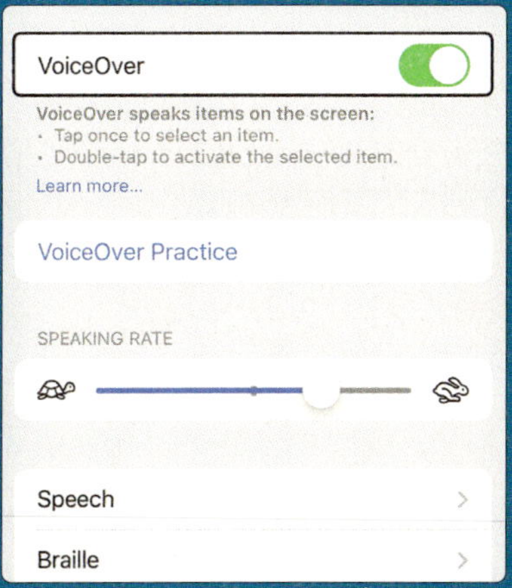

The News App

If you regularly trawl the web for news and features on subjects that interest you, the News app should be a welcome addition. It gathers stories from numerous sources into one place for quick and easy reading.

NEWS *in Focus*

1 Today's date, which is always important on a digital news app.

2 This is Today, the News app's main page. Scroll for top stories, trending stories and more.

3 You can watch videos directly from the News app. Just tap the Play button and the video plays, right there in the story.

4 Stories in the News app are tagged with how long ago they were uploaded to the Internet, so you know how recent your stories are.

5 Front-page news stories are usually illustrated with photos, videos or other such graphics. If you scroll the page, you get to see a range of news stories, trending stories, top videos and articles selected especially for you.

6 This is the Today icon. It takes you back to the screen shown here.

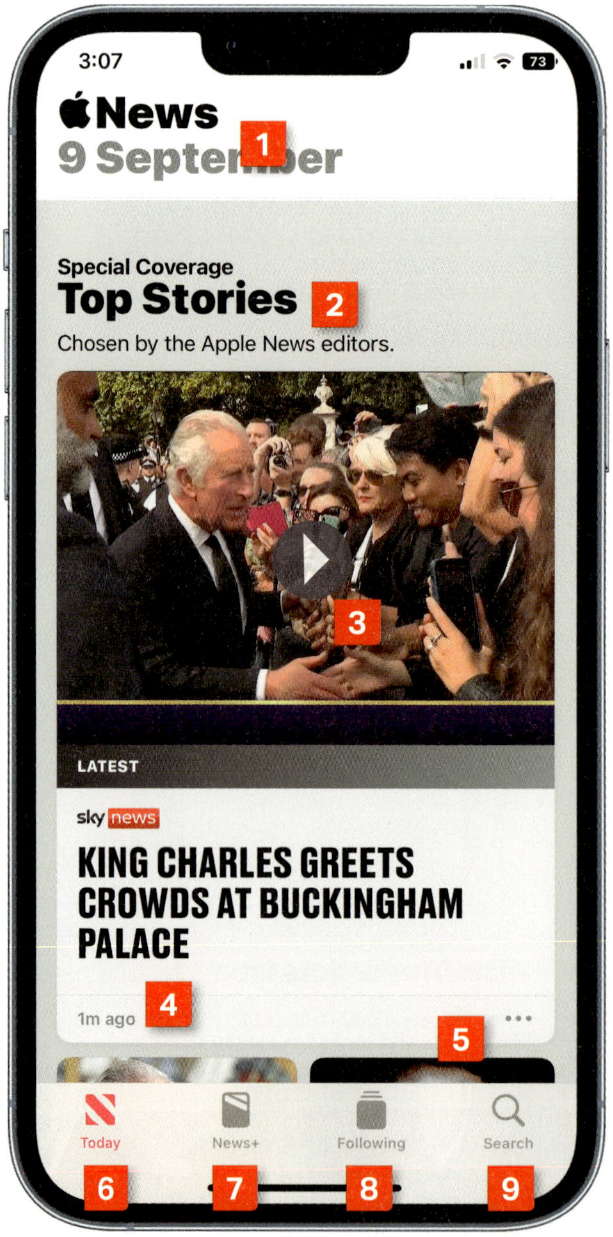

7 This icon reads 'News+', and is your gateway to Apple's paid-for subscription service that collates news, features and information from magazines and newspapers from all over the world. Your first month is free.

8 Tap the Following icon for a list of news sources and subjects you currently follow. From there, you can add new sources and subjects, delete those you're no longer interested in, search the News app, review your saved stories and manage the channels and topics you've blocked.

9 Tap here to search the News app and its articles for words or phrases.

Plus/Max Sized iPhones

When you turn the News app into landscape mode you get a sidebar showing the channels you're following and more.

Getting started with News

To get the most from News, first set it up to your specific requirements.

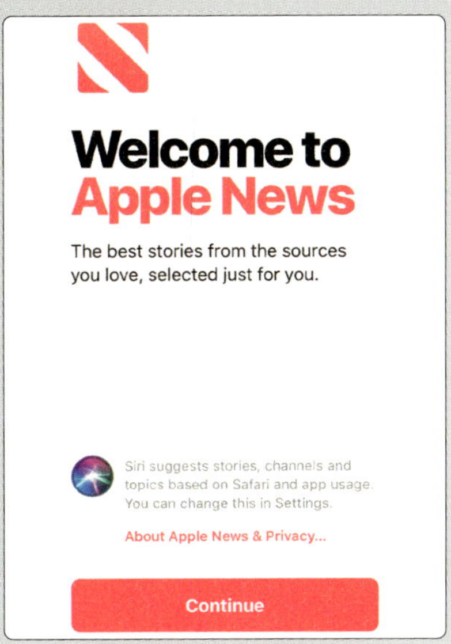

Tap Continue to open the News app. It's on the Today page. Tap Channels (bottom right) to see Siri's suggestions. Tap the heart icon next to topics you like and the crossed heart next to ones you dislike. Slide an option left to remove or ignore it. Pull down to search.

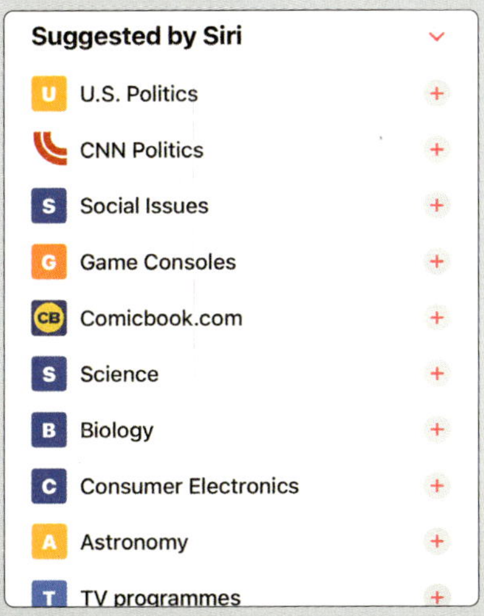

Under Suggestions, tap See All. You're shown a list of subjects Siri thinks you might like, based on your Safari browsing history and what you've done in other apps. Tap the heart for subjects that interest you, and the crossed out heart for those you don't want to see.

Today and Spotlight/Weekend icons

1 On the Today screen, tap a news story to open it on your iPhone, so you can read it in its entirety. With the news story open, you can also change the font size (top right icon showing two 'A's). Tap the chevron, top left, to go back to the Today screen.

2 At the top of an open news story is the three-dots icon. Tap it and use the thumbs icons for liking and disliking a story. This helps Siri tailor stories and suggestions to your tastes. You can also copy and save a story, alongside many more options.

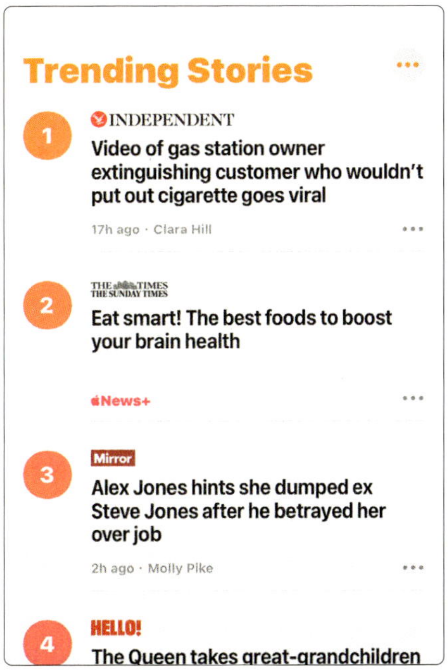

3 Scroll down the Today screen for more categories. Top Stories are today's most important news items. For You is news and features tailored to your tastes. Trending Stories are tales doing the rounds on social media. Videos are collected on the Today screen too.

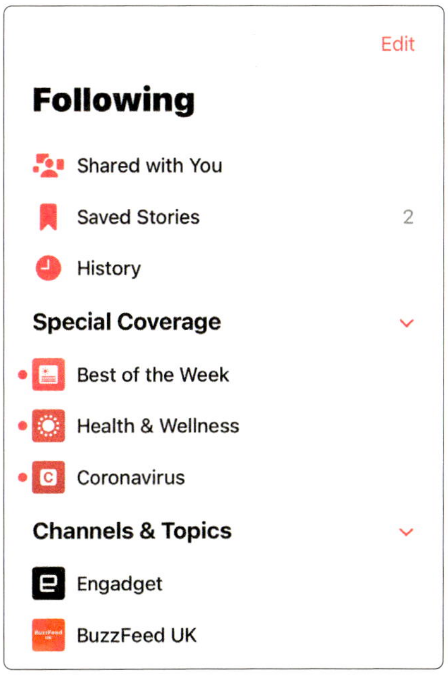

4 Tap the Following icon for a list of news sources and titles you're currently following. Tap and hold one for a pop-up that lets you go to, unfollow or block a channel. Scroll down and tap Discover Channels & Topics for suggestions of more things to follow.

The FaceTime App

Your iPhone's FaceTime app can make audio and video calls, to Android and Windows devices as well as other Apple gear. As FaceTime calls are made over the Internet, they're free. You can even make group calls, with several people appearing on screen at once for a party chat. Look out for new Live Captions, Handoff and SharePlay features too.

First Steps with FaceTime

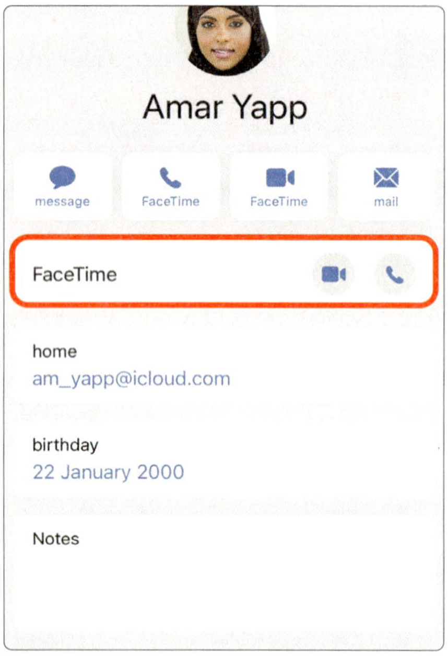

1 To start a FaceTime conversation from the Contacts app, first find the contact card of the person you wish to call. If that person's email or phone number are registered with FaceTime, you can see FaceTime icons for both audio (the telephone receiver) and video (the camera). Tap one to make the call.

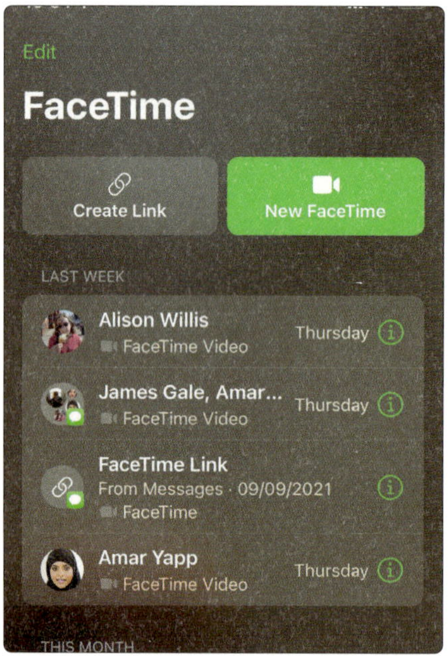

2 There are several ways of starting a FaceTime call from the FaceTime app. Tap the New FaceTime button (top right). Add the name of the person you want to call (or their phone number or email address if they're not in your Contacts), then tap a button for either a video or audio FaceTime call.

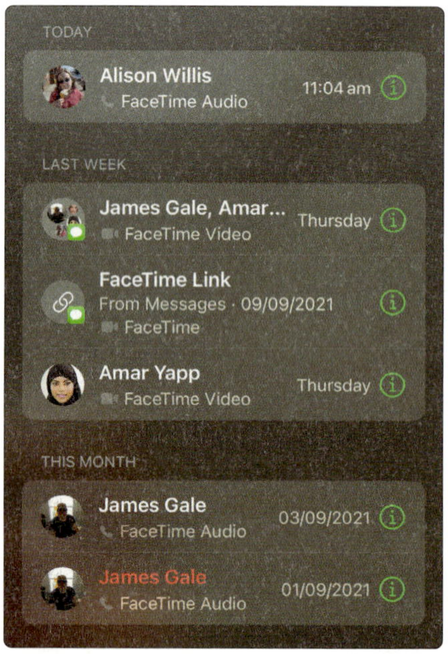

3 The FaceTime app also shows a list of recent FaceTime calls, showing whether they were audio or video. If you tap one of these, you can make that same call again. A name in red means the call was not answered. If you tap the 'i' to the right of the name, you get their Contacts card within the FaceTime app.

Portrait Video

Hold the iPhone sideways and you can video chat in Landscape Mode, as shown. If you have an iPhone XS or later, you can activate Portrait Mode, with the background blurred. Just tap your own video feed, then tap the silhouette icon in the top-left corner to activate and deactivate Portrait Mode. Tap the arrows icon to shrink your window again.

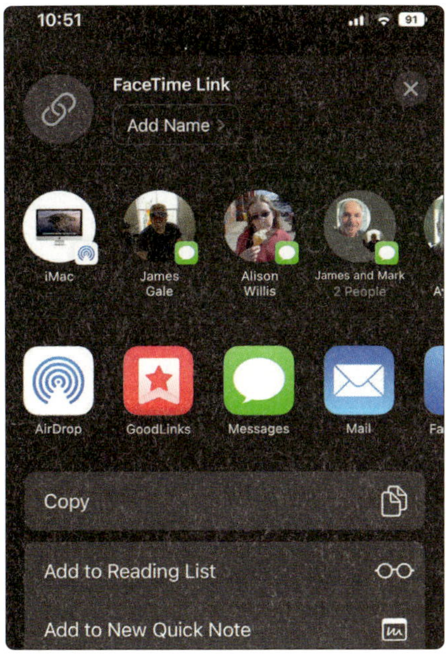

4 Another way to start a FaceTime chat is tap the Create Link button (top left). You can then add names manually, add them from the suggestions offered by the FaceTime app, and send them by Messages, Mail and more. The recipient can then initiate a FaceTime call with you from their end.

5 During a FaceTime video call, tap the screen to show and hide controls. The icons on the small screen (you) are for effects and to switch cameras respectively. The icons on the main screen (them) are Speaker on/off; mic on/off; camera on/off; SharePlay, and the red 'X' to end the call.

6 The white button at the bottom-left of the screen takes a live photograph of the person you're calling, which is found in your Photos app. This is a photo, not a screenshot, so the FaceTime controls do not appear in the picture. If the button is not there, go to Settings > FaceTime and turn FaceTime Live Photos on.

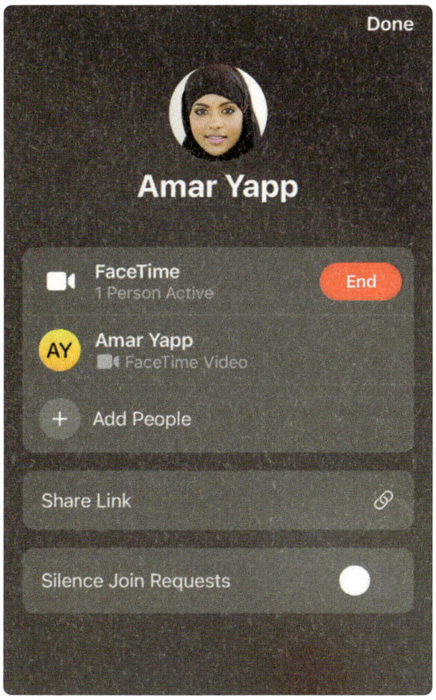

7 Tap the screen to show the controls and tap the 'i' icon (top right) to see the full range of options. You can end the call, or add more people by tapping the Add People link or by tapping Share Link and then sending it to others, who can then ask to join the conversation, turning it into a group chat.

8 The icon that looks a bit like a five-pointed star, found in the bottom left corner of the screen or at the bottom left of your picture, is for effects. Tap it and you can choose all sorts of fun things to modify your video feed. Tap the arrows icon to return to the chat, and the effects icon to remove the effects.

Windows & Android

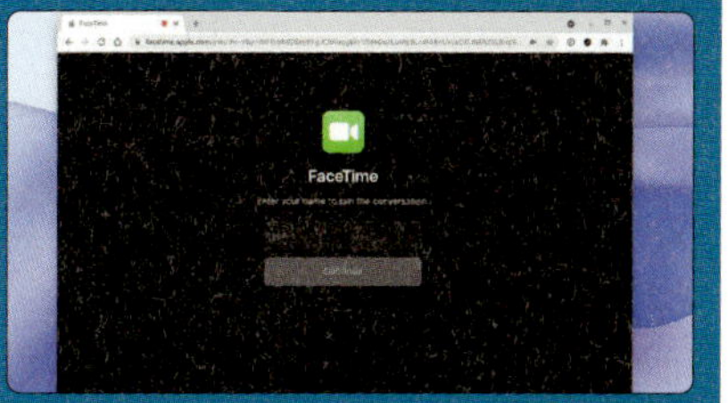

It's now possible to answer FaceTime calls on Windows and Android devices. You can't download a FaceTime app and initiate calls on those devices, but when the Apple user is on at least iOS 15, iPadOS 15 or macOS Monterey, FaceTime Links can be sent to non-Apple devices and answered on the Google Chrome web browser.

First of all, an Apple user needs to make a link using the Create Link button in FaceTime, then send it to the Android or Windows user, probably by email. When they get the link, they need to open it in Chrome. They can then join the FaceTime call in the usual way, right from their browser.

Group FaceTime Chats

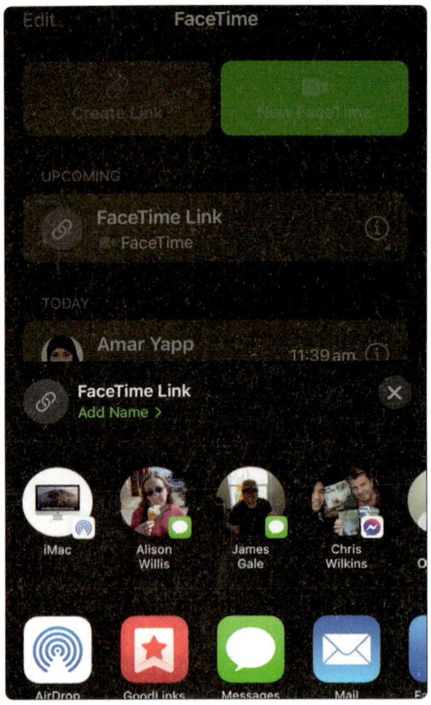

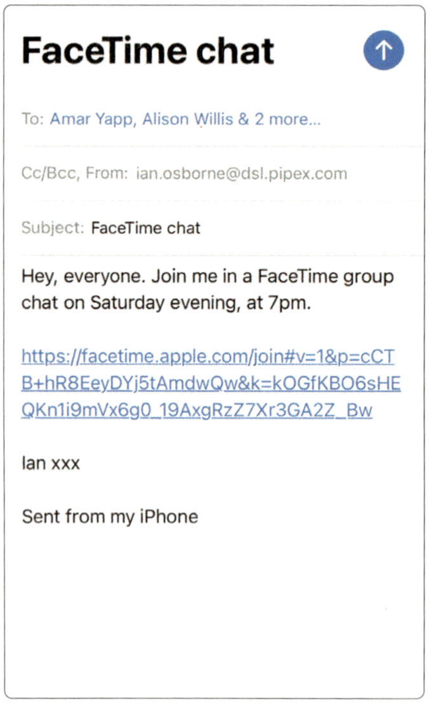

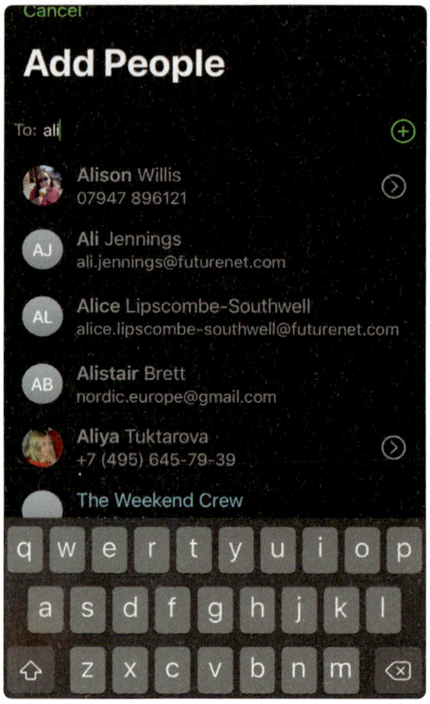

1 The easiest way to start a Group Chat is to open the FaceTime app, tap Create Link and then send it to those you want to invite, either by tapping Add Name or using the buttons below it to send it by email, Messages and more.

2 By swiping up, you can send the link via various apps. Recipients tap the link to join the chat. You can also copy the link and then send it to people you want to join a group chat at a later time; maybe by email or as a Calendar event.

3 During a one-to-one call, you can also invite another person to join. Tap the screen to show the FaceTime app's controls, swipe the control panel down and tap Add Person. Type their details and then tap send.

4 You can watch a group chat in Grid View. To switch between views, tap the screen to get the controls, tap the names of the people in the chat and tap the Grid View button.

5 You can even Group FaceTime from an Apple Watch or a HomePod speaker, though as these devices don't have built-in cameras, you are limited to audio chat only.

Handoff

As long as you're running at least iOS/iPadOS 16 and/or macOS Ventura, you can Handoff a FaceTime call to another Apple device. Just move the device you're calling on near to your iPhone, Mac or iPad, unlock the second device and look for the FaceTime icon appears. Tap/click on it, then tap/click the Switch button on the item you're calling on. The call – and connected Bluetooth earbuds or speakers – are transferred. It's great for when you're on a call while walking home, for example, and want to switch to your Mac when you arrive.

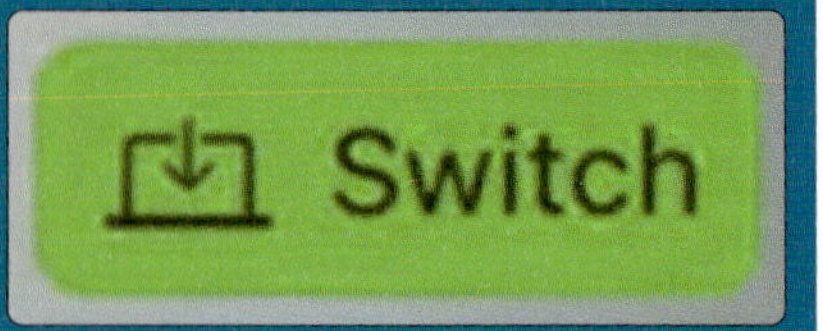

Mic Modes

There are new microphone modes to choose from in FaceTime audio calls. While in conversation, open the Control Centre in the usual way and tap the Mic Mode button. As well as the Standard option, you can also opt for Voice Isolation or Wide Spectrum. Voice Isolation focuses the outgoing sound on your own voice, cutting out ambient noise in the background. During a keynote demonstration, Apple successfully conducted a FaceTime call with a leaf blower being used in the background. Wide Spectrum does exactly the opposite, taking in sounds from all around the room, and not just your own voice. Just the thing if you have music on that you want to share over video chat, for example.

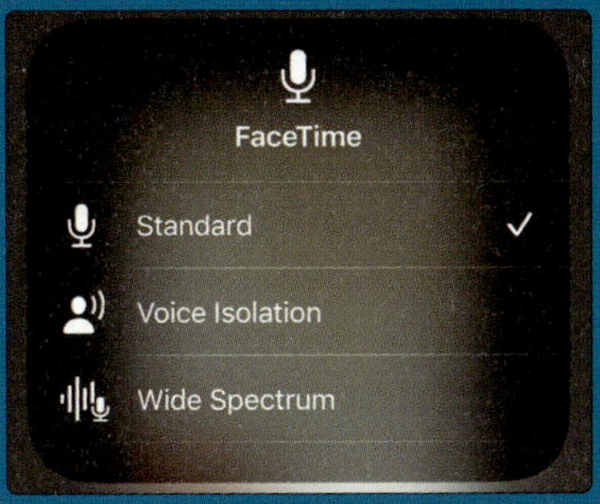

Live Captions

In iOS 16 (also iPadOS 16 and macOS Ventura), Apple introduces Live Captions, which appear in FaceTime calls using speech-to-text technology. To switch them on, go to Settings > Accessibility > Hearing > Live Captions, and switch it on. Requires iPhone 11 and later, iPad model with A12 Bionic and later, and Mac with Apple silicon.

Settings

In Settings > FaceTime, you can switch Speaking prominence on or off, depending on whether you want the person who last spoke to be more prominent, turn the Live Photos button on and off and also activate Eye Contact, which makes it look like a person is looking directly at you instead of at their own screen.

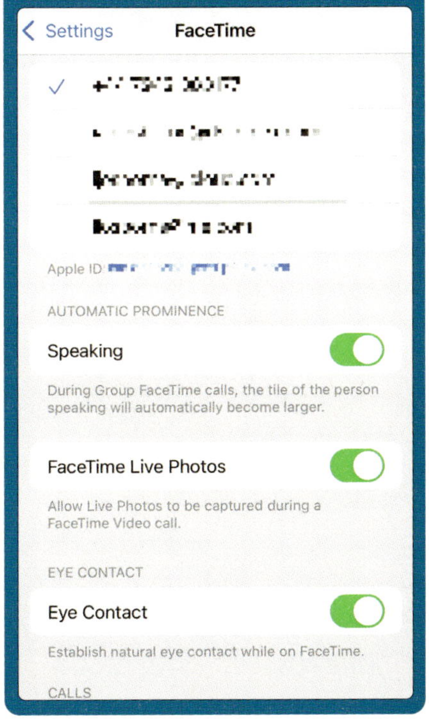

SharePlay

With SharePlay, you can get together with your friends to watch a movie or listen to an album together over FaceTime. During a FaceTime call, tap the SharePlay button (the one that looks like a person in the corner of a TV screen) to see a list of apps that you have installed on your iPhone that support SharePlay. Tap one of them to open it, and choose the movie, show, music or other type of media you'd like to share.

When you've chosen, the other person or people involved in the call are invited to SharePlay with you. This they can choose to do or not do, as they please. If they accept your SharePlay, your media is also played on their Apple device, with the FaceTime call still in operation. The media is played in sync, so there's no danger of someone (for example) announcing a movie spoiler just before everyone else has seen it.

Apps that are compatible with SharePlay include Music, Apple TV, TikTok and more. Obviously, to share something you're enjoying through a subscription service like Apple Music or Apple TV+, all parties have to be a subscriber.

The Home App

In iOS 16, Apple rebuilt the Home app from the ground up. It's now much more comfortable to use, allowing you to explore your connected devices with ease. It's great fun to control household appliances from your iPhone too.

HOME *in Focus*

1 Tap this waveform icon to record a message which is then sent to every intercom device connected to your Home app.

2 The Plus icon opens a pop-up, from which you can add a HomeKit-compatible accessory; or add a scene or group of instructions to your accessories activated with a single tap.

3 Tap here to access a list of your accessories, your Home settings, options to edit the Home view and reorder sections, and access to rooms you've set up with HomeKit accessories.

4 These status icons give important information gleaned from your HomeKit-compatible accessories. You can tell at a glance, for example, whether a light is on, what the temperature is or whether a motion sensor is picking up movement.

5 The Home app now groups connected cameras and shows them all in one place. Conversely, 'I'm Leaving' might turn them all off.

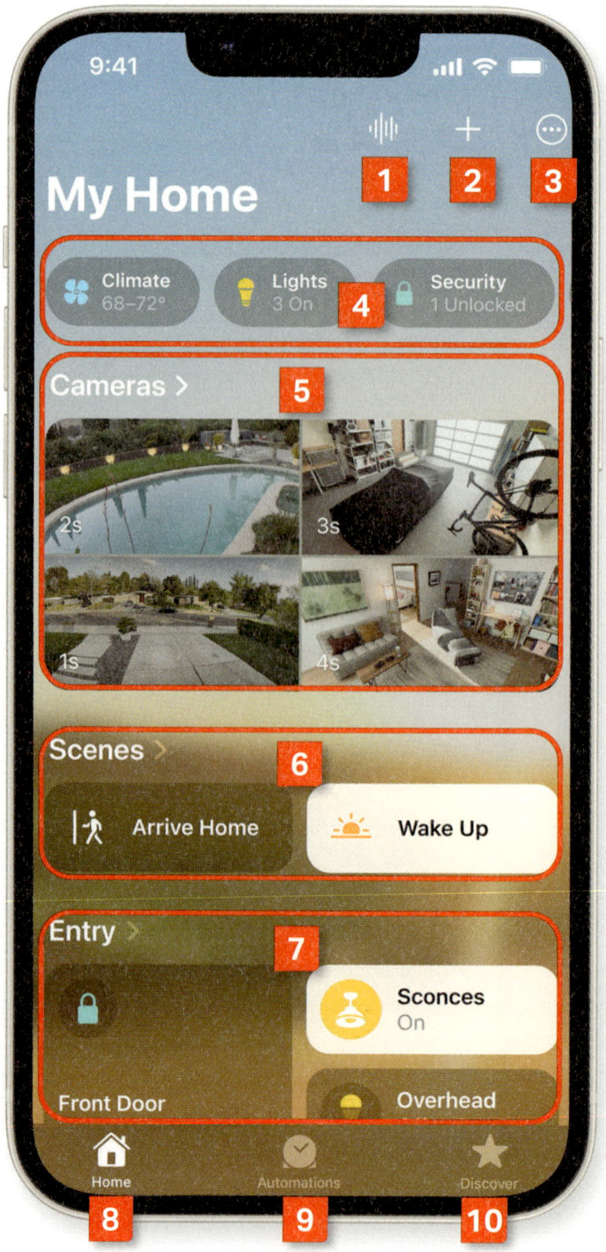

6 A scene is a series of actions activated together. For example, 'I'm Home' might turn on HomeKit-compatible lights, use a HomeKit-compatible plug socket to switch on the TV or stereo and turn on the heating. Conversely, 'I'm Leaving' might turn them all off.

7 Scroll the page up and you can see the various rooms you've set up with HomeKit-compatible gear, giving you access to the entire home directly from the Home tab.

8 The Home icon here takes you to your home's overview, as seen here. On this screen, you can add new scenes and accessories, as well as activating and controlling those you've already added.

9 Here you can set accessories to function automatically at given times or use Apple TV or HomePod to control them when your iPhone or other Apple devices aren't nearby, and more.

10 The Discover tab is where you learn more about the connected home and HomeKit. Take a look; there's plenty to learn.

Adding HomeKit accessories

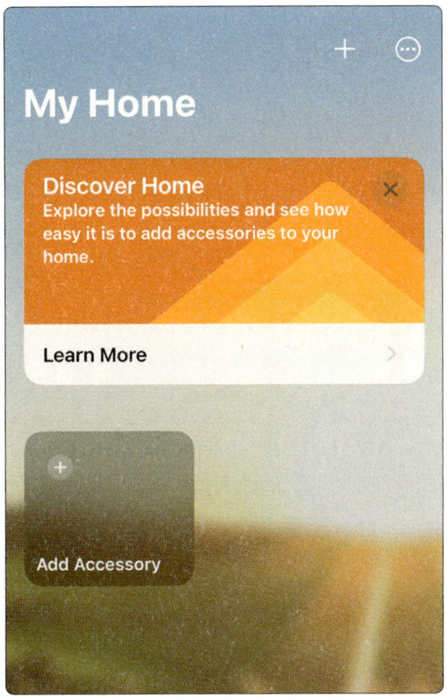

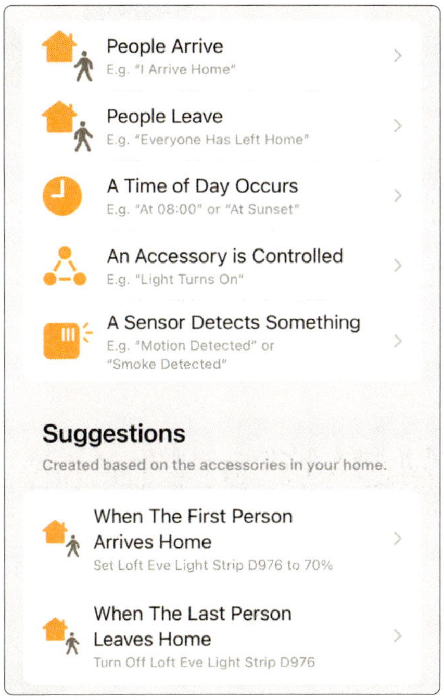

1 When you first open the Home app, you see this screen. The app is currently empty, as no accessories have been added. To change the name (currently My Home) or the wallpaper, tap the three-dots icon and select Home Settings.

2 On the Home screen, tap '+' then select the Add Accessory option. Use the iPhone's camera to scan the HomeKit Code that comes with the device; then follow the on-screen instructions to add it to your Home app.

3 The bottom middle icon (Automation) lets you set timers, actions and more. What these timers and actions do depends on what kit you've incorporated into your Home app. You need to read their instructions for details.

Using gadgets and scenes

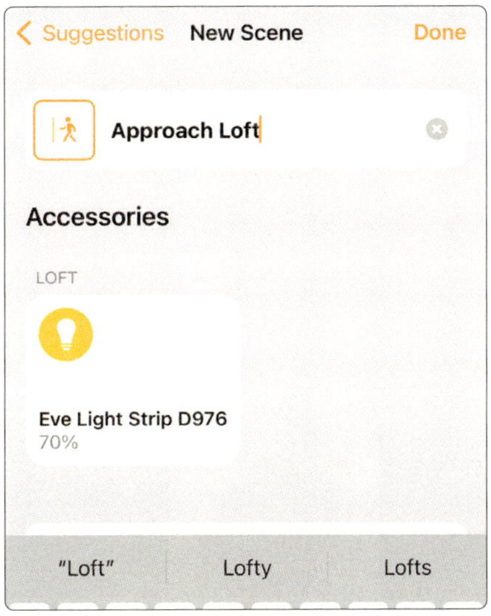

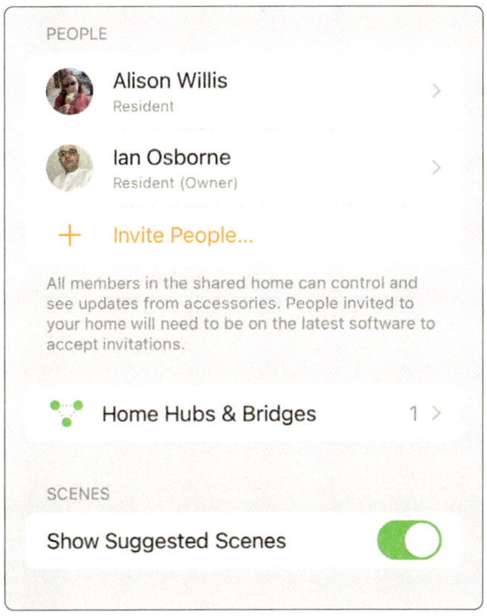

1 When you've added some accessories, you can access their controls directly from the Home app, without having to open their own companion app. You can also set up automations involving that particular gadget, again from their Home app controls.

2 To set up a scene, on the Home app's front page tap '+' and choose Add Scene. Give it a short title. Tap Add Accessories and choose which of your gadgets you want to include, and follow the on-screen instructions to construct a scene around them.

3 If more than one person in the house needs to control the HomeKit accessories, you can share Home app settings. In the Home tab, tap the three-dots icon and choose Home Settings. Under People, tap the Invite link to invite others to share your app.

The iTunes App

You can buy and download media for your iPhone at the iTunes Store. You can also buy or rent movies and TV shows and sample short snippets of songs before buying them. It's your one-stop shop for digital entertainment.

ITUNES *in Focus*

1 Tap here for a pop-up window that lets you filter music according to its genre. Available genres include Blues, Classical, Country, jazz, metal, rock, greatest hits and more. Choose the Tones option to view ringtones.

2 Tap the Featured tab to see what's hot and what's new. The Charts tab gives you the best selling songs, albums and music videos on the iTunes Store.

3 Tap here for your wish list, songs you've identified using Siri (see the Siri guide for more details) and tracks you listened to as previews.

4 Scroll this line of albums left and right for more options, or tap See All to open the New Music page.

5 The iTunes Store's shop window. Tap a price to buy a song or album or tap the cover or name of the item for more details. On the information screen, you can also play a sample of the song by tapping its name.

6 This icon opens the iTunes Store's Music page. This is where you can buy new music to listen to on your iPhone.

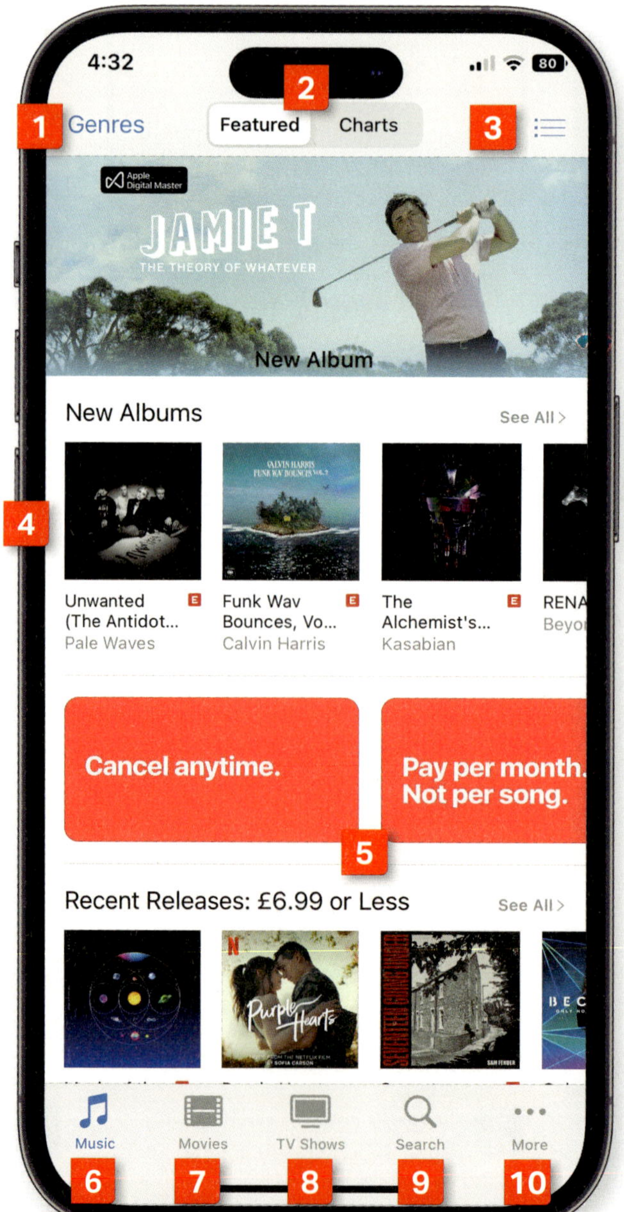

7 Tap here if you're interested in buying or renting movies. This part of the iTunes Store adds a rental option for renting movies instead of buying.

8 This icon takes you to the TV Shows section, where you can buy individual shows or an entire season of a programme you like.

9 The Search option. It searches throughout the iTunes Store, so search results can potentially show music, movies, TV shows, books and more, regardless of where you were in the store when you did the search.

10 This icon gives access to the ringtones section of the store, the Genius option for suggestions of new music, movies and TV, a list of purchased items and a view of your current downloads from the App Store.

iTunes Store Gift cards

You can redeem an iTunes Store Gift Card by scrolling up and tapping Redeem at the foot of the screen.

The App Store App

The App Store is where you download and install new apps for your iPhone. You can get games, productivity software, entertainment applications and more. Many App Store apps are free too.

APP STORE *in Focus*

1 The App Store's Today screen gives you the pick of the best of the new releases, chosen every day by Apple's editors. Scroll up for the apps that were chosen on previous days.

2 Tap here to get to your account details, redeem a card, send an app as a gift, update apps, and check on the apps you've previously purchased, or sign out of the App Store.

3 These are the apps, and a feature highlighting a range of apps, that have been chosen by Apple's editors as the choice of the day. Tap one for information on that particular app, and the opportunity to get it.

4 Tap here to get to the Today screen, as seen here. The Today screen is a great way of finding out what's new and exciting on the App Store, so you will probably want to visit it often.

5 Gaming apps have their own category, which you reach by tapping the Games icon.

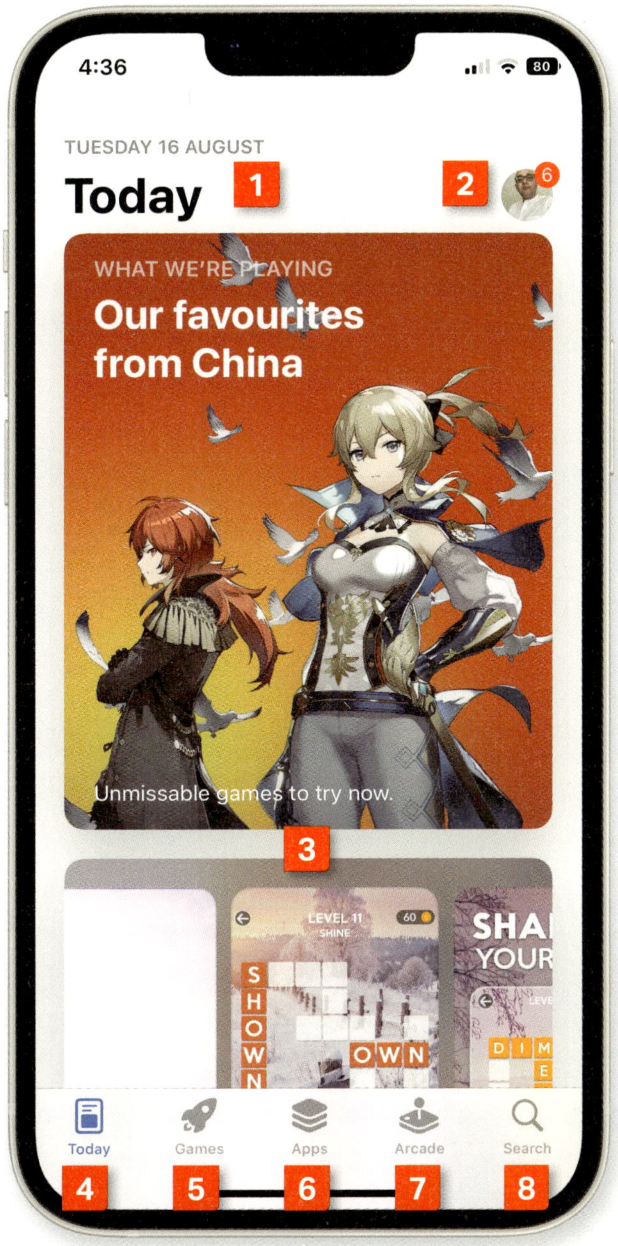

6 Tapping the Apps icon takes you to the apps page, where you find non-gaming apps. Scroll up and down and browse by category if you wish. Scroll this page all the way to the bottom to redeem iTunes gift cards.

7 This icon takes you to the Apple Arcade subscription service. For a set monthly fee of £4.99/$4.99/4,99 €, you can play ad-free games on Macs, iOS devices, iPads and Apple TV. You can play as many or as few as you want. It's a little like Apple Music, but for great gaming experiences.

8 You can search for an app or a game using the search field. You can search for an app by name, by what it does (e.g. word processor), by the developer and more.

Updates

If you're not using automatic updates, when app updates are available, a badge appears on the App Store icon and also next to Item 2.

The Find My App

The Find My app arose from the fusion of two older applications, Find My Friends and Find My iPhone. With it, you can find lost or stolen Apple devices, including iPhones, iPads and Macs, and wipe them clean if they're lost for good. You can also locate your friends or family members on the map; just the thing if you're all on a day out and at risk of losing each other.

The People tab

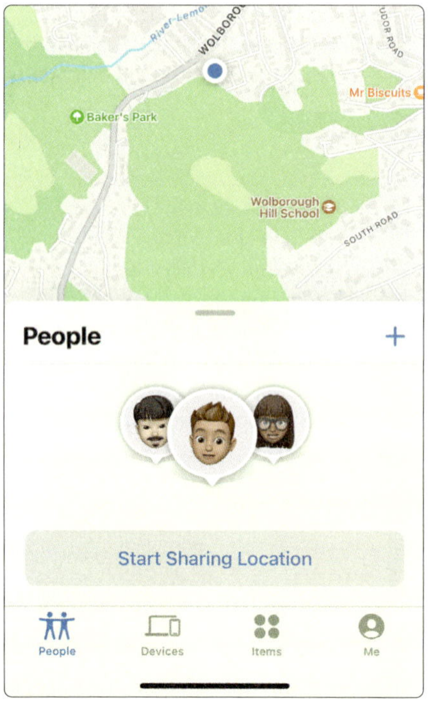

1 Tap the People icon at the foot of the screen. To start sharing your location with friends or family members, tap Start Sharing Location. Enter the name, Apple ID email, or phone number of the person you want to share with.

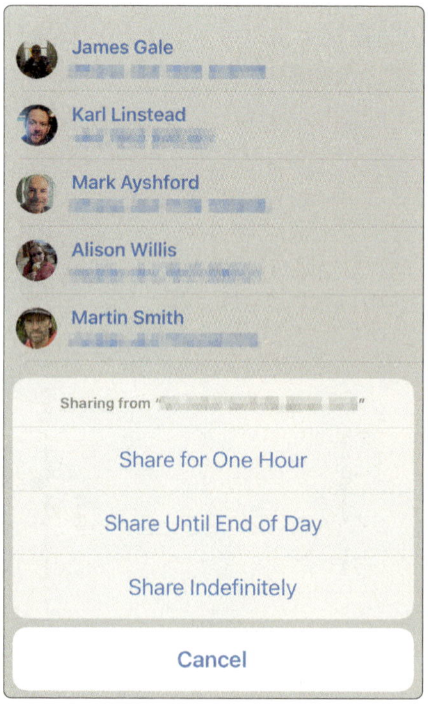

2 As is usual, you can tap the + sign to the right and select a person from your Contacts app. Add as many people as you wish, and tap the Send link. Then you can choose whether to share for an hour, the rest of the day or indefinitely.

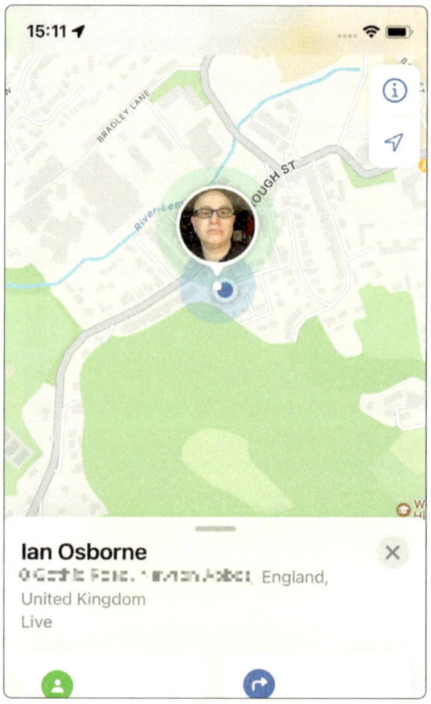

3 The people you shared your location with can now see you as a blue spot on the map. Pinch and spread to zoom in and out. Tap a name for options. From here, you can tap Contact to bring up their card from your Contacts app.

Returning the favour

When someone shares their location with you, you're given a notification. Tap this and you can quickly and easily choose to return the favour, and share your location with them.

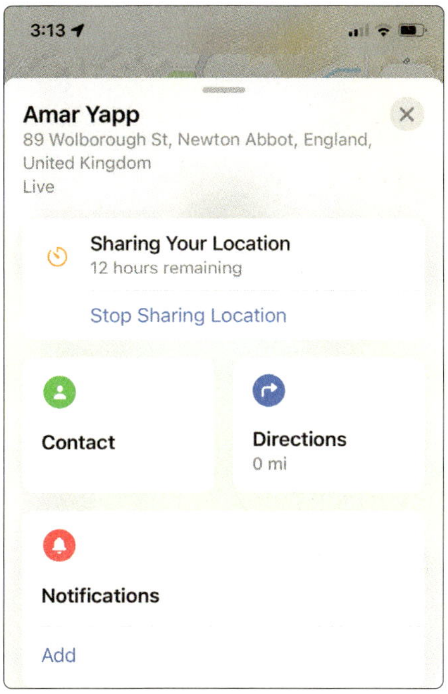

4 Other options available on this screen are: ask for their location, stop sharing your own or remove them from the people you're sharing with. Tap Notifications to let them know when you leave or arrive.

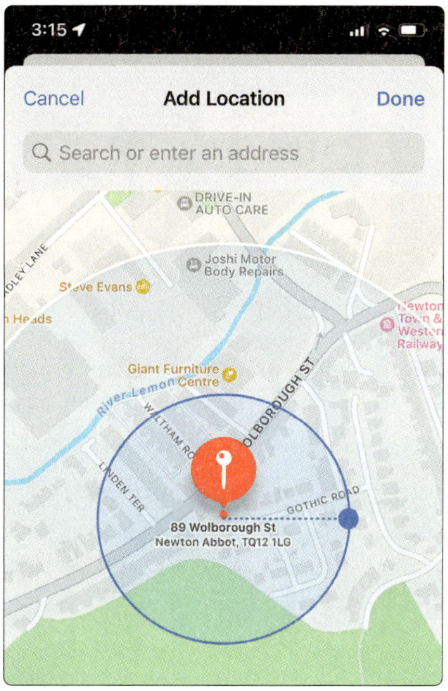

5 Still on the Notifications screen, tap the name of someone whose location you're sharing, then tap one of the options atop the screen. You can choose a location and be notified when they leave, arrive or is not there.

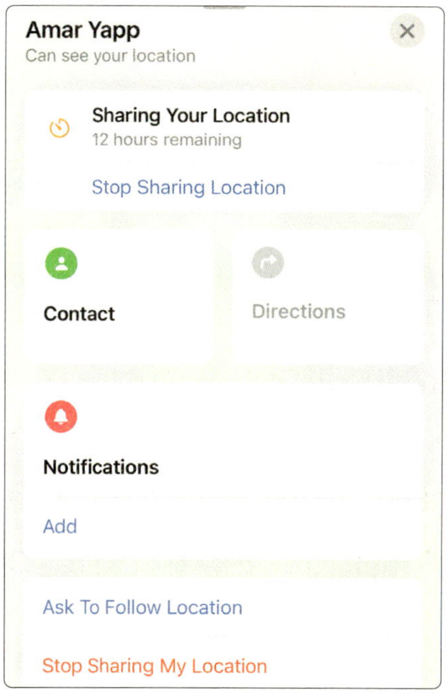

6 Tap a friend's name, that isn't currently sharing their own location with you, and then tap Ask To Follow Location to request they do so. If they comply, they also appear on the map, along with yourself and others who are sharing.

Devices and Items

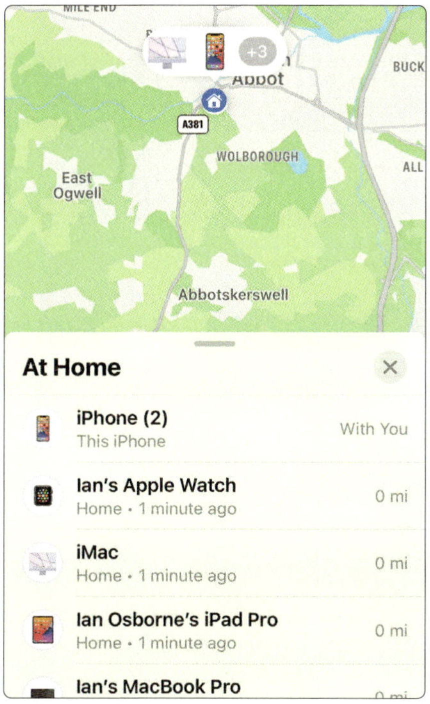

1 You can trace the location of your devices, such as Macs, iPads and iPhones, through the Devices icon at the foot of the screen. Items such as AirPods and AirTags, are located using the Items icon.

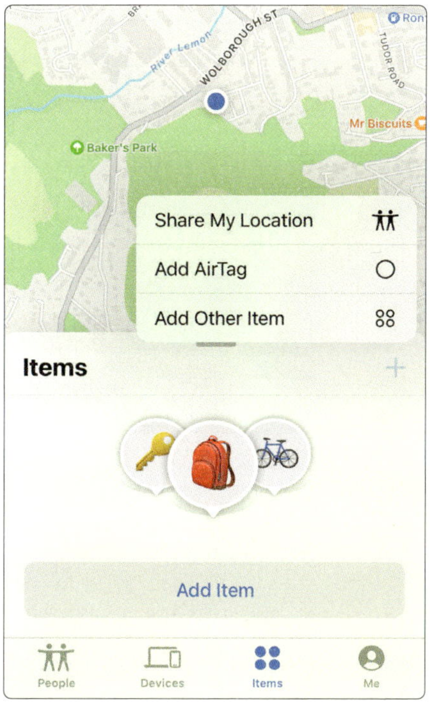

2 Devices shows Apple gear signed into the same Apple ID as your iPhone. Items must be added manually; tap Items at the foot of the screen, tap '+' and follow the on-screen and supplied instructions.

The Me tab

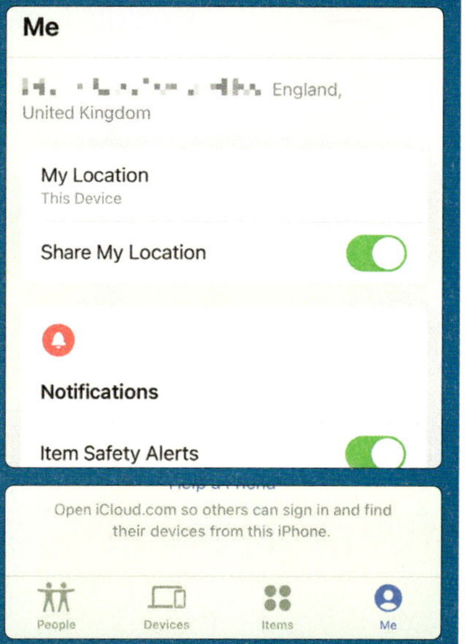

Tap the Me tab at the foot of the screen for a range of options and info. You're told where you are, given the option of naming that location (work, home, school, and so on), and can also stop sharing your location too.

Your iPhone's Advanced Functions

Are you ready to take things further? Your iPhone's advanced features are great, and make your life much easier. iCloud Drive and the Files app let you store your data online, you can organise and delete existing apps as well as downloading new ones, use features like Live Text and Siri, and more.

Done
THU 25
Messages
Calendar
Photos
Weather
Camera
iTunes Store
Stocks
Maps
News
Reminders
Clock
Notes
Books
App Store
Health
Home
Wallet
Settings
Watch

iCloud Drive

iCloud Drive is Apple's own cloud computing service and it comes free with the iPhone. With iCloud Drive, you can sync your documents across all of your Apple devices and even access them through a web browser; they're all found on your iPhone in the Files application. If your free space isn't enough, you can buy more for a set monthly fee.

An introduction to iCloud Drive and the Files app

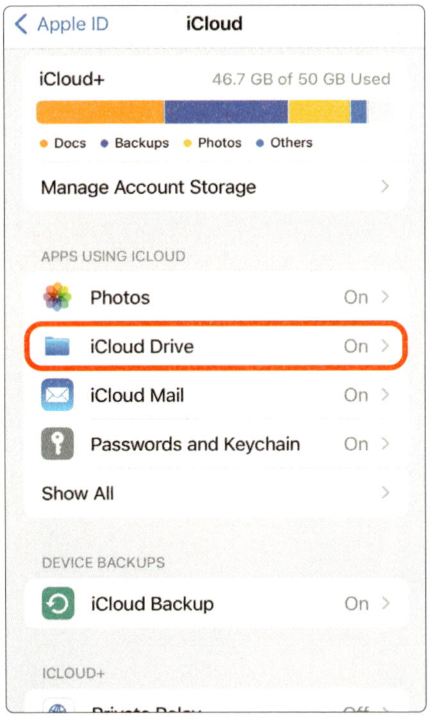

1 In the Settings app, tap your name at the top of the screen, tap iCloud and scroll down to iCloud Drive. If it isn't on already, turn it on. You can now save your files in the cloud and access them from any Internet device.

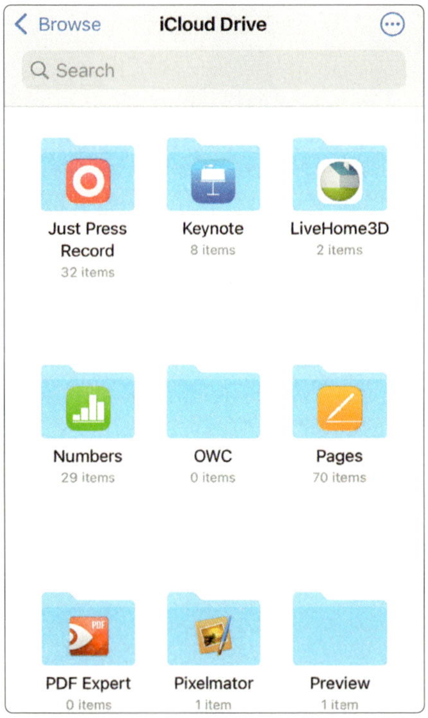

2 Open the Files app and under Locations, tap iCloud Drive. Here you see the files stored on your iCloud Drive, arranged by their apps. iCloud Drive is also accessible through other Apple devices, and www.icloud.com.

3 You can open an iCloud document on your iPhone, if you have the iPhone version of the app that created it. Just open the folder for the app in question (here we're looking at Pages) and tap a document to open it.

Documents contained in your iCloud Drive are kept in sync across your devices. If you make a change on one device, when you open that particular document on another, that change is already there. So, for example, you can work on a document on your Mac at home, then edit it on your iPhone on the bus.

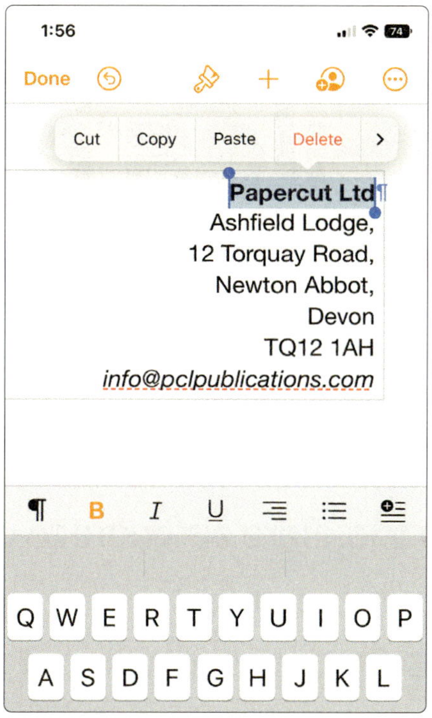

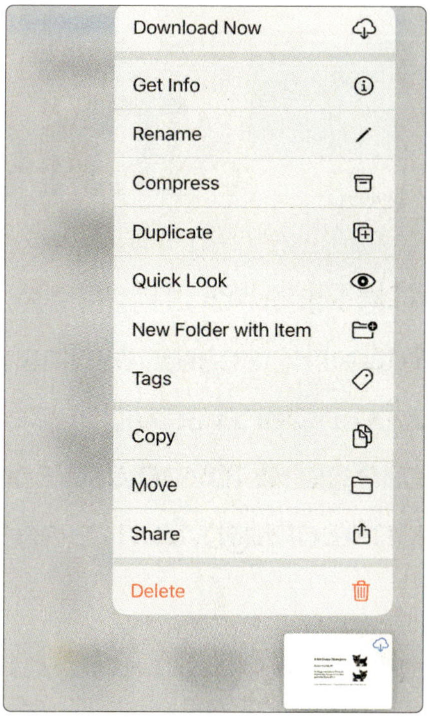

4 When you open an iCloud document on your iPhone, it's downloaded to your smartphone. It then opens in the usual way, so you can edit, modify and generally work on the document on your iPhone.

5 Edits and changes you make on the iPhone are also made on the cloud copy of the document. This means if you edit it on the go on your phone, then open it on your Mac at home, the changes are there.

6 Tap and hold a document until you get the pop-up menu. From here, you can copy the document, duplicate it, delete it, rename it, share it, move it to another folder, and more. If you don't see all the options, scroll up and down.

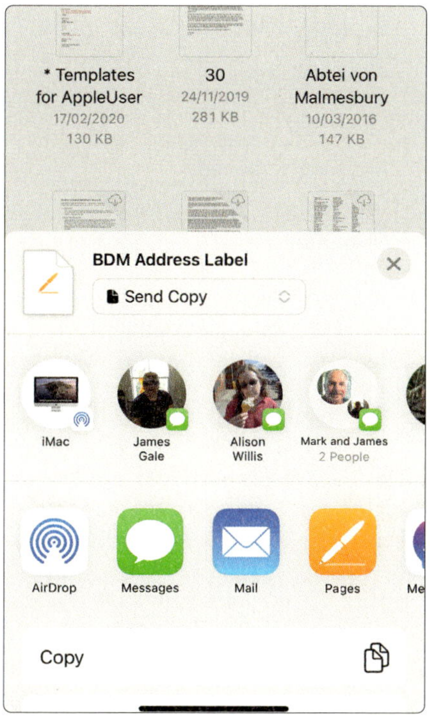

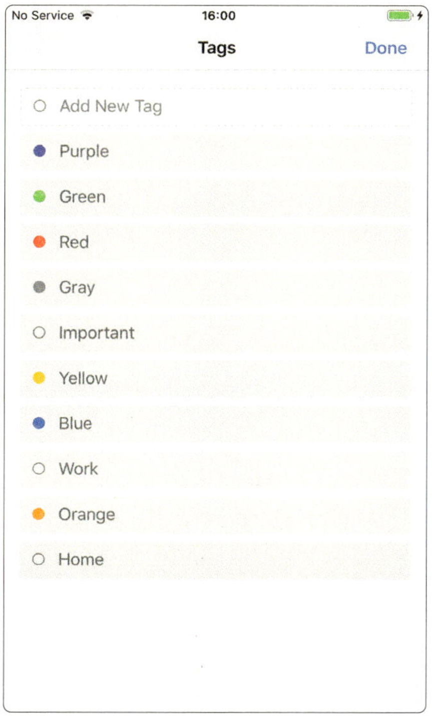

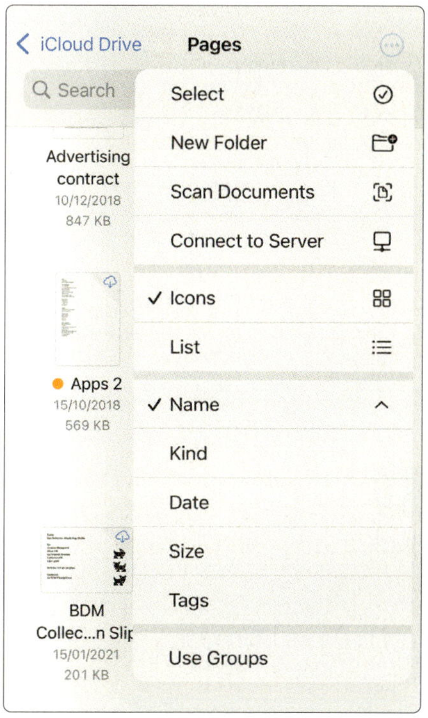

7 This pop-up menu also lets you share a document, right from your Files app. You can email it, add it to Notes, send it to another Apple device with AirDrop and let others collaborate on it using Add People.

8 The menu that pops up when you tap and hold iCloud docs also lets you tag a document with a coloured icon. Tagged documents can be found by tapping their colour in the Tags section in the Browse window.

9 Open an iCloud Drive folder and tap the three-dots icon in the top-right corner, above the search field. This opens a menu from where you can create a new folder, connect to an external server, change how document icons are displayed and more.

The Files App

The Files app boasts an impressive range of features. It boasts excellent, Mac-like searches, the ability to read external drives, sharing folders and zipping and unzipping files, which is great for sending them by email. You can use it to browse and download the files you have stored in your iCloud Drive cloud storage space too. Here's a guide to getting more from Files.

Features of the Files app

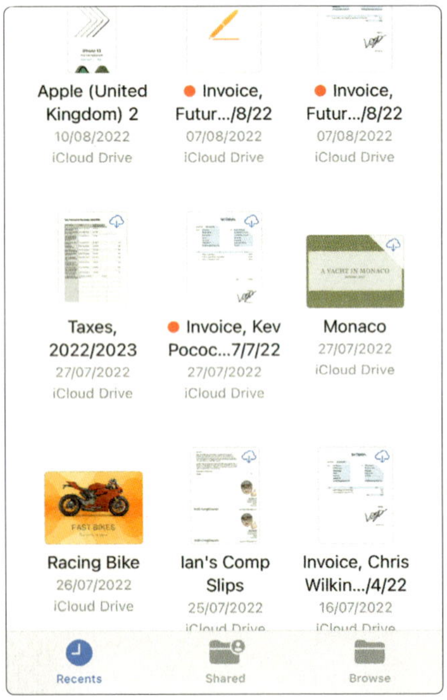

1 When you first open the Files app, you see three icons at the foot of the screen. The Recents icon shows you documents you've recently opened, and Shared gives access to those you've shared with other people. The Browse icon lets you look through your files.

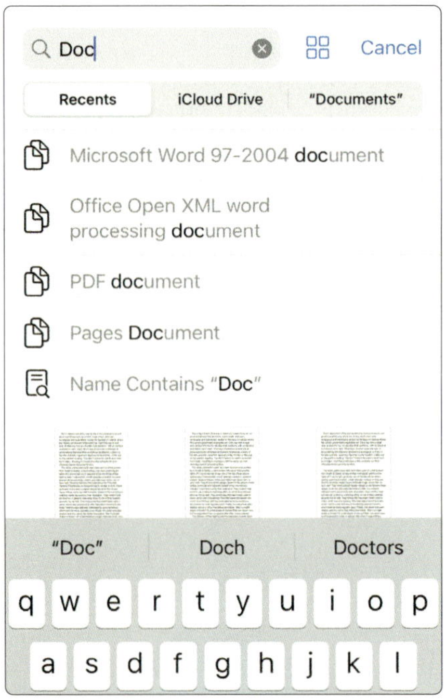

2 The Files app has an improved search facility. You can restrict your search to recents, files on iCloud Drive, or the specific app whose folder you've opened, and can also add 'tokens' to restrict the search to (for example) specific file types or production dates (e.g. 'last week').

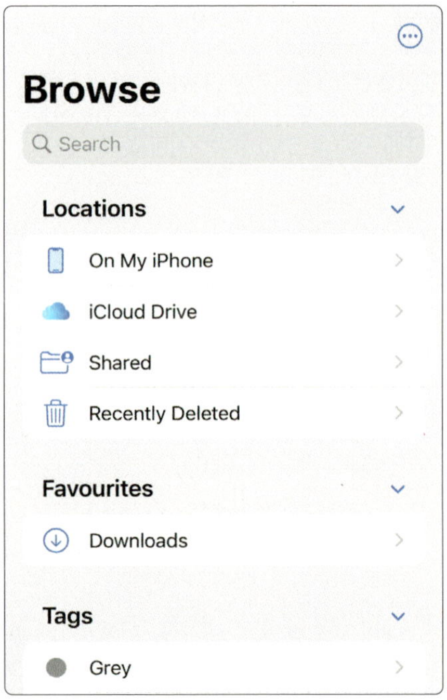

3 The first four options on the Browse screen include On My iPhone (documents you've stored locally) iCloud Drive (documents stored on your iCloud service), Shared (files shared with you) and Recently Deleted (recover things you've deleted in error).

The Cloud icon

If a document is stored on your iCloud but not on your iPhone, there's a Cloud icon in the top right corner of its thumbnail. Tap the thumbnail to download the document to your iPhone, and then open it so you can edit and modify it on your phone, with your changes synced to iCloud.

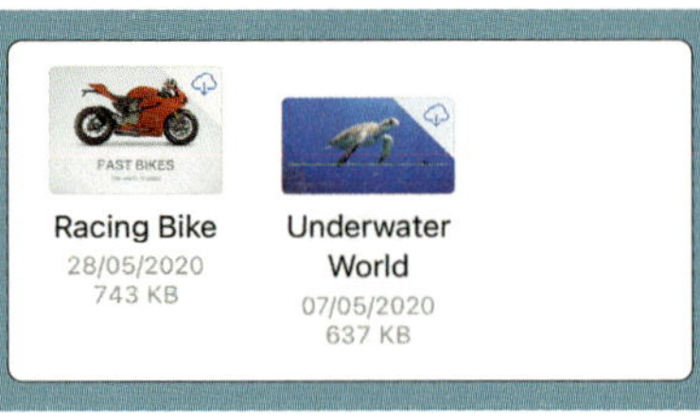

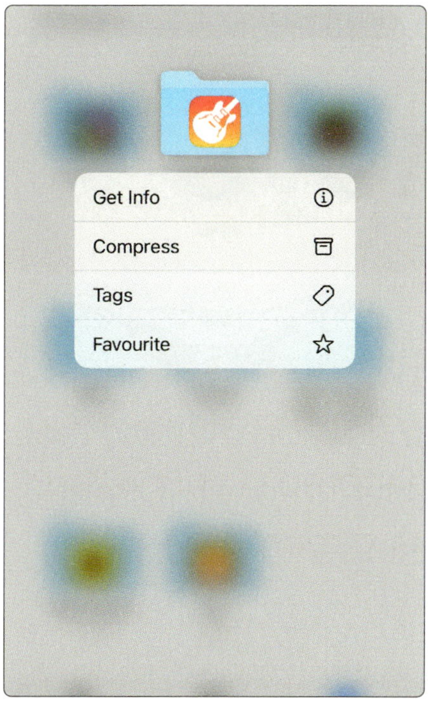

4 Tap and hold a folder in the Files app for a pop-up menu. Tap Favourites to add the folder to your Favourites. These appear on the first page of the Browse page, for easy access. To remove the item from Favourites, tap and hold the folder in iCloud Drive and then tap Unfavourite.

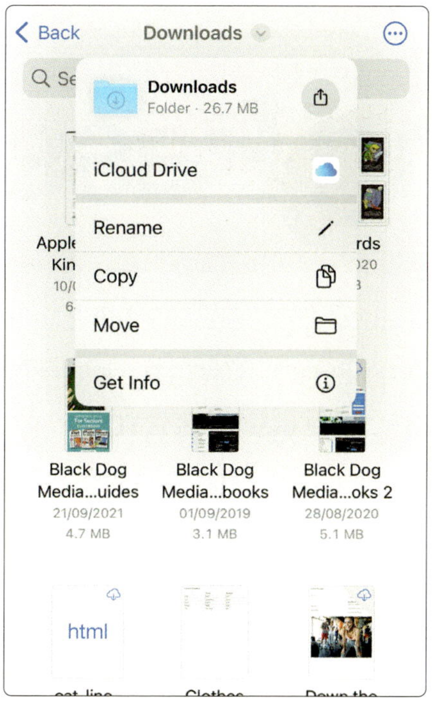

5 The Downloads folder, which is in iCloud Drive, and also your Favourites by default, shows items you've downloaded on your iPhone, from Safari for example. These items are, of course, synced with your Mac and other iOS devices, where they're also found in Downloads.

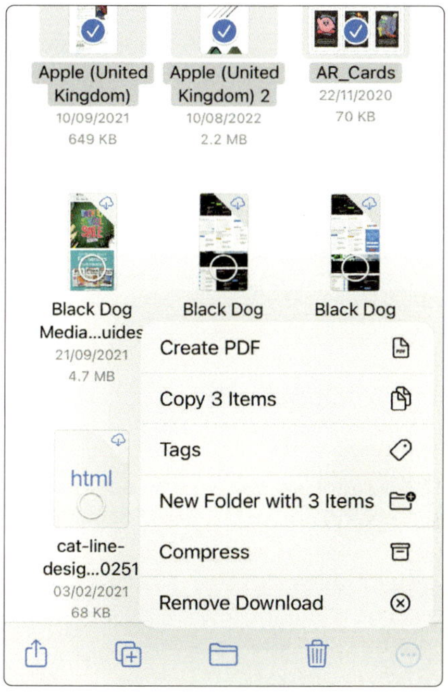

6 Tap the three-dots icon (top right) then Select on the pop-up menu. Tap one or more items or folders. A group of icons appear at the foot of the screen. You can share, duplicate, move, or delete selected files. The new three-dots icon (bottom right) brings up a contextual menu.

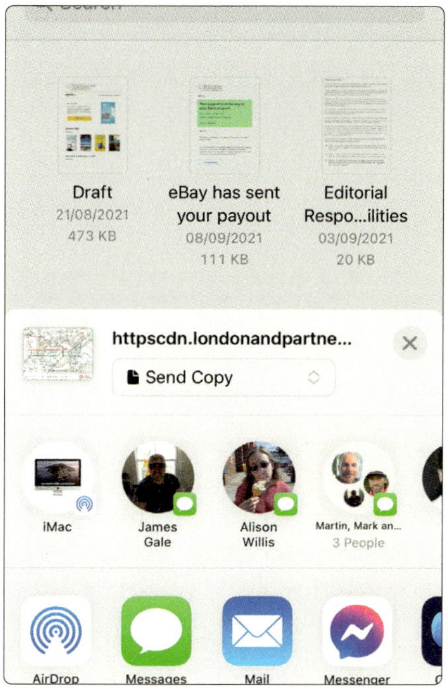

7 To share a document stored on your iCloud with other people, tap and hold it, then tap Share in the pop-up. Choose a method of sharing, such as Mail, Messages, AirDrop and more. Choose the iWorks app that created the document and a collaboration option is available.

Compress files

You can compress a folder by tapping and holding it and then selecting Compress from the pop-up menu. To compress a group of files, tap the three-dots icon (top right), select them, tap the three-dots icon in the bottom right, then select the Compress option.

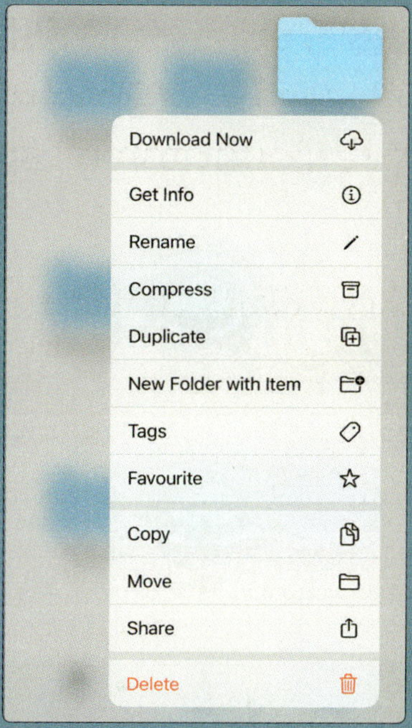

A compressed archive is shown as a Zip file. Tap to uncompress it, or tap and hold it for the pop-up menu, which again lets you carry out a range of tasks. Zipping files and then tapping the pop-up's Share option is great for sending a group of files by Messages, email or more.

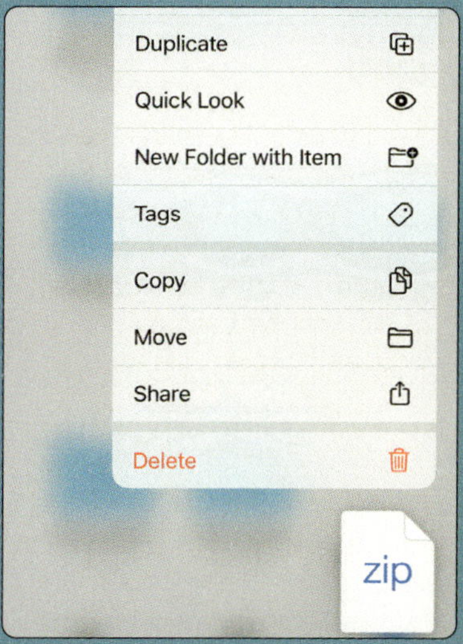

Using Passkeys

Having to log into websites and apps can be annoying, but with Passkeys, the procedure is greatly simplified. A feature arriving with iOS 16, iPadOS 16 and macOS 13: Ventura, Passkeys is a new authentication method that uses Touch ID or Face ID to sign in. Passkeys are synced through iCloud, and you can even use them on non-Apple devices using a QR code.

Sign in with Passkeys

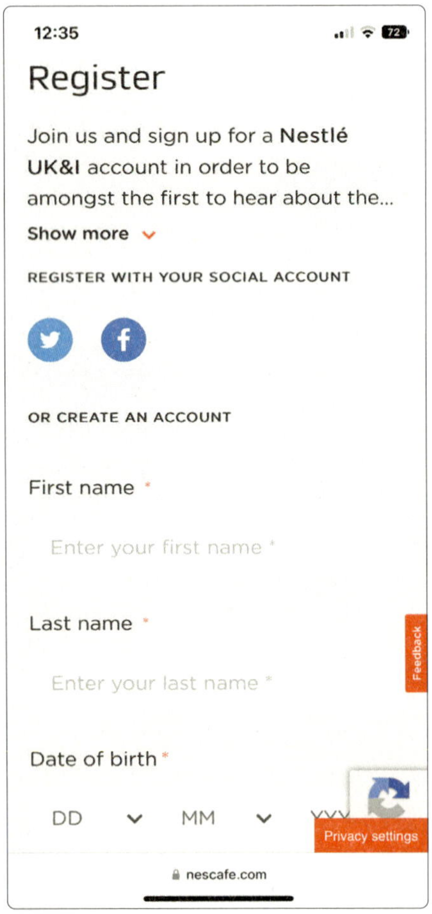

1 If you don't already have an account on the site you're trying to use, create one in the usual way, with a username and a password. Procedure differs from site to site, so follow the on-screen instructions to register an account.

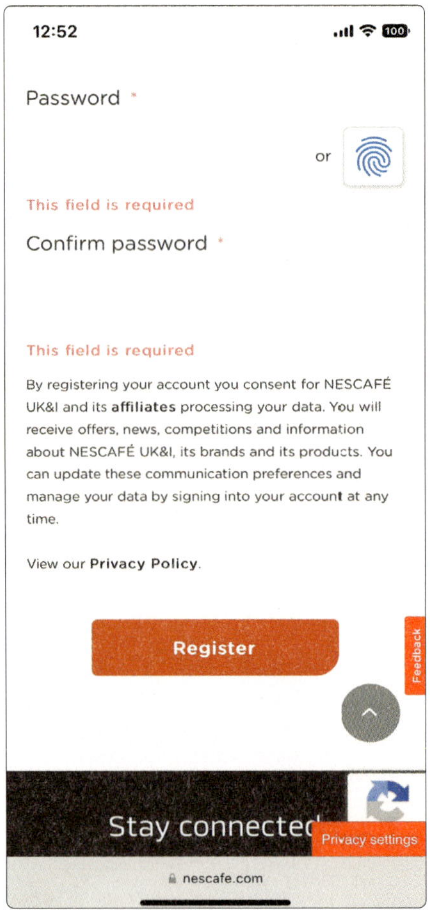

2 Once again, details vary from site to site, but on the Nestlé site, you can add a Passkey instead of entering and re-entering a passcode. All you have to do is tap the fingerprint icon instead of entering passwords into the password field.

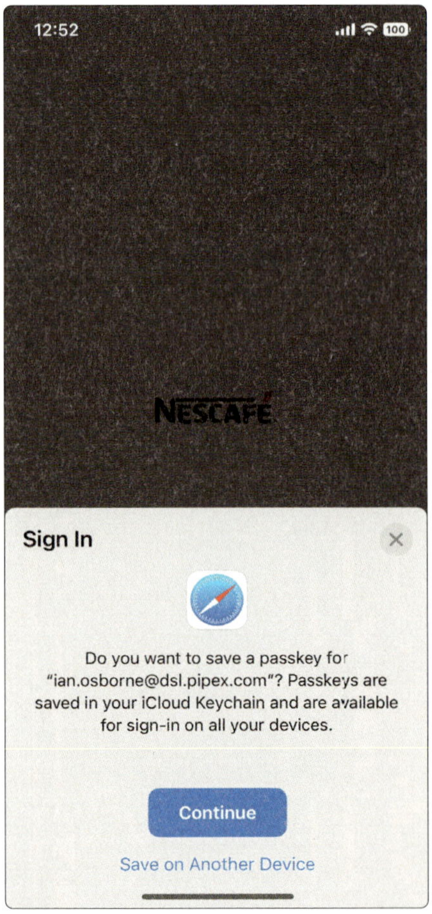

3 The site invites us to set up a Passkey for the site and the account in question. When this is done, the Passkey is saved in your iCloud Keychain, and therefore are available for use on all your compatible devices. Tap Continue.

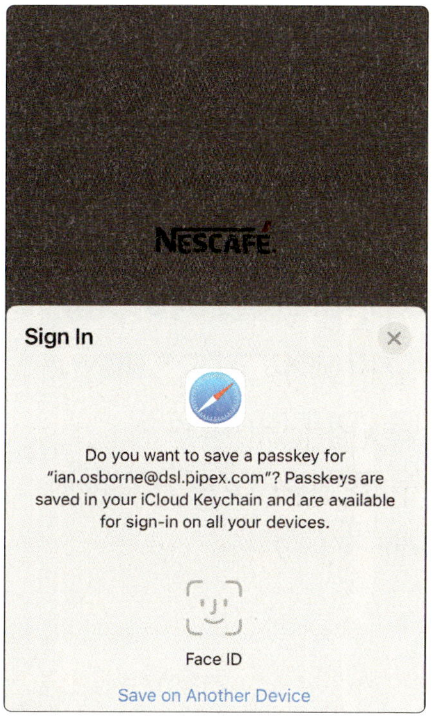

4 We're now invited to log in using the iPhone's Face ID feature. All you have to do is point the front-facing TrueDepth camera at your face, and Face ID confirms your identity. A tick confirms this, and you move to the next stage.

5 You must now prove you're a human being, and not an automated sign-up bot trying to register accounts with the site for malicious purposes. Just follow the on-screen instructions, and select the images as instructed, then tap Verify.

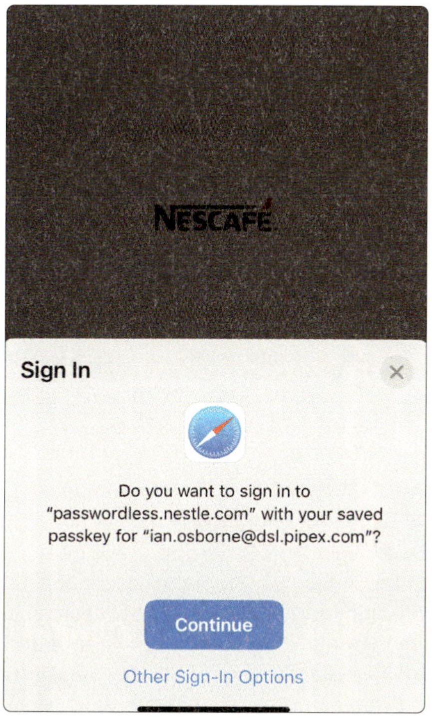

6 To complete our registration, we have to open an email sent by the site. Tap a key to complete your registration. Next time you want to log in to the site in question, you're invited to do so using your passkey. Tap Continue to do so.

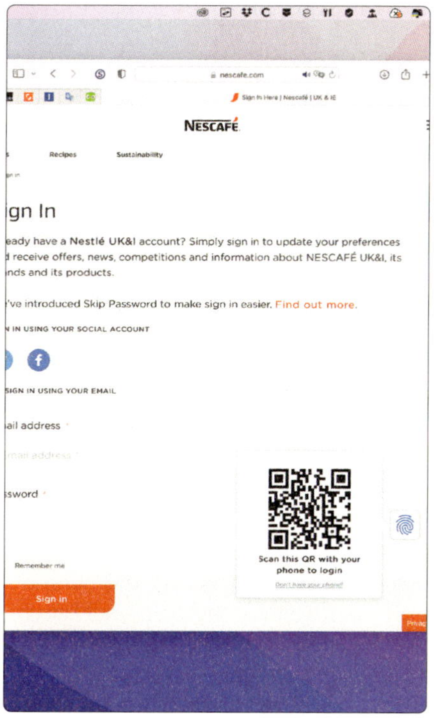

7 Logging in on our Mac, we clicked the fingerprint option. We were invited to scan a QR code on our iPhone, which got us in through Face ID. If you don't have your phone handy, they can send you a 'Magic Link' instead.

More about Passkeys

Passkeys can only be used on websites that have made them available. On Passkeys-compatible websites, you can log on using your Face ID, Touch ID or device's passcode, without having to enter your username and password. This has a number of advantages. As your Passkey never leaves your device, phishing attacks – whereby a user is conned into giving away his or her login details – are almost impossible. And because the Passkey information is never kept on an external server, it can't be leaked after a hacking attack on the website either. All in all, it's more secure than using a username and a password to log in.

A Passkey digital key is unique to the site it was created for. You have to create Passkeys on a per-site basis, but this isn't any great problem. Once it's been made, it can be used on the site it was created for as often as you like. Passkeys are designed to work in apps as well as on the web, but again, the developer has to make them available. Because they're cross platform, you can use your Passkeys on a Mac, iPad and Apple TV as well as on your iPhone, though these devices must be running macOS Ventura/iPadOS 16/ iOS 16 too.

Passkeys can be used on non-Apple devices too, as long as you have your iPhone with you. You can sign in on these devices using your iPhone, by scanning in a QR code, and then unlocking with Face ID or Touch ID. It's simple.

Apple hopes Passkeys will eventually take over from passwords completely over time, but at the moment they're only available on a limited number of sites, including BestBy, Nestcafé, Namecheap, Cloudflare, GitHub, Bitwarden, AOL, Dropbox, Facebook, GoDaddy, Google, ID.me, Twitter, WordPress and more. Naturally, further websites – and apps – will be added over time.

Stay Organised

If you want to upgrade your iPhone to the free iOS 16 operating system, follow this guide. It's always a good idea to keep iOS and your apps up to date, to take advantage of new features. Upgrading your iPhone's operating system is as easy as following these simple steps, which work whenever Apple releases a new version of iOS for your iPhone.

Updating iOS and Apps

1 When a new version of iOS is available, the Settings app is badged. Open it, go to General > Software Update and your iPhone checks with Apple to check if there's a new version for you. If there is, it gives you an option to Download and Install. Tap the link to do so.

2 The update downloads. When advised to do so, tap Install Now; you might need to connect your iPhone to a power source if the battery is low. After your update has installed, your iPhone restarts. Of course, if you turn on Automatic Updates, all this is done for you.

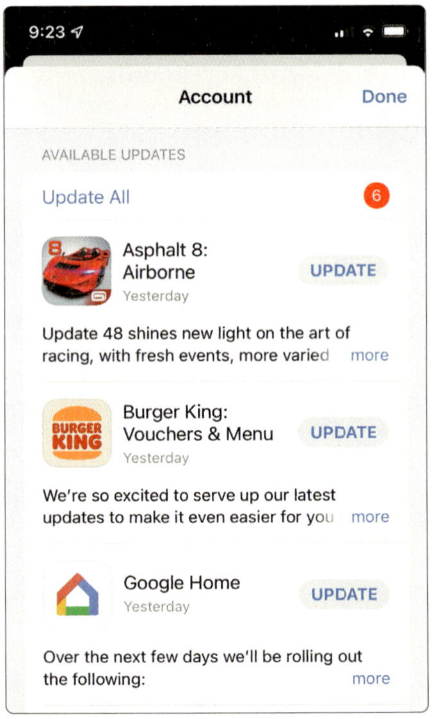

3 When app updates are available, your App Store app is badged. Open it, and tap the badged icon in the top-right corner. On the next screen, you can update individual apps by tapping their Update button, or tap the Update All link to update all the apps at once.

The iPhone's iOS operating system is regularly updated, as are the apps that run on it. New updates can bring new features, and also fix bugs that might have caused problems with the older version of the app or iOS, so it's always worth keeping your iPhone up-to-date. It's best to do this at home on your Wi-Fi network, so you don't use up your mobile data downloading new versions of apps.

Arranging apps

1 To change the order of the app icons on your home screen, first of all, tap and hold on an individual app. A pop-up window appears.

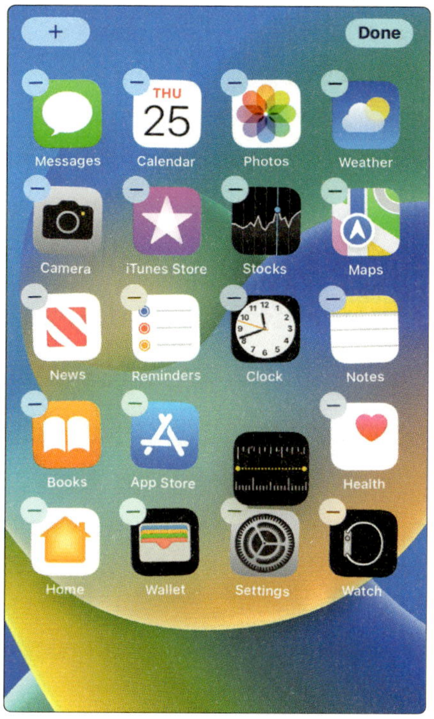

2 Tap Edit Home Screen. The app icons wobble and show a X in the corner. You can drag them to rearrange. Tap Done when you've finished.

Deleting apps

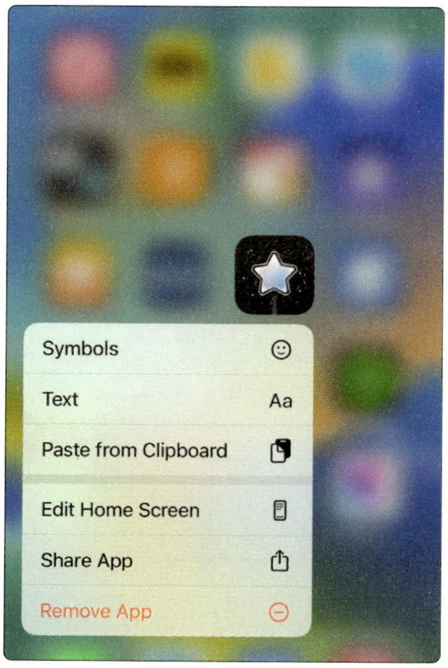

1 The simplest way to delete an app or widget is to tap and hold its icon and, from the pop-up menu, select the Delete App option. It disappears.

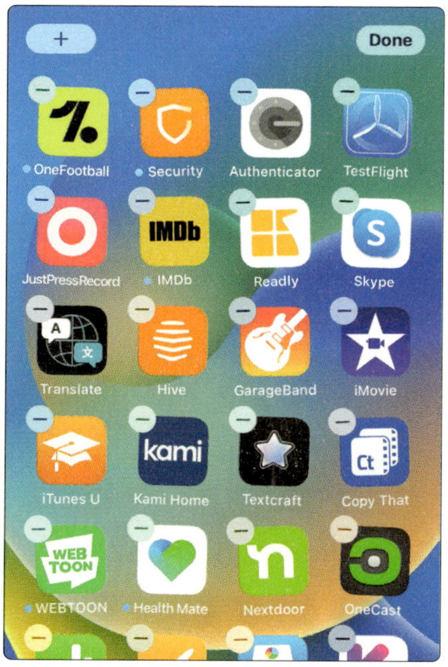

2 If you have several to delete, tap Edit Home Screen instead. Tap the - on every app or widget you want to delete, then tap Done (top right).

Offloading apps

If you need to delete an app without losing its data, go to Settings > General > iPhone Storage. Scroll down and tap the app you want to offload.

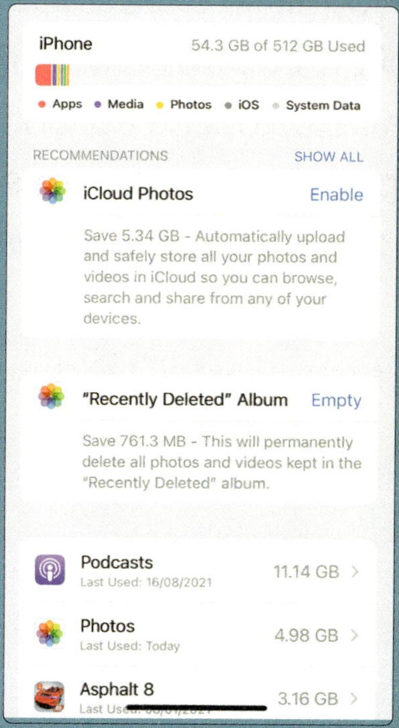

Tap Offload App and the app itself is removed, but data such as your settings or saved games are not. When you download the app again, it's still there.

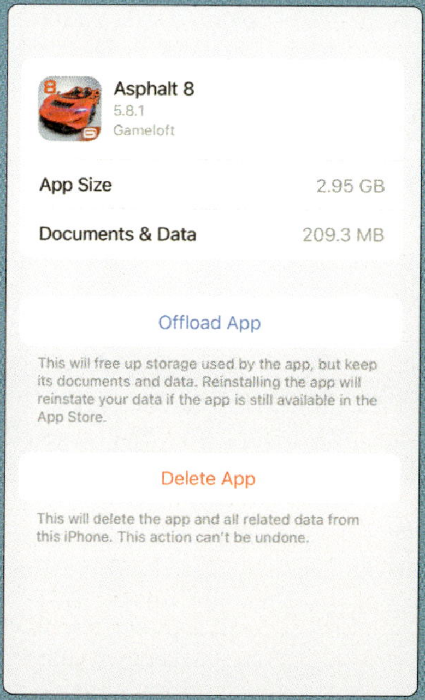

Using Live Text

Live Text is a great feature that lets your iPhone identify and copy editable text from your environment, simply by pointing your camera at it. You can also copy text from photographs you've already taken. When you've copied the text, you can paste it into any app that uses editable words, such as Notes, Mail, Messenger and more. You can even copy handwriting.

Using Live Text

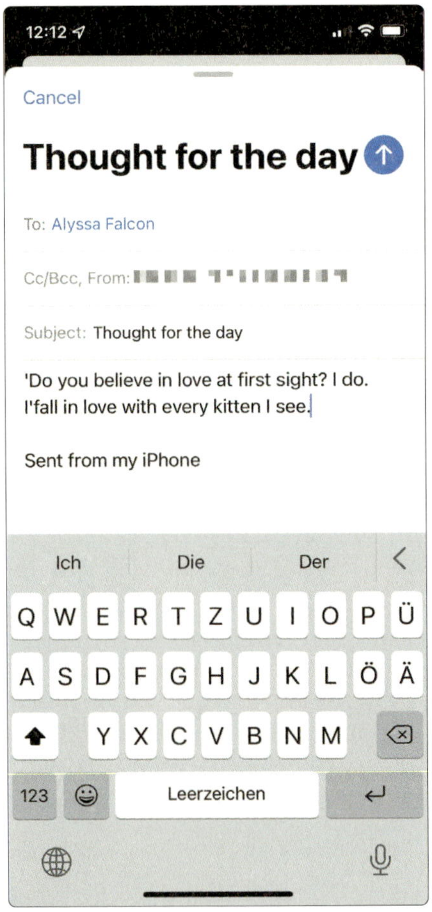

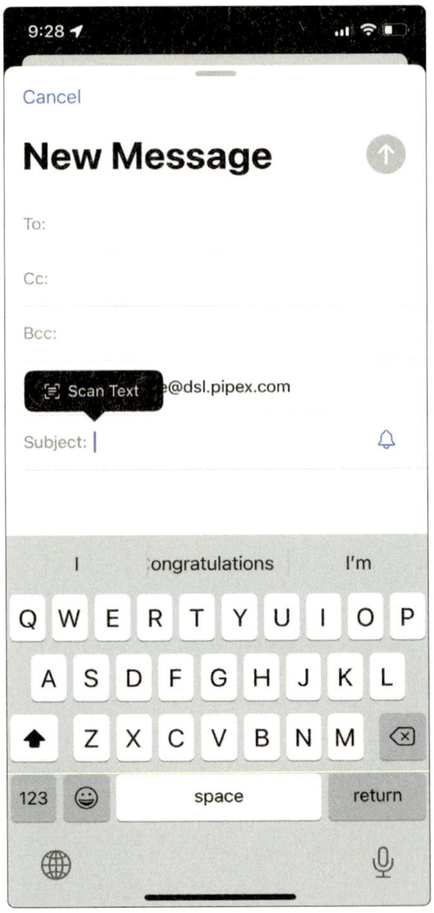

1 Point your iPhone's camera at text or numerals, and tap the icon that appears (bottom-right). A menu gives options regarding the text. You can also tap and drag to select a portion of the text instead of all of it.

2 You can copy and paste it into any app that uses text, or share it directly to that app. It sometimes needs a little editing after it has been imported, especially if the original text is presented in an unusual font.

3 Tap a text field in an app that utilises text and in a pop-up menu, you can select Scan Text. You can then use your camera to copy text from your environment, directly into the app's text field.

4 Live Text can read from photos you've already taken too. Just open the picture in question in the Camera app, and tap a piece of text. You can drag handles to select the exact text you want to highlight.

5 You can copy previously non-editable text from photographs in a variety of places on your iPhone. Here, for example, we're copying from a picture found on a website using the Safari app.

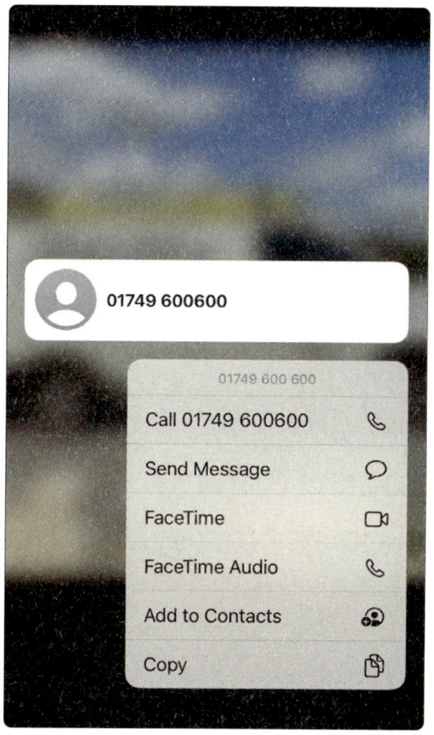

6 If you tap and hold on a telephone number in the Camera app or in a photo you've previously taken, Live Text reads the number and gives you a pop-up from which you can call, message and more.

7 You can also tap and hold a URL to open the site in Safari, or tap and hold an email address for a menu that lets you send an email, send a message, make a FaceTime call, copy the address and more.

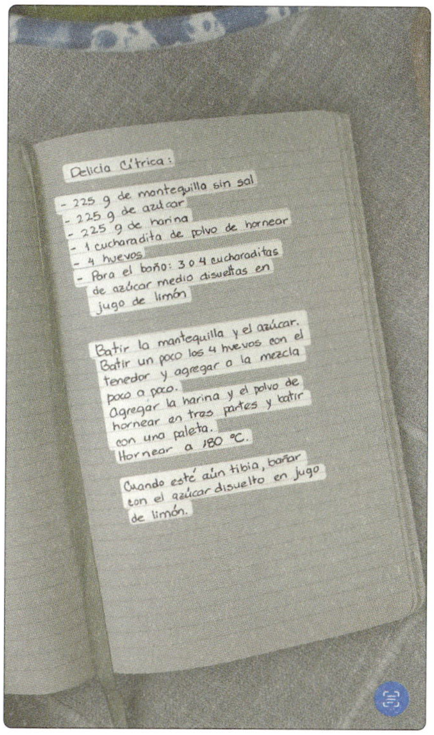

8 Live Text can even copy and paste handwritten text. Just the thing if you want to send a recipe from your notebook by email. Handwritten text might require a little editing before it's completely correct.

In Videos too

In iOS 16, you can pause a video on any frame that contains text, and tap it for options to copy, translate, look up, share and more, just like you can with a photograph.

Using Spotlight

Spotlight Search can do more than you think. When you type a Spotlight search, it searches throughout your phone. Search for an app and you can launch it without tapping it on the Home screen. Search for a person, and you can get taken straight to that individual's Contacts card. It does an excellent job of looking for pictures in your Photos app too.

Searching for Photos

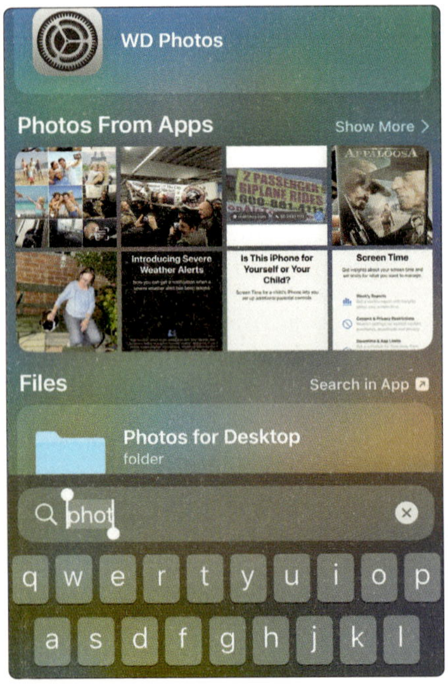

1 Type (or at least, start to type) 'Photos' and you can open the Photos app, or see photographs taken from apps, including the Photos app. Tap Show More next to Photos from Apps to see more pictures.

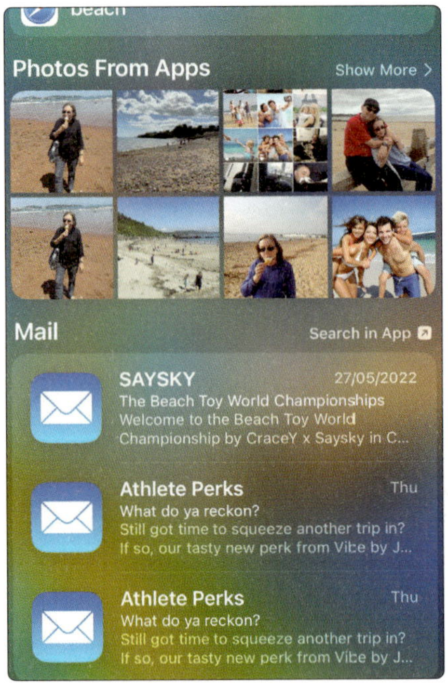

2 You can look for specific subjects within your photos if you wish. Here we've searched for 'beach'. In the search results are pictures taken from the Photos app; tap Search in App and you'll see the results in Photos.

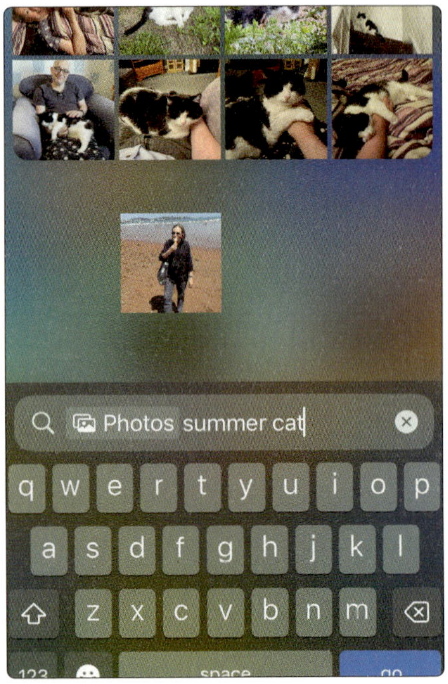

3 You can be more specific too. By searching for 'Summer Cats', for example, we see pictures of cats that were taken during the Summer months. Of course, we could use that search in other apps too, such as Mail and Safari.

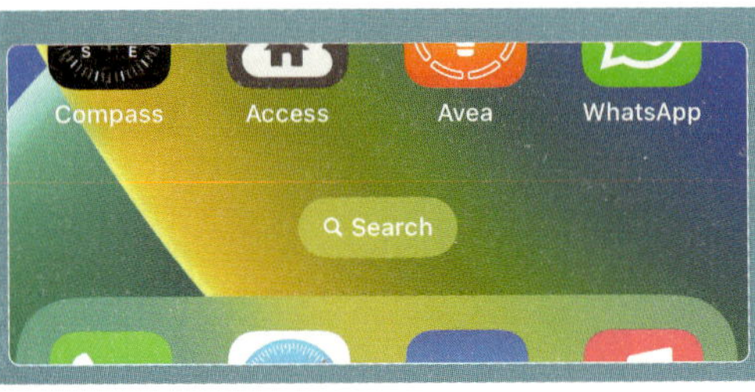

Accessing Spotlight

To access the Spotlight feature on your iPhone, swipe down from the Lock screen or the Home screen. In iOS 16, it's also found at the foot of each home screen, under the app icons.

Other Spotlight Features

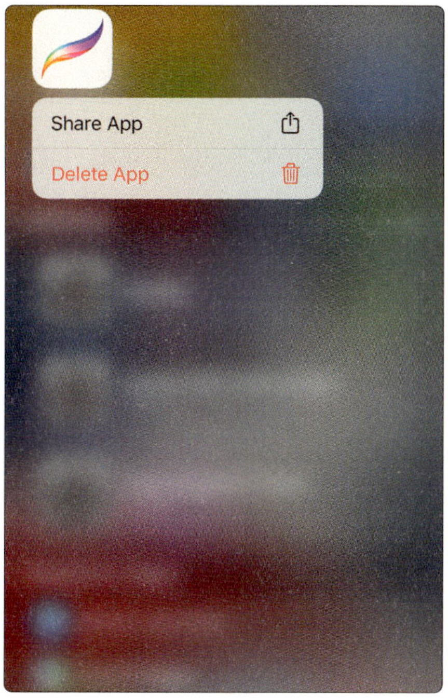

1 Install and delete apps; enter the name of an app you don't have; tap the App Store link to go straight to the app's page. To delete an app, type its name then tap and hold its icon. From the pop-up, share or delete it.

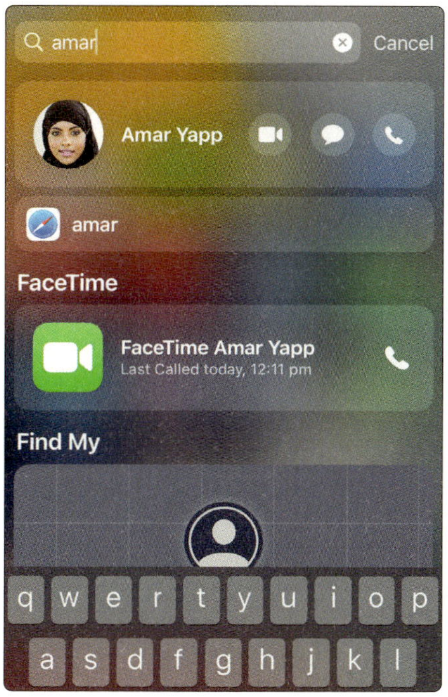

2 Search for someone in your Contacts app, and you see their name and/or photograph in the results screen. You can send a message, start a video or audio call from here, or tap the name and see more details.

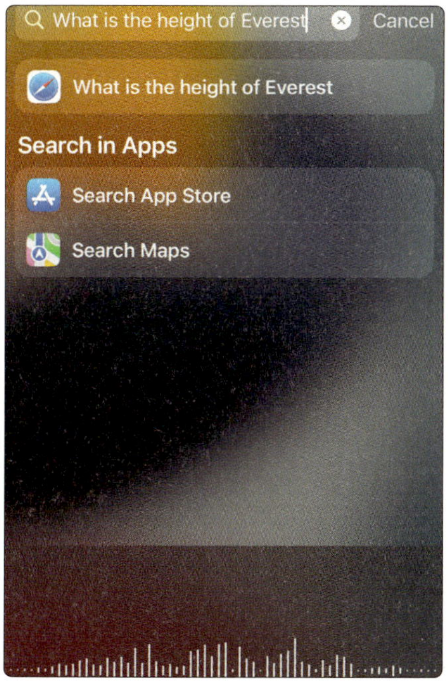

3 Tap the mic in the Search field to dictate your search instead of typing it. You can ask questions in Spotlight, and potential sources of an answer are offered. Tap Safari, for example, and the question is automatically searched for.

New in iOS 16

New Spotlight features for iOS 16 include accessing Spotlight directly from the Home Screen, expanded rich results, intelligent suggestions, and image results from apps like Messages, Notes, and Files. You can also take actions like starting a timer or running a shortcut right from Spotlight.

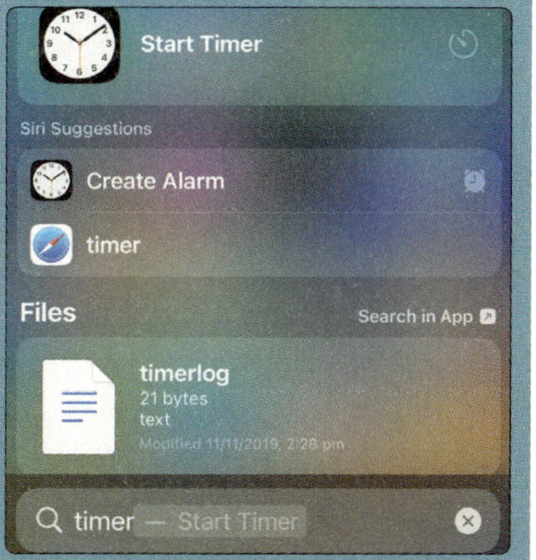

Customising Spotlight

To customise your Spotlight feature, go to Settings > Siri & Search. Ignore the first set of controls, collectively labelled Ask Siri, and instead scroll down to Content from Apple. Here you can choose whether to include Apple-curated content in the Spotlight search. Just tap the switch labelled Show in Spotlight to turn this content on and off.

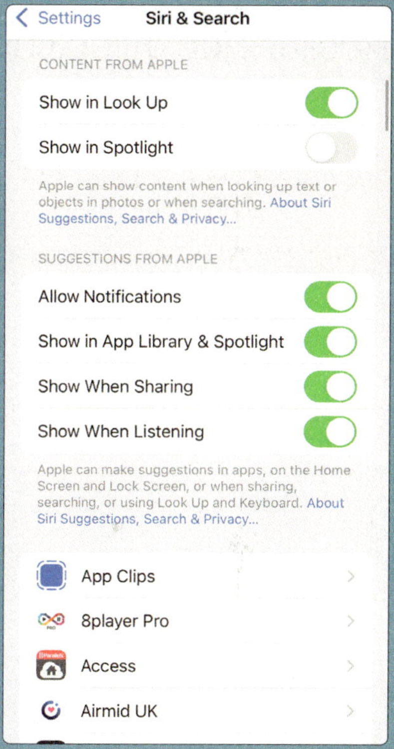

Scroll down further, and you can see a list of all the apps on your iPhone. If you want to exclude one of them from the Spotlight search, tap on that app for a series of options. It's the section labelled 'While Searching' we're interested in here. If you turn off the first option, Show App in Search, the application in question will no longer appear in Siri suggestions when you search in Spotlight. If you turn off the second option, Show Content in Search, content drawn from that app will no longer appear in Spotlight searches. For example, if you turn off Show Content in Search for the News app, Spotlight searches will no longer offer stories drawn from the News app.

Screen Time

With Screen Time, you can check what you've been doing on your iPhone and for how long, plus set limits for your own, or your children's iPhone usage. If you're worried about spending too long on social media, this feature is for you.

SCREEN TIME *in Focus*

1 To open Screen Time, go to Settings > Screen Time. You can also get to the Widgets screen by swiping right from the Lock screen, or the Home screen, and tapping the Screen Time widget near the bottom.

2 A summary of how you've been using your iPhone on each day of the week. Tap a bar to see how much you used it on that day. Also shown is your daily average time, and whether this is up or down.

3 This link takes you to a more detailed breakdown of what you've been doing with your phone, and when.

4 Tap here to schedule downtime for your iPhone. During this time, only apps you choose to exclude can be used. It's great if you think you're spending too much time on your iPhone.

5 Tap here to limit the time you spend on certain apps or categories of apps. At last, you can break that Facebook habit with a little help from Screen Time.

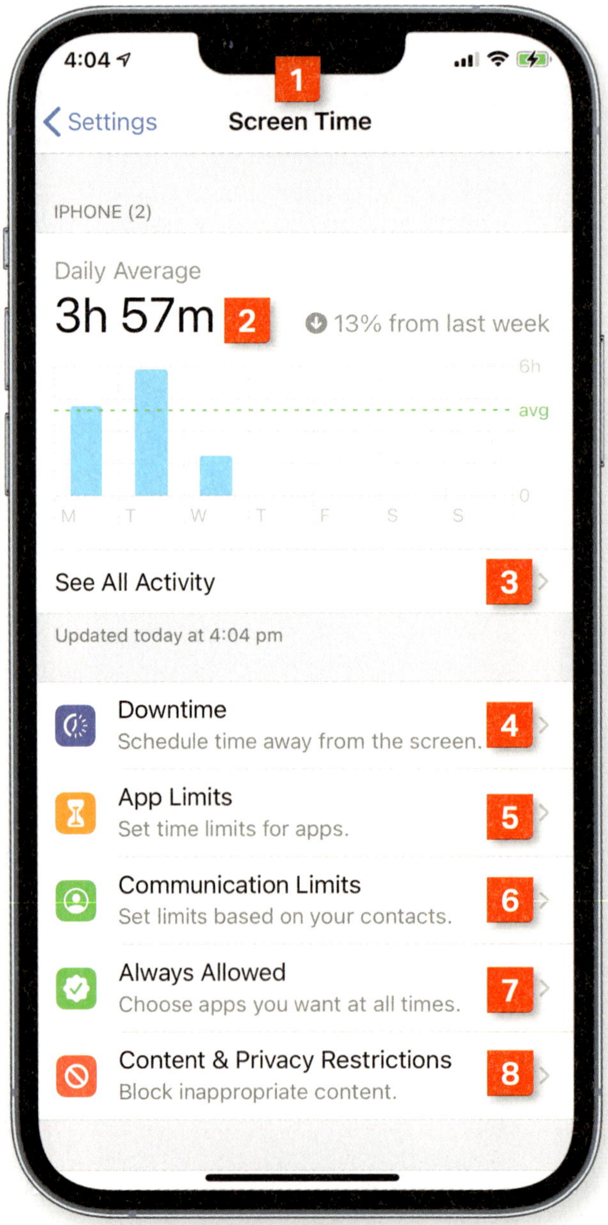

6 This option lets you limit your interactions with specific contacts, both during 'regular' and downtime periods. Again, this lets you limit your own iPhone use.

7 Tap here to identify apps you wish to exclude from downtime, or time limits. Phone, Messages, FaceTime, and Maps are always allowed by default, but you can edit this list.

8 Tap here for passcode-protected restrictions that can be used to block any inappropriate content. Just the thing if your kids are allowed to use your iPhone.

More options

Scroll the Screen Time page up for two more useful options. Share Across Devices combines Screen Time settings for all your Apple gear that's signed into the same Apple ID, and Turn Off Screen Time switches the feature off completely.

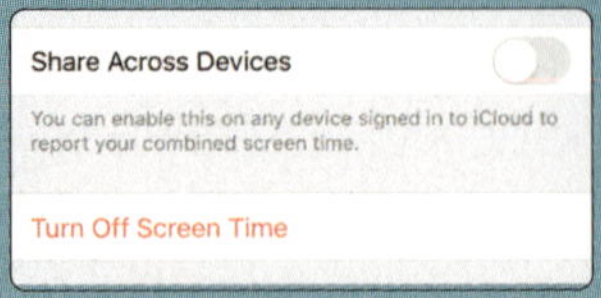

Setting up and using Screen Time

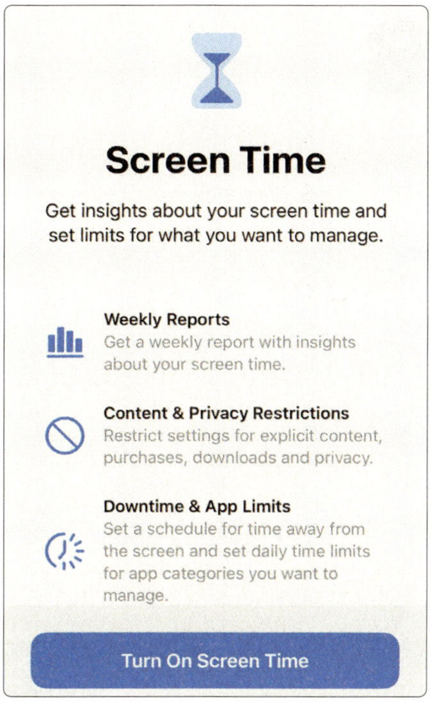

1 First of all, go to Settings > Screen Time. The first time you open this setting, you get a window telling you what this new iPhone feature can do. Have a read, then tap Continue.

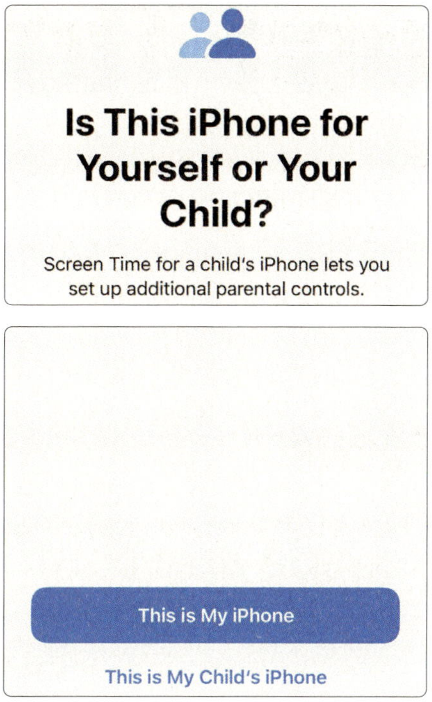

2 Screen Time lets you monitor and regulate your child's iPhone use as well as review your own. If this is your child's iPhone, you can tap this option and set up various parental controls.

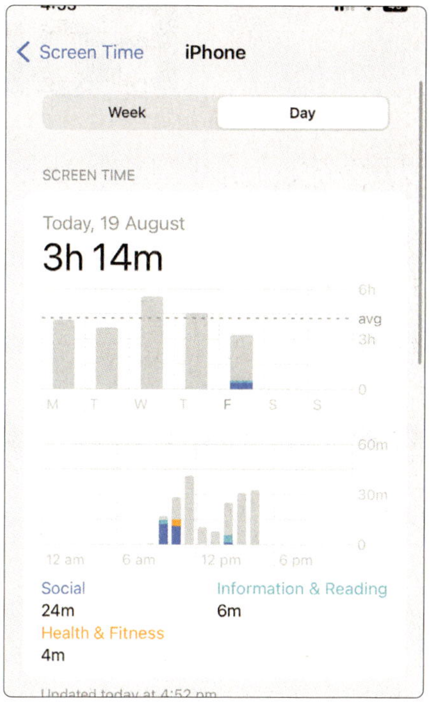

3 Tap the graph for more details. Tap the tabs at the top to switch between today and the last seven days. If you have more than one Apple device, tap Devices (top right) to choose one.

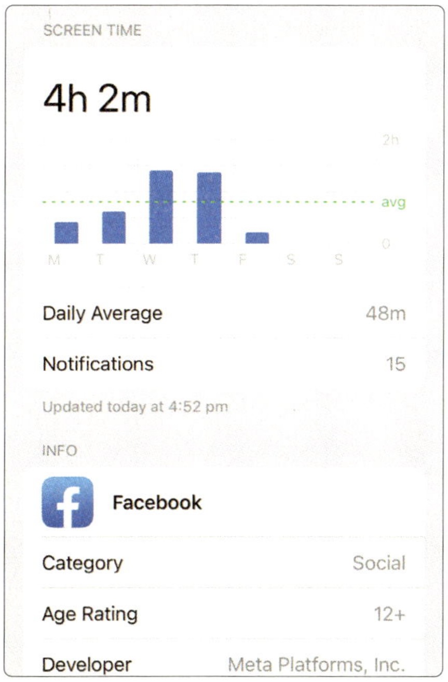

4 Tap on an app in this overview to see how long you've been using it recently, broken down by time on the Today view and by days on the Last 7 Days page. Tap Add Limits to limit the time you can spend on this app.

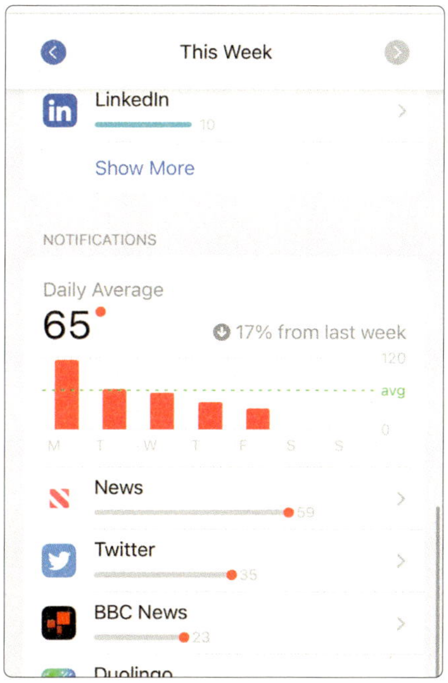

5 Scroll up on the summary page and you can see how many times you've picked up your iPhone during the last day or the last seven days and also how many notifications you've received on your iPhone in that time.

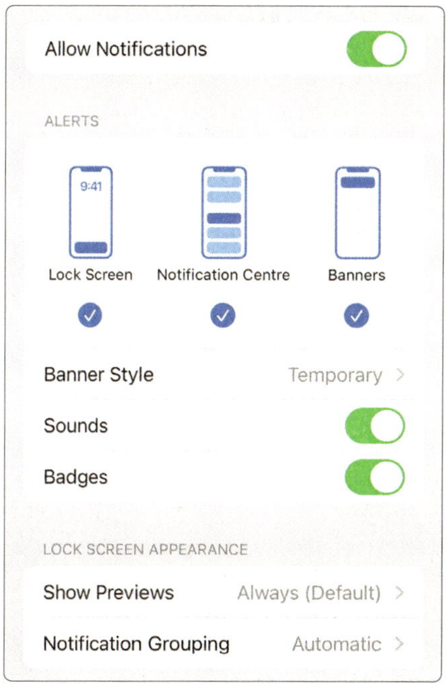

6 Tap an app listed under 'Notifications' and you can change your notifications settings for that app. For example, you can choose what sort of notifications you want and whether they make a sound on arrival.

Focus Filters

Focus Filters is a new feature introduced with iOS 16. It lets you fine-tune your content by filtering apps like Calendar, Mail, Messages and Safari to make sure only relevant content comes through when a Focus is active. In a Work Focus, for example, you can set Calendar to show only professional calendars, and Safari limited to work-related tab groups.

Using Focus Filters to hide app content

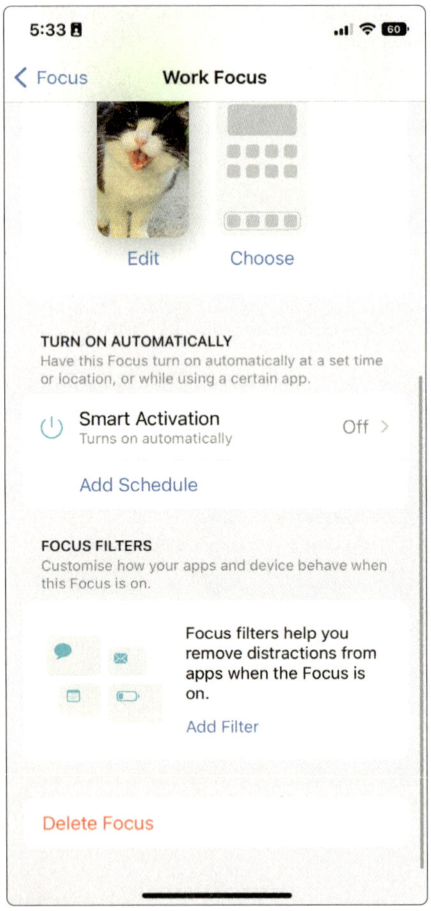

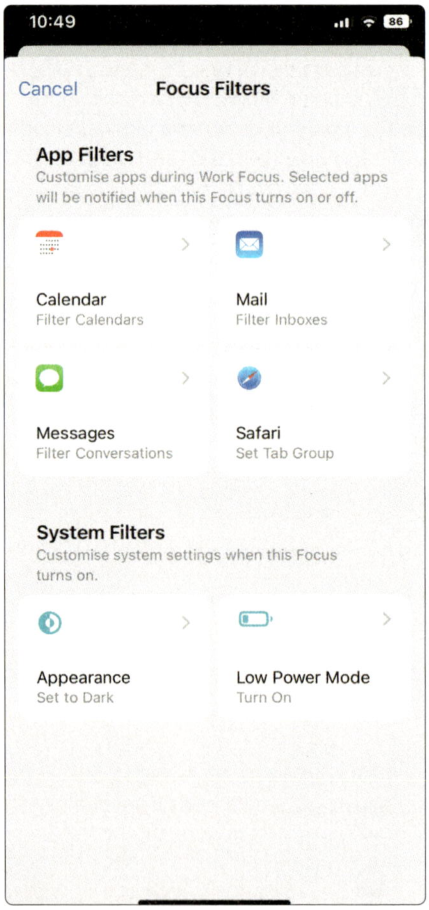

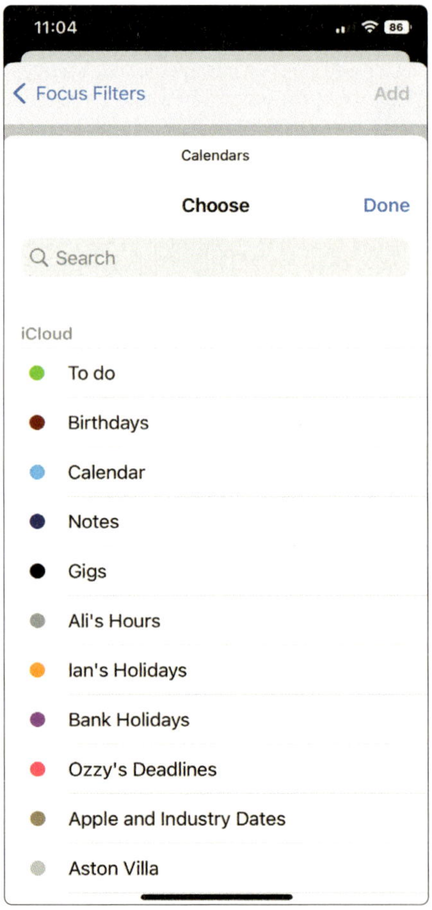

1 To customise a Focus, open the Settings app and select the Focus option. Choose the Focus you want to customise, or press the + screen in the top-right corner to start a new Focus from scratch. To use Focus Filters, scroll the screen up to find the Focus Filters section.

2 Tap Add Filter and you arrive at this screen, from where you can apply filters to four apps, namely Calendar, Mail, Messages and Safari. You can also set System Filters, allowing you to set the appearance of your iPhone to Dark Mode or turn on Low Power Mode.

3 Tap Calendar and you can choose which calendars to show with the Focus in question. For example, for the Work Focus, you can restrict the Calendar app to showing your professional calendars. When you've set your filter, tap Add in the top-right corner (this is true for all the filters).

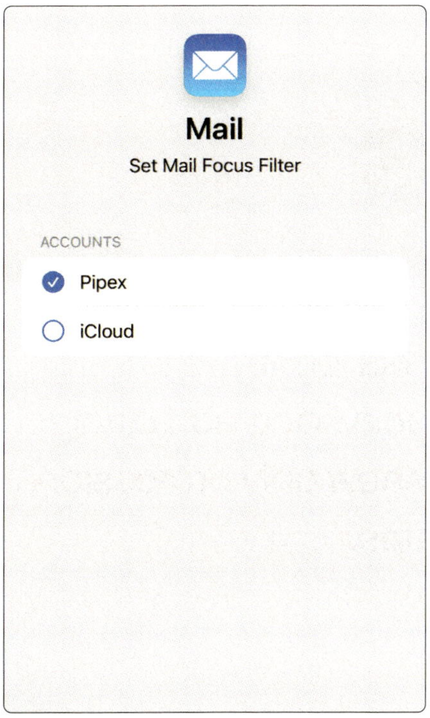

4 You can also filter inboxes in the Mail app. If you have several different accounts set up in Mail, you can choose which are shown while a Focus is active. Just the thing if you don't want work emails while you're not working.

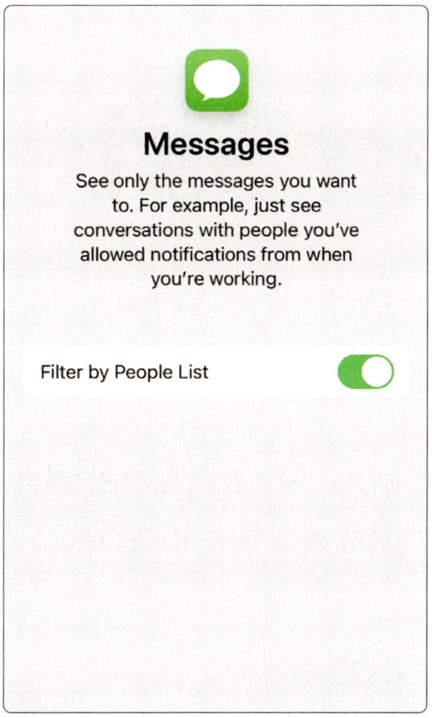

5 The Focus Filter for the Messages app is very simple. Turn it on and you see only the messages from people you wish to allow notifications from. While the focus is active, only they give you notifications when a message arrives.

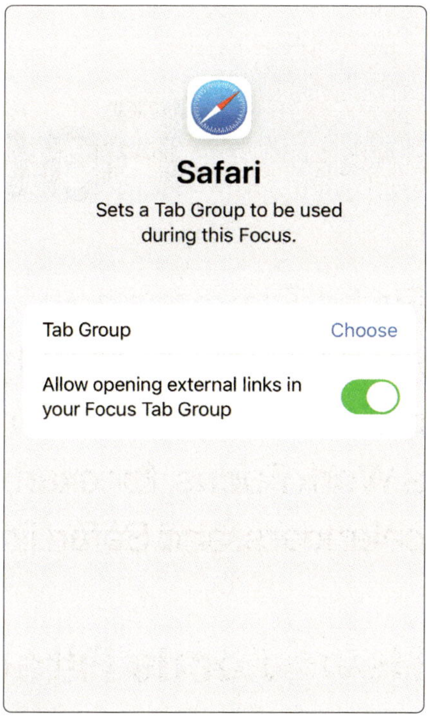

6 In the Safari, you can set a filter to only show certain tab groups. If you're revising for an exam, you might have a tab group related to your studies. Turning this on stops you wasting time on other sites.

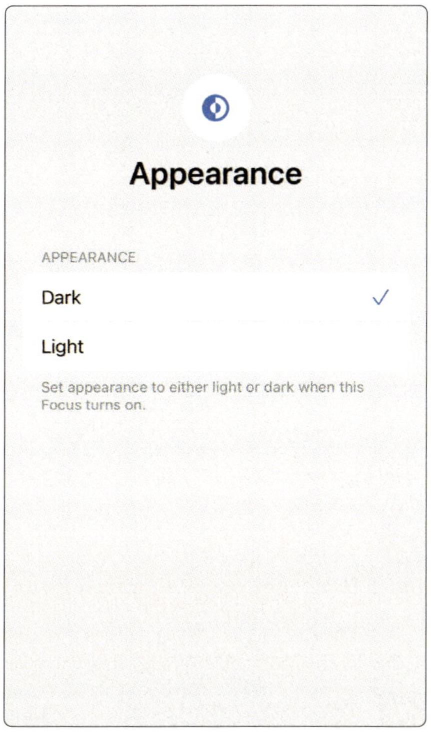

7 There are two options to change system settings when the focus is active. The first is your iPhone's appearance. You can have the focus set it to Light Mode or Dark Mode too.

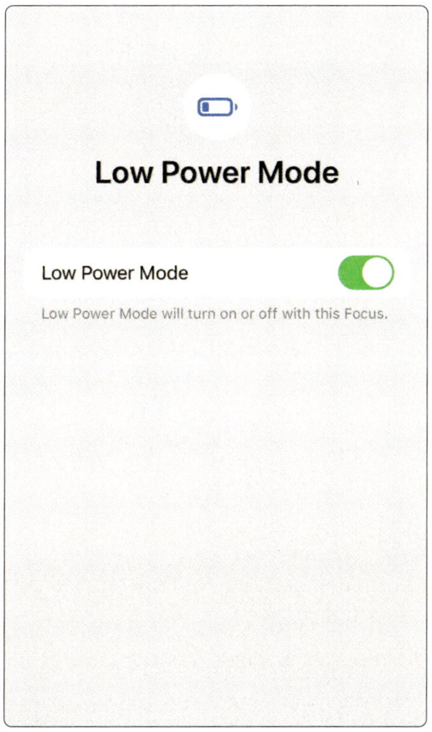

8 Add the Low Power Mode setting to your focus and you can have your iPhone switch to Low Power Mode while the focus is active. It's great for the hour before bedtime, when you want to relax.

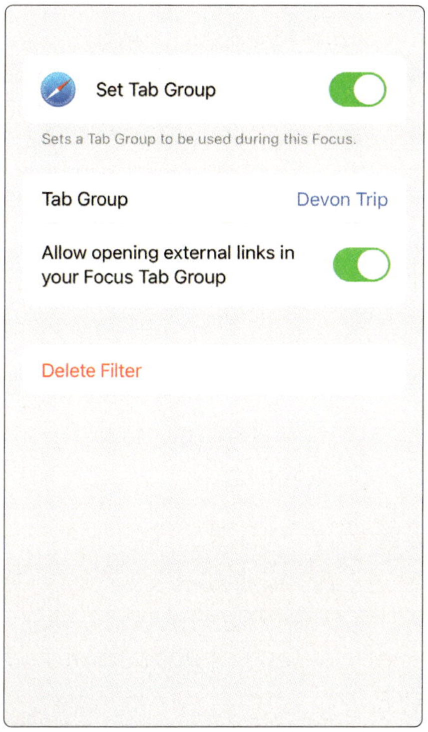

9 To remove a Focus Filter from your Focus setting, go to Settings > Focus and tap the focus in question. Tap the Focus Filter, which is now displayed on this page, then tap Delete Filter.

Using Siri

Siri has a great new compact design. Your personal digital assistant no longer takes over the whole screen, but lets you concentrate on what you're doing. What follows is a short guide to activating and using Siri, and using some of its more advanced features like setting alarms, checking appointments, looking things up and identifying a song.

How to activate and speak to Siri

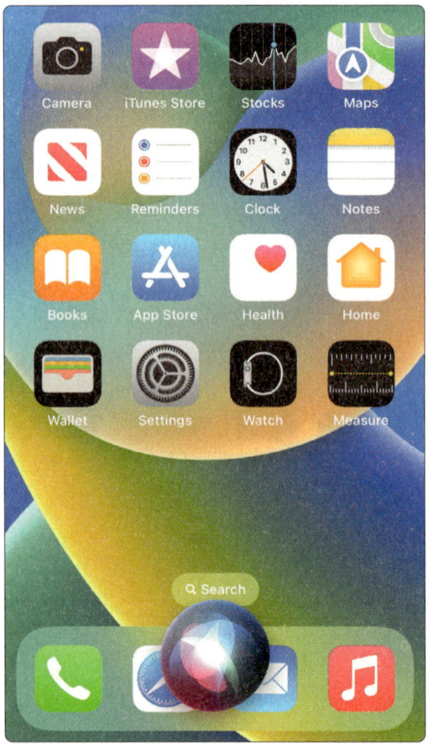

1 To open Siri, hold down the Side button or the Home button on older iPhones. Siri now appears at the foot of the screen, as you can see here.

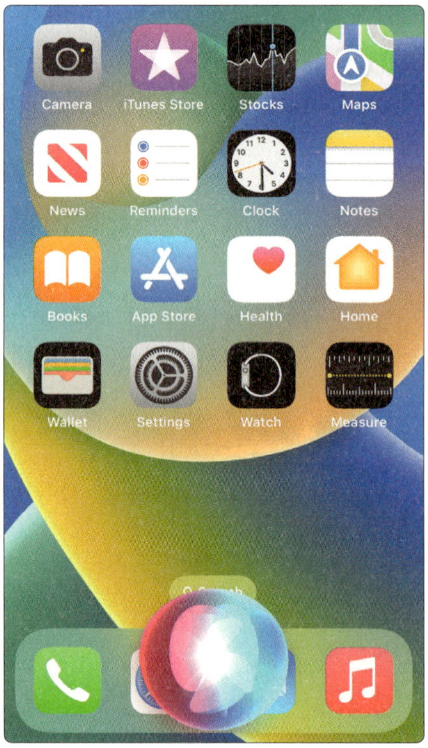

2 Begin speaking and the coloured icon reverberates to let you know that Siri can hear you. If it doesn't, tap it to talk to Siri again.

3 You can also access Siri by saying "Hey Siri" and then speaking your request. Tap the answer shown to open the app that created it.

Siri learning

The more you use Siri, the more it learns about you, your voice and the sort of words you use. The digital assistant gets used to your accent and also your way of speaking. Over time, Siri has become better at understanding natural language and expressions, making it easier to use and far more useful to you.

What Siri can do for you

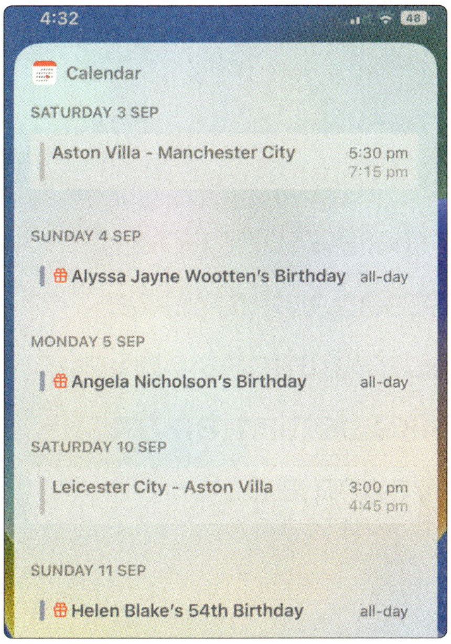

Check appointments

Siri can tell you if you have any appointments on any particular date, or even within a time frame. Say to Siri something like "What's my schedule for April?" and it tells you how many appointments you have in that month and lists them on screen. If you want to be more specific, say "What are my appointments today?" or "What's my schedule for June 19th?"

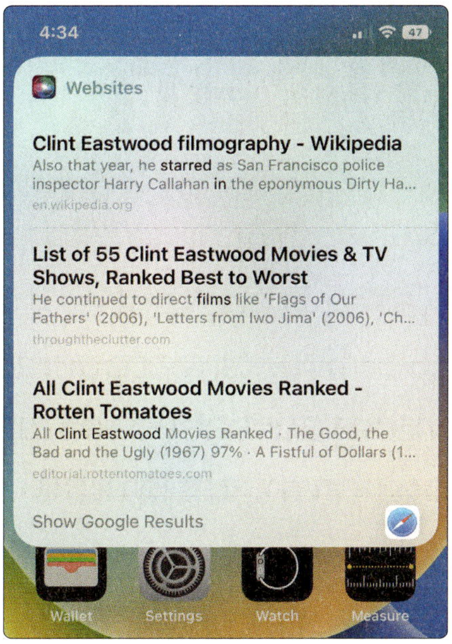

Look things up

To look things up using Siri, speak to Siri as you would if you were asking a human being. For example, 'Which planet is the largest?' 'Why does snow fall?' or 'What movies has Clint Eastwood starred in?' Siri uses the source it thinks best able to answer the question. If you want to use a particular search engine, simply say the name before the question: "Google, how far is it to the Sun?"

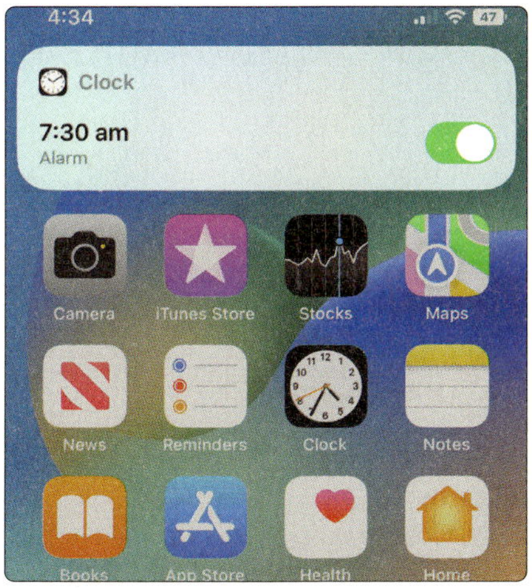

Turn alarms on or off

Siri makes common tasks easier but don't forget there are many other things that your personal assistant can help you with. Rather than fumbling about late at night to turn your morning alarm on or off, simply raise the phone to your ear, wait for the beeps and say "Turn on (or off) my alarm". Siri confirms it.

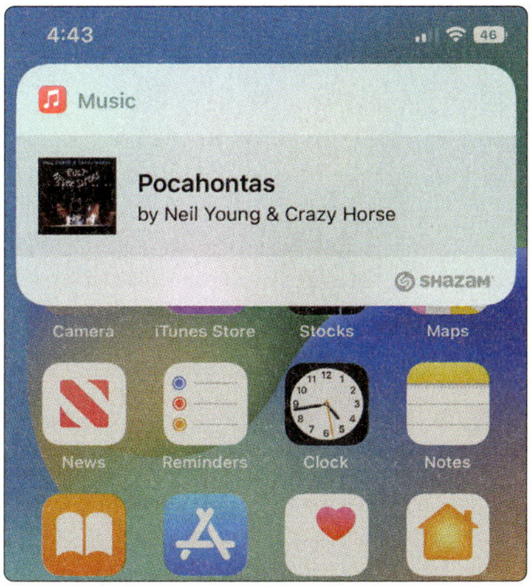

Identify a song

Siri is not only there to search for content on the web, it also lets you identify a song using the Shazam audio recognition software. While a song is playing, activate Siri and ask, "What is this song?" Siri searches, finds the title and then links you to its entry in iTunes to give you the chance to buy it.

Siri dictation commands

Siri also understands dictation as well as words, so if you are dictating an email, for instance, this useful list of dictation commands that Siri recognises will prove very useful.
New line - Move to the next line
New paragraph - Start a new paragraph
All caps - Make the next word all uppercase
All caps on ... all caps off - Make part of what you say uppercase
No caps - Make the next word lowercase
No caps on ... no caps off - Make sure part of what you say is all lowercase
Space bar - Prevent a hyphen from appearing in a normally hyphenated word
Period - .
Comma - ,
Apostrophe - '
Exclamation mark - !
Question mark - ?
Ampersand - &
Asterisk - *
Open parenthesis - (
Close parenthesis -)
Open bracket - [
Close bracket -]
Open brace - {
Close brace - }
Dash: -
Hyphen -
Em dash —
Percent sign - %
Copyright sign - ©
Registered sign - ®
Section sign - §
Dollar sign - $
Cent sign - ¢
Pound Sterling sign - £
Degree sign - °
Caret - ^
At sign - @
Pound sign - #
Greater than sign - >
Less than sign - <
Forward slash - /
Back slash - \
Vertical bar - |
Smiley - :-)
Frowny face) - :-(
Wink - ;-)

Notifications

Notifications have had a minor refresh in iOS 16. By default, incoming notifications now arrive on a roll at the foot of the screen, which is far less intrusive than before. Notifications are sent by applications on your iPhone. For example, the Mail app might send a notification when an email arrives, or Facebook when a post is added to your feed.

Using the Notification Centre

1 Notifications now arrive as a roll at the foot of your screen. Swipe it up to review them, or down to replace them with a Notification Count. Get to Notification Centre on an unlocked phone by swiping down from the top of the screen.

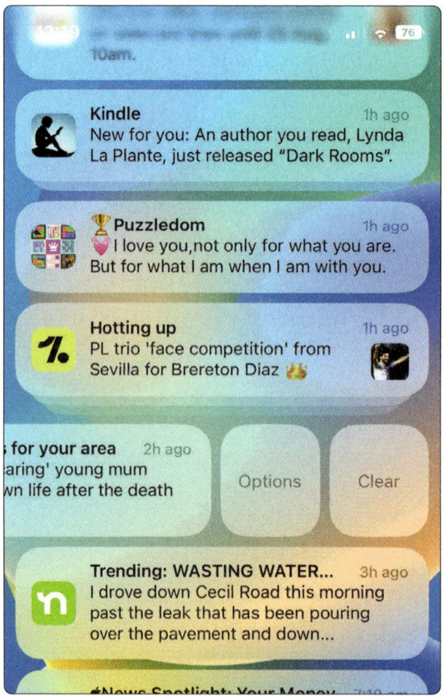

2 To clear a single notification, swipe it left and tap the Clear button. To delete all notifications received from a given app, tap the X next to the app name and then the Clear button that replaces it. All those notifications go.

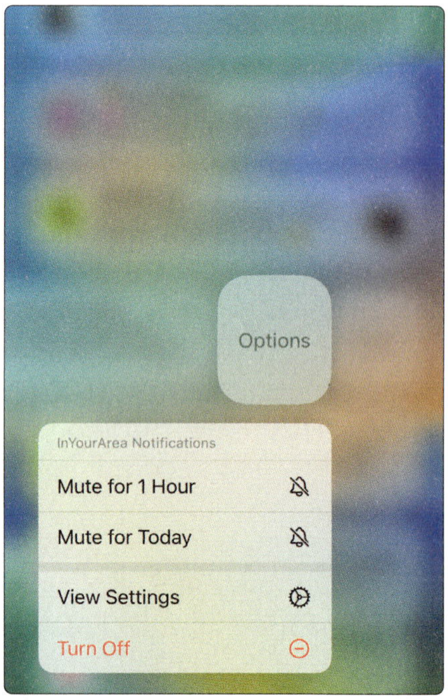

3 Swipe an incoming notification left and tap Options to mute notifications from that app for an hour or the rest of the day, view the settings for that app's notifications or turn off notifications for that app altogether.

Notification options

If you swipe a notification left, you get the Options and Clear buttons. However, if you continue to drag it even further left, you can swipe it off the screen entirely, deleting it without having to tap the Clear button.

Organising your notifications

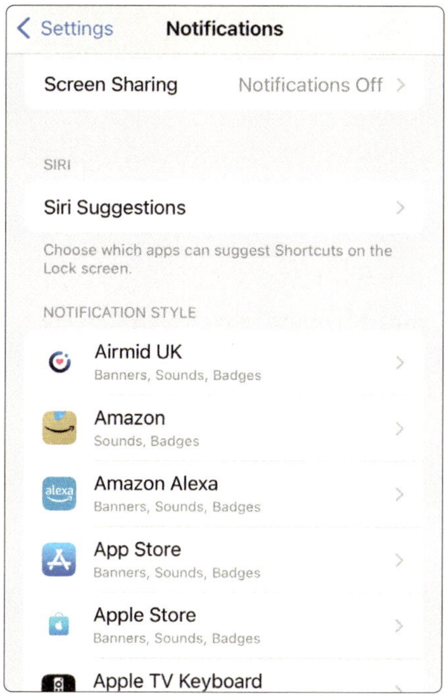

1 Go to Settings > Notifications and scroll up for a list of apps that produce notifications. Tap one. Alternatively, swipe a notification from the Notifications Centre and tap Options > Settings to get directly to that app's settings.

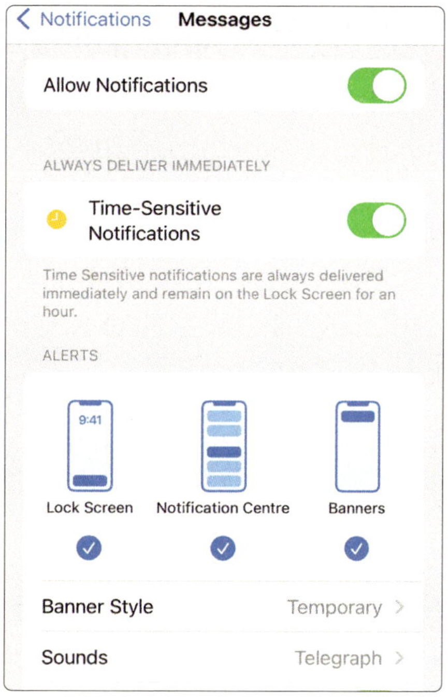

2 You can edit the way that app sends notifications. These changes are fairly self-explanatory. The changes can be implemented on an app-by-app basis, so you can switch off notifications on one app but retain them for the others.

3 Turning Badges on puts a red circle on the app's Home screen icon, showing how many notifications it currently has. Show as Banners puts an incoming notification on the screen as a temporary or persistent bar (your choice).

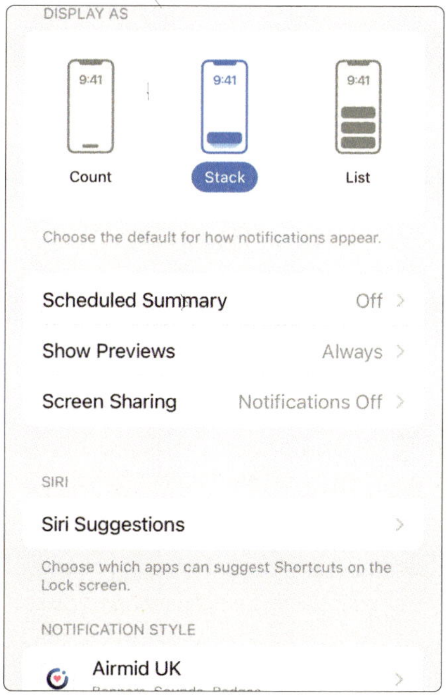

4 At the top of Settings > Notifications, there's a new option; Display As. It's set to present notifications as a stack at the foot of the screen, but you can replace them with a counter or go for List to do it the old way.

Previewing

1 Tap and hold a notification for a preview of the item to which it refers. A notification that's sent by the News app, for example, gives a preview of the news story to which it refers. Tap it to read the article in the app.

2 Preview a Message or Mail notification and you can reply from within the notification, instead of having to access the app itself. It's a very convenient way of sending a quick reply to an incoming message or mail.

Accessing Notifications when in-app

1 Many iPhone applications send notifications can be accessed while using another application. When one arrives, access it by placing your finger on the notification and swiping down.

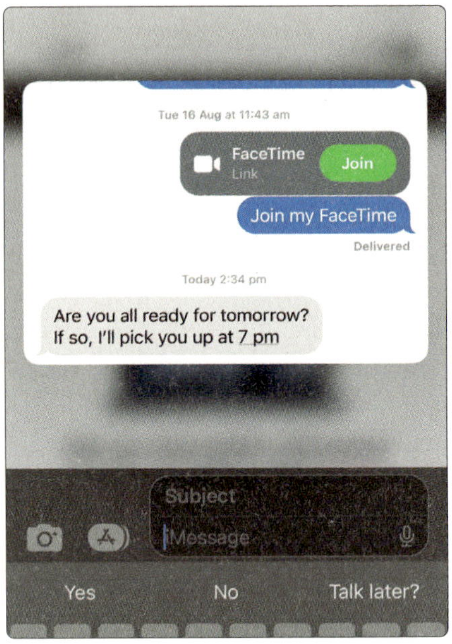

2 Tap the notification to be taken straight to the app. Here, swiping down the notification lets you reply to a message, whilst tapping it takes you directly to the Messages app.

Using application-based notifications

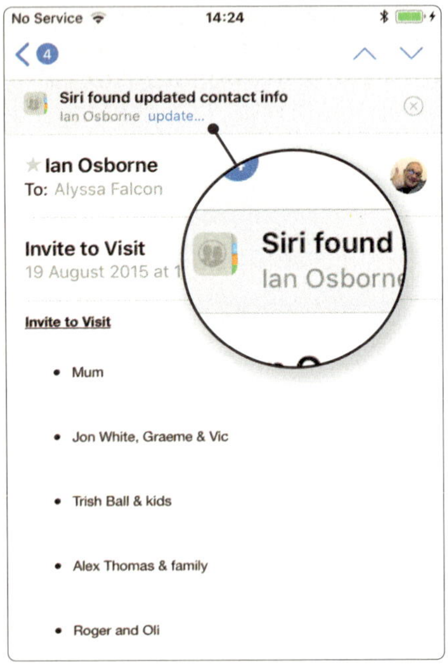

1 Open the Mail app and check through your mail. When a mail contains additional contact details that you don't already have in your Contacts app, you receive a notification like the one shown here.

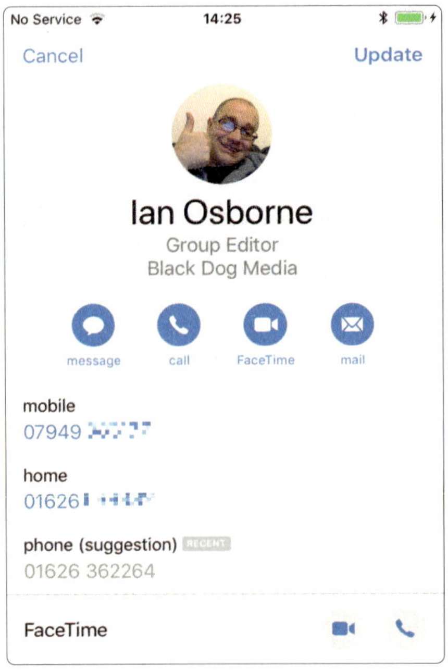

2 If you tap the notification, you're shown the contact card for the person in question, with the new information gleaned from the email shown as a suggestion. If you accept the change, tap Update (top right).

Notification Summary

If you'd prefer non-urgent notifications, such as tweets and Facebook notifications from friends, to appear at a more convenient time – for example, outside working hours – you can bundle these non-urgent notifications and have them sent when you choose.
First of all, Open the Settings app and then tap the Notifications option. At the top of this list is an option called Scheduled Summary. Tap this, and on the next screen, tap the switch to turn on this option. You're shown an intro screen explaining how Notification Summary works and what it achieves. Tap the blue Continue button to start the setup process.

You're then invited to choose which apps to include in the summary. Tap Show More at the bottom of this screen and you're shown all the apps you can bundle in this way. Direct messages and time-sensitive notifications are always sent immediately. Tap the circle next to the apps whose notifications you wish to bundle, then tap 'Add [X] Apps' at the foot of the screen.

Next, you must set a schedule. You can choose when you receive your summary. You can choose more than one time; just set a time for your first and second summaries, then tap Add Summary if you want to add more. Your bundle of notifications that aren't time sensitive, sent by the apps you chose earlier, are sent at these times.

When you're done, tap Turn On Notification Summary and you're finished. You can edit your choices, including arrival times and apps in the summary, in Settings > Notifications > Scheduled Summary. You can turn it off by tapping the Scheduled Summary switch here too.

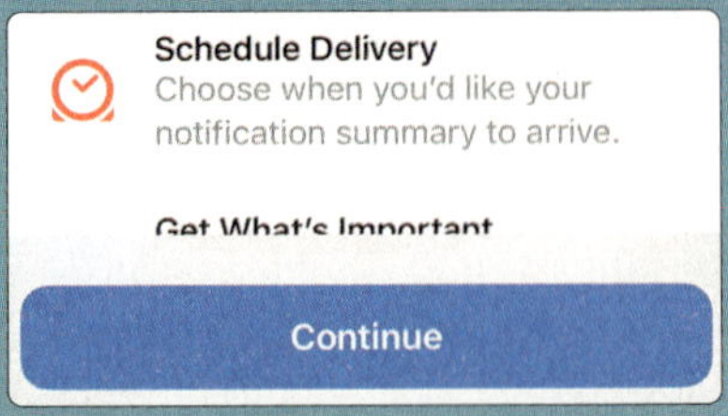

AirDrop & BT

AirDrop is great for sharing files wirelessly, and with Bluetooth you can pair and connect your iPhone with wireless devices such as speakers, headphones and keyboards. Here's how to use both these features.

Using AirDrop for file transfer

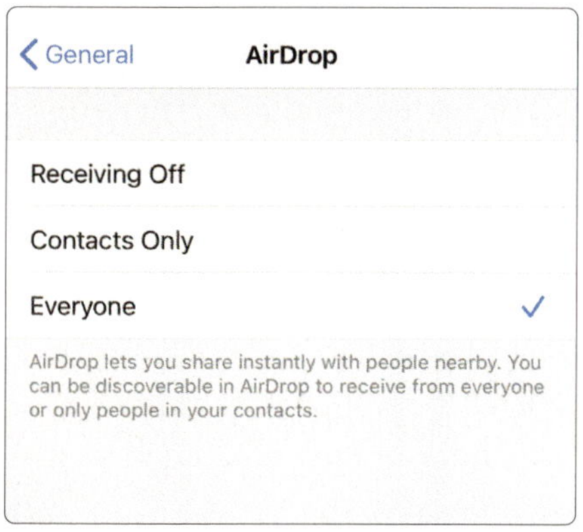

1 Send files to other Apple devices using AirDrop. Switch on Wi-Fi and Bluetooth, then go to Settings > General > AirDrop and decide whether receiving via AirDrop is on or off, share only with Contacts, or share with everyone.

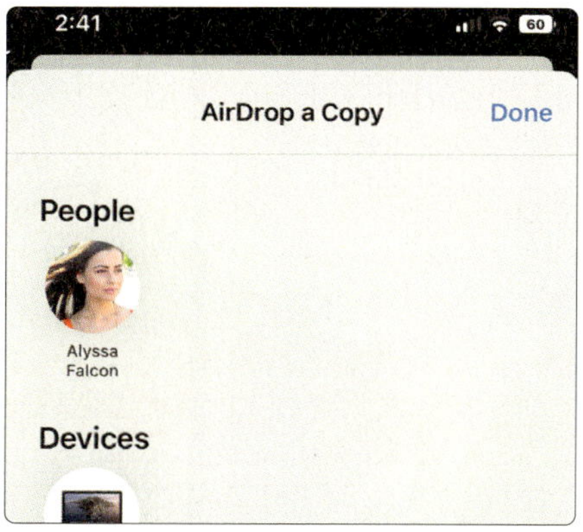

2 Select a file, photo, or video you want to send by AirDrop, and open it. Tap the Sharing icon (the page with the up-pointing arrow), and then tap AirDrop in the pop-up window. Tap the person to which you want to send the file, and it's sent.

3 If you accept AirDrops from everyone, when you're sent an AirDrop file, you have to accept it first. AirDropped files are accessible from their host apps: Safari links open via Safari, photos via the Photos app, etc.

Pairing and Unpairing with Bluetooth

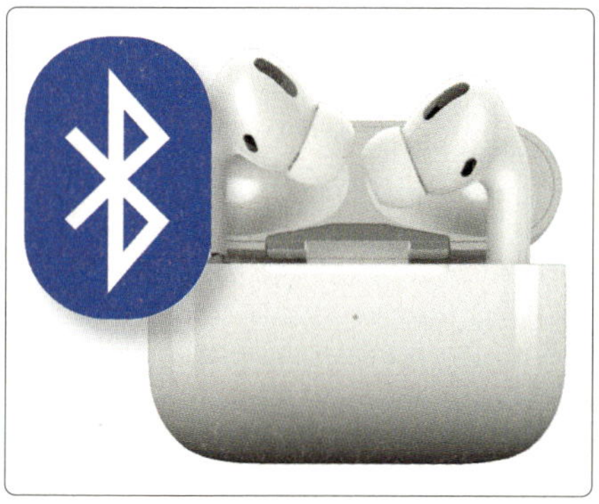

1 Bluetooth can wirelessly connect your iPhone with devices such as speakers, headphones and keyboards. The item you wish to pair with must be put in Pairing Mode. To do this, follow the manufacturer's instructions.

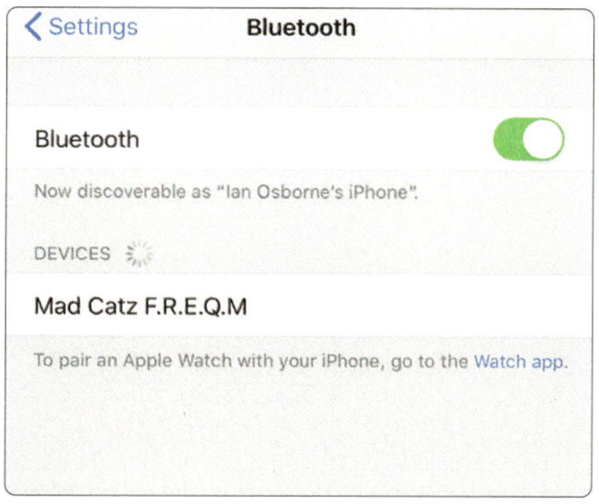

2 Go to Settings > Bluetooth, and the device you're pairing should be listed. Tap it and the two devices pair. Pairing only needs to be done once. You don't have to pair your Bluetooth device every time you use it.

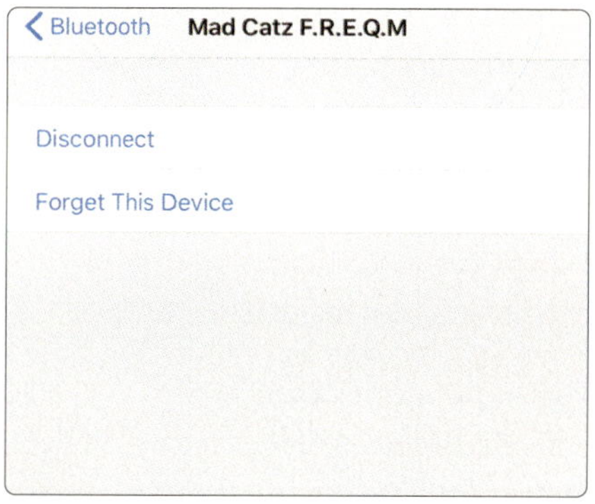

3 To unpair a device, in Settings > Bluetooth, tap the 'i' icon next to the device in question. You can then disconnect it (assuming it's currently connected) or tap 'Forget this Device' to unpair it completely.

More Great iOS 16 Features

What else does Apple's latest iPhone operating system have to offer?

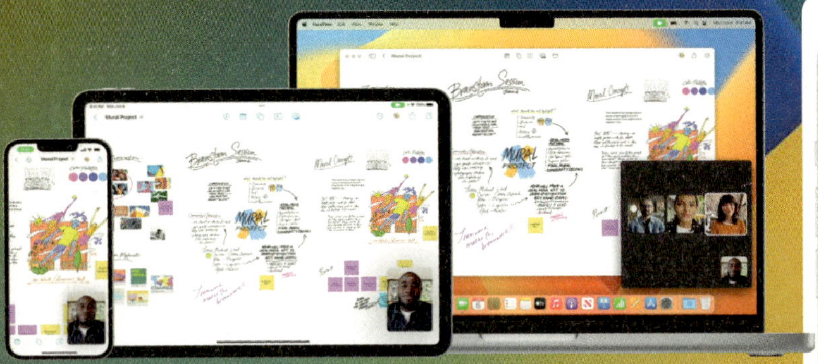

The Freeform App

It's coming soon, but it wasn't ready in time for iOS 16, iPadOS 16 and macOS Ventura. The Freeform app helps you work collaboratively across your Apple devices by offering a flexible digital canvas available to all parties during a FaceTime chat. Ever been in a meeting where ideas were expressed on a whiteboard? If FaceTime video chat can replace the meeting, Freeform supplies the whiteboard. You can add images, notes, scribbles, documents, web links, PDFs and more. Edits are made in real-time, and everyone can pitch in with their ideas. The Freeform app is due for release 'later this year', and will probably arrive with an iOS 16 update.

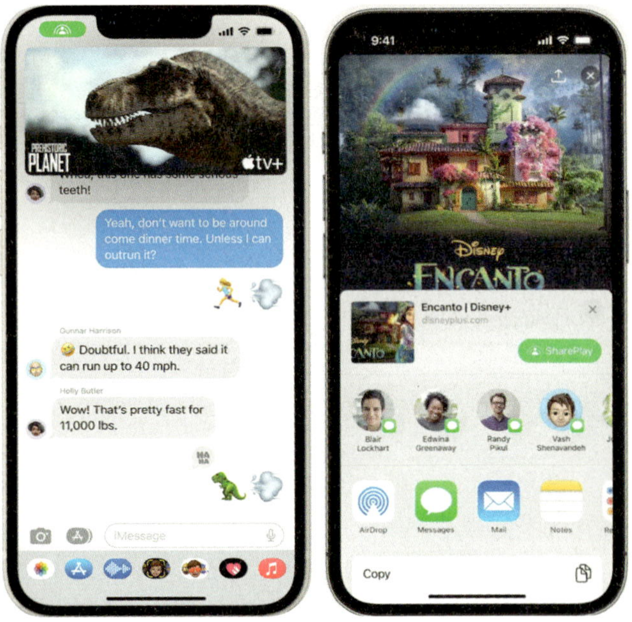

SharePlay in Messages

With iOS 16, you can SharePlay from the Messages app. Now you can watch a movie or a TV show or listen to music while chatting about it with your friends in the Messages app. You're always fully synced, so you're all in the same place in the video or music as you chat, and you also get shared playback controls.

Door Detection

A new accessibility feature helps users who are blind or have very poor vision. Door Detection can identify and warn about closed glass doors which might otherwise not have been seen. It uses the LiDAR Scanner, and is available on iPhone 12 and later.

Switch Controllers

We've been able to use our Sony and Microsoft gamepads with our iPhones for a while now, but with iOS 16, we can also use those built for the Nintendo Switch – both the Joy-Cons that come with the console, and the Switch Pro controllers that are sold separately. Just the thing for playing Mario Kart: World Tour on your iPhone.

Music on Lock Screen

When you're listening to your music on your iPhone, the controls now appear as a widget on the lock screen. You get to see the album art at a decent size, and can pause, play, rewind or fast forward your tunes without having to unlock your phone.

Visual Look Up

If you tap and hold an object within a photo, it's automatically cut out and copied. You can then use it as a sticker in another app. Tap the Copy button to copy it, ready to paste it somewhere else, or tap the Share button to send it through iOS's regular Sharing facilities.

My Sports

A new section in the News app lets you follow your favourite teams and leagues, and get related stories from hundreds of national and local publications. You can also watch highlights and get the latest scores, fixtures and rankings in your news feed.

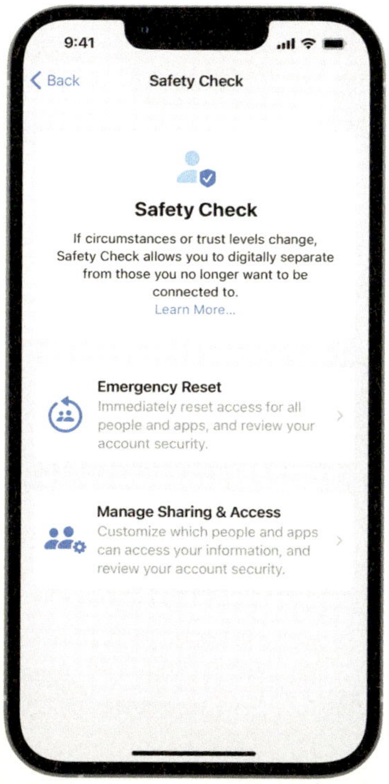

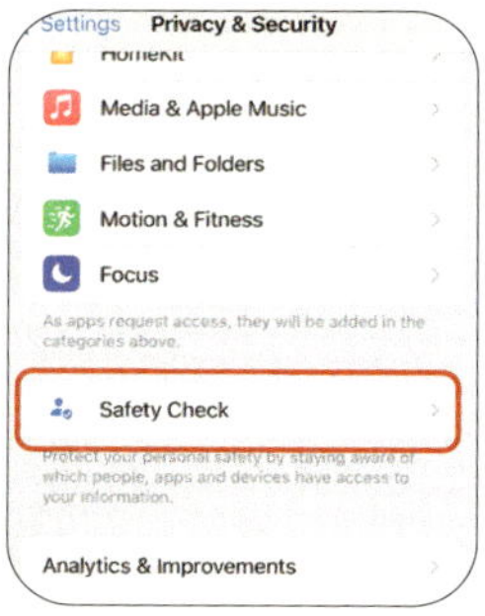

Safety Check

Safety Check can help those whose personal safety is at risk from domestic or intimate partner violence by quickly removing all access they've granted to others. It's in Settings > Privacy & Security, and lets you reset access for people and apps.

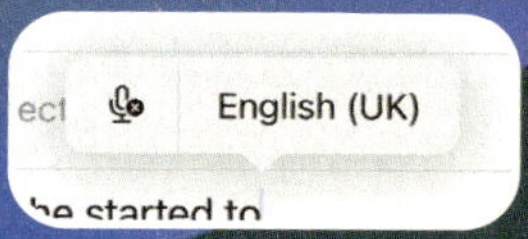

Dictation with Keyboard

When using the Dictation text-to-speech feature, the virtual keyboard remains on the screen, so you can seamlessly switch from using your voice and typing. It's great for when you need to add a non-standard word such as a place name, which is likely to be incorrectly rendered.

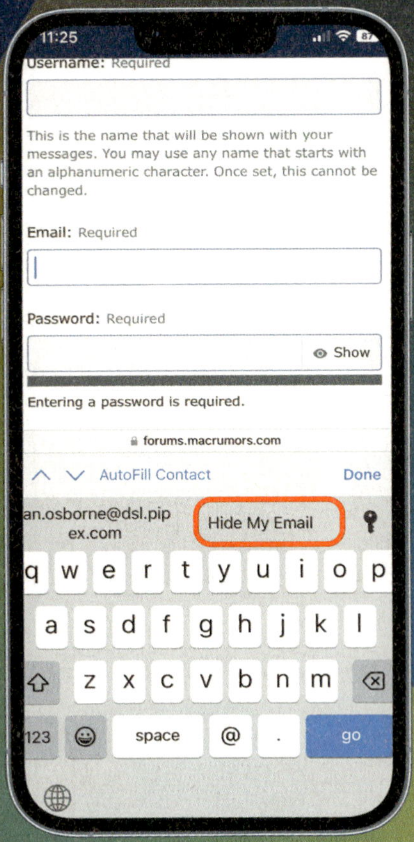

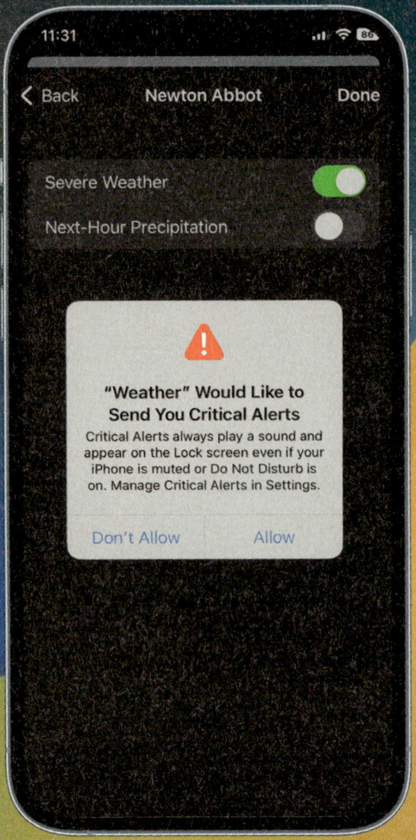

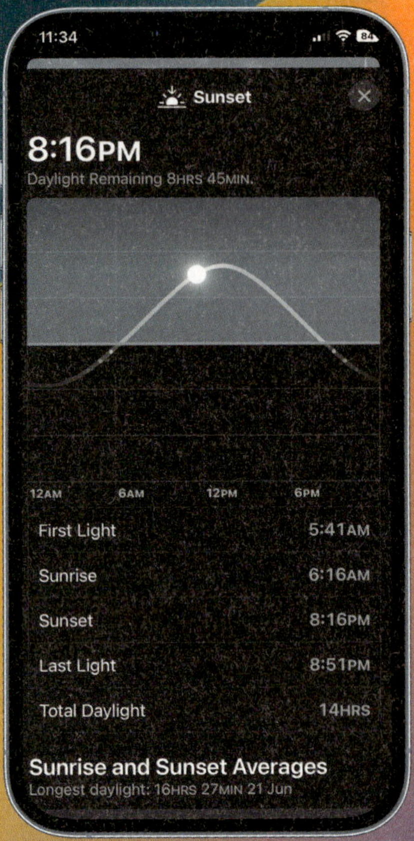

Hide My Email

iCloud+ is a range of features available to those who subscribe to iCloud, as opposed to only using the free service. One such feature is Hide My Email, which lets you keep your email address private when signing up for online accounts. It's now available from the QuickType keyboard.

Weather Enhancements

The Weather app can now give you notifications, namely Severe Weather alerts that warn you if you're heading for a hurricane or something similar, and Next-Hour Precipitation, to let you know if it's likely to rain soon. Also new are tappable tiles that open up a more detailed data set than is available on the main Weather page.

New Languages

The Translation app now offers support for the Turkish, Thai, Vietnamese, Polish, Indonesian and Dutch languages.

New in CarPlay

Powered by iOS 16, CarPlay can provide content for multiple dashboard screens. Deeper integration means you can control the radio and change the in-car temperature directly through CarPlay, and you can personalise your dashboard by choosing different gauge cluster designs. Cars compatible with the new CarPlay features are expected late next year.

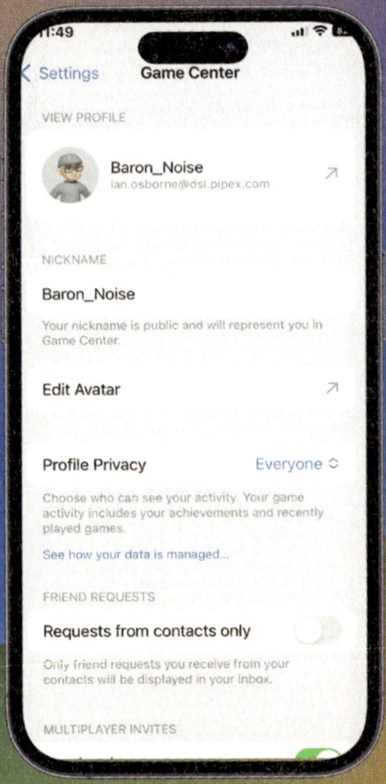

Game Center

You can access Game Center's tools in the Settings app. With a redesigned dashboard that shows friends' activity and accomplishments from games in one place, it's easy for players to jump in to play with or compete against their chums.

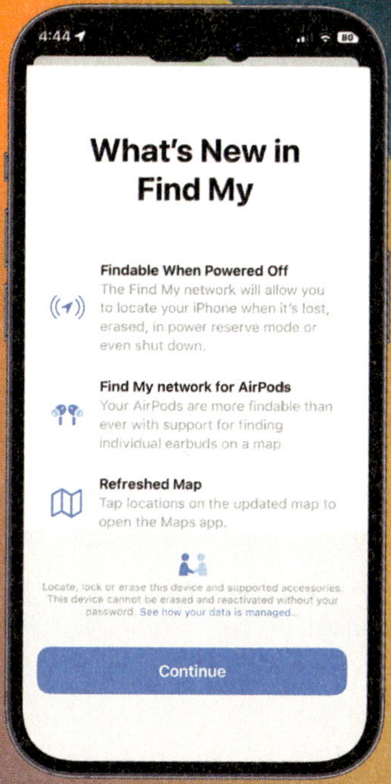

New in Find My

There are a few new features in the Find My app. There's a Find My network for AirPods, which can find individual pods if you lose just one. You can tap the locations in the Find My app to open the Maps app, and you can locate your iPhone when it's lost, erased, in power reserve mode or even shut down.

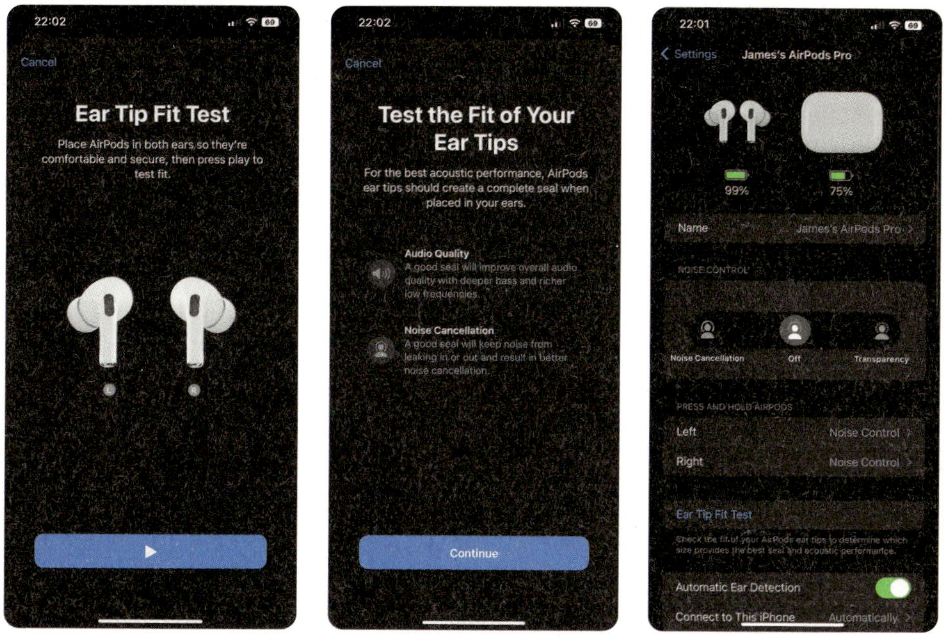

Ear Tip Fit Test

If you're lucky enough to own a set of AirPods, you can use a new Settings feature to make sure they're a good fit. Open Settings > [the name of your AirPods], and select Ear Tip Fit Test. Follow the on-screen instructions to make sure you're using the correct set of silicon tips on your pods. It improves the sound as well as making them less likely to fall out.

New Ping Tone

Swipe the screen up on your Apple Watch for its Control Centre. Tap the icon that looks like an iPhone making a noise and it pings your iPhone. The ping tone has changed, making it easier to tell where it's coming from.

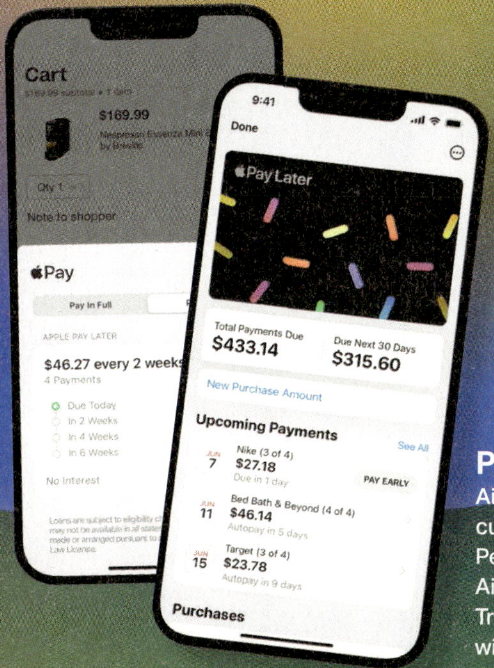

Apple Pay Later

American iPhones can split the cost of an Apple Pay purchase into four equal parts, paying them over six weeks with no interest charged and no fees incurred. It's available everywhere Apple pay is accepted. Upcoming payments are organised through Wallet.

matter

Why Matter Matters

The smart home is great, but differing standards can be confusing. Apple has joined forces with other connected home industry leaders to create a new cross-platform standard, called Matter. The new standard is based on Apple's HomeKit, and will be supported by a wide variety of brands. There's already over 130 products in the pipeline.

Personalised Spacial Audio

AirPods 3, AirPods Pro and AirPods Max users can customise their listening experience with Personalised Spacial Audio. Available through the AirPods' Settings page, it uses the iPhone's TrueDepth camera to scan your face like it does with Face ID, and then scans each of your ears. The iPhone then uses this information to create a personal profile used to fine-tune the audio output from your AirPods to better suit your ears, removing detail imperfections caused by reflections and echoes.

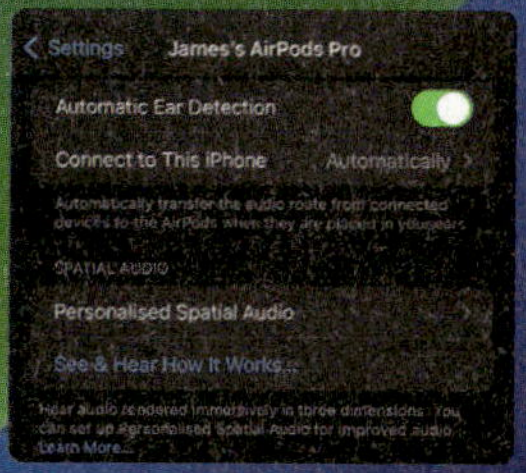

The iOS 16 iPhone Guidebook
2022 | ISBN: 978-1-914404-82-5

Published by: Papercut Limited
Visit us at: **www.pclpublications.com**
Managing Editor: James Gale
Production Director: Mark Ayshford
Editor: Ian Osborne
Design: Martin Smith, Mark Ayshford
Editorial: Ian Osborne, James Gale
Printed and bound in Great Britain by: Acorn Web Offset Limited
Print services supplied by: Media First (International) Ltd
UK & International Newsstand distribution by:
Seymour Distribution Limited, 2, East Poultry Avenue, London EC1A 9PT
Digital distribution by: Zinio, Pocketmags, Readly.com

Papercut Limited
Registered in England & Wales No: 04308513

ADVERTISING – For our latest media packs please contact:
Richard Rowe - richard@tandemmedia.co.uk
Will Smith - will@tandemmedia.co.uk

INTERNATIONAL LICENSING – Papercut Limited has many high quality publications and all are available for licensing worldwide. For more information email: jgale@pclpublications.com